The Great Escape
of the Boer Pimpernel

A formidable combination: General Christiaan de Wet on his Arabian stallion, Fleur. (War Museum of the Boer Republics, Bloemfontein)

The Great Escape of the Boer Pimpernel

Christiaan de Wet
The Making of a Legend

Fransjohan Pretorius
Translated and adapted by Stephan Hofstätter
Assisted by Wilhelm Snyman

2001
UNIVERSITY OF NATAL PRESS
Pietermaritzburg

Published by
University of Natal Press
Private Bag X01
Scottsville 3209
South Africa
Email: books@nu.ac.za
http://www.unpress.co.za

© 2001 Fransjohan Pretorius

All rights reserved. No part of this publication may be reproduced or transmitted, in any form or by electronic or mechanical means, including information storage and retrieval systems, without permission in writing from the publishers.

ISBN 0 86980 994 6

Cover design by Jason Askew

Typeset and designed by University of Natal Press
Printed and bound by Interpak Books, Pietermaritzburg

Contents

List of Illustrations vii
List of Maps ix
Abbreviations x
Timeline xi
Preface xv

Introduction The making of a legend 1
Chapter 1 Three cheers for Oom Christiaan 7
Chapter 2 Cornering the fox 17
Chapter 3 Under their noses 23
Chapter 4 The fugitive attacks 43
Chapter 5 Crossing the line 63
Chapter 6 Give us this day our daily bread 75
Chapter 7 Pinned against the Vaal 83
Chapter 8 'Boer brigands of the veld' 93
Chapter 9 'A just and sacred cause' 101
Chapter 10 Wide open 111
Chapter 11 Across the Vaal 121
Chapter 12 Surprised! 133
Chapter 13 No sign of the Boers 143
Chapter 14 Scorched earth 161
Chapter 15 Over the neck 173
Chapter 16 Wandering about the bush 191
Epilogue The most spectacular guerrilla warfare modern
    times have seen 197

Bibliography 211
Index 225

I should like to dedicate this work to my colleagues in the Department of History and Cultural History at the University of Pretoria: Johan Bergh, Karen Harris, Jackie Grobler, Marié van Heerden, Karina Sevenhuysen, Lizé Kriel and Charlotte van Niekerk – for their collegeality, understanding and support while I was on commando with De Wet.

Illustrations

General Christiaan de Wet on his Arabian stallion, Fleur .... *Frontispiece*
Lieutenant-General Sir Archibald Hunter 26
General Philip Botha 27
Commandant A.M. Prinsloo 27
C.C.J. (Stoffel) Badenhorst 28
Commandant Alex Ross 28
President M.T. Steyn 30
Slabbert's Nek from the inside of the Brandwater Basin 34
'Steyn and De Wet on the journey to the Transvaal (July 1900)' 35
Brigadier-General C.P. Ridley 45
The farmhouse of Cornelis Wessels on Blesbokfontein 55
General Piet de Wet 56
De Wet on a dark brown horse 65
The trucks wrecked near Serfontein Siding on 21 July 1900 66
Danie Theron 69
'On the track of De Wet' 85
Brigadier-General R.G. Broadwood 86
Commandant Danie Theron and his men capturing a
  train near Holfontein 96
J.S. Stowe 97
Colonel Lord Algernon Gordon Lennox 98
Marthinus Prinsloo 106
Lord Methuen 117
Field-Cornet J.A. van Zyl 125
Captain Gideon Scheepers 133
An incident during Methuen's surprise attack 139
Major-General H.L. Smith-Dorrien 151
General Piet Liebenberg 152
Colonel E.H. Dalgety 161
The moment when a British shrapnel shell burst over a
  Boer gun team 165
President Steyn with an escort 174
Lord Kitchener 176
Field-Marshal Lord Roberts 183
Olifant's Nek in the Magaliesberg mountain range 184

vii

Lieutenant-General Ian Hamilton 185
Commandant Lukas Steenekamp 193
De Wet on Fleur with some of his men 203
De Wet addresses the Boer inhabitants of Potchefstroom 203
Probably the most famous photograph of Christiaan de Wet 204
'De Wet addressing the burghers on the scheme for invading
 the Cape Colony' 205

Maps

The Brandwater Basin, July 1900 25
The exit from Slabbert's Nek, 15–18 July 1900 33
Over the undulating hills of the Free State, 17–23 July 1900 51
British and Boer positions on the Vaal River, 6 August 1900 113
The hunt continues in the Transvaal, 6–11 August 1900 122
De Wet escapes over Olifant's Nek, 11–14 August 1900 144
Ian Hamilton's march, 8–14 August 1900 179
The first De Wet hunt, 15 July – 14 August 1900................ 206

Abbreviations

CA	Central Archives, Pretoria
CO	Colonial Office
FA	Free State Archives, Bloemfontein
GOC	General Officer Commanding
HTD	Hoofd der Telegraafdienst (Chief of Telegraph Service)
IOP	Intelligence Officer, Pretoria
JPE	Journal of the Principal Events connected with South Africa
Leyds	Dr W.J. Leyds Archive
LRP	Lord Robert's Papers
MGP	Military Governor, Pretoria
OC	Officer Commanding
PRO	Public Records Office, London
SA Telegrams	South African Telegrams and Letters sent by Field-Marshal Lord Roberts, Dec. 1889 – Dec. 1900
TA	Transvaal Archives, Pretoria
WMC	War Museum Collection, Bloemfontein
WO	War Office

Timeline

1880–1881: Anglo-Transvaal War. Peace talks held after Battle of Majuba (27 February 1881).

29 December 1895: Dr Jameson launches an abortive raid into the Zuid-Afrikaansche Republiek.

1899

9 October: Transvaal issues ultimatum to Britain.

11 October: Ultimatum expires and war breaks out.

12 October: Boers invade Natal in bid to isolate or wipe out the British forces threatening the republics on their borders, and to occupy suitable positions in enemy territory where the Boer forces could halt the advance of British reinforcements moving up from the coast. First military contact of the war – General Koos de la Rey captures armoured train at Kraaipan on the western front.

13 October: Boers besiege Mafeking in the Cape Colony.

14 October: Boers begin surrounding Kimberley leading to siege of the town.

20 October: Battle of Talana Hill, Natal.

21 October: Battle of Elandslaagte, Natal. Boers encounter British cavalry charge for the first time.

30 October: Battle of Ladysmith, Natal. De Wet achieves first Boer success on Natal front at Nicholson's Nek.

2 November: Boers besiege Ladysmith in Natal.

10 December: Battle of Stormberg, Cape Colony. British force under Lieutenant-General Gatacre defeated by General J.H. Olivier.

11 December: Battle of Magersfontein, Cape Colony. British forces under General Methuen sent to relieve Kimberley are repulsed.

15 December: Battle of Colenso, Natal.

1900

10 January: Arrival in South Africa of two leading personalities of the war – Lord Roberts and Lord Kitchener.

15 February: Kimberley relieved.

18–27 February: Battle of Paardeberg, which results in the surrender and capture of General Cronjé. De Wet made chief commandant on western front.

28 February: Ladysmith relieved.

13 March: Roberts enters Bloemfontein, the Free State capital.

17 March: Mafeking relieved. Boer council of war at Kroonstad decides to adopt guerrilla tactics.

28 May: Roberts announces annexation of the Free State as the Orange River Colony, dating it 24 May to coincide with Queen Victoria's birthday.

29 May: President Kruger leaves Pretoria and heads for Machadodorp.

31 May: Roberts enters Johannesburg.

5 June: Roberts occupies Pretoria.

7 June: De Wet captures the biggest booty of the war at Roodewal. The war is far from over, despite British annexation.

16 June: Roberts launches scorched earth policy.

4–7 July: De Wet, President Steyn and the Free State forces are driven into the Brandwater Basin.

15 July: De Wet and Steyn escape with 2 000 men through Slabbert's Nek.

20 July: De Wet and his brother General Piet de Wet part company.

21 July: De Wet crosses the Bloemfontein–Pretoria railway.

30 July: General Marthinus Prinsloo surrenders.

3 August: Danie Theron captures a train carrying the American consul-general.

6 August: De Wet crosses the Vaal at Schoeman's Drift.

14 August: De Wet crosses the Magaliesberg at Olifant's Nek.

21 August: De Wet recrosses the Magaliesberg and makes his way back to the Free State.

1 September: Roberts announces annexation of the Transvaal.

20 October: President Kruger sets sail (he got on board on the 19th) for Europe from Portuguese East Africa.

15 November – 14 December: Second De Wet hunt.

29 November: Kitchener succeeds Roberts as Commander-in-Chief in South Africa.

1901

21 January – 11 March: Third De Wet hunt.

7 August: Guerrilla warfare continues unabated. Kitchener issues proclamation threatening banishment of all Boer leaders still in the field after 15 September.

1902

7 March: De la Rey captures Methuen at Tweebosch.

9 April: Transvaal and Free State government representatives meet at Klerksdorp.

14 April: Boer government representatives meet Kitchener and Lord Alfred Milner in Pretoria.

15 May: Discussions of Boer peace delegates commence at Vereeniging.

31 May: Peace treaty signed in Pretoria.

Preface

There is a tale about a boy who, during the Anglo-Boer War, sold postcards of General Christian de Wet. He had a successful little business going because the famous escapades of the Boer Pimpernel were big news in Britain. One day one of his clients, an elderly woman, opened her envelope and, displeased, turned to the boy and said: 'But there's no picture of De Wet in here!' 'Good heavens,' he replied, 'he must have escaped again!'

With the recent centenary of the Anglo-Boer War, it is appropriate that the figure of General De Wet be taken out of the envelope again. This book tells the story of how De Wet became a legend in his time: how from July to August 1900 he, along with 2 000 men (which rapidly grew to 2 500), managed to evade the elaborate net Lord Roberts had so carefully prepared to ensnare him. In so-doing De Wet ran rings around 50 000 British troops.

This remarkable tale has been taken off the shelf from among other Afrikaans books. Stephan Hofstätter's translation of the work into English, assisted by Wilhelm Snyman, has lent a new dimension to this chapter in the history of the Anglo-Boer War. For this I should like to express my admiration and heartfelt gratitude. Where apppropriate, text in German and Dutch was rendered into English by the translators.

Long ago my parents shared with me the adventures of De Wet across the plains of the Free State and the wintery savannahs of the Western Transvaal. I would like to express my sincere gratitude for the many years they spent on sentry duty. Many thanks too to my wife, Laurette, and to Little Laurette, Nicolaas and Hermann, who have had to put up with me during the commemoration of the war.

Fransjohan Pretorius
Department of History and Cultural History
University of Pretoria

'We pay homage to the courageous Boer men and women . . . (who) had the courage to take on a Goliath in defence of their freedom. We pay homage to them because . . . they asserted the right of all colonised people to independence.'
– President Thabo Mbeki at the official launch of the Anglo-Boer War Centenary Commemorations at Brandfort, 9 October 1999

'A Boer commando travelled light, light and fast. De Wet's commando moved like a hunting cat on the veld. One minute the men lay there: formless, huddled around the small fires of cow-dung, sipping coffee, or trying to sleep, wrapped up against the cold in their blankets; behind them squatted the African servants of the better-off burghers; ponies picked at the bare veld, hobbled by foreleg and halter. The next minute the raiding party was on the move, bobbing heads under slouch hats, Mausers erect, bandoliers swathed across the men's shoulders, strips of biltong (dried meat) and pouches of flour tied to the saddle-bow. De Wet's commando was not a majestic fighting machine, like a British column. It was a fighting animal, all muscle and bone: in one sense the most professional combatant of the war.' – Thomas Pakenham

'The English were exceedingly angry that we had escaped from them on the Vaal river, for they had thought that they had us safely in their hands. That we should have succeeded in eluding them was quite beyond their calculations.' – De Wet

'We seek him here, We seek him there, Those Frenchies seek him everywhere. Is he in heaven? – Is he in hell? – That demmed, elusive Pimpernel.'
– Baroness Orczy

INTRODUCTION
The making of a legend

CHRISTIAAN RUDOLF DE WET was perhaps the most famous Boer general of the Anglo-Boer War of 1899–1902. The conflict which erupted on the eve of the twentieth century between the mighty British Empire and two tiny Boer republics was an absurdly unequal contest – one which the British expected would be over by Christmas. Instead it dragged on for close on three years and, in Rudyard Kipling's famous phrase, taught the British 'no end of a lesson'. This come-uppance, which ultimately led to a revamp of the British Army before World War I – both in the upper echelons of its administration and in field tactics – was in no small measure due to the inspired leadership of legendary figures such as De Wet.

De Wet was born on 7 October 1854 on the farm Leeuwkop near Smithfield in the newly established Republic of the Orange Free State, the sixth of Jacobus Ignatius and Aletta Susanna Margaretha's 14 children. Although he received but a few months' formal education, his military apprenticeship began at the tender age of 11, when he served with his father in the second war against the Basotho in 1865. In 1873 he married Cornelia Margaretha Kruger, a strong, steadfast woman who shared his profound religious convictions. Their union produced eight sons and eight daughters. De Wet was a restless spirit and frequently on the move. In the 1870s he worked as a transport rider on the Kimberley diamond fields. Later, during the Anglo-Transvaal War of 1880–1881, he served as acting-commandant for the Heidelberg district of the Transvaal and took part in the famous storming of Majuba Hill on 27 February 1881. This military experience obviously stood him in good stead when the Boers went to war with Britain again almost two decades later.

De Wet had little taste for public life, but his dynamic personality and firm convictions often attracted the attention of his fellow citizens. In 1885 he was elected to the Transvaal *Volksraad* (parliament). After only one session he returned to the Free State, where he was elected a *Volksraad* member for the Upper-Modder River ward in 1889, a constituency he represented for nine years. De Wet was not a born orator, speaking with a slight lisp, but his terse, impassioned delivery always left a strong impression on his listeners. Though part of a less conservative element in the *Volksraad*, he wholeheartedly identified himself with the upsurge of Afrikaner nationalism during the years preceding the outbreak of the Anglo-Boer War. During the presidential elections of 1896 he supported the successful candidate, the young judge and fervent patriot Marthinus Theunis Steyn, against Scottish-born Sir John George Fraser. De Wet was in unison with Steyn's Boer republicanism.

As Britain's imperial ambitions in southern Africa grew increasingly aggressive, Boer republicanism gained momentum. Despite peace efforts by the Free State, this clash of irreconcilable differences caused tensions to escalate to a point where both sides considered war inevitable. With the intention of launching a pre-emptive strike, the Zuid-Afrikaansche Republiek (ZAR) declared war on Britain on 11 October 1899 and, together with its ally the Orange Free State, invaded two neighbouring self-governing British colonies, Natal and the Cape Colony. Now there was no turning back.

De Wet's rise to prominence in the war was nothing short of meteoric. He reported for duty on his white stallion, Fleur, as an ordinary burgher (citizen) of the Heilbron commando. But soon afterwards the commandant fell ill and De Wet was elected acting-commandant. In this capacity he achieved the first Boer success on the Natal front: on 30 October, with a small force of 300 burghers, he drove the British from their positions at Nicholson's Nek (the Battle of Ladysmith). This dramatic victory brought him to Steyn's attention and in December De Wet was appointed *vecht-generaal* (combat-general) under General Piet Cronjé on the western front.

At first the Boers continued to enjoy numerous successes, but the war took a decidedly different turn when British reinforcements began to pour into the country and advanced inexorably on the republican capitals Bloemfontein and Pretoria. Pinned down by the British on the banks of the Modder River and greatly outnumbered, Cronjé was forced to surrender on 27 February 1900. This left De Wet in charge of the remaining Free State forces on the western front.

By now it was clear trench warfare could no longer stem the enemy advance and De Wet switched to guerrilla warfare, before long achieving some of the spectacular successes that would earn him a worldwide reputation as a master of surprise hit-and-run tactics which are still the subject of case studies by military academies around the globe.[1] By the middle of 1900 De Wet was Commander-in-Chief of all the Free State forces and, together with Steyn, had come to be regarded as the heart and soul of the republic's bitter struggle to cling to its independence.

De Wet's capture now became a prerequisite for ending the war and in July 1900 the first of three so-called De Wet hunts was launched. Several British columns (eventually more than 50 000 troops) were sent to track down De Wet and his force of 2 000–2 500 men. Miraculously, the Free State commander not only gave his pursuers the slip but succeeded in wreaking havoc on British supply lines at every opportunity. In the process De Wet acquired worldwide fame for being something of a Scarlet Pimpernel – running rings around his pursuers on the African veld, often coming to within an inch of capture yet always managing to slip through the net at the last moment, leaving a number of prominent British generals red-faced and empty-handed.

The first hunt was also the crucible in which De Wet's legendary status, both at home and abroad, was forged. The Boer commander's powerful leadership, equanimity in the face of danger and brilliant reconnaissance methods, not to mention his uncanny ability to assess military situations and swiftly turn adversity to his own advantage, earned him the admiration and respect of a core of burghers who remained loyal to their commander to the bitter end. In Britain, too, he was hailed as a formidable opponent, and his spectacular successes, daring will-o'the-wisp tactics, remarkable mobility and unpredictability won him many admirers in pro-Boer Europe. It was a legacy which was to prove enduring. In the 1916 uprising, the nationalist Irish Volunteers christened their slouch hats 'De Wets',[2] and streets in the Netherlands bear his name to this day.[3]

By the end of the war, almost two years – and two hunts – later, De Wet was still at large, and still determined to continue the struggle. But the remaining Boer leaders believed the time had come to negotiate. Britain's infamous scorched earth policy had laid waste to both republics and their civilian populations had been herded into concentration camps, leading to the death of an estimated 27 000 Boer women and children and more than 14 000 Africans. De Wet, then acting president of the Free State, was privately persuaded to agree to peace. In terms of the peace agreement of Vereeniging, signed on 31 May 1902, the Boer republics would lose their independence and become British colonies, with the possibility of being granted self-government under the British crown at a later date. It was with a heavy heart that De Wet took these bitter tidings back to his faithful burghers still holding out in the Free State.

De Wet now left for Europe with fellow generals, Louis Botha and Koos de la Rey, to raise funds for Boer widows and orphans. On board the ship to Southampton, De Wet wrote his war memoirs *De Strijd tusschen Boer en Brit,* published in English under the title *Three Years War* and translated into several languages, including Russian. De Wet was surprised by the warm reception he received from the British public; on the continent he was virtually treated as a war hero. But in the end the trip bore little financial fruit.

On returning to South Africa De Wet, now impoverished by the war, went back to farming and in 1907 was appointed minister of agriculture in what had become the Orange River Colony. Although De Wet participated enthusiastically in preparing the ground for the establishment of the Union of South Africa in 1910 with Louis Botha as its first prime minister, his rejection of Botha's vision of an active role for South Africa in the British Empire caused the relationship between the two former generals to become increasingly strained. When Botha invaded German South West Africa following the outbreak of World War I in Europe, De Wet took the lead in an Afrikaner rebellion against the government and raised a force of about 5 000 men. After clashing with government troops, De Wet was surrounded near Winburg. Once again the legendary Pimpernel managed to slip through the net prepared for him, but this time his pursuers were motor driven, not mounted, and De Wet was eventually captured at Waterbury near Vryburg. He was sentenced to six years' imprisonment for sedition, but, backed by popular opinion and after giving assurances of good conduct, he was released after serving only six months and settled down to the quiet life of a farmer for the rest of his days. De Wet died on 3 February 1922 on the farm Klipfontein near Dewetsdorp, and despite his participation in the rebellion was given a state funeral and buried next to his spiritual father Marthinus Steyn at the foot of the National Women's Monument in Bloemfontein.

The Boer Pimpernel's great escape during the first hunt which was launched to capture him, was one of the more interesting and significant episodes of the war. Yet up to now no detailed account has appeared in English. The present work is a translation from Afrikaans and an adaptation of *Christiaan de Wet-Annale 4: Die Eerste Dryfjag op Hoofkmdt. C.R. de Wet,* published in 1976. Meticulously researched, drawing mostly from eyewitness accounts, letters, diaries and telegrams – many of which, especially on the Boer side, have never been consulted before – as well as interviews with war veterans, the book attempts to shed new light on the operations of the legendary Boer general whose war memoirs have too often been regarded as the last word on the subject.[4] What's more, every effort has been made to bring to life this dramatic and intriguing chapter of South Africa's history in a language and style which should appeal to the military history buff and general reader alike.

Notes
1. Peter Stiff in foreword to *Three Years War* by Christiaan de Wet, p. 4.
2. Bill Nasson, *The South African War 1899–1902,* p. 67.
3. Ibid, p. xi.

4. The diary of Dr Oskar Hintrager, a German jurist who accompanied the Free State artillery, and the memoirs of Hendrik Ver Loren van Themaat, a Dutch volunteer who fought for the Boers, have proved particularly valuable sources. Unfortunately, the dates supplied by both are often incorrect. These errors, not taken into account by later writers, can be deduced by an examination of British and other Boer sources, as well as by following the logical sequence of events.

CHAPTER ONE

Three cheers for Oom Christiaan

7 JUNE 1900. On a featureless plain sweeping down to the Rhenoster River in the Orange Free State, the muffled sound of hooves pounding the dusty veld echoed into the distance. A Boer commando was closing in on its prey. Just before dawn the leading horseman stopped to scan the horizon, but it was pitch black out there. No matter – he knew this part of the country like the back of his hand; his own farmstead stood but a few kilometres off.

It was hard to distinguish him from the 80-odd men under his command: the stocky figure sitting bolt upright on his white mount, Fleur, and sporting a neatly clipped black beard with streaks of grey – the same colour as the koppies now beginning to emerge in the distance – looked just like an ordinary burgher.[1] Hardly a sight to strike fear into the hearts of his adversaries. Yet at 45, the diminutive general's ability to launch lightning strikes and make daring getaways when outnumbered – such as at Sannah's Post on 31 March 1900 – had already earned him the reputation of being something of a military wizard.

Today Christiaan de Wet's target was the British depot at Roodewal railway station, where a mountain of supplies had piled up after retreating Boer forces dynamited the bridge across the Rhenoster River. When they had set out, none of the burghers, let alone their general, had the slightest idea they were about to capture the biggest booty of the entire war. Now, less than 1 km away from their target, De Wet ordered his troops to unlimber the single field gun they had brought along for the assault. After scouting the depot, De Wet sent a note to the enemy: surrender or face defeat. He received a curt refusal; it was time to attack.[2] As artillery and rifle fire began to rake the veld, a faint red line appeared on the horizon.

This was not supposed to happen. Not to the British anyway. Barely three months ago, on 13 March, their newly appointed supreme commander, Field-Marshal Lord Frederick Sleigh Roberts, had triumphantly paraded through the streets of the Free State capital, Bloemfontein, at the head of a victorious army. There had been humiliating reverses of course: the débâcle in Natal at Talana shortly after the war broke out, which cost a brave but foolish General Penn Symons his life; the infamous 'Black Week' two months later, when British troops were massacred at Stormberg and Magersfontein in the Cape and Colenso in Natal; and the protracted sieges of Mafeking, Ladysmith and Kimberley. But that was before Lord Roberts arrived in South Africa. After crossing the Orange River early in February 1900 with a majestic force of about 40 000 men, including an entire cavalry division and 100 field guns,[3] the British war machine had gradually pulverized all opposition. Lieutenant-General John French's dramatic cavalry swoop to relieve Kimberley on 15 February and General Piet Cronjé's surrender with 4 000 men at Paardeberg on 27 February dealt the republican cause a staggering blow. The very next day Sir Redvers Buller – who until then had suffered some of the worst setbacks in the war in his efforts to liberate Ladysmith – finally tasted success. On 5 June, less than three months after entering Bloemfontein, Roberts occupied the second republican capital, Pretoria. The Boers were supposed to be defeated, crushed. And now Roodewal.

What Roberts had failed to grasp was that although the set-piece battle phase of the war was drawing to a close, the Boer old guard had already been replaced by young hotheads like De Wet who had switched to guerrilla tactics. What for Britain was supposed to be a short colonial war would now turn into an agonisingly protracted affair.

De Wet's ideas on guerrilla warfare had already begun to take shape in his mind some months before his raid on Roodewal. The night before the fall of Bloemfontein, Free State president Marthinus Steyn and his government fled north to Kroonstad on one of the last trains to steam out of the capital.[4] Four days later, on 17 March, the town hosted a war council attended by, amongst others, Steyn and De Wet, Transvaal president Paul Kruger, as well as his generals Koos de la Rey and the frail old warrior who would die soon afterwards, Commandant-General Piet Joubert. The agenda was nothing less than how to evade defeat. With burghers in both republics deserting in droves (12 000–14 000 surrendered between March and July)[5] and the British inflicting defeat after defeat, there was certainly no simple answer.

At the war council Steyn, Joubert, Kruger and De la Rey spoke forcefully in favour of a new, mobile warfare. De Wet seconded Joubert's proposal that the best tactic would be to harass the enemy from behind, capturing isolated detachments, raiding supply convoys and cutting communication lines. The officers also recognised that Roberts' army, scattered over a vast area and far from its supply bases, would become increasingly dependent on the single-track railway to Pretoria. It was the very lifeline of his campaign, one rendered more vulnerable with every step his troops advanced.

This would soon become De Wet's principle target. But there were two crucial requirements: since mobility was the key to fighting a war when vastly outgunned and outnumbered by the enemy, the Boers would have to abandon their wagon laagers. De Wet found himself repeatedly issuing this warning during the next six months, often in vain. Secondly, the Boers needed a corps of crack troops, burghers committed to the struggle and who would not turn tail and flee at the first whiff of cordite or the sight of a column of cavalry bearing down on them. They had to be battle-hardened troops capable of forming small self-sufficient raiding parties eager to harry the enemy at every opportunity. With this in mind, De Wet had already taken the highly original if unorthodox step of dissolving the demoralised Free State forces with the order to reassemble at the Sand River on 25 March. The gamble paid off as the burghers who rejoined did so with renewed vigour. Although the new style of combat would not entirely replace conventional strategy for some time, the days of defensive trench warfare were numbered.

Almost immediately De Wet achieved some notable successes behind enemy lines. At the end of March he captured seven guns (which were to come in very handy later) and over 100 fully loaded wagons and carts when he ambushed the cavalry commander Brigadier-General Robert Broadwood at Sannah's Post, a stone's throw from Roberts' headquarters in Bloemfontein. In what was to become a classic in the annals of warfare, more than 500 British troops were killed, wounded or taken prisoner. In April De Wet swooped south to Reddersburg, on the way persuading burghers who had laid down arms to re-enlist. There he captured an entire British garrison of 600 Royal Irish Rifles charged with bringing the southern districts firmly under British control.[6] Next he attacked a force of 2 000 men stationed at Wepener on the Basutoland border. They were mostly loyalist Cape Afrikaners and De Wet seemed to relish subjecting them to a particularly ferocious siege until a column of reinforcements arrived from Bloemfontein two weeks later to relieve them. Now Roberts tried to use an encircling movement to trap the Boer commander, but De Wet, relying as usual on information supplied by his élite scouting corps, managed to slip away in the nick of time, heading north towards the government seat at Kroonstad.[7]

These engagements certainly helped retard plummeting Boer morale and De Wet has been credited for keeping the war effort from foundering completely.[8] But they did little to impede Roberts' march on Pretoria. It was not until the end of May – when, in De Wet's words, British forces had begun to 'swarm over our country'[9] while he had barely 8 000 mounted burghers to contain them[10] – that the Free State commander was forced to rely solely on guerrilla tactics. By then Boer morale had truly reached its nadir, and De Wet's spectacular successes in June in the face of overwhelming odds breathed new life into the republican cause on both sides of the Vaal.

Until 3 May, however, Roberts could not budge. It had been almost two months since his hitherto unstoppable war machine had ground into Bloemfontein – and ground to a halt. The first setback was a typhoid epidemic. The troops were supposed to spend a short while recuperating from heavy fighting and a murderous march in sweltering heat on half rations. But the British soldiers had been exposed to the unhealthy water of the Modder River, where numerous draught animals belonging to the Boers had been lying dead since the Battle of Paardeberg on 18 February. By early April almost 1 000 men had died from the disease in what was to become the first of many outbreaks.[11] Transport and supply problems caused further delays, and exacerbated the epidemic. While the generals and their staff were amply provided for with champagne and cigars, the rest of the army was hardly in a position to feed its troops and their mounts. The enormous garrison would have to wait until sufficient baggage mules, forage carts and supply trains to replenish it had trundled into town before Roberts could bag the main prize: Pretoria. It would be checkmate, he was sure of it.

By the time Roberts was able to resume his march, the retreating Boer forces had dug trenches along the rivers in their path in the vain hope of repulsing the invaders: first at the Vet River just north of Bloemfontein; then the Sand River; and finally Kroonstad's last line of defence, the Valsch River. Outnumbered by cavalry and horse artillery, the defenders were obliged to abandon each successive position and instead content themselves with dynamiting the railway bridges and culverts they crossed as they fled north. Still to come were the Rhenoster River and the Vaal River itself. But first Roberts had to make one last pit-stop. On 12 May he occupied Kroonstad, his main column remaining there for over a week while his engineers repaired his principle supply artery: the railway from Bloemfontein. A few days later, on 17 May, he received a cheery telegram from Baden-Powell: 'Happy to inform you Mafeking successfully relieved today.'[12] It had been the last garrison town still pinned down by the enemy, months after the relief of Kimberley and Ladysmith. The Boers had been dealt yet another psychological blow; now there was nothing to stop the British from sweeping to victory.

It certainly looked that way for Roberts' 40 000-strong army thundering through the northern Free State: during the last 90 km march to the Vaal River he encountered virtually no opposition. Spearheaded by French's cavalry and accompanied by the field-marshal himself in a covered wagon, the main invasion force advanced on the central front, rarely straying far from the railway. Meanwhile, Sir Archibald Hunter's column swooped down on the Vaal River, 80 km to the west, and Sir Ian Hamilton advanced

30 km to the east with two mounted brigades – including Broadwood's cavalry – and two infantry brigades.[13] The job of mopping up the eastern Free State in their wake was entrusted to a senior divisional commander, Major-General Sir H.E. Colvile, who had lost one of his brigades to Ian Hamilton. With only Hector MacDonald's Highland Brigade at his disposal, Colvile found himself inadequately equipped for the task of dealing with De Wet and his raiders – a failure that eventually led to his sacking.

Still, by the end of May, Roberts controlled all the most important strategic points along the Bloemfontein–Pretoria line. On 28 May he annexed the Free State, dating the event 24 May to coincide with Queen Victoria's birthday. Henceforth the republic would be known officially in British circles as the Orange River Colony, although the Boers never recognised the annexation. In any event, with Buller's Natal divisions – another 20 000 men – poised to cross into the Transvaal from the south-east, Roberts now felt ready to pounce on Pretoria.[14]

Battered and demoralised, the Transvaal's army was in no position to offer much resistance and on 31 May Johannesburg surrendered, lest fighting take place in the streets. Apart from a few minor skirmishes, the only significant engagement took place two days before, at Doornkop, west of the city. The ridge overlooking Krugersdorp was held by several hundred burghers under Ben Viljoen and De la Rey. In what was to be one of the last true set-piece battles of the war, Ian Hamilton – who in the meantime had joined French's cavalry west of the railway – ordered a spectacular but reckless extended frontal assault, without proper artillery support. His Gordon Highlanders took the hill, but paid dearly in casualties.

The fall of Pretoria five days later must go down as one of the great anti-climaxes of the war. Formidable fortifications erected at great cost, with state-of-the-art field telephones, were all but abandoned. The president had fled east by rail to Machadodorp with the republic's gold and ammunition reserves – rolling stock would be the seat of government until Kruger left for Europe in September. There was no sign of the Boer forces. Roberts took part in his second triumphal march in three months and made the enemy capital his new headquarters, the Transvaal to be formally annexed on 1 September. He was convinced the war was over.

In reality, De Wet and Steyn were if anything more active than ever in the north-eastern Free State in resisting British occupation. Not that they were being left to their own devices. Roberts had left behind some 20 000 troops to pacify the territory in the wake of his conquering army. Steyn and what remained of his government were relentlessly driven east, first evacuating Kroonstad for Heilbron and finally, toward the end of May, finding some respite and a telegraph line to the Transvaal at President Koppie, north-east of the town. In the meantime, the Transvalers fighting on Free State soil had been driven back to their homeland. But all this only served to strengthen De Wet's resolve. On 26 May he launched a fresh recruitment drive, requesting the magistrate of Potchefstroom to order all Free Staters in the Transvaal to join his commandos.[15] He now threw himself wholeheartedly into implementing the new mobile warfare outlined at the Kroonstad council just over two months ago. Five days later his brother, General Piet de Wet, scored the first major coup by capturing the entire 13th Imperial Yeomanry Battalion near Lindley, which included a number of prominent young aristocrats. They had been sent to reinforce Colvile, who was advancing on Heilbron to the north and supposed to have the district under control. It was a major blow to British prestige.

Roberts' second miscalculation was assuming the Transvaal commandos were a spent force. He was not entirely wrong – at the beginning of June this would have been a pretty accurate assessment. But the next few days would change everything. After the fall of Johannesburg, several prominent Boer officers, including Louis Botha and Ben Viljoen, told Kruger it was time to concede defeat. Pretoria could not hold out against Roberts, and to defend it would lead to severe loss of life and terrible devastation. Kruger was dismayed and immediately communicated these views to Steyn.[16] Steyn's response was read out to a war council held in Pretoria on 2 June. He did not mince his words: the Free Staters would never surrender. The enemy had occupied their capital, slaughtered their livestock and ravaged their land; and yet they continued to fight. And now that the war had spilled over into the Transvaal, Kruger was prepared to sue for peace.[17] It was tantamount to accusing his northern allies of betrayal. De Wet, for his part, sent a tersely worded telegram to Botha, urging him to resume the struggle. The Free Staters, he assured Botha, were at that moment poised to disrupt British supply lines north of Kroonstad.[18]

Steyn's telegram was like a match to gunpowder: suddenly all talk of surrender evaporated and the Transvalers were full of fire again. The war council agreed on a fighting retreat. After abandoning the capital and engaging with the British in the hills east of Pretoria on 11 and 12 June (the Battle of Diamond Hill or Donkerhoek), Botha and the forces he could muster pulled back towards Kruger's headquarters at Machadodorp, where he would fight the last great battle of the war. De la Rey, for his part, set about launching his own guerrilla campaign in the Western Transvaal.

De Wet lost no time fulfilling his pledge to Botha. On the evening of 1 June he set off with about 800 men from his laager at President Koppie to nab the supplies damming up at Roodewal station. *En route* the commando received a welcome windfall. On the afternoon of 3 June, De Wet's scouts sighted a supply convoy of 56 wagons travelling up the Rhenoster

River with a small escort of 160 infantrymen without artillery. As it turned out, the provisions were destined for Colvile's Highland Brigade, now at Heilbron.[19] That night De Wet and his men advanced silently along the river to the enemy encampment at Swavelkrans, surrounding the Highlanders at dawn. They surrendered without a fight.

On the evening of 6 June, De Wet was ready to pounce on the main prize. First he divided his men into three groups. Commandant Lucas Steenekamp was ordered to take 300 men and attack the British camp at Vredefort Road Station further north to prevent reinforcements from being sent down the line to Roodewal, while General Christoffel Froneman, also with 300 men and supported by two field guns, would tackle a larger force at the Rhenoster River bridge. De Wet would lead the assault on Roodewal himself. His scouts had informed him the station was poorly defended by fewer than 100 men, so he judged 80 burghers with one field gun a sufficient force.[20]

Early the next morning De Wet launched his assault. For once, however, his legendary scouts were wrong: almost 170 men – post-office workers, a railway pioneer corps company and some Anglo-Indian volunteers – defended the station, barricaded behind an ingenious, hastily constructed breastwork of mailbags, bales of clothes and bully beef tins.[21] A fierce exchange of fire ensued. Fortunately for De Wet, the defenders had no artillery. His Krupp, removed to a safe distance under a hail of bullets, soon shot the station's corrugated iron buildings to pieces.[22] When Froneman joined the fray with two more field guns after heavily defeating the 4th Derbyshires at the Rhenoster River, the British were forced to put up a white flag, fearing their vast ammunition supplies would be hit.[23]

In the meantime, Steenekamp caught the garrison at Vredefort Road Station napping: he bagged 38 prisoners without firing a shot.[24] This, along with the 140 British casualties and 486 prisoners taken by Froneman, brought De Wet's total tally for the day to 800 prisoners, with almost 180 casualties.[25] De Wet put the Boer casualties at one dead and four wounded:[26] by anyone's standards a resounding success, just two days after the fall of Pretoria and a week after the Transvaal forces were ready to throw in the towel.

The booty, too, surpassed all expectations. Ammunition cases, food hampers and bales of clothing were piled high in enormous quantities: winter uniforms, greatcoats, warm underwear, tobacco, coffee, sugar, chocolates, cakes – the list was endless. And a large consignment of champagne and cigars. Soon the burghers were dressed in smart new winter outfits, some quaffing champagne and puffing on cigars. Then someone proposed a toast: 'Three cheers for Oom Christiaan!'[27]

It was dark by the time the commando rode out of Roodewal. The burghers took all the loot they could carry and another 600 cases of ammunition to be buried on De Wet's farm. The rest was torched. When the procession was about 1 500 paces away the shells exploded, and the men wheeled round to see a curtain of flame leap into the sky. 'It was the most beautiful display of fireworks I have ever seen,' De Wet remarked later.[28]

Notes
1. Thomas Pakenham, *The Boer War*, p. 331.
2. Christiaan Rudolf de Wet, *Three Years War*, p. 104.
3. Pakenham, p. 312.
4. Nasson, p. 163.
5. Ibid., p. 167.
6. Ibid., p. 168.
7. Ibid., p. 170.
8. Pakenham, p. 387.
9. De Wet, p. 87.
10. De Wet, p. 98. The burghers were constituted as follows: Boshof, 25 men under Field-Cornet C.C.J. Badenhorst (TA, N.J. de Wet Collection 13: Telegram, Badenhorst – De Wet, 25.5.1900. De Wet incorrectly supplies the figure of 27 men, p. 98); Jacobsdal, 40 men under Commandant H.P.J. Pretorius; Fauresmith, 70 men under Commandant P.J. Visser; Bethulie, almost 100 men under Commandant F.J. du Plooy; Bloemfontein, 200 men under Commandant Piet Fourie; the burghers of the districts of Ficksburg, Bethlehem, Harrismith and Vrede; incomplete commandos of Rouxville, Smithfield, Wepener, Ladybrand, Winburg, Kroonstad and Heilbron. Burghers from districts such as Philippolis and Hoopstad, with some exceptions, virtually disappeared from the military arena.
11. Nasson, p. 163.
12. TA, LRP 31: Baden-Powell – CSO, Taungs, 17.5.1900, p. 156. Compare this to the illustration of exuberant British in the streets of London in H.W. Wilson's *With the Flag to Pretoria*, II, pp. 616–617.
13. Major-General Horace Smith-Dorrien's 19th Brigade and Major-General Bruce Hamilton's 21st Brigade.
14. Pakenham, p. 422.
15. TA, N.J. de Wet Collection 13: De Wet – Magistrate, Potchefstroom, 26.5.1900.
16. TA, Leyds 757: Kruger – Steyn, 19:30, 31.5.1900, p. 163.
17. TA, Leyds 757: Steyn – Kruger, 14:30, 1.6.1900, p. 166; Nasson pp. 181–182.
18. TA, N.J. de Wet Collection 13: De Wet – Botha, 1.6.1900, p. 2; C.W.L. de Souza, *No Charge for Delivery*, p. 43.
19. L.S. Amery (ed.), *The Times History of the War in South Africa, 1900–1909*, IV, p. 262; compare C.J. Barnard, 'Studies in the Generalship of the Boer Commanders' in *Military History Journal*, 2(5), June 1973, p. 152.
20. Barnard, p. 153.
21. Pakenham, p. 435.
22. Barnard, p. 153.
23. De Wet, p. 105; TA, Lord Roberts Papers 11: Captain Grant, 'Roodewal Station, 7 June 1900', p. 126. Compare PRO, WO 105, LRP 11 for the same source.
24. TA, Leyds 734: Oorlogsbericht, 10:00, 11.6.1900, p. 7; De Wet, p. 109.

25. The *Cape Times*, 21.6.1900; Ibid., 6.7.1900, leader page; De Wet, p. 109; TA, Leyds 734: Oorlogsbericht, 10:00, 11.6.1900, p. 7.
26. De Wet, p. 109.
27. Barnard, p. 154.
28. De Wet, p. 108.

CHAPTER TWO
Cornering the fox

THE FIREWORKS DISPLAY which lit up the Free State veld for the Boers proved just as illuminating for the British: the war was far from over, that much was clear now. By preventing sorely needed supplies from reaching their destination, De Wet was retarding Roberts' attempts to deal the Boer forces north of the Vaal a final, crippling blow. What was more, De Wet had destroyed 18 km of rail and cut the telegraph line to Pretoria. The result was that just two days after occupying the Transvaal capital, Roberts was practically cut off from the outside world, believing for a few days that De Wet had recaptured Kroonstad.[1] For a week, communication with Cape Town could only take place with great effort and after considerable delays via Natal.

De Wet's coup at Roodewal also haemorrhaged the British treasury: more than £100 000 worth of food, clothing and ammunition destined for the front had gone up in flames.[2] The war was fast becoming Britain's most expensive military campaign since the Crimean War and would wind up costing taxpayers £205 million, with supplies and transport accounting for almost £80 million of the total expenditure.[3]

De Wet did not stop there. The very next day, 8 June, he sent a patrol to capture 38 British infantrymen marching to Kroonstad, bringing the Free State bag to almost 1 300 prisoners in just over a week. Moreover, his daring raids were encouraging more Free Staters to take up arms again and spurring on the Transvaal commandos. The main advance of the British army now became of secondary importance to Roberts: if he was to bring the war to a speedy conclusion he would first have to hunt down De Wet.[4]

The wheels had already been set in motion a few days earlier. Lieutenant-General Lord Methuen, the commanding officer of the 1st Infantry Division, who was patrolling the area west of Kroonstad, arrived in the eastern Free State a day after Piet de Wet's sensational capture of the Imperial Yeomanry at Lindley on 31 May.[5] Although Methuen's column was too late to rescue the Yeomanry, Roberts ordered him to secure the area between Kroonstad, Lindley, Heilbron and Heilbron Road Station, lamenting the fact that small bands of raiders were preventing urgently needed supplies from arriving in Heilbron.[6] Methuen was barely in a position to carry out this order when De Wet surprised the Highlander convoy at Swavelkrans two days later. Roberts, who referred to the incident as 'a terrible blundering', was incensed: 'It is absurd that our garrisons are being shut up and that the country is being dominated by the few Boers De Wet has with him,' he fumed.[7]

With the news of De Wet's three-fold attack on British communication lines in the northern Free State on 7 June, Roberts' impatience increased sharply. The same day he ordered the commanding officer of Vereeniging to hasten south with all available troops, without endangering the town, to restore telegraphic communications with Bloemfontein.[8] (As it happened this was only achieved a week later.) And the next day Roberts sent no less a personage than his Chief of Staff, Lord Horatio Herbert Kitchener of Khartoum, along with Major-General H.L. Smith-Dorrien's 19th Brigade, 10 field guns and mounted infantry to bring the situation along the railway under control. If anyone was up to the job, it was Kitchener. This time, however, he was about to meet his match.

Kitchener's first taste of success came on 11 June, a day after he united with Methuen.[9] Advancing on the Boer commander with a force De Wet estimated at around 12 000–15 000 men,[10] the British drove the Free Staters from their positions in the koppies near Roodewal.[11] Seven Boers, cut off from their force retreating west of the railway line, were taken prisoner.[12] It was not long, however, before De Wet and his commandos were once again harrying the occupying forces. On 13 June General Froneman overran a British garrison north of the Rhenoster River bridge and captured 58 British soldiers and 300 Africans employed to work on the railway line[13] and who now joined the Boers' growing entourage of prisoners of war (POWs). That night Kitchener himself narrowly evaded capture when Froneman's men halted his train at the same outpost[14] – a clear indication, if one was needed, that the British had not snuffed out all resistance in the eastern Free State.

Roberts decided sterner measures were called for. On 16 June he launched what would later become known as the infamous scorched earth policy. The wanton destruction inflicted on the region by 'small parties of raiders' could not, declared Roberts, take place without the connivance of their fellow citizens. 'The houses in the vicinity of the place where the damage is done will be burned,' he warned, 'and the principle civil residents will be made prisoners of war.'[15]

This was only the latest in a whole barrage of proclamations the British commander had fired at the Boers. As early as February, when Roberts first crossed the Orange River, the British stated their quarrel was with the Boer governments, not their burghers. Should they lay down arms and remain at home, no penalties would be imposed and requisitioned goods would be paid for. On 15 March Free State burghers were informed they would be granted a free pass home if they laid down arms and pledged to desist from hostilities.[16] Continued resistance to British occupation following annexation led Roberts to place the Free State under martial law on 31 May.[17] The next day he issued a stern proclamation: all inhabitants of the Orange River Colony who had not surrendered arms within 14 days would be 'liable to be dealt with as rebels and to suffer in person and property accordingly'.[18]

The deadline came and went, yet De Wet's burghers paid scant heed to these threats. Roberts now decided that burning their farms was the only way to bring them to their senses and starve them of support and supplies. Their leader would be the first to be made an example of[19] and on the morning of 16 June, De Wet's farmstead near Roodewal was razed to the ground.[20]

The next day Roberts ordered his commanders in the field to post strong garrisons at Lindley, Heilbron and Frankfort to secure any vulnerable positions along the railway, and to organise four flying columns – commanded by Methuen, MacDonald, Ian Hamilton (to be sent back across the Vaal) and General R.A.P. Clements at Winburg south of Kroonstad – which would continually sweep through any Free State districts still offering resistance.[21]

Despite these measures, De Wet showed no sign of letting up and a week later was still cutting telegraph lines, attacking supply convoys and wrecking the railway at every opportunity,[22] somehow always managing to shake the enemy columns sent to pursue him. It was becoming clear a more specific strategy was called for and Roberts decided to launch a determined, concerted effort to force the Free State commandos into a corner.

There was already a broad cordon in place. The road south was barred by Lieutenant-General Sir Leslie Rundle's 8th and Colonial Divisions, controlling a line from Winburg (garrisoned by Clements) to Ficksburg. Methuen had in the meantime been ordered to secure the railway through Kroonstad. Central to Roberts' strategy, however, was to drive the Free Staters east and pin them against the Basutoland border. If he succeeded they would have no choice but to surrender or be defeated. And this could very well signal the end of the war. Indeed, rumours were doing the rounds at the time that President Kruger was willing to stop fighting if Steyn would agree to do the same.[23] In London, the *Daily Telegraph* claimed most of the burghers in the Transvaal would 'enter into *pourparlers* the moment De Wet's operations collapse'.[24] Roberts certainly took these sentiments seriously enough to inform Buller – who had crossed the northern Natal border into the Transvaal on 10 June – that there could be little talk of the Transvalers laying down arms until the Free Staters were eliminated as a military force.[25] He thus ordered Buller to occupy Standerton on the Durban–Johannesburg line at the earliest opportunity[26] to sever the only remaining telegraph line and transport link between the Boer republics. When Buller's mounted infantry entered Standerton on 22 June, the last escape hatch in the east was rapidly slamming shut. Now, instead of swinging south across the Vaal to attack the Free Staters, as originally envisaged, Buller was allowed to advance north towards the Delagoa Bay railway for the assault on Botha's forces further east.[27] Buller nevertheless occupied Greylingstad 10 days later, thereby controlling the Durban–Johannesburg line. Thus, along with the Basutoland border, the eastern frontier was effectively sealed.

Roberts now unleashed his flying columns. On 21 June he ordered Clements to join forces with Major-General A.H. Paget's 20th Brigade stationed at Lindley and drive the Free Staters east towards Bethlehem. Roberts' stern warning was that they must on no account be allowed to double back towards the central railway, as he believed Methuen's force – the only troop concentration in that direction – would not be sufficient to contain them.[28] Meanwhile, advancing on the Free Staters from the north was the aptly-named Sir Archibald Hunter, who had been given command of Roberts' main mobile force of three divisions to capture De Wet after Ian Hamilton broke his collar bone in a riding accident. Hunter left Heidelberg on 28 June and was joined *en route* at Frankfort on 2 July by MacDonald and his Highlanders from Heilbron.[29]

Steyn and his government had in the meantime moved to Bethlehem and De Wet, after engaging with the advancing British at the farm Elandsfontein on 3 July, fell back and prepared to defend the town. After carefully reconnoitring the surrounding countryside, he personally instructed his officers which positions their commandos should take, while Bethlehem's inhabitants were informed of the impending battle. Soon a long procession of women and children (and a few men, according to De Wet[30]) were heading for the sanctuary of a mountainous region south of Bethlehem known as the Brandwater Basin. The British attacked on 6 July, but in the few remaining hours before sunset the Boers were able to hold them off. The next day, however, Paget and Clements launched a ferocious artillery barrage and by noon the Boer left flank had fled. Once word was received that Hunter's vanguard was approaching from the north, the right flank also gave way and an orderly retreat was ordered. With every other avenue of escape closed to them and with the British snapping at their heels, De Wet and his men had no choice but to follow in the footsteps of the refugees.[31]

Notes

1. Pakenham, p. 437.
2. TA, Leyds 734: Oorlogsbericht, 10:00, 11 June 1900, p. 7; Amery (ed.), IV, p. 265; De Wet states that he had read in the newspapers afterwards that he had inflicted a loss of three quarters of a million sterling on the English government (De Wet, p. 106), but the author was unable to find this reference in the English South African newspapers he consulted (June to December 1900) or *The Times* of London (June 1900 to March 1901).
3. Darrell Hall, *The Hall Handbook of the Anglo-Boer War*, pp. 254–255.
4. Pakenham, p. 437.
5. Ibid., p. 436.
6. TA, SA Telegrams II: No. C1881, Roberts – Methuen, via OC, Kroonstad, 2.6.1900, p. 77; compare PRO, WO 108/239 for the same source.
7. TA, SA Telegrams II: No. C1900, Roberts – Methuen, 4.6.1900, p. 80; compare PRO, WO 108/239 for the same source.
8. TA, SA Telegrams II: No. C1961, Roberts – OC, Vereeniging, 7.6.1900, p. 85; compare PRO, WO 108/239 for the same source.
9. Major-General Sir Frederick Maurice and M.H. Grant, *Official History of the War in South Africa, 1899–1902*, III, p. 132.
10. De Wet, p. 112.
11. Amery (ed.), IV, p. 266.
12. Ibid.; Maurice and Grant, III, p. 138; De Wet, pp. 113–114.
13. De Wet, pp. 116–117.
14. Pakenham, p. 437.
15. British Blue Books (hereafter Cd.) 426, *Proclamations issued by Field-Marshal Lord Roberts in South Africa*, 16 June 1900, p. 10.
16. Hall, p. 189.
17. Cd. 426, 31 May 1900, p. 8.
18. Cd. 426, 1 June 1900, p. 8.
19. TA, SA Telegrams II: Roberts – Kitchener, 14.6.1900, pp. 105–106; compare PRO, WO 108/239 for the same source.
20. TA, LRP 35: No. A942, Methuen – Roberts, 16.6.1900, p. 128; compare PRO, WO 105, LRP 14 and LRP 27: No. 65 for the same sources.
21. TA, SA Telegrams II: No. Q1527, 17.6.1900, pp. 115–116; compare PRO, WO 108/239 for the same source; Amery (ed.), IV, p. 299 incorrectly supplies the date 14 June.
22. De Wet, p. 119.
23. TA, SA Telegrams III: No. C2176, Roberts – Buller, 20.6.1900, p. 6; compare PRO, WO 108/240 for the same source.
24. TA, Acquisition 1016: News Cuttings II, the *Daily Telegraph,* 12.7.1900.
25. TA, SA Telegrams III: No. C2176, Roberts – Buller, 20.6.1900, p. 6; compare PRO, WO 108/240 for the same source.
26. TA, SA Telegrams III: No. C2114, Roberts – Buller, 15.6.1900, p. 11; compare PRO, WO 108/240 for the same source.
27. TA, SA Telegrams III: No. C2667, Roberts – Buller, 24.6.1900, p. 15; compare PRO, WO 108/240 for the same source; TA LRP 18: No. 287, Buller – Roberts, 23.6.1900, p. 147.
28. TA, SA Telegrams III: No. C2337, Roberts – Hunter, 27.6.1900, p. 23; compare PRO, WO 108/240 for the same source.

29. TA, SA Telegrams III: No. C2476, Roberts – Buller, 3.7.1900, p. 39; compare PRO, WO 108/240 for the same source.
30. De Wet, p. 124.
31. TA, Leyds 728 (h): Report No. 22, received 15.7.1900, De Wet – Transvaal Government, Machadodorp, sent 9.7.1900; De Wet, pp. 124–125.

CHAPTER THREE

Under their noses

LOOKING BACK at the events of the past month, Lord Roberts was justifiably pleased with himself. After the violent sea change which had come over the eastern Free State in June, that troubled region was at last beginning to show signs of calming down. In fact, his plan had succeeded admirably: De Wet and the remainder of the Free State forces, along with President Steyn and his government, had sought refuge in the natural fortress of the Brandwater Basin. With the imminent arrival of Hunter's column in Bethlehem it was simply a matter of time before they were forced to surrender. The end of the war, certainly in the Free State, was in sight after all. Roberts decidedly thought so. 'We are now established upon a most momentous, and what I trust will prove a most successful phase of the campaign,' he cabled the British high commissioner in Cape Town, Sir Alfred Milner. 'The two forces of the enemy are completely separated by nearly 200 miles. The Orange Free Staters, about 7 000 in number, are concentrated in hilly country. If there be a stand they ought to be brought to terms and if they are able to break through our troops, only small bodies of them will, I hope, get away.'[1]

Hilly country! In fact, the Boers were enclosed by a giant 120 km horseshoe formed by the Witteberge ('white mountains') in the west and the Roodeberge ('red mountains') in the east. Guarding these stony battlements was a tangle of kloofs, crevices and 'isolated kopjes standing like sentinels to bar the way'.[2] A 65 km stretch of the Caledon River in the south, the frontier with Basutoland, neatly sealed the Boers' mountain citadel. At the base of the semi-circle, the Small Caledon River and the Brandwater River flow into the Caledon River a few kilometres from one another, the former from the east through the Roodeberge and the latter from virtually directly north where the Witteberge and Roodeberge meet.

For a week the Boer forces spread out 'in an unusually extended laager'[3] to guard the entrances to their rugged lair. The only major routes, in or out, were through four passes: Commando Nek near Ficksburg in the west, Slabbert's Nek and Retief's Nek in the north and Naauwpoort's Nek in the east. Access could also be gained via a number of barely traversable tracks, such as Nel's Poort and Wit Nek in the Witteberge,

23

Bamboeshoek east of Retief's Nek, and Golden Gate east of Naauwpoort's Nek (the latter in such poor condition it was practically never used by wagons).[4]

The task of keeping an eye on British troop movements was entrusted to the Theron Verkenningskorps (TVK for short), one of two specially trained scouting corps De Wet had at his disposal. Captain Danie Theron and his 200 or so scouts, who had left the Transvaal to join the Free Staters as they were retiring toward Bethlehem at the end of June, were ordered to position themselves at Retief's Nek outside the Brandwater Basin.[5] The scouts were a strangely cosmopolitan crew. Comprising mainly Afrikaners (including policemen from Johannesburg and Pretoria), Dutchmen and Germans, the corps also enjoyed the services of an Irishman, a Bulgarian, a Greek, an Arab and a handful of Russians. A motley band of warriors if ever there was one, but Theron managed to maintain strict discipline and turn his corps into one of the most professional reconnaissance units of the war.[6] This was in fact one of the reasons De Wet was often one step ahead of the enemy. The Free State acting attorney-general, Jacob de Villiers, later commented on 'the marvellous superiority of our scouts, who grown up in the veld, have all their senses fully trained. The English scouts are shot down from day to day. Consequently they are so "wild" that they can't do good work.'[7] What was more, during the hunt which was to follow, De Wet's scouts constantly found themselves fighting rearguard actions to allow the wagon convoy to escape under enemy fire, as well as launching a series of successful raids on British supply lines.

While Theron's scouts guarded the northern approach to the Brandwater Basin, their wagons were sent ahead to Fouriesburg, a small town nestling in the heart of a fertile valley between the Small Caledon River and the Brandwater River. The town became the new home for the women and children who had fled Bethlehem, including Steyn's wife and children, as well as the last seat of the Free State government; thereafter it would have to function in the field. At Fouriesburg the women set up a temporary hospital where wounded burghers could be tended to.[8]

Although the ordinary burghers viewed their sojourn in the basin as a welcome respite from the war,[9] De Wet was less sanguine. The British were creeping up on them. On 9 July Hunter arrived in Bethlehem, and the next day was appointed overall commander of all five columns converging on De Wet. These included Paget's 20th Brigade; Broadwood's 2nd Cavalry (800 lancers, six guns of the RHA and one Vickers-Maxim); Ridley's 2nd Mounted Infantry (1 400 men, six guns of RHA and three Vickers-Maxims); and MacDonald's Highland Brigade (three battalions). In Bethlehem there were a further two batteries of Royal Field Artillery and two five-inch guns. Meanwhile Clements and his 12th Brigade were on their way back towards Senekal to meet their supply column, and

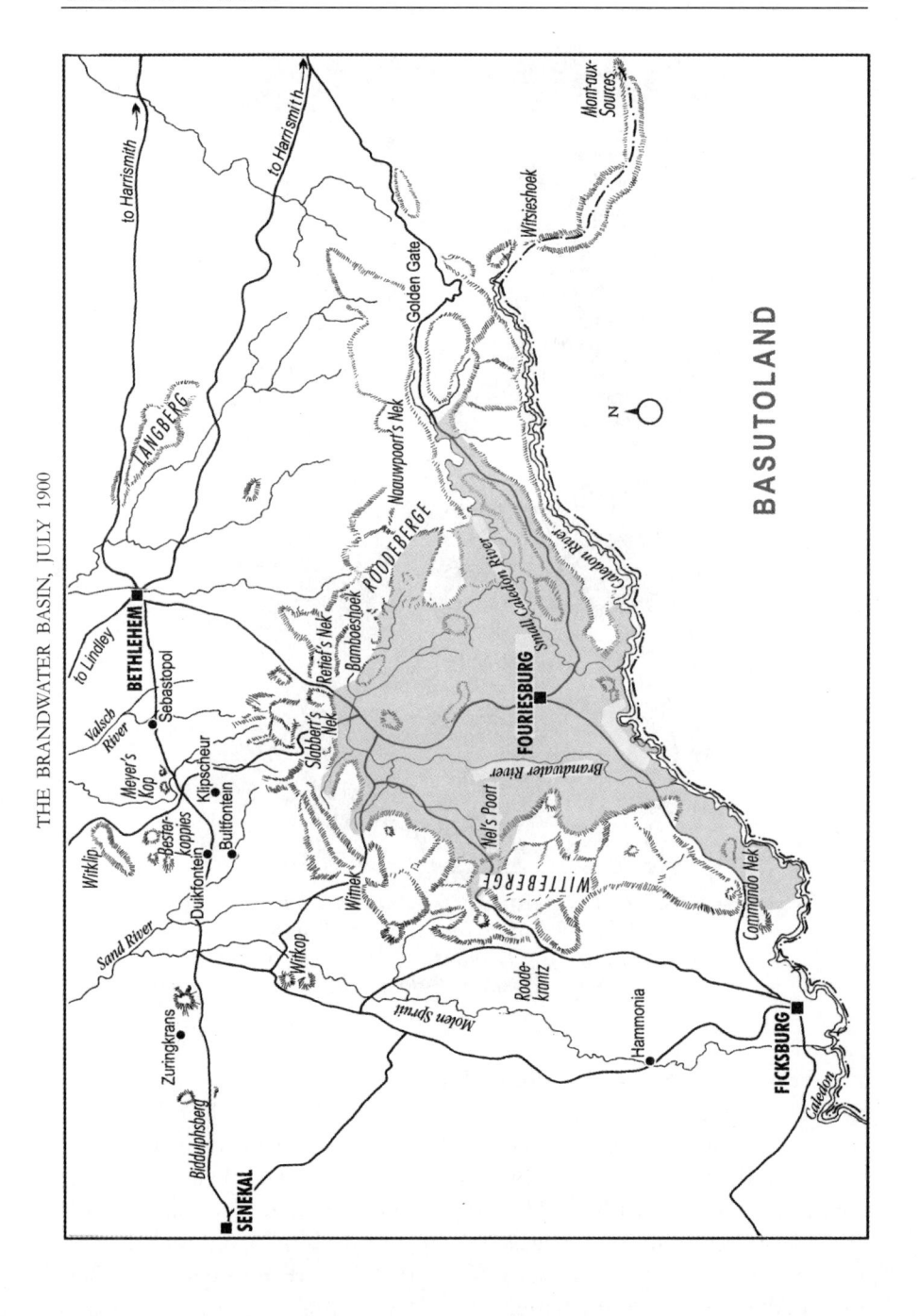

THE BRANDWATER BASIN, JULY 1900

Lieutenant-General Sir Archibald Hunter, who trapped the Free State forces in the Brandwater Basin. (From: C.N. Robinson, Celebrities of the Army, *London, 1900, p. 105)*

Rundle with his 8th and Colonial Divisions controlled the Ficksburg–Biddulphsberg line, charged with guarding Wit Nek, Roodekrantz, Moolman's Kloof and Commando Nek to prevent the enemy from breaking out in the south. The 21st Brigade of Major-General Bruce Hamilton (not to be confused with Ian Hamilton) would be ordered to march south from Reitz to Bethlehem at a later date, and Colonel Cunningham was expected from Heilbron around 18 or 19 July with one battalion (500 mounted infantry and one battery RFA).[10] With this large force at his disposal, Hunter had been ordered by Roberts to 'prevent the enemy from getting south of the Winburg–Trommel–Ficksburg line, capture Steyn and De Wet and break up the Free State's Forces'.[11]

Though De Wet and a good number of his officers correctly assumed that to remain where they were was to court disaster, this view was not shared by everyone. At a war council held in Steyn's tent between Retief's Nek and Slabbert's Nek,[12] the president informed the gathering he had ordered the commandos of Vrede and Harrismith, who were guarding the Drakensberg passes, to cross the Roodeberge and join the rest of the Free State forces.[13] But De Wet made it clear he vehemently opposed any suggestion of making a stand in the mountains.[14] Finally a decision was reached: the basin would not be defended; apart from a livestock guard, the rest of the commandos would slip through the British net under cover of darkness.

The plan was to divide the burghers into three groups. The first, De Wet's, would cross Slabbert's Nek and head north-west toward Kroonstad and Vredefort.[15] It would consist of 2 000 men, including Steyn and the rest of his government. General Philip Botha, eldest brother of Louis Botha, would serve as combat-general over the force, but De Wet was *de facto* in command. This force consisted of the Heilbron commando under Commandant L. Steenekamp, the Kroonstad commando under Commandant F. van Aard, 500 burghers of the Bethlehem commando under Commandant Michael Prinsloo, 150

General Philip Botha, eldest brother of General Louis Botha, was De Wet's senior officer in command of the 2 000 burghers who left the Brandwater Basin on 15 July 1900. (From: P.H.S. van Zyl, Die Helde-Album, *Johannesburg, 1944, p. 120)*

Commandant (later General) A.M. Prinsloo who, with his Bethlehem commando, accompanied De Wet in his escape from the Brandwater Basin on 15 July 1900. De Wet is said to have declared that if he had had a hundred men of the calibre of 'Rooi Michiel' Prinsloo he would surely have taken London. (From: J. Malan, Die Boere-Offisiere van die Tweede Vryheidsoorlog 1899–1902, *Pretoria, 1990, p. 50)*

C.C.J. (Stoffel) Badenhorst was only a field-cornet with a few burghers from Boshof under his command when he accompanied De Wet out of the Brandwater Basin, but he deservedly rose to the rank of general in April 1901.
(From: C.C.J. Badenhorst, Uit den Boeren-Oorlog, 1899–1902, *Amsterdam, 1903, frontispiece)*

Commandant Alex Ross who led the Frankfort commando during the escape from the pursuing British forces in July–August 1900. (From: P.H.S. van Zyl, Die Helde-Album, *Johannesburg, 1994, p. 246)*

Frankfort burghers under Commandant A. Ross, 25 burghers from Boshof under Field-Cornet C.C.J. Badenhorst, a number of Griqualand West rebels under Field-Cornet J.A. van Zyl and a group of Potchefstromers who had joined the Free Staters at the end of May.[16] The TVK and another élite scouting corps of 30 men led by Gideon Scheepers would accompany them.

Another group of 2 000, under the command of the fighting preacher, General Paul Roux, was to cross Slabbert's Nek a day after the first party and head toward Bloemfontein, then move through the southern districts with the aim of persuading the burghers there to take up arms again.[17]

On the same day a third group under General J. Crowther was to head for the area north of Bethlehem and join forces with the Vrede and Harrismith commandos to resume the struggle in the north-eastern Free State under General F.J.W.J. Hattingh.[18]

Only a small commando would remain in the Brandwater Basin to guard the livestock. This task was entrusted to Marthinus Prinsloo (formerly a general) and his Witteberg burghers, whose intimate knowledge of the terrain made them ideally suited to carry it out. They were ordered to position themselves at Slabbert's Nek, Retief's Nek and Naauwpoort's Nek without their wagons to enable them to flee easily in the face of any large-scale British offensive.[19]

There were good reasons for leaving the Brandwater Basin besides escaping from a trap. First and foremost, De Wet was to advance north-west toward Vredefort with the intention of resuming raids on the railway, if possible with the co-operation of the burghers operating on the western border of the Transvaal. The ammunition he had buried on his farm near Roodewal would come in handy for this purpose. Secondly, De Wet wanted to swell his ranks. He therefore chose the burghers of the northern districts to accompany him so that they could recruit and re-enlist family and friends along the way. General Roux, too, would be accompanied by burghers from the southern districts for the same reason. De Wet actually intended to work his way down the Bloemfontein–Pretoria railway line to unite with Roux in the southern Free State, but was forced to abandon this plan later when the British began to hunt him down in all earnest.

Then there was the question of a long overdue meeting between Steyn and Kruger. On 31 May, when the Transvaal generals were facing utter defeat in conventional warfare, Kruger had cabled Steyn urging him to come to Machadodorp at once to discuss a more effective military strategy.[20] As it turned out, Steyn's visit to President Kruger at Watervalonder some six weeks later was one of the results of the trek from the Brandwater Basin, which has led some writers to claim it took place with the express purpose of bringing the two leaders together. This is highly unlikely. Although Steyn did intend to see Kruger if and when circumstances permitted, the meeting was only decided upon after De Wet and Steyn had escaped from the Brandwater Basin, and then only because the British columns pursuing De Wet prevented him from heading south to join forces with Roux and instead forced him toward the Transvaal. For the same reason, De Wet was unable to dig up the ammunition he had captured at Roodewal and buried on his farm.[21]

De Wet also intended his burghers to team up with their Transvaal allies where possible. Joint guerrilla initiatives, whereby the advancing British would be attacked from the rear and their supply lines disrupted, were mooted as early as May, and again in June and July. But Roberts' rapid advance along the central railway soon put paid to these plans. By the end of May, Botha and his forces had been obliged to retreat over the Vaal River, leaving De Wet and his commandos to launch guerrilla

President M.T. Steyn, who, together with his Executive Council, accompanied De Wet and his commandos on their epic journey through the Free State and Western Transvaal. (Transvaal Archives Depot)

attacks on the British in the region of Frankfort and Heilbron without the help of the Transvalers – a series of raids which culminated in De Wet's spectacular coup at Roodewal, an event which in turn led to Roberts sending part of his army back across the Vaal to deal with De Wet, thus taking some of the heat off the Transvalers.

By mid-June the two republics still cherished the hope of joint operations. After the British took Klerksdorp and Ventersdorp, General Piet Viljoen of the Heidelberg commando entered the Free State and made contact with De Wet and Froneman[22] and, in the light of subsequent events, it is likely joint operations were discussed. Then, on 13 June, after the Transvalers found themselves retreating in the face of the British advance at Diamond Hill, Kruger approached Steyn and asked him if the Free Staters could launch a rear attack against the British at Vereeniging or Johannesburg since the Transvalers were having to contend with the main force of the enemy.[23] Steyn replied that De Wet and his men were tied up in the Free State.[24]

Soon, however, the tables were turned. On 21 June, a week before Hunter left Heidelberg to advance on the Free State forces, Botha predicted the British would attempt to drive De Wet from the central railway. He thus ordered General Viljoen to advance post haste with the Heidelberg commando from the east towards Vereeniging to disrupt British telegraph and transport links there.[25] Viljoen, who feared Hunter would soon drive De Wet into a corner, asked Botha on 1 July for permission to come to De Wet's aid by heading toward Vereeniging to slip behind the British forces in Johannesburg and Pretoria.[26] Botha consented, but the next day their plans suffered a serious setback when Buller occupied Greylingstad. Botha now ordered Viljoen to collaborate with the Standerton and Bethal commandos and deal with Buller first,[27] and only then advance directly to Vereeniging to pursue the British force on its way to the Free State. Nevertheless, Botha did believe the Transvalers should put some of their own military plans on the backburner rather than allow the British to knock De Wet out of action and he ordered Viljoen to hasten to De Wet's aid at the greatest possible speed as soon as he could.[28] For the moment, however, his hands were tied and his assistance restricted to warning De Wet that Hunter was bearing down on him from Heidelberg and suggesting he move in the direction of Vredefort, where De la Rey's men from the Western Transvaal would come to his aid. This they did indeed do, but only after De la Rey's brilliant victory at Silkaat's Nek just 30 km west of Pretoria on 11 July, when the Transvaal general ordered General Piet Liebenberg and Commandant C.M. Douthwaite to hasten in the direction of Potchefstroom with 300 men.[29] This is precisely the direction De Wet did take, though only after leaving the Brandwater Basin. The actions of Liebenberg's men, the so-called western border burghers, would soon become a crucial factor in his own operations and attempts to evade the British columns sent to pursue him.

But on Friday 13 July, few of the burghers in the Brandwater Basin had any inkling of what lay ahead because De Wet and Steyn had kept their intentions secret to avoid any possible leaks. In fact, for the past week their laager had resembled a rest camp rather than a military bivouac, and many burghers believed they were destined to remain in this tranquil sanctuary for some time to come. But today, as one surprised burgher noted in his diary, 'there was something in the offing': De Wet was putting his plan into operation.[30]

The next night, 14 July, Theron's scouts were unexpectedly ordered to abandon their posts and cross back into the Brandwater Basin through Retief's Nek. A strange sight awaited them: instead of the glow of homely campfires and the routine preparations for a night's rest, they were confronted by a large force of Boers standing ready to depart.[31] The arrival of the scouts was the moment De Wet had been waiting for. Without further ado he gave the order to saddle up and soon the dark valley echoed with the sound of creaking ox wagons and pounding hooves as a great convoy of wagons, carts and horsemen made their way towards Slabbert's Nek and freedom, De Wet himself riding at the helm.

On numerous occasions wagon delays forced the convoy to halt. Then the troopers would dismount and set the grass alight to keep the biting cold from gnawing at their bones.[32] That the burghers were prepared to trek out of the Brandwater Basin into the icy void of a Free State winter's night without the slightest idea of where they were headed bears testimony to the extraordinary faith De Wet inspired in his men. The commandos who stayed behind were just as puzzled when the long line of wagons and horsemen thundered past.[33] What none of the burghers knew was that President Steyn and the Free State government had also departed with De Wet's group. That day Steyn had taken leave of his wife and children in Fouriesburg,[34] leaving Alfred B. Roberts behind as a representative of the government.[35] It would be two years before Mrs Steyn laid eyes on her husband again.

The first attempt to break through the British cordon was a false start. Commandant J.H. Olivier had been ordered to occupy the koppie to the right of Slabbert's Nek to cover the exodus. But he had returned to the Brandwater Basin instead, reporting that his presence on the koppie was no longer necessary as the British force which had been advancing that morning from Bethlehem in a westerly direction had returned to the town. Just as the vanguard cleared Slabbert's Nek, the order was given to dismount and set up camp for the night: two of De Wet's scouts had spotted a British troop concentration at Meyer's Kop,[36] due north of Slabbert's Nek and directly in the path of the advancing Boer convoy. As it turned out it was Ridley's 2nd Mounted Infantry, sent from Bethlehem that ss-morning to reinforce a British detachment involved in a skirmish at Meyer's Kop. De Wet would have to wait until the coast was clear.

On Sunday morning, 15 July, De Wet and his burghers settled down to a church service held on the slopes of Slabbert's Nek, conducted by General Roux.[37] While the burghers sat or kneeled on the grass, President Steyn occupied a chair a few metres from the pastor. Roux's text was Isaiah 66, verse 8: 'Did ever a land bring forth its people in a single day?' He exhorted his burghers to set aside personal concerns and think of their country and their people. Without painful suffering and sacrifice, he said, no nation could be born. And what the burghers had hitherto endured was nothing compared to the trials which lay ahead. 'Who knows how long it will take', concluded Dominee Roux, 'before we can once again be gathered together as we are today.'[38] His words were to prove prophetic.

THE EXIT FROM SLABBERTS NEK, 15–18 JULY 1900

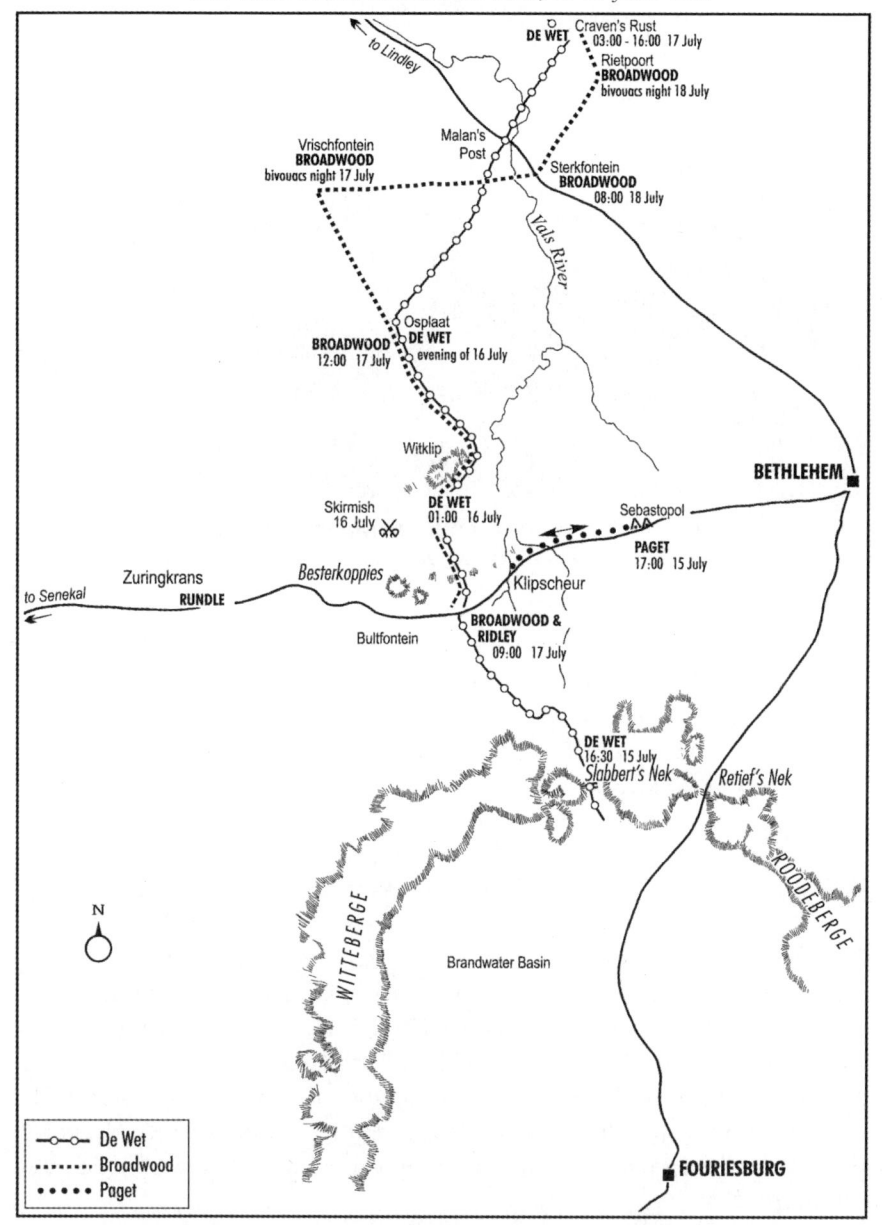

Slabbert's Nek from the inside of the Brandwater Basin – De Wet's escape route on 15 July 1900.

At 16:30,[39] after receiving intelligence from his scouts about British positions,[40] De Wet's entourage of 2 000 men accompanied by the artillery and some 400 wagons and carts set off once more.[41] The procession that squeezed through Slabbert's Nek and spilled onto the sprawling Free State veld was indeed a strange sight. A small commando of burghers and scouts rode ahead. They were followed by President Steyn and his councillors, then De Wet and his second-in-command, General Louis Botha's brother General Philip Botha. Next came the artillery – two Krupps and two Armstrongs (of Lieutenant P.J. Strydom, Captain W.H. Muller, Corporal Bruwer and Bombardier C. Borslap), and a Maxim and the ox- and mule-drawn carts carrying the baggage and ammunition of the various commandos. Then came a large number of Cape carts belonging to the burgers, some of whom followed on horseback, though most rode to the left and right of the great train of wagons to tend their pack animals and stay clear of the dust trail.[42] Theron and his scouts formed the rearguard.[43] From end to end the entire entourage stretched a good few kilometres.[44]

It was not long before the sun set. Under the cloak of darkness the Boers advanced, tense and silent, toward enemy-controlled territory, first veering slightly south, later west and finally turning north.[45] The burghers had received strict instructions not to light a match during the trek for fear of betraying their position to the enemy. When an *agterryer* (African military servant) broke the rule, De Wet immediately ordered him to be flogged.[46]

A painting by the contemporary German artist, J. Schlattmann, entitled 'Steyn and De Wet on the journey to the Transvaal (July 1900)' – probably depicting them passing through Slabbert's Nek. (From: W. Vallentin, Der Burenkrieg, *Vol. II, Leipzig, 1903, facing p. 192)*

Occasionally the troopers dismounted so as not to wear out their horses,[47] or were ordered to halt so that the wagons drawn by plodding oxen were given time to catch up. Meanwhile, veld fires set by the British as beacons glowed in a semi-circle in the distance before the advancing Boers. Now and then their route took the Boers past a sleeping or deserted farm house, and on one occasion, when crossing the road from Bethlehem to Senekal,[48] they came within 3 km of Paget's brigade camped on the farm Sebastapol. The British were blissfully unaware that De Wet was escaping right under their noses.

The Free State commander was the first to reach the prearranged rendezvous – a deserted hollow under a koppie called Witklip on a farm by the same name.[49] There, in the early hours of the morning, the weary burghers dismounted, fed their horses and drifted off to sleep against their saddlebags while the icy air from the nearby vlei chilled them to the bone.

It was a remarkable feat, but only one of many escapes in the month to follow during what was to become known as the first De Wet hunt. Remarkable, but not miraculous – because a series of blunders by the British had contributed significantly to De Wet's success.

When Hunter arrived in Bethlehem on 9 July, his plan was to consolidate the position of the British forces in the north-eastern Free State, then launch a concerted attack on the Boers holed up in their mountain stronghold. This daunting task was made more difficult by woefully inadequate field intelligence. The maps of the area at his disposal were virtually useless,[50] and Hunter was forced to rely on local guides as well as information supplied by escaped POWs and the British Resident Commissioner of Basutoland, Sir Godfrey Lagden.[51] The Lovat Scouts, too, were sent on reconnaissance sorties[52] but did little to plug the gaps. Such scanty knowledge of extremely difficult terrain, Hunter cabled Roberts, meant the possibility should not be excluded that the enemy could escape and would have to be pursued.[53]

Not that Hunter had any intention of letting this happen. He sent his troops to occupy two out of three northern exits from the Brandwater Basin, and Rundle's 8th and Colonial Divisions still controlled the Ficksburg–Biddulphsberg line, guarding the western and southern exits of the Witteberge.

Before launching an attack, however, Hunter would await the arrival of further supplies and two more brigades – Bruce Hamilton's 21st, ordered to leave Reitz just north of Bethlehem on 13 July, and Clements' 12th. In fact, Clements' attack from the west at Nel's Poort, Hamilton explained to Roberts, would signal the start of the joint offensive. If he had not heard from Clements by 18 July, Hunter would assume that was the day to launch the assault. This decision, as it turned out, would give the Boers the opportunity to escape.

By the time Hunter arrived in Bethlehem, Clements was already desperately short of provisions and ammunition, especially 15-pounder shells. That same morning he struck out toward Senekal to intercept his supply convoy advancing from Winburg. On 13 July he cabled Hunter to say he expected his convoy to meet him at Zuringkrans east of Biddulphsberg on 18 July. He apologised for the delay he was causing but promised to be at Nel's Poort on 20 July[54] – two days later than Hunter had envisaged and a full five days after De Wet had made good his escape. Though Clements' concern over supplies was apparently justified, it came at a highly inopportune moment for the British and exposed him to much harsh criticism later.

Clements was by no means the only British commander who placed a high premium on a full stomach and a loaded gun. Hunter, too, was not a man to skimp on provisions. And because he was incapable of feeding his troops and mounts from the surrounding countryside (at that stage only Rundle had achieved this distinction),[55] Hunter's brigades charged with guarding the northern necks of the basin were reliant on supply columns sent from Heilbron and Winburg – in both cases a 12-day plod there and back. Although it would indeed have been risky to send his troops into unknown and difficult terrain to occupy the Witteberge and Roodeberge passes without adequate supplies, Hunter has been accused of exaggerating these concerns. *The Times History*, for example, argues there was no reason why Paget's 20th Brigade 'should not have been sent on 9 July to eat their supplies outside Slabbert's Nek',[56] the only exit from the basin not occupied by the British and the very route De Wet chose for his escape.

Even more supplies were needed for the main assault. On 14 July Bruce Hamilton arrived from Reitz with supply columns sent all the way from Heidelberg in the Transvaal and five days later Colonel J.S. Ewart arrived with a convoy that had been sent to fetch supplies in Heilbron.[57] Furthermore, on 11 July Hunter had sent Brigadier-General J.P.R. Gordon and his 3rd Cavalry Brigade and about 1 400 mounted infantry back to Heilbron because, he declared, he needed to conserve supplies and the topography was not suited to mounted combat.[58] This, despite the possibility, of which he was fully aware, that De Wet could break through the British cordon and would have to be pursued. These delays, and the gaps they left in the British cordon, did not go unnoticed by De Wet's wily scouts and Hunter was the first to admit he was partly responsible for allowing the Free Staters to get away.

Another stroke of luck for De Wet was a telegram sent on 14 July to Lord Roberts by Lagden in Maseru, Basutoland. He told the chief he had received reports that the Boers would force their way through the British line in the south, near Ficksburg, with the intention of wrecking the railway near Bloemfontein.[59] Ironically, just the day before Lagden had warned Roberts that the road from Bethlehem had to be carefully guarded as the movements of the enemy could be disguised by 'strategic moves by which they say they can always deceive British forces'.[60] Lagden clearly did not take his own warning very seriously. Roberts immediately warned Hunter that the Boers could be preparing to escape over Commando Nek in the south, and suggested that Rundle's divisions in the area be reinforced.

On the same day Rundle – who in the meantime had moved towards the Witteberg passes[61] – was reinforced by 400 mounted men of the Colonial Division and one gun from Clement's force.[62] Thereupon Rundle made his way to Ficksburg, where he would have at his disposal on 17 July four battalions, 10 guns and 1 600 mounted troops. At Witkop and opposite Wit Nek (not to be confused with Witklip) he left General B. Campbell behind with two companies of the Imperial Yeomanry, two sections RFA, the 2nd Grenadier Guards, four companies of the 2nd Scots Guards, 700 troops of the Colonial Division and half of the 21st Field Hospital.[63]

As it turned out, De Wet had sent a number of wagons in the direction of Commando Nek to divert attention from the northern passes. On 15 July, Rundle's troops were kept busy all day by a Boer force at Roodekrantz in the south-west and just before sunset, while De Wet's convoy was crossing Slabbert's Nek, the British spotted a Boer commando without wagons crossing the Witteberge a few kilometres further back at Nel's Poort, out of range of the British artillery. Rundle believed they were reinforcements who had arrived late, not for a moment suspecting the truth: it was a red herring, and the British had swallowed it whole.

The prize for the biggest blunder, however, must go to Paget. Lagden's telegram prompted Hunter to send Paget's 20th Brigade to reinforce the south-western line on 15 July.[64] Broadwood received similar orders and his cavalry departed on the same day.[65] At 13:00 Paget set off on the Bethlehem–Senekal road – directly in the path of De Wet's escape route, which could easily have been blocked. After crossing the Valsch River later that day, Paget set up camp for the night with his entire force on the farm Sebastapol, a mere 16 km north of Slabbert's Nek.[66] The rumours of a Boer break-out in the south probably caused Paget to drop his guard. Whatever the reason, he sent no scouts to Slabbert's Nek and posted no pickets for the night. He had left the door wide open.

De Wet's escape from the Brandwater Basin was one of the most significant events of the war. He had led 2 000 men – about a quarter of the remaining Free State forces – 400 wagons and heavy artillery, as well as President Steyn and the Free State government, to safety. In the nick of time too, for two weeks later Marthinus Prinsloo was forced to surrender with 4 400 men who had stayed behind. Not only had Hunter failed to capture De Wet; he now had to inform Roberts that the Boer Pimpernel would probably resume his guerrilla activities with renewed vigour.

Notes

1. TA, Milner Papers, FK 1204: No. 872, Roberts – Milner, 16.7.1900, p. 942.
2. Amery (ed.), IV, p. 310.
3. W. van Everdingen, *De Oorlog in Zuid-Afrika, Tweede Tydvak, Tweede Deel*, p. 6.
4. Maurice and Grant, III, p. 293.
5. H. Ver Loren van Themaat, *Twee Jaren in den Boeren Oorlog*, p. 138; G.S. Preller, *Kaptein Hindon: Oorlogsavonture van 'n Baasverkenner*, pp. 129–130. De Wet, p. 127, states Danie Theron's corps consisted of 80 men, a figure which is incorrect for this stage of the war.
6. J.H. Breytenbach, *Komdt. Danie Theron: Baasverkenner van die Tweede Vryheidsoorlog*, pp. 180–181 and p. 185.
7. M.C.E. van Schoor, 'The Diaries and Recollections of Jacob Abraham Jeremias de Villiers', *Christiaan de Wet-Annale*, 8, 23.7.1900, p. 18.
8. TA, Acquisition 235 (II): Slegtkamp's manuscript, p. 136.
9. Ver Loren van Themaat, p. 140; Van Everdingen, p. 5.
10. TA, LRP 37: No. A112, Hunter – Roberts, 13.7.1900, p. 150; compare PRO, WO 105, LRP 17 for the same source; TA, South African Dispatches II: Report by Hunter on Operations in Eastern Districts of Orange River Colony, p. 20; compare PRO,

WO 32/7998 for the same source; TA, South African Dispatches II: Account by Roberts of Operations in Orange River Colony and Transvaal, 14 June to 10 October 1900 (hereafter referred to as Roberts' Account) p. 3; compare PRO, WO 32/8000 for the same source; Maurice and Grant, III, pp. 292–293; P.A. Nierstrasz, *La Guerre Sud-Africaine, 1899–1902: Der Süd-Afrikanische Krieg,* II, Band 5, p. 989.

11. TA, SA Telegrams III: No. C2630, Roberts – Hunter via GOC, Kroonstad, 10.7.1900, p. 53; compare PRO, WO 108/240 for the same source.
12. FA, WMC 155/13/1 (f): G. Boldingh, 'Het Verraad van Generaal Prinsloo', p. 20; G. Boldingh, *Een Hollandsch Officier in Zuid-Afrika,* p. 13. G. Kriek, an adjudant to Commandant P.H. de Villiers (FA, Renier Collection, 119.8) recounts that the meeting took place on the farm of the erstwhile MP Fanie Viljoen. According to Kriek the meeting did not take place in a tent: 'It was curious to see this group sitting in a circle. How those of us who waiting for our officers a short distance away wished we could hear what was being discussed.' Because Boldingh was actually present at the war council his testimony has been accepted by the author.
13. FA, WMC 155/13/1 (f): G. Boldingh, 'Het Verraad van Generaal Prinsloo', p. 20; TA, Leyds 728 (g): Telegram No. 27, A.B. Roberts – Meyer, 8.7.1900.
14. De Wet, p. 127.
15. FA, WMC 155/13/1 (f): G Boldingh, 'Het Verraad van Generaal Prinsloo', p. 20; De Wet, p. 127; TA, Acquisition 235 (II): Slegtkamp's manuscript, p. 136.
16. De Wet, p. 127; TA, N.J. de Wet Collection 13: Telegram, Badenhorst – De Wet, Frankfort, 25.5.1900; TA, N.J. de Wet Collection 2: Minutes of War Council held at Vereeniging, 24.5.1900, p. 38; FA, WMC 155/13/1 (f): G. Boldingh, 'Het Verraad van Generaal Prinsloo', p. 21; J.N. Brink, *Oorlog en Ballingskap,* p. 81.
17. De Wet, p. 127; FA, WMC 155/13/1 (f): G. Boldingh, 'Het Verraad van Generaal Prinsloo', p. 20.
18. De Wet, pp. 127–128.
19. Ibid., p. 128.
20. TA, Leyds 757: Kruger – Steyn, 19:30, 31.5.1900, p. 163.
21. See Fransjohan Pretorius, 'Kommentaar op "Die Strategiese Oogmerke van Genl. C.R. de Wet Tydens die Eerste Dryfjag, Julie – Augustus 1900"' in *Historia,* May 1977, 22(1), pp. 23–24.
22. TA, Leyds 734: Oorlogsbericht, 07:00, 18.6.1900, p. 20.
23. TA, Leyds 727 (a): Telegram No. 27, Kruger – Steyn, 13.6.1900.
24. TA, Leyds 727 (a): Telegram No. 2, Steyn – Kruger, 14.6.1900, received 15.6.1900.
25. TA, Leyds 727 (e): Telegram No. 21, Botha – Viljoen, 21.6.1900.
26. TA, Leyds 750 (a): Telegram No. 14, P. Viljoen – L. Botha, 1.7.1900.
27. TA, Leyds 750 (a): Telegram No. 15, L. Botha – P. Viljoen, 3.7.1900.
28. Ibid.
29. TA, De la Rey Collection 17: Herinneringe van genl. De la Rey, letter, De la Rey – Kruger, 21.7.1900, p. 49 and p. 47.
30. FA, WMC 155/13/1 (a): Diary, G. Boldingh, quoted in Van Everdingen, p. 9.
31. Ver Loren van Themaat, p. 139.
32. Ibid.
33. Van Everdingen, p. 10.
34. N.J. van der Merwe, *Marthinus Theunis Steyn: 'n Lewensbeskrywing,* II, p. 106 and p. 109.
35. FA, WMC 155/13/1 (a): Dagboek, G. Boldingh, 13.7.1900.
36. Van Schoor, 'Diaries of Jacob de Villiers', 15.7.1900, p. 12.
37. Ibid.; Brink, p. 81; [O. Hintrager], *Steijn, De Wet und die Oranje-Freistaater, Tagebuchblätter aus dem Süd-Afrikanischen Kriege,* p. 50 asserts incorrectly that the service was conducted by Dominee J.J.T. Marquardt; compare Oberholster, p. 79.

38. Oberholster, p. 79; compare [Hintrager].
39. Van Schoor, 'Diaries of Jacob de Villiers', 16.7.1900, p. 13; compare FA, WMC 155/13/1 (f): G. Boldingh, 'Het Verraad van Generaal Prinsloo', p. 22; P.S. Lombard, *Uit die Dagboek van 'n Wildeboer*, p. 61.
40. TA, Acquisition 1250: Herinneringe van G. Scheepers, recorded by C.P. van der Merwe.
41. In his memoirs De Wet puts the number of burghers who accompanied him at 2 600 but Jacob de Villiers notes in his diary on 15 July that about 2 000 burghers were present. His figure is supported by a report by Philip Botha to his brother Louis Botha (TA, Leyds 758 (a): Telegram, no number, P. Botha – L. Botha, no date) and in a statement by Piet de Wet two weeks later after his surrender at Kroonstad (TA, WO – Acquisition JPE: Intelligence Reports, 29.7.1900, p. 44). Furthermore, Philip Pienaar and Oskar Hintrager, who both took part in the trek, arrived at the figures of 2 000 and 2 100 respectively (P. Pienaar, *With Steyn and De Wet*, p. 139; [Hintrager], p. 52). British figures are 1 500 (TA, SA Telegrams III: No. C2855, Roberts – OC, Kroonstad, 18.7.1900, p. 75.) and 1 800 (TA, LRP 38: Paget – Roberts, 16.7.1900, p. 114.) and even 2 000 (TA, SA Telegrams III: no number, Roberts – OC, Heilbron, 19.7.1900, p. 78), which also indicates De Wet may have exaggerated. During the trek a number of burgers joined the convoy, which is probably how De Wet arrived at his figure. H. du Cane, *The German Official Account of the War in South Africa*, II, p. 310 also supplies the figure of 2 000.
42. [Hintrager], p. 51; compare Oberholster, p. 80; TA, LRP 39: Telegram, Barton – Roberts, 23.7.1900, p. 166; compare PRO, WO 105, LRP 22 for the same source; Amery (ed.), IV, p. 317; Du Cane, p. 310.
43. TA, Acquisition 285, Danie Theron Collection: No. 41, Statement, J. Versteeg, 28.8.1939.
44. [Hintrager], p. 52.
45. Ibid.
46. Ibid.; Pienaar, pp. 139–140; Van Schoor, 'Diaries of Jacob de Villiers', 16.7.1900, p. 13.
47. Ver Loren van Themaat, p. 143.
48. C.P. van der Merwe: imparted to author on site, 4.12.1972.
49. [Hintrager], p. 52; F. Klinck-Lütetsburg, *Christiaan de Wet: De Held van Zuid-Afrika*, p. 177.
50. Amery (ed.), IV, p. 319.
51. TA, LRP 38: Telegram, Lagden – Roberts, 15.7.1900, p. 63 and p. 66; compare PRO, WO 105, LRP 18 for the same source.
52. Amery (ed.), IV, p. 320.
53. TA, SA Telegrams III: No. C2720, Roberts – Buller re Hunter – Roberts, 13.7.1900, p. 61; compare PRO, WO 108/240 for the same source.
54. TA, LRP 38: Clements – Hunter, 13.7.1900, p. 90; compare PRO, WO 105, LRP 17 for the same source.
55. Amery (ed.), IV, p. 318.
56. Ibid. p. 323.
57. TA, South African Despatches II: Report by Hunter on Operations in Eastern Districts of Orange River Colony, pp. 20–21; compare PRO, WO 32/7998 for the same source.
58. TA, South African Despatches II: Report by Hunter on Operations in Eastern Districts of Orange River Colony, p. 20 and p. 25; compare PRO, WO 32/7998 for the same source. Amery (ed.), IV, p. 319 supplies the date 10 July.

59. TA, LRP 38: Lagden – Roberts, 14.7.1900, p. 61; compare PRO, WO 105, LRP 18 for the same source.
60. TA, LRP 38: Lagden – Roberts, 13.7.1900, p. 58; compare PRO, WO 105, LRP 18 for the same source.
61. TA, SA Telegrams III: No. C2634, Roberts – Rundle, 10.7.1900, p. 54; compare PRO, WO 108/240 for the same source; Maurice and Grant, III, p. 294.
62. TA, LRP 37: No. A131, Hunter – Roberts, 14.7.1900, p. 153; compare PRO, WO 105, LRP 17 for the same source.
63. Maurice and Grant, III, p. 295.
64. TA, South African Dispatches II: Report by Hunter on Operations in Eastern Districts of Orange River Colony, p. 21; compare PRO, WO 32/7998 for the same source.
65. TA, LRP 10: Operations Report by Broadwood, 'The Chase of De Wet' (henceforth Broadwood, 'Chase of De Wet'), 15.7.1900, p. 94; compare PRO, WO 105, LRP 10 for the same source.
66. TA, LRP 8: Paget's Report on Engagement at Witklip, 16.7.1900, p. 117; compare PRO, WO 105, LRP 9 for the same source.

CHAPTER FOUR

The fugitive attacks

ON THE MORNING of Monday 16 July, the sun found the burghers sleeping peacefully in the lee of Witklip koppie west of Bethlehem, exhausted after a tense night march through enemy controlled territory. Little did they know that but a few hours hence their position would be betrayed, that soon they would be fleeing for their lives across the Free State and driven right up to the Vaal River, where a circle of hills straddling the banks would form their next natural sanctuary.

When the British camp was roused at 06:00[1] Paget had no idea he had just allowed De Wet to slip through his fingers. Two hours after reveille he continued his march west as planned, sending scouts to reconnoitre the hilly area ahead known as Besterkoppies, due south of Witklip[2]. It was not long, however, before they ran into a Boer patrol in the hills and came under fire. Meanwhile, local Africans informed Paget that a commando on its way to Lindley from Slabbert's Nek had crossed the Senekal road that night.[3] This would not be the last time Africans would be used as a source of intelligence by either Boers or British during the first De Wet hunt. At this stage, however, no one was aware the Free State commander, let alone the republic's president, was among the group spotted.[4] It was nevertheless dawning on the British that some Boers must have escaped through one of the northern passes out of the Brandwater Basin. A short while later this was confirmed beyond doubt by Paget's scouts; a Boer laager had been sighted.[5]

The Boers were certainly not expecting their presence to be detected so soon, and pandemonium ensued. In fact, De Wet would probably have launched a good many more raids on British positions on his way to the railway line had it not been for Paget's scouting party. As it happened, he now had to direct his martial fury against his burghers. Some were instantly gripped by a blind panic, snatching their possessions and saddling up or hurriedly hitching oxen to carts, preparing to flee in a disorderly stampede. It took some harsh words from their commander, and probably a few blows from his sjambok too, to prevent pandemonium from taking over and to get the wagons to form up in an orderly convoy.[6] Eventually the procession set off along the wagon road skirting Witklip, heading north in the direction of Lindley. De Wet immediately began to prepare for a rearguard action; the British could attack at any moment and would have to be delayed until the wagon convoy was safe.

First, De Wet cut the telegraph line to Bethlehem, a move which would pay off handsomely. For it was not until later that afternoon that Hunter, still in Bethlehem, received word that the Boers had slipped through his cordon. He immediately ordered Ridley to rush to Paget's aid with his 800 mounted infantry, but the rescue party did not arrive until the next morning.[7] Clements, being resupplied further east at Zuringkrans, may have been in a position to send help, but Paget could not reach him. Next, Hunter tried to communicate directly with the chief in Pretoria,[8] but to no avail.

De Wet now personally supervised the placement of his artillery along the ridge that ran parallel to the road. Bruwer would cover the departing burghers from the eastern tip with one gun while Borslap and Strydom were placed in the middle of the ridge with two guns and a Maxim.[9] The position commanding the western spur, likely to be the frontline of defence, would be occupied by Captain Muller with one gun, joined by Steyn and De Wet to boost troop morale.[10] As a decoy De Wet ordered 300 Heilbron burghers to occupy the mealie field directly in front of Witklip. If the ridge could be held until nightfall the convoy would have made good its escape.

By noon Broadwood's cavalry brigade of 1 500 men arrived from Bethlehem, and the two British commanders now devised a plan to drive the Boers from their position and cut off the laager's line of retreat. Broadwood would attack the Boer right flank while Paget positioned four guns on a low hill 3,6 km south of the assumed Boer position.[11] Though the British now outnumbered their foe, they faced an extended battle line, making it difficult to execute their preferred flank attack. Furthermore, the topography left them relatively vulnerable: the broad plain between Witklip and Besterkoppies formed a gradual incline towards the British; their position, though hilly, thus afforded little effective cover from Boer artillery fire.[12]

De Wet's decoy worked. Unaware of the shells about to rain on his men, Paget launched a determined assault on the Boers in the mealie field ahead of Witklip, who were soon forced to fall back to the ridge.[13] A number of Heibronners risked being cut off from their comrades and a detachment of 20 men under Alex Ross of the Frankfort commando was sent to rescue them. Despite murderous fire, they succeeded in covering the Heilbronners' retreat.[14] A mounted infantry squadron of Roberts' Horse with a Maxim-Nordenveldt was sent after the advance guard. Muller, followed by the rest of the Boer gunners, promptly unleashed an artillery barrage on the British infantry advancing across the plain, who were soon forced to beat a hasty retreat.[15] The mounted infantry, too, were obliged to fall back behind the British lines under covering fire from the guns Paget had brought closer to support the attack.[16] These guns in turn were subjected to a Boer barrage so fierce that Paget decided to withdraw them again. Broadwood's attack on the Boer right flank had in the meantime also been repulsed.[17] Now the British brought the 38th Royal Field Artillery battery into play. Fire was so effective that in no time the Boer guns were momentarily silenced. Strydom's Armstrong was nearly lost when a shell burst on the rock shelf just behind it while the Bethlehem burghers were struggling to remove the gun to safer ground.[18]

For the rest of the day the battle turned into an artillery duel. Although the Boers occupied the best position, their shelling caused little damage because unlike the ridge they held, they were firing into soft ground. Furthermore, their shrapnel often exploded too high. And 'well-timed shrapnel', as one of Paget's men remarked dryly, 'would have been very damaging'.[19] Throughout the engagement British pom-pom fire was so heavy the Boers were often only able to operate their guns while their adversaries were reloading.[20] Yet they managed to hold the ridge,[21] miraculously suffering only three casualties – less than a third of the British losses. At the end of the day, eight or nine British soldiers had been wounded and one officer killed,[22] while one Boer was killed (Koos Papenfus from Frankfort) and two were wounded.[23] As happened so often during the war, nightfall signalled the end of hostilities and a relieved Boer rearguard was able to leave behind the veldfires caused by heavy shelling and head north to catch up with the laager outspanned at Osplaat.

The next morning, 17 July, instead of setting off in hot pursuit at first light, Broadwood decided to await Ridley's arrival. This cost the British valuable time and exposed Broadwood to just censure,[24] though to be fair,

Brigadier-General C.P. Ridley, commander of the 2nd Mounted Infantry Brigade, who joined Broadwood on 17 July 1900 on the first De Wet hunt. (From: L.S. Amery, The Times History of the War in South Africa, *Vol. III, London, 1905, facing p. 388)*

it must be remembered the British were not accustomed to dealing with a night-time flight. Ridley finally trotted in at 09:00. Now, along with Broadwood's cavalry (including six Royal Horse Artillery guns), 200 mounted Bushmen detached from Paget's force (he stayed behind) and the RHA's 'P' Battery, the British had a force of 2 500 men and 12 guns with which to hunt down De Wet.[25]

What Broadwood was unaware of was that the 3rd Cavalry Brigade was also advancing on De Wet. Then again, the 3rd Cavalry also did not know this at the time. On 11 July Hunter had sent the 3rd Cavalry, at that stage commanded by Brigadier-General J.P.R. Gordon, back north to Heilbron in order to conserve dwindling supplies for his assault on the Brandwater Basin. On his arrival in Heilbron on 15 July, Gordon was summoned to the Transvaal to take over the 1st Cavalry Brigade, and Lieutenant-Colonel M.O. Little of the 9th Lancers was put in charge of the 3rd Cavalry,[26] including the RHA's 'R' Battery. That day Roberts ordered Little to change direction and head south toward Winburg via Kroonstad. Roberts, acting on Lagden's advice that the Boers would try to escape through Rundle's line in the south and unaware De Wet would slip past Paget in the north that very night, believed the 3rd Cavalry would be well placed 'should De Wet force Rundle's line'.[27] On the afternoon of Monday 16 July, while the Boer laager was fleeing from Witklip, Little unwittingly found himself bearing down on them from the north.

Broadwood did not waste any time after Ridley arrived with reinforcements, and his trackers were soon on De Wet's trail. It was no easy task, however. The Boers had a 14-hour head start in terrain they were intimately familiar with, and the British scouts were forced to scour the veld for hoof prints and wagon tracks or scale koppies along the way to scan the horizon in the hope of spotting the departing Boers.[28] Local Africans were also interrogated whenever possible. At noon Broadwood arrived at Osplaat, the last Boer bivouac, but their quarry had already fled and the trail was cold. Broadwood decided to rely on earlier information and continue on toward Lindley.

The Boers had in fact left almost 12 hours before. Once the artillery, the last of the rearguard, had caught up with the rest of the laager, man and beast were given a short rest and the opportunity to replenish themselves. At 01:00 on 17 July the order was given to saddle up.[29] Soon the long wagon train was once again rumbling across the veld in the dead of night. Although De Wet was still ultimately heading in the direction of Vredefort, he now decided on a diversionary tactic and the convoy swung north-east, crossing the Valsch River and outspanning at Craven's Rust a few hours later – a move which threw Broadwood off course. De Wet himself remained behind with a commando in case the British cavalry had taken up the chase, but the precaution proved unnecessary and De Wet and the artillery joined the laager early that morning.[30]

While Broadwood was being led astray, the Boers took the opportunity to recuperate from the previous days' exertions, remaining at Craven's Rust until the evening of 17 July. Some of the burghers whose farms were nearby, including Piet de Wet, paid their homes a short visit. During this sojourn, Steyn told De Wet they should invade the Cape Colony. De Wet agreed in principle,[31] but it appears as though he put the idea on hold until a suitable opportunity should present itself; he would not be diverted from his chosen course. Later De Wet undertook some reconnaissance work and spotted Colonel Ewart's supply convoy destined for Hunter at Bethlehem. Ewart set up camp that afternoon about 20 km south-west of Lindley on the main road to Bethlehem – a hair's breadth from the route taken by De Wet early that morning.[32] Hunter had in fact ordered Ewart to do his best to cut off the Boers, presumed to be advancing on Lindley.[33] Although one of his patrols was involved in a short skirmish with a small Boer detachment, during which one burgher was killed,[34] Ewart was in no position to tackle the main force, especially since he was unaware of the proximity of Broadwood's brigade. Indeed, he was in more danger of being attacked himself.

It was the colonel's lucky day; for once De Wet decided not to strike. Instead he returned to camp, where preparations were being made for the next night march that would take the Free Staters in a northerly direction, past Lindley and back on track towards Vredefort.[35] At 18:00 the wagons and commandos departed, covered by Theron and his scouts.[36] Although the enemy stubbornly refused to take up the chase, this precaution often averted disaster in the coming weeks and it was not until after midnight that the scouts followed, reaching the well-protected laager site on the farm Riversdal shortly before dawn on 18 July.[37] Here the Boers would spend the day and hold a war council before continuing north-east to outspan on the farm Karroospruit for the night.[38]

Broadwood was still at least two steps behind. By the morning of 18 July he had probably received reports that De Wet had passed east of Lindley and he decided to veer east himself to rendezvous with Colonel Ewart, whom he ordered to stay put instead of continuing south toward Bethlehem. Broadwood later said he was motivated by the fear that De Wet might try to nab Ewart's convoy.[39] Be that as it may, Broadwood and Ridley replenished their troops and horses from Ewart's supplies, and commandeered the 1st Derbyshire Regiment and the 76th Royal Field Artillery battery to guard their baggage.[40] This gave Broadwood a combined force of more than 3 000 troops, most of them mounted, as well as 14 guns and a couple of Maxim-Nordenveldts.[41] But he remained in the dark about De Wet's movements. 'Not yet certain where the Boers are heading for,' he cabled Hunter later that morning,[42] before trying to pick up their trail in a north-easterly direction. A long march, constantly interrupted by having to gather intelligence from local Africans, brought him no closer to his quarry. That evening, with De Wet at Karroospruit, Broadwood had hardly progressed any further north than the night before.[43]

On the morning of Thursday 19 July, De Wet's scouts reported sighting a British formation of some 400 men advancing on Lindley from the west. De Wet could not resist the temptation. Instead of continuing his secret flight he now veered south and switched to the attack.[44] Just after dawn, De Wet, accompanied by Philip Botha, set off with 500 burghers and two guns commanded by Strydom and Muller, determined to capture the entire formation.[45]

This was in fact Little's 3rd Cavalry, a brigade of almost 800 men who had been sent to reinforce the southern cordon around the Brandwater Basin. But on finding out on the afternoon of 17 July that the Boers had escaped over one of the northern necks, Roberts immediately ordered Little to hasten to Broadwood's aid instead.[46] The next morning, 18 July, Little had set off at a stiff pace towards Lindley while Roberts cabled the commanding officers of Kroonstad, Bethlehem and Heilbron to send messengers to inform Broadwood and Little they ought to 'get into communication with each other and arrange for concerted action'.[47] That evening Little had set up camp less than 30 km north-west of Lindley, continuing the next day (19 July). But in what was to be the first of a series of British communication glitches that played into De Wet's hands, Broadwood never received the message.[48]

At noon on 19 July the Boers encountered the enemy's left flank — Little's 'C' Squadron — at Paardeplaats, 11 km north-west of Lindley. A British patrol, with the exception of one man, narrowly escaped being ambushed.[49] Strydom and Muller immediately let rip at the fleeing horsemen from an exposed position at a range of 3 000 m, which brought Little's brigade to a standstill.[50] Now Little sent another squadron, accompanied by an artillery battery and a Maxim machine-gun, to reinforce 'C' Squadron.[51] In so doing, Little employed precisely the same tactic the Boers were fond of using: the Boer attack on the left flank was turned into a frontal assault by the British. This paid off handsomely. Although there were no casualties, the Boer guns were immediately silenced and had to be removed to safer ground 600 m back.[52]

Their new position robbed the Boer gunners of a direct line of fire,[53] but at 14:00 they nevertheless launched a fresh round of shelling[54] while the rest of the Boers, now divided into two groups, attempted to encircle the enemy.[55] The Kroonstad burghers commanded by Commandant Frans van Aard and 25 Boshof burghers under Field-Cornet C.C.J. Badenhorst were sent around the British right flank. Their order, recalled the field-cornet, was to 'storm the enemy's laager'.[56] Little sent his mounted infantry and a Maxim to counter the attack.[57]

While the British were thus engaged, De Wet used the opportunity to reach a ridge on their left flank unobserved[58] and launch a ferocious surprise attack from behind,[59] forcing Little to frantically withdraw his forces from the central and right flank to reinforce the left. All available men joined the fray but it was to no avail and as Philip Botha's men surrounded the camp, the British raised the white flag.[60] The Boers, apparently, had won the day. Then, without warning, victory was snatched from under their noses. Instead of allowing his men to press home their advantage, Botha ordered them to abandon their positions.[61] He had received a report, probably from Piet de Wet, that the enemy was attacking their laager at Karroospruit and had been instructed to come to their aid.[62] Strydom and Muller's guns also hastened to the laager.[63]

The surprise attack on the Boer laager was in fact launched by Broadwood's 2nd Cavalry, blithely ignorant of De Wet's sortie to the south. Little, who communicated sporadically with Roberts[64] and thus knew Broadwood's force was nearby, actually heard the 2nd Cavalry's guns roar into action. Inexplicably, he failed to get in touch with the brigade's commander.[65]

The engagement at Paardeplaats did not end there, however. Small bands of Boers continued to harry Little's brigade and the ridge De Wet had occupied could only be taken with considerable effort,[66] while the Kroonstad and Boshof burghers still proved troublesome on the right flank until they were subjected to artillery fire. But as daylight faded, the Boers gradually melted away.[67] All except the Kroonstad and Boshof burghers, that is. For some reason they had not received Botha's order to retire and were cut off from their comrades.[68] It would be some time before they saw them again.

The British now set up camp on the battleground of Paardeplaats and counted their losses – three officers and seven men wounded, with five missing.[69] The Boer side suffered five casualties.[70]

Broadwood meanwhile had shaken off his tardiness; even before De Wet's scouts spotted Little's brigade that morning, his camp was a hive of activity. At 06:00 he cabled Hunter: 'Enemy's movements rather puzzling but I think now I have ascertained he is marching on Heilbron so am following at daybreak.'[71] Perhaps his newfound zeal had something to do with a startling discovery: De Wet himself was part of the potential bag. Two days before, on the night of 17 July, one of Ewart's officers riding through Lindley heard that De Wet's scouts under Gideon Scheepers had been seen in town that day. De Wet's name was also being bandied about.[72] But Roberts did not set much store by these rumours. Earlier that day he had cabled Buller, informing him of the Boer break-out through

Slabbert's Nek. 'They are not, I believe, under De Wet,' he confided.[73] The next morning he sent a telegram to his commander in Bloemfontein, Lieutenant-General T. Kelly-Kenny, reporting that Piet de Wet and President Steyn were accompanying the Boer force.[74] But by the morning of 19 July Broadwood, who had scoured the district for any scrap of information he could glean on the Boer force, came to a startling realisation: 'All news points to Steyn and both De Wets being with the force,' he cabled Hunter.[75] Roberts received the news late that afternoon – a full four days after De Wet and his entourage squeezed through Slabbert's Nek.[76]

Strange to say, Broadwood knew less about the movements of his own side – more specifically the 3rd Cavalry Brigade. This is clearly illustrated by his request that morning to the brigade's former commanding officer, Brigadier-General Gordon, for co-operation in capturing De Wet.[77] Little had in fact taken over command from Gordon four days before and already been instructed to hasten to Broadwood's aid. Even more remarkable is the fact that the two cavalry commanders, who were a stone's throw from one another, failed to communicate at all for another five days – even though both were ostensibly acting under Lord Roberts' orders.[78] Roberts actually believed until the afternoon of 20 July – when the commanding officer of Kroonstad put him in the picture – that Broadwood and Little had both received his orders and were chasing De Wet in concert.[79]

At dawn on 19 July, Broadwood set off after De Wet with a mounted force and the Royal Horse Artillery, leaving his supply convoy and more cumbersome Royal Field Artillery behind to catch up later.[80] Now the hunt began in all earnest. Broadwood knew who he was chasing and where his quarry was heading. Well, not quite. The snippets of information he had so scrupulously gathered along the way did little more than confirm that despite his brigade's various detours, they were more or less on the right track. The low rises and small ridges in this part of the country, however, proved quite a hindrance, as De Wet and his men easily slid from view. But time after time, as an American war correspondent F.H. Howland, who was accompanying the British forces, observed, it was thanks to 'Broadwood's shrewd judgement in discriminating between the true information and the false' that the trail was found again[81] – only to turn cold. The troops, understandably, were becoming despondent. Then Broadwood received encouraging news: the Boers were but a few hours ahead. The British were in fact rapidly approaching the laager at Karroospruit from the east just as De Wet was about to run straight into Little's left flank.[82]

That same morning, after De Wet set off to capture the 3rd Cavalry, the Boer laager at Karroospruit, which had apparently been left in charge of Piet de Wet, fell prey to a strange lethargy. Many burghers slept late[83]

THE FUGITIVE ATTACKS 51

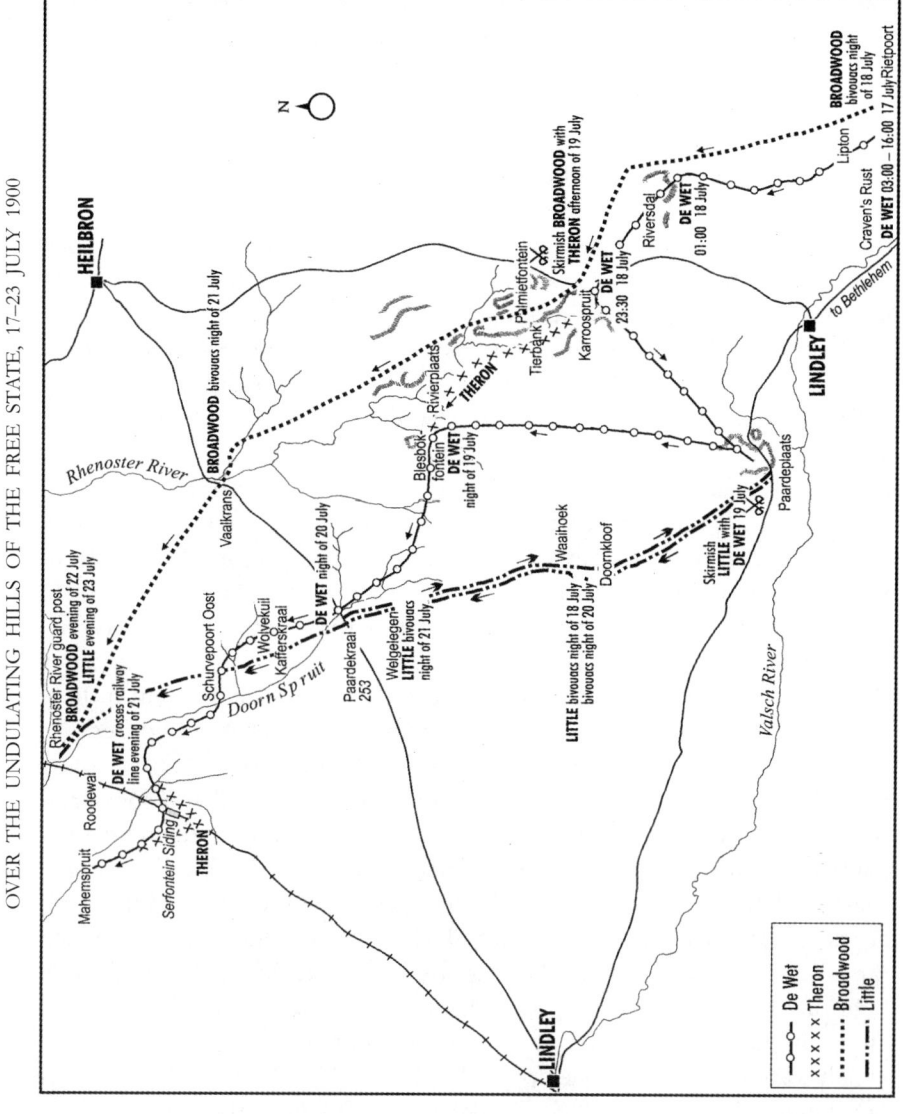

OVER THE UNDULATING HILLS OF THE FREE STATE, 17–23 JULY 1900

and when the order was given to inspan and trek north, the Boers, oblivious to the imminent danger, unhurriedly struck camp. At 13:00, a horseman raced into the laager with the news that British troopers had been spotted a short way off.[84] It was Broadwood's advance guard, now a mere 6 km away. 'We had run them down at last,' declared Howland.[85] The laager suddenly sprang to life, and even the burghers who until then had been behaving as though they were on a picnic now demonstrated just how quickly the Boers could get a wagon convoy formed up and ready to belt off into the distance. It was a facility which would get them out of many a tight corner in the weeks to come.[86]

Meanwhile, Danie Theron prepared to cover the escape with a rearguard action. First he addressed his men on a rise near the spruit. 'Today will bring much suffering,' he warned, 'and we shan't be able to hold our positions. But to grant the wagons sufficient time to escape we must keep the enemy at bay as long as possible, then fight as we retire.'[87]

This was a pattern which would often be repeated: a rearguard action, and lives sacrificed, to buy enough time for the wagons to scuttle to safety. Previously at the Kroonstad conference on 17 March, it had been agreed that the war effort must continue without large wagon laagers; only wagons ferrying food and ammunition should accompany the Boers.[88] But as the Free State force was being driven towards Bethlehem in June and the first week of July, the wagon convoy grew unobserved because the burghers were determined to prevent their possessions from falling into the hands of the British, who were confiscating all transport and beasts of burden. This put De Wet in a delicate position. He could sympathise with his burghers' desire to retain and protect the few possessions they had left, but as their Commander-in-Chief he was now saddled with an extra responsibility. 'It was an indescribable burden,' he complained bitterly.[89] What was worse, the wagons hampered his ability to launch lightning strikes and swiftly evade his enemy's grasp. Even Roberts was aware of the delays caused by such a large number of wagons and carts,[90] which were threatening to scupper the Boer cause. But De Wet knew his burghers well enough not to risk force in removing the wagons. This could only spell mutiny, especially following the fall of Bethlehem.[91] After crossing Slabbert's Nek no burgher would be prepared to leave his wagon and oxen in the veld. Only bitter experience during the hunt taught the burghers the error of their ways. As Dominee J.D. Kestell aptly put it: 'How differently De Wet could have acted in the months during which he was forced to bear responsibility for a wagon laager if he had at his disposal only a swift mounted commando which could continually surprise the enemy.'[92] When De Wet took the enemy by surprise he almost always met with resounding success, and it was usually when the British surprised the wagon laager that Boer casualties were high.

The wagon laager was a curse, then, but for now it could not be dispensed with. And today the unenviable task of holding the enemy at bay until the wagons could escape was once again entrusted to Theron and his scouts. Theron divided his force, complemented by burghers from the Bethlehem, Heilbron and Frankfort commandos,[93] into 12-man detachments. Their horses were tethered well out of sight of the approaching enemy, with the detachments positioned about 750 m apart[94] behind rocky outcrops and the walls of stone enclosures all along a low ridge. This created the illusion of an extended line of more than 10 km protecting the Boer laager and, together with the fact that the Boers were ordered to fire in salvoes, meant the British could never establish the strength of the Boer line of defence with any accuracy. A British flank attack or encircling movement was thus rendered virtually unworkable.[95]

It was not long before Broadwood and Ridley made their appearance. They had gone ahead with a detachment of scouts and halted atop a hillock little more than 1 km from Theron's position, just in time to see the Boer wagons disappearing over the horizon. And that was their downfall. For while the British were preoccupied with scouring the distant hills with their binoculars, Theron's men suddenly let rip from their shelters behind the nearby ridge, which the British mistakenly believed was part of the distant hill.[96] Luckily for the British, the Boers aimed too high. Twice. For a second round of Mauser fire also whistled over their heads. 'Take cover men!' Broadwood ordered, without for a moment losing his composure. But the third volley found its mark and a British trooper tumbled to the ground.[97] Broadwood immediately brought his artillery into position, and while the cavalry swiftly dismounted, led their horses to safety, and took cover behind a kraal wall. A moment later British bullets were whistling over the heads of the Boers.[98]

The British artillery joined the fray around 14:00.[99] The Boers responded by calling off Muller and Strydom's guns at Paardeplaats, where they were shelling Little's brigade, and ordering them to cover the rearguard action here at Karroospruit.[100] As it happened, a shortage of ammunition and the fact that they were unable to advance much closer than 6 km rendered the guns relatively ineffective. This in itself was not too disastrous. In a typical Boer rearguard action, it was enough for the artillery to bare their teeth while the riflemen held their positions for as long as was tenable before falling back to the next position to be defended, all the while buying time for the wagon laager to escape.[101] Thus it happened that when a large number of Australians poured into a breach on the British left flank, dislodging the Boers from their position, Theron, who was on the central front, immediately ordered his men to abandon the ridge. Although two British field guns blazed away at them, the Boers got away in small groups without suffering any casualties. For a short while they regained their breath in the lee of the hill before crossing a vlei to take cover along a stony ridge on another hill.[102]

Now 800 troopers under Colonel H. de B. de Lisle tried to encircle the Boer rearguard from the British right flank,[103] reinforced by Ridley's mounted infantry in the middle.[104] In no time the Boers came under heavy fire and were forced to abandon their second position, tearing across a broad expanse with a long ridge running along their right. De Lisle's cavalry, which had been working its way round the fleeing Boers, suddenly appeared on the same ridge, forcing the Boers to run the gauntlet of a hail of Lee-Metford bullets. But they took the precaution of spreading themselves out and managed to emerge unscathed.[105] Meanwhile Ridley was advancing in a straight line in the middle, from one forward position to the next.[106]

Even when out of range, the Boers kept galloping ahead. Then Danie Theron thundered: 'TVK, in position!'[107] This encouraged more burghers to join the scouts and soon a spur jutting from the ridge De Lisle had used to bring the Boers under fire became their third rearguard stronghold. Now the British crept forward carefully at a range of 180 m, finding a Mauser bullet whistling past their ears the moment their heads popped out from behind an anthill.[108] De Lisle nevertheless put the Boer rearguard under constant pressure and it was with some relief that the Boers watched the cloud of dust kicked up by their laager departing north-west behind the hills south of the Rhenoster River fade with the setting sun.[109]

Although the British felt obliged to halt their pursuit as soon as it grew dark,[110] Theron remained behind with about 30 scouts to cover the Boer rearguard's nocturnal retreat. The rest of the scouts, under the command of Lieutenant Barney Enslin, now followed in the laager's tracks. As it was pitch dark by then, the burghers occasionally galloped into fences or bodies of water. It was close to dawn by the time this group reached the outspan site at Blesbokfontein to catch up with the rest of the burghers, including those involved in De Wet's attempt to capture Little's brigade.[111]

Ridley and Broadwood now controlled the Boer positions, having driven their adversaries some 10 km north-west along the Rhenoster River[112] and suffering 20 casualties along the way, including the death of a Western Australian major.[113] According to Broadwood, eight Boer corpses were found on the battlefield,[114] though their losses may have been higher because the deceased were removed by their comrades whenever possible, as in the case of Theron scout Hendriks, from Doetinchem in the Netherlands.[115] Field-Cornet Strydom from Frankfort and a certain Van Vuuren also died that day.[116] Just before midnight the rest of the British artillery arrived with their supply convoy and the British could enjoy a well-earned rest.[117]

The Boers were in no mood to fight another rearguard battle to protect the wagon laager, and on the morning of 20 July it was sent west toward

The farmhouse of Cornelis Wessels on Blesbokfontein, where Generals Christiaan and Piet de Wet parted ways on 20 July 1900.

Honingspruit, accompanied by the Heilbron commando, outspanning at Andries B. Wessels' farm Paardekraal near the main road between Kroonstad and Heilbron at noon.[118] The remaining commandos were ordered to stay at Blesbokfontein, a farm belonging to Cornelis Wessels, until Theron and the rest of his scouts arrived.

Cornelis Wessels now invited De Wet, Steyn and his councillors to join him for breakfast at his farmstead. Christiaan's brother, Piet de Wet, had by then become heartily sick of the war. Over a month before he had been court-martialled for offering to surrender to the British, but Roberts had rejected his terms and he had rejoined the struggle. On 19 July, during the battle at Karroospruit, Piet de Wet apparently still fought like a tiger, according to one account firing at the British 'until the oil on his gun started smoking'.[119] But deep down he believed the Boer cause was hopeless. The next morning Piet de Wet rode up to Cornelis Wessels' simple whitewashed farmhouse and, midway through breakfast, called Christiaan outside. Piet asked his brother if he wanted to continue fighting. De Wet was enraged. 'Are you mad?' he spluttered before turning on his heels and storming back into the house, 'quite unaware that Piet de Wet had that very moment mounted his horse, and ridden away to follow his own course'.[120] Six days later General Piet de Wet and his staff laid down their weapons in Kroonstad.[121]

If anything, De Wet himself seemed more determined than ever to keep fighting at all costs. After breakfast he and Steyn scaled a koppie on

General Piet de Wet, who believed from at least early June 1900 that the Boer cause was hopeless. The day after he put up a brave fight on 19 July, he asked his brother, Christiaan, whether he wanted to continue the struggle. 'Are you mad?' was the answer he got. Six days later Piet de Wet and his staff laid down their weapons in Kroonstad. (From: Lady Maud Rolleston, Yeoman Service, London, 1901, frontispiece)

the farm to see if the British were snapping at their heels again, but the only thing visible in Broadwood's direction was a lonely pillar of smoke.[122] Broadwood, as it happened, had continued advancing along the northern bank of the Rhenoster River instead of swinging west to follow the Boers;[123] for the moment at least they were out of danger. Later that afternoon Theron and his men arrived at Blesbokfontein, probably confirming that the British were headed in the wrong direction. De Wet ordered his men to follow the laager to Paardekraal.

For De Wet it had been a week of successes and defeats for which both sides must take credit and blame. The virtual breakdown in communication on the British side undoubtedly helped De Wet slip past a combined force of 4 000 troops converging on him from two directions, and to switch from hunted to hunter along the way. But if Broadwood had not surprised the laager at Karroospruit, De Wet would certainly have achieved even greater success.[124]

Broadwood's achievement can be explained in part by his smart tactical decision to swoop down on the laager with squadrons of mounted men unencumbered by baggage and heavy artillery, which only caught up with the cavalry at midnight.

The Boers, on the other hand, were also plagued by numerous delays. A day before the attack, a military tribunal was held to try a burgher who had accidentally killed two scouts. Their subsequent funeral was a further hold-up.[125] The Boer horses, too, were in a deplorable state and sorely in need of rest. In these circumstances extra vigilance was needed, yet De Wet apparently relaxed his guard, believing he had shaken his pursuers by his tactical changes in direction.[126] The fact that his scouts were unable to give the laager sufficient warning the next day indicates he did not take the threat seriously enough to take appropriate precautions. But his biggest blunder was probably leaving a battle-weary Piet de Wet in charge.[127] Had the Free State commander's brother shown more vigilance in monitoring British troop movements and been more energetic in getting the laager on the move, Broadwood may well have failed to catch them off guard.

Despite these mistakes, when De Wet rode into Paardekraal at sunset on 20 July with Theron and his scouts, he was still two steps ahead of his pursuers and hungry to fight another day.

Notes

1. E. Childers, *In the Ranks of the CIV*, p. 147.
2. TA, LPR 8: Paget's Report on Engagement at Witklip, 16.7.1900, p. 117; compare PRO, WO 105, LRP 9 for the same source; visit to the site by the author, accompanied by C.P. van der Merwe, 4.12.1972.
3. TA, LPR 8: Paget's Report on Engagement at Witklip, 16.7.1900, p. 117; compare PRO, WO 105, LRP 9 for the same source.
4. Paget was under the impression that the Boers were under the command of a certain Swanepoel – probably Commandant Hans Swanepoel; TA, LRP 38: No. C6, Paget – Roberts, 16.7.1900, p. 114; compare PRO, WO 105, LRP 21 for the same source.
5. TA, LPR 8: Paget's Report on Engagement at Witklip, 16.7.1900, p. 117; compare PRO, WO 105, LRP 9 for the same source.
6. [Hintrager], p. 53.
7. TA, South African Dispatches II: Report by Hunter on Operations in Eastern Districts of Orange River Colony, p. 21; compare PRO, WO 32/7998 for the same source.
8. TA, LRP 38: No. C6, Paget – Roberts, 16.7.1900, p. 114; compare PRO, WO 105, LRP 21 for the same source.
9. FA, WMC 155/82/1: O. Hintrager, Kriegs-Tagebuch (manuscript), map, p. 130; [Hintrager], p. 53; Oberholster, p. 82.
10. [Hintrager], p. 53; Pienaar, p. 143; Amery (ed.), IV, p. 322.
11. TA, LRP 8: Paget's Report on Engagement at Witklip, 16.7.1900, p. 118; compare PRO, WO 105, LRP 9 for the same source.
12. Childers, p. 149.
13. TA, LRP 8: Paget's Report on Engagement at Witklip, 16.7.1900, p. 118; compare PRO, WO 105, LRP 9 for the same source; Childers, p. 148.
14. TA, G.S. Preller Collection 81: Die Oranje-Vrystaat-kommando's 1858–1915, Frankfort-kommando, p. 2; Lombard, p. 61.
15. TA, LRP 8: Paget's Report on Engagement at Witklip, 16.7.1900, p. 19; compare PRO, WO 105, LRP 9 for the same source; [Hintrager], p. 53.
16. TA, LRP 8: Paget's Report on Engagement at Witklip, 16.7.1900, p. 119; compare PRO, WO 105, LRP 9 for the same source.
17. Ibid.; TA, LRP 10: Broadwood, 'Chase of De Wet', 16.7.1900, p. 94; compare PRO, WO 105, LRP 10 for the same source; Amery (ed.), IV, p. 321.
18. C.P. van der Merwe in conversation with the author on site, 4.12.1972; compare [Hintrager], p. 53, who also mentions the incident.
19. Childers, p. 150.

20. [Hintrager], p. 53.
21. TA, LRP 8: Paget's Report on Engagement at Witklip, 16.7.1900, p. 119; compare PRO, WO 105, LRP 9 for the same source; TA, LRP 38: No. 6, Paget – Roberts, 16.7.1900, p. 114; compare PRO, WO 105, LRP 21 for the same source; TA, Acquisition 1250: D. de Witt, 'Die Trek naar die Bosveld', recorded by C.P. van der Merwe, p. 2.
22. TA, LRP 8: Paget's Report on Engagement at Witklip, 16.7.1900, p. 121; compare PRO, WO 105, LRP 9 for the same source.
23. Van Schoor, 'Diaries of Jacob de Villiers', 17.7.1900; TA, G.S. Preller Collection 81: Die Oranje-Vrystaat-kommando's 1858–1915, Frankfort-kommando, p. 2; Lombard, p. 61.
24. Amery (ed.), IV, pp. 414–415.
25. TA, LRP 10: Broadwood, 'Chase of De Wet', 15 and 17.7.1900, pp. 93 and 95; compare PRO, WO 105, LRP 10 for the same source; TA, LRP 8: Paget's Report on Engagement at Witklip, 16.7.1900, p. 120; compare PRO, WO 105, LRP 9 for the same source; TA, LRP 37: No. A106, Hunter – Roberts, 17.7.1900, p. 154; compare PRO, WO 105, LRP 17 for the same source; TA, South African Dispatches II: Roberts' Account, 14 June to 10 October 1900, pp. 3 and 4; compare PRO, WO 32/8000 for the same source; The *Natal Witness*, 13.10.1900: F.H. Howland, 'The Chase of De Wet'; F.H. Howland, *The Chase of De Wet and Other Later Phases of the Boer War as seen by an American Correspondent*, pp. 121–122. Howland's claim that the two British commanders were 'inferior in artillery' compared to De Wet is patently false. In Hunter's above-mentioned telegram to Roberts he puts Broadwood's combined force at 2 300, but was at that stage apparently unaware that Broadwood also had part of Paget's mounted force with him.
26. TA, WO Acquisition, JPE 5: Quarter-Master-General's Diary, 19.7.1900, p. 29.
27. TA, SA Telegrams III: No. C2783, Roberts – Kelly-Kenny, 16.7.1900, p. 67; compare PRO, WO 108/240 for the same source.
28. Howland, p. 122.
29. [Hintrager], pp. 53–54; Lombard, p. 62.
30. [Hintrager], p. 54. The claim made by Lombard (p. 62) that they had outspanned at 14:00 thus appears incorrect, the more so because Ver Loren van Themaat (p. 144), one of the scouts furthest to the rear, had already encountered the large wagon laager just after sunrise that morning.
31. Van Schoor, 'Diaries of Jacob de Villiers', 17.7.1900, p. 15.
32. TA, LRP 39: No. B1187, GOC, Kroonstad – Chief of Staff, 18.7.1900, p. 15; compare PRO, WO 105, LRP 22 for the same source; B. Moeller, *Two Years at the Front with the Mounted Infantry*, p. 84.
33. TA, LRP 38: No. C6, Paget – Roberts, 16.7.1900, p. 114; compare PRO, WO 105, LRP 21 for the same source; Moeller, p. 84.
34. Moeller, p. 84.
35. Van Schoor, 'Diaries of Jacob de Villiers', 18.7.1900, p. 15; TA, WO Acquisition, JPE 5: Intelligence Reports, 29.7.1900, p. 44; Ver Loren van Themaat, p. 145.
36. Ver Loren van Themaat, p. 145.
37. Van Schoor, 'Diaries of Jacob de Villiers', 18.7.1900, p. 15; [Hintrager], p. 54; Ver Loren van Themaat, p. 145; De Wet, p. 132; Nierstrasz, II, Vol. 5, p. 994.
38. FA, Sen. D.J. Malan Collection 60.22: No. 95, Oorlogsdagboek van D.J. Malan, 18.7.1900; Van Schoor, 'Diaries of Jacob de Villiers', 19.7.1900, p. 16; Nierstrasz, II, Vol. 5, p. 995.
39. TA, LRP 37: Broadwood – Hunter, 19.7.1900, p. 160; compare PRO, WO 105, LRP 15 for the same source.

40. Ibid.; TA, LRP 37: No. A173, Hunter – Roberts, 19.7.1900, p. 162; compare PRO, WO 105, LRP 17 for the same source; TA, LRP 10: Broadwood, 'Chase of De Wet', 18.7.1900, p. 96; compare PRO, WO 105, LRP 10 for the same source; Moeller, p. 85; Amery (ed.), IV, p. 416.
41. Amery (ed.), IV, p. 416.
42. TA, LRP 37: Broadwood – Hunter, 18.7.1900, p. 156; compare PRO, WO 105, LRP 15 for the same source.
43. Howland, p. 123; TA, LRP 37: Broadwood – Hunter, 06:00, 19.7.1900, p. 160; compare PRO, WO 105, LRP 15 for the same source; Amery (ed.), IV, p. 415.
44. De Wet, pp. 132–133.
45. [Hintrager], p. 56; De Wet, pp. 132–133; TA, Leyds 758 (a): Telegram, no number, P. Botha, Sterkstroom – L. Botha, no date (probably 17.8.1900), no page; Lombard, p. 63; compare TA, WO Acquisition, JPE 5: Staff Diary, 3rd Cavalry Brigade, 19.7.1900, p. 29 which incorrectly mentions three guns on the Boer side.
46. TA, WO Acquisition, JPE 5: Quarter-Master-General's Diary, 19.7.1900, p. 29; TA, South African Dispatches II: Roberts' Account, 14 June to 10 October 1900, p. 4; compare PRO, WO 32/8000 for the same source; F.F. Colvin and E.R. Gordon, *Diary of the Ninth Lancers during the South African Campaign, 1899–1902*, p. 129. Amery (ed.), IV, p. 416 claims that Little received his orders at Rosepan, a few kilometres south of Paardekraal.
47. TA, SA Telegrams III: No. C2855, 12:30, 18.7.1900, p. 75; compare PRO, WO 108/240 for the same source.
48. TA, LRP 39: No. 1217, GOC, Kroonstad – Roberts re Little's report, 21.7.1900, p. 17; compare PRO, WO 105, LRP 22 for the same source.
49. Colvin and Gordon, p. 130; TA, WO Acquisition, JPE 5: Staff Diary, 3rd Cavalry Brigade, 19.7.1900, p. 29; Amery (ed.), IV, p. 417.
50. [Hintrager], p. 56; Colvin and Gordon, p. 130.
51. Colvin and Gordon, pp. 130–131.
52. TA, WO Acquisition, JPE 5: Staff Diary, 3rd Cavalry Brigade, 19.7.1900, p. 29; Colvin and Gordon, p. 131.
53. [Hintrager], p. 56.
54. TA, WO Acquisition, JPE 5: Staff Diary, 3rd Cavalry Brigade, 19.7.1900, p. 29.
55. TA, Leyds 758 (a): Telegram, no number, P. Botha, Sterkstroom – L. Botha, no date, no page; TA, WO Acquisition, JPE 5: Staff Diary, 3rd Cavalry Brigade, 19.7.1900, p. 29.
56. C.C.J. Badenhorst, *Uit den Boeren-Oorlog, 1899–1902*, p. 43.
57. Colvin and Gordon, p. 131.
58. TA, Leyds 758 (a): Telegram, no number, P. Botha, Sterkstroom – L. Botha, no date, no page; [Hintrager], p. 56; Colvin and Gordon, p. 131.
59. TA, WO Acquisition, JPE 5: Staff Diary, 3rd Cavalry Brigade, 19.7.1900, p. 29.
60. TA, Leyds 758 (a): Telegram, no number, P. Botha, Sterkstroom – L. Botha, no date, no page; compare Van Schoor, 'Diaries of Jacob de Villiers', 20.7.1900, p. 17.
61. Badenhorst, p. 43.
62. TA, Leyds 758 (a): Telegram, no number, P. Botha, Sterkstroom – L. Botha, no date, no page; compare Van Schoor, 'Diaries of Jacob de Villiers', 20.7.1900, p. 17.
63. [Hintrager], p. 56.
64. TA, LRP 39: No. 1217, GOC, Kroonstad – Roberts re Little's report, 21.7.1900, p. 17; compare PRO, WO 105, LRP 22 for the same source.
65. Colvin and Gordon, p. 132.
66. Ibid., p. 131.

67. Ibid.
68. Badenhorst, p. 43. Lombard, p. 63; TA, WO Acquisition, JPE 5: Staff Diary, 3rd Cavalry Brigade, 19.7.1900, p. 29; TA, SA Telegrams III: No. C2933, Roberts – Buller, 21.7.1900, p. 85; compare PRO, WO 108/240 for the same source.
69. TA, WO Acquisition, JPE 5: Staff Diary, 3rd Cavalry Brigade, 19.7.1900, p. 29.
70. Amery (ed.), IV, p. 417.
71. TA, LRP 37: Broadwood – Hunter, 19.7.1900, p. 160; compare PRO, WO 105, LRP 15 for the same source.
72. TA, LRP 39: No. B1187, GOC, Kroonstad – Chief of Staff, 18.7.1900, p. 15; compare PRO, WO 105, LRP 22 for the same source.
73. TA, SA Telegrams III: No. C2822, Roberts – Buller, p. 72; compare PRO, WO 108/240 for the same source.
74. TA, SA Telegrams III: No. C2838, Roberts – Kelly-Kenny, 18.7.1900, p. 73; compare PRO, WO 108/240 for the same source.
75. TA, LRP 37: Broadwood – Hunter, 19.7.1900, p. 160; compare PRO, WO 105, LRP 15 for the same source.
76. TA, LRP 37: No. A172, Hunter – Roberts, 19.7.1900, p. 160; compare PRO, WO 105, LRP 17 for the same source.
77. TA, LRP 37: Broadwood, Rietpoort – Hunter, Bethlehem, 19.7.1900, p. 160; compare PRO, WO 105, LRP 15 for the same source.
78. Amery (ed.), IV, p. 417.
79. TA, SA Telegrams III: no number, Roberts – GOC, Kroonstad, 14:00, 20.7.1900, p. 82; compare PRO, WO 108/240 for the same source.
80. TA, LRP 10: Broadwood, 'Chase of De Wet', 19.7.1900, p. 97; compare PRO, WO 105, LRP 10 for the same source.
81. Howland, p. 123.
82. FA, WMC 155/13/1 (g): G. Boldingh, 'De Guerilla in den OVS', p. 11; Howland, p. 123.
83. FA, Sen. D.J. Malan Collection 60.22: No. 95, Oorlogsdagboek van D.J. Malan, 19.7.1900.
84. Van Schoor, 'Diaries of Jacob de Villiers', 20.7.1900, p. 16; compare Ver Loren van Themaat, p. 146.
85. Howland, p. 124.
86. F. Rompel, *Uit den Tweeden Vrijheidsoorlog, Schetsen en Portretten*, p. 9; Ver Loren van Themaat, p. 146; Van Schoor, 'Diaries of Jacob de Villiers', 20.7.1900, p. 16.
87. Ver Loren van Themaat, p. 146.
88. TA, Kommandant-Generaalstukke (KG) 353 (1): Extract uit de Notule van de Krygsraad, te Kroonstad gehouden op Zaterdag, den 17den Maart 1900; The *Natal Witness*, 12.7.1900: 'A Council of War'. The latter is by Captain Allum, Norwegian attaché to the Boer republics; Amery (ed.), IV. p. 26; C.J. Barnard, *Generaal Louis Botha op die Natalse Front 1899–1900*, p. 152; TA, G.S. Preller Collection, 134: Documents of Jacob de Villiers, p. 77.
89. De Wet, p. 134.
90. TA, SA Telegrams III: No. C2894, Roberts – OC, Heilbron, 20.7.1900, p. 80; compare PRO, WO 108/240 for the same source.
91. De Wet, p. 134.
92. J.D. Kestell, *Christiaan de Wet: 'n Lewensbeskrywing*, p. 86.
93. Van Schoor, 'Diaries of Jacob de Villiers', 20.7.1900, p. 17; TA, G.S. Preller Collection 81: Die Oranje-Vrystaat-kommando's 1858–1915, Frankfort-kommando, p. 2; FA, Renier Collection 119.512: Oorlogsherinneringe van W.J.J. Potgieter, re-

corded by M. Potgieter; TA, Acquisition 1250: D. de Witt, 'Die Trek naar die Bosveld', recorded by C.P. van der Merwe, p. 2.
94. Ver Loren van Themaat, p. 146; H.J.C. Pieterse, *Oorlogsavonture van Genl. Wynand Malan*, p. 79.
95. Ver Loren van Themaat, p. 147; Pieterse, p. 80.
96. Howland, p. 125.
97. Howland, pp. 125–126; Ver Loren van Themaat, p. 147, is probably referring to the same incident.
98. Howland, p. 126; Ver Loren van Themaat, p. 147.
99. Howland, p. 126; [Hintrager], p. 56; Lombard, p. 63.
100. [Hintrager], p. 56; Lombard, p. 63.
101. Pieterse, p. 80.
102. Howland, pp. 126–127; Ver Loren van Themaat, p. 148.
103. TA, LRP 10: Broadwood, 'Chase of De Wet', 19.7.1900, p. 97; compare PRO, WO 105, LRP 10 for the same source; Howland, p. 127.
104. Howland, p. 127.
105. Ver Loren van Themaat, p. 148.
106. Howland, p. 128.
107. Ver Loren van Themaat, p. 149.
108. Ibid.; compare TA, LRP 10: Broadwood, 'Chase of De Wet', 19.7.1900, p. 97, in which Broadwood, who had positioned himself at the central front, reports that De Lisle's Australians rushed into the right flank and engaged with the Boers at a range of about 90 m. Two such widely differing statements are difficult to reconcile. But since Ver Loren van Themaat was actually present, his version could be considered more reliable.
109. Ver Loren van Themaat, p. 149.
110. TA, LRP 39: Broadwood – GOC, Kroonstad, 21.7.1900, p. 19; compare PRO, WO 105, LRP 15 for the same source.
111. Ver Loren van Themaat, p. 151; Van Schoor, 'Diaries of Jacob de Villiers', 20.7.1900, p. 17; Lombard, pp. 63–64; *Nieuwe Rotterdamsche Courant*, 25.7.1900; TA, LRP 39: No. B1227, GOC, Kroonstad – Military Secretary, Chief, Pretoria, re telegram Bullock, Honingspruit, 22.7.1900, p. 21; compare PRO, WO 105, LRP 22 for the same source.
112. Howland, p. 128; The *Natal Witness*, 13.10.1900: F.H. Howland, 'The Chase of De Wet'.
113. PRO, WO 108/231 VI: No. C600, COC, Lines of Communication – Secretary of State for War, 23.7.1900, p. 47. Major H.G. Moor and four men were killed, while Lieutenant F.W. Stanley of the 10th Hussars and 14 men were wounded.
114. TA, LRP 39: Broadwood – GOC, Kroonstad, 21.7.1900, p. 19; compare PRO, WO 105, LRP 15 for the same source; TA, LRP 10: Broadwood, 'Chase of De Wet', 19.7.1900, p. 97; compare PRO, WO 105, LRP 10 for the same source.
115. Ver Loren van Themaat, p. 151.
116. TA, G.S. Preller Collection 81: Die Oranje-Vrystaat-kommando's 1858–1915, Frankfort-kommando, p. 2; Lombard, p. 63.
117. Howland, pp. 128–129.
118. Van Schoor, 'Diaries of Jacob de Villiers', 20.7.1900, p. 17. The farm belonged to Andries B. Wessels, who together with his brother Barend J.S. Wessels of the farm Rivierplaats, were joint Volksraad members for Mid Valsch River. Furthermore, Andries B. Wessels took part in the trek as field-cornet of the Kroonstad commando. The house which was built in 1872 stands to this day, although it has been

altered with face brick. Wynand G. Wessels, the son of Andries B. Wessels, was still living there when the author interviewed him on 6.12.1972.

119. TA, Acquisition 1250: D. de Witt, 'Die Trek naar die Bosveld', recorded by C.P. van der Merwe, p. 2.
120. De Wet, p. 133.
121. Piet de Wet later took up arms against the Boers as leader of the Heilbron section of the Orange River Colony Volunteers.
122. De Wet, p. 133; Van Schoor, 'Diaries of Jacob de Villiers', 21.7.1900, p. 17.
123. TA, LRP 39: No. B1227, GOC, Kroonstad – Military Secretary, Chief, Pretoria via Natal re telegram Broadwood, 22.7.1900, p. 19; compare PRO, WO 105, LRP 22 for the same source.
124. Compare TA, Leyds 758 (a): Telegram, no number, P. Botha – L. Botha, no date; Van Schoor, 'Diaries of Jacob de Villiers', 20.7.1900, p. 17; also compare F. Pretorius, 'Die Twee Skermutselinge van C.R. de Wet op 19 Julie 1900' in *Christiaan de Wet-Annale*, 2, October 1973, p. 159.
125. Van Schoor, 'Diaries of Jacob de Villiers', 18.7.1900, pp. 15–16; Lombard, pp. 62–63.
126. Ver Loren van Themaat, p. 146.
127. Danie Theron had a great deal of authority that day because the skirmish developed into a rearguard action, which had become his designated field of expertise. But it does seem as if Christiaan de Wet initially left Piet de Wet in command of the Boer laager and commandos. The heliographer Lombard reported that during the fight against Little, Steyn had sent him to see Piet de Wet in the northern position (Lombard, p. 64), while D.J. Malan noted in his diary: 'This afternoon khakis are after us at Thos Naudé. I am in the laager with Piet de Wet.' (FA, Sen.s D.J. Malan Collection, 60.23: No. 93, Oorlogsdagboek van D.J. Malan, 19.7.1900). M. Davitt, *The Boer Fight for Freedom*, p. 449, incorrectly asserts that Commandant Nel was in command of the one Boer group, as Nel had already handed in his resignation in June 1900. Moreover, Davitt's description of the period 16– 23 July is vague and nebulous.

CHAPTER FIVE

Crossing the line

DE WET HAD TO SEE his laager safely over the Bloemfontein–Pretoria railway line in order to reach the comparative safety of the hills along the Vaal River around Reitzburg and Vredefort and to launch further attacks on British supply lines, hopefully in co-operation with Liebenberg's burghers in the Western Transvaal. This was easier said than done. De Wet's string of successes in June along that line, and especially the bonfire of British supplies at Roodewal on 7 June, left no doubt in the minds of the British about the need to keep the line heavily guarded. Piet de Wet had warned earlier that the entire Free State force would be captured along the railway.[1] This was certainly not far fetched. As Oskar Hintrager, the German jurist who accompanied the Free State artillery, put it: 'The railway is synonymous with the proximity of the English.'[2] Meticulous planning and careful reconnaissance were needed to avoid disaster.

Soon after sunrise on Saturday 21 July, the Boers set off for the railway from Paardekraal along the eastern bank of the Doornspruit.[3] De Wet sent out reconnaissance patrols in all directions to ensure the laager was not surprised again. Captain Gideon Scheepers and his scouts, along with some of Theron's men, where sent ahead to find a suitable crossing point.[4]

The rest of Theron's scouts formed a rearguard in two sections; one north and the other south of the wagon train.[5] The northern flank was especially vulnerable because of the presence of Broadwood's large force, and at one point the scouts there were forced to take up positions to protect the laager.[6] But Little did not leave the southern flank in peace and a charge by the 17th Lancers, supported by a pom-pom, forced a group of scouts to retire. The advantage of these engagements, however, was that by early afternoon, despite rolling hills which impeded long-range vision, De Wet was well informed about the positions of the two British cavalry brigades.

Mindful of the danger his men were in, De Wet ordered the trek to continue without pause until they had crossed to the western bank of the Doornspruit to outspan on Henrik Serfontein's farm Schurwe Poort Oost.[7] Theron's rearguard caught up with the wagons during the river crossing[8] and were able to join the rest of the burghers, enjoying a brief rest before the convoy set off again after dark. Not far off was the railway line, with Honingspruit Station to the south-west, Serfontein Siding virtually due west and Roodewal north-west.

While De Wet was waiting for word from Scheepers about the most suitable crossing point, he received a report from some burghers that there was a British camp at Honingspruit Station and another north of Serfontein Siding at Kaallaagte. If this was true, the Boers would be captured or only able to cross the line with 'fierce fighting', according to De Wet. This caused some consternation among Steyn and his councillors. But De Wet was intimately familiar with the terrain and refused to heed the warning until he had received intelligence from his own scouts. Sure enough, when Scheepers and his men returned they reported seeing six or so British tents at Honingspruit Station and four at Kaallaagte, guarded by small pickets.[9] The burghers had thus greatly exaggerated the British presence along the line. Steyn and his councillors let out a sigh of relief.

Just before sunset, De Wet began to arrange the convoy in formation. Philip Botha was ordered to line up the wagons in six adjacent rows to shorten the length of the procession and ensure the operation ran smoothly. De Wet himself rode at the head of the wagons accompanied by Steyn in an advance guard that probably included Scheepers and his scouts.[10] The convoy was protected by flank commandos of 200 men each, the left commanded by Michael Prinsloo and the right by Philip Botha,[11] with orders to wreck the railway in the event of the unexpected appearance of a British armoured train. Some of Theron's scouts were among these commandos; they were told to hand over any spare horses to fellow burghers accompanying the wagons. Apparently most of the combatants, along with the Boer artillery, were ordered to position themselves behind the convoy to cover its departure from the rear, as happened at Witklip and Karroospruit.[12] Theron and his scouts formed the final rearguard again.

It was dark by the time the convoy set off, heading due west over the plain toward Serfontein Siding.[13] Twenty minutes east of the line, De Wet ordered the flanks, about 5 km apart, to advance on the railway south and north of the siding respectively. The section in the centre also proceeded, followed by the wagons and carts, until De Wet called a halt a short distance from the line. He now took 15 burghers and rode ahead to cut the telegraph line,[14] which was usually done by firing a bullet into the telegraph pole and pulling it to the ground. Just then a train from Kroonstad came, bearing down on the group of saboteurs. As De Wet had no dynamite at hand to blow up the rails, he laid stones on the tracks. But the locomotive's cow-catcher simply swept this ineffectual barrier aside and the train steamed on into the night. A short while later another train departed from Serfontein Siding, this time smashing into the stones and grinding to a halt. A man carrying a lantern emerged to inspect the dam-

De Wet on a dark brown horse – unusual because the general is always associated with his white stallion, Fleur. The dark horse proved useful for his nocturnal excursions. (Suid-Afrikaanse Akademie vir Wetenskap en Kuns, Pretoria)

age, but boarded the train unmolested after clearing the tracks.[15] De Wet, as it turned out, had ordered his men to hold their fire as he believed an outbreak of fighting ahead of the wagons would have caused pandemonium.[16] Presently the advance guard, followed by six rows of wagons, began to cross the railway at Serfontein Siding.[17]

On the right flank, Philip Botha ordered his men to 'occupy the line and let nothing more through'[18] – probably after the two trains heading north had passed. Botha's men wrecked the line with equipment brought along for this purpose and remained in position until word arrived that De Wet and Steyn were safely across. Then, just as the last wagons rolled over the railway, De Wet received a report from Theron on the left or southern flank: a train had been captured. De Wet immediately raced to the scene, allowing the wagons to proceed without him.[19]

The Bethlehem commando was the first to reach the line south of Serfontein Siding just before the train from Kroonstad appeared; they let it pass unhindered.[20] A short while later Theron's scouts, led by Theron himself, left the rearguard and joined the Bethlehem burghers. Just then another locomotive pulling between 29 and 32 supply wagons[21] – transporting 100 Welsh Fusiliers and two officers to Pretoria[22] – began to approach a long rise about 4 km north of Honingspruit Station. Eventually it slowed virtually to walking pace. Then, for no apparent reason, the train screeched to a halt. An officer alighted. Theron scout Wynand Malan tried to disarm the man, but he fired a shot.[23] The Boers immediately let rip at the train. In the ensuing confusion a number of Welsh Fusiliers leaped from the carriages and flattened themselves on the ground to return fire. The skirmish did not last long. Malan and a number of Dutch volunteers launched a flank attack and the Welsh soon surrendered. Ninety-eight men were taken along as prisoners of war and four wounded men were left behind. De Wet put Boer casualties at one man seriously wounded,[24] but there is evidence suggesting a certain E.J.A. van der Heide of the Bethlehem commando was killed during the engagement.[25]

The train not only contained ammunition but was heavily laden with oats and flour destined for the front. Theron's scouts and the Bethlehem burghers made good use of the opportunity to replenish their own dwindling provisions. Word of the capture spread fast and soon groups of mounted burghers hungry for booty began to appear on the scene.[26]

De Wet ordered the wounded British soldiers to be placed in a wagon, which was removed at a safe distance of 200 m before the train was torched. Again a lack of readily available transport – the wagons and carts were already too far ahead – forced De Wet to sacrifice a good deal of valuable ammunition.[27] Now it was important for the Boers to put some distance between themselves and the scene of destruction. De Wet and Theron gathered their men together and headed north-west after the convoy,[28] which at 02:00 had outspanned at Mahemspruit about 10 km up

The trucks wrecked and set on fire by Danie Theron's corps near Serfontein Siding on 21 July 1900. (From: H. W. Wilson, After Pretoria: The Guerilla War, *Vol. I. London, 1901, p. 55)*

ahead.[29] Throughout the night detachments of Boers kept arriving, some only reaching the bivouac at dawn on Sunday, 22 July.[30]

Oddly enough, in De Wet's report to the Transvaal government he dates the crossing 24 July.[31] This is contradicted by a number of primary British sources. On the Boer side, the personal testimony of Chris van Niekerk (later commandant) is probably the most irrefutable proof that the British sources were correct: 'On July 21st – I remember it well because it was my late father's birthday – we crossed the line under the cover of darkness.'[32]

Thus Piet de Wet's predictions of doom and gloom had not come to pass. On the contrary, De Wet had led the entire Boer force across the line virtually unharmed, seized or destroyed a substantial quantity of British supplies and ammunition and taken 98 prisoners. And their pursuers where nowhere to be seen. De Wet, a devout Christian, ascribed his success to the guiding hand of a 'Higher Power'.[33] But there were other, more prosaic, reasons.

For one thing, Roberts had not pursued the Boers more vigorously because once again, as with Lagden's telegram, he had fallen victim to false intelligence – this time from Major-General A.F. Hart, the commanding officer at Heilbron. On Friday 20 July, Hart reported to Roberts that the Boer force had been spotted the previous night east of Heilbron, and was presumably heading for the Transvaal.[34] This caused Roberts to suspect De Wet was escorting Steyn to see Kruger on the Delagoa Bay railway.[35] He thus informed Buller in Standerton in the Eastern Transvaal to see to it that Major-General Clery was at Greylingstad north-east of Heilbron no later than Sunday 22 July.[36] If Clery could engage the Boer force this would give Broadwood time to catch up with De Wet. What's more, he ordered General French to be in position with his cavalry and the mounted infantry of Major-General E.T.H. Hutton at the confluence of the Olifants River and Steenkoolspruit on 22 July to block De Wet should he slip past Clery.[37] Roberts also cabled Broadwood and Little on 20 July, informing them of his plans based on the information received from Hart, concluding with the stern warning: 'I shall be much disappointed if you do not manage to keep in touch with and overtake him [De Wet] within the next few days.'[38]

The main threat to De Wet, however, was Broadwood. The cavalry commander knew the Boer force had disappeared behind the hills south of the Rhenoster River after the extended rearguard action from Karroospruit.[39] Strange to say, Broadwood had failed to pursue them. The reasons for his conduct are hard to determine.

On 20 July Broadwood buried his dead with full military honours[40] before preparing to resume the hunt. He decided to repeat his tactic of the day before and loaded as many provisions as possible into lighter wagons and carts for a rapid advance; the bulk of his supply convoy could catch up later. Arranging this took some time and it was only at noon that the 2nd Cavalry and Ridley's mounted infantry were ready to depart. De Wet had thus built up a substantial head start, with his laager already outspanned at Paardekraal. After some of his patrols engaged Boer detachments at the rear of his main force,[41] Broadwood unaccountably proceeded to march along the northern bank of the Rhenoster River. By the next evening, 21 July, he had only progressed as far as Vaalkrans on the Kroonstad–Heilbron road, while the Boers were already crossing the railway further west at Serfontein Siding.[42]

The excuse Broadwood offers for his bizarre behaviour hardly holds water: 'My orders', he explained later, 'were to prevent De Wet from reaching the Transvaal and I believed Methuen to be in the vicinity of Kroonstad with a large force.'[43] But which order was Broadwood referring to? It could hardly have been the one issued on Friday 20 July, because it was precisely at that point that communication with Broadwood was causing the British command innumerable headaches. If he was referring to Roberts' order of 18 July, then Broadwood had not carried it out. In the first place he had not been told to tarry in the vicinity of the Boer force to prevent it from crossing into the Transvaal; Roberts had stressed it was of the utmost importance 'that this party should be overtaken and dealt with'.[44] The order clearly called for offensive action, not the defensive approach Broadwood had adopted. Secondly, Broadwood took no notice of Roberts' instruction that he should link up with Little and act jointly in the hunt for De Wet. It is thus entirely plausible that communication glitches meant Broadwood never received Roberts' orders in time and that in compiling his report after the event he had exploited Roberts' mistake concerning De Wet's whereabouts to absolve himself.[45]

Broadwood's remark that he believed Methuen was in Kroonstad – implying he could rely on the support of the 1st Division commander – was a clear indication of the communication problems bedevilling the British at that stage. Eight days before, on 12 July, Methuen had been ordered into the Transvaal[46] to clear the road to Rustenburg, where a garrison commanded by Baden-Powell was stationed. On 16 July he reached Krugersdorp and two days later, accompanied by Smith-Dorrien's column of infantry, headed west to force his way through a sizable Boer force blocking Olifant's Nek, the southern pass through the Magaliesberg mountains to Rustenburg.[47] Broadwood was therefore relying on a division he presumed was still in his vicinity, but with which he had no contact. It was not the first time during the hunt that Broadwood was not entirely up to date concerning the movements of his allies.[48] With an adversary such as De Wet these errors were bound to cost him dearly.

For Roberts, the disappointment he had been determined to avoid was greater than he could have foreseen. He now had to hear that De Wet had not only led the Boer forces north-west and crossed the railway, but had managed to capture a supply train and, as in the case of Roodewal six weeks previously, cut the British commander's most important telegraph line. The chief, who had been ready to move his headquarters east from Pretoria along the Delagoa Bay line closer to the eastern front,[49] thus had to hear the ill tidings via Natal from the commanding officer in Cape Town, who in turn had received the news from Kelly-Kenny, commander of the British communication line up to Kroonstad.[50]

The Boer camp, understandably, was elated. On 22 July, the morning after the successful crossing, De Wet mounted a wagon and, with his entire force assembled and Theron at his side, began to praise the scouts and their leader for their bravery. It turned out that one of the scouts had leaped aboard the moving train and disconnected its pneumatic break.[51] The names of Theron scout Wynand Malan[52] and a certain Otto[53] have been linked to this deed. Whoever was responsible, it was a fine example of the dash needed if the Boers were to enjoy any success against a foe which vastly outnumbered them. 'If today I had at my disposal 1 000 men like Danie Theron,' De Wet declared, 'I'd be walking straight to Cape Town now.'[54] Then he announced that a military council decision had been taken to promote Captain Theron to commandant; in future the scouts would have one field gun at their disposal.[55] The exuberance of the Boers following the announcement struck the German artilleryman Oskar Hint-

Danie Theron, leader of the TVK (Theron Verkenningskorps or scouting corps) who was promoted to commandant on 22 July 1900 after capturing a train the previous evening while De Wet's force was crossing the Bloemfontein–Pretoria railway line near Serfontein Siding. (Transvaal Archives Depot, Pretoria)

rager. 'For the first time since I'd been in South Africa I saw some enthusiasm, for among Theron's people there are foreigners and young Afrikaners. The real country Boer is as unfamiliar with enthusiasm as he is with dejection. The waves of his emotional life know neither crest nor trough. He is serene and unperturbed by anything – as though nothing could get at him.'[56] But the Bethlehem burghers were certainly not unmoved when De Wet, according to one, accused them of offering but 'feeble assistance' to Theron's scouts during the capture. They now resolved to show their leader they were capable of seizing a train themselves without the aid of his much-vaunted scouts.[57]

After the ceremony, the trek north-west toward Vredefort resumed. That afternoon the convoy crossed the Rhenoster River again to spend the night near Wonderheuwel,[58] where a gentle winter rain set in that would continue falling the next morning, making the road treacherous for the wagons and carts to negotiate.[59] Before sunrise on Monday 23 July, the Boers set off again, outspanning on the farms Klein-Bloemfontein and Vlakkuil[60] later that day, while heliographers climbed a nearby koppie and unsuccessfully tried to communicate with their counterparts in the Transvaal.[61] Ahead of the Boers, the undulating Free State landscape was broken by a series of tall hills around Reitzburg and Vredefort on both sides of the meandering Vaal River. A more stark contrast to the terrain they had been traversing could hardly be imagined. De Wet did not immediately seek refuge behind this natural shelter as he first wished to find out what the British forces, now massing along the railway near Roodewal, intended doing.[62]

He also wanted to form a clearer picture of the lay of the land ahead and led a 50-man commando on a reconnaissance mission in the direction of Vredefort.[63] Before he left, De Wet sent a few cart-loads of wheat to be ground at a mill in the town belonging to a certain Mr Mackenzie[64] – a decision which was to spark off one of the more bizarre skirmishes of the war. When De Wet returned to his laager later that afternoon he received a report that a large British column heading from Rhenoster River bridge to Vredefort had set up camp less than 13 km away at a farm called Klipstapel.[65] This was in fact Broadwood's brigade, a little further away on the farm Shepstone, but nevertheless catching up fast. And the first Boers to bear the brunt of his advance would be the drivers of five loads of freshly ground flour.

Notes

1. De Wet, p. 136.
2. [Hintrager], p. 58.
3. Lombard, p. 64; Ver Loren van Themaat, pp. 152–154 and map p. 145. Doornspruit is a tributary of the Rhenoster River.
4. Ver Loren van Themaat, p. 153; H.J.C. Pieterse, p. 86; De Wet, p. 134.
5. De Wet, p. 134; Ver Loren van Themaat, p. 154.
6. FA, Renier Collection, 119.512: Oorlogsondervindinge van W.J.J. Potgieter, recorded by M. Potgieter.
7. Lombard, p. 64; Ver Loren van Themaat, p. 154.
8. Ver Loren van Themaat, p. 154.
9. De Wet, p. 134.
10. Van Schoor, 'Diaries of Jacob de Villiers', 23.7.1900, p. 17; [Hintrager], p. 57; De Wet, p. 135; Pieterse, p. 87.
11. Van Schoor, 'Diaries of Jacob de Villiers', 23.7.1900, p. 17.
12. [Hintrager], p. 57.
13. De Wet, p. 135; FA, Renier Collection 119.512: Oorlogsondervindinge van W.J.J. Potgieter, recorded by M. Potgieter.
14. De Wet, p. 135.
15. Van Schoor, 'Diaries of Jacob de Villiers', 23.7.1900, pp. 17–18.
16. De Wet, p. 135.
17. Ibid.; Van Schoor, 'Diaries of Jacob de Villiers', 23.7.1900, p. 18.
18. FA, Renier Collection 119.119: W.J. Cilliers, 'Theron-Verkenningskorps', memoirs recorded 5.12.1949.
19. De Wet, p. 135.
20. Ver Loren van Themaat, pp. 155–156.
21. The *Cape Times*, 17.8.1900: 'The Destroyed Train'.
22. TA, WO Acquisition, JPE 5: Staff Diary, Lines of Communication, 22.7.1900, p. 34; The *Cape Times*, 17.8.1900: 'The Destroyed Train'.
23. Pieterse, p. 89.
24. De Wet, p. 135.
25. M.J. Grobler, *Met die Vrystaters onder die Wapen*, p. 150; TA, Acquisitions 1250: D. de Witt, 'Die Trek naar die Bosveld', recorded by C.P. van der Merwe, p. 3; Ver Loren van Themaat, p. 157.
26. TA, Leyds 730 (e): Telegram No. 46a, received 15.8.1900, De Wet – Transvaal government via Grobler, no date; FA, Renier Collection 119.70: M.H. Wessels, 'Danie Theron en die Trein wat hulle gevang het', memoirs recorded 8.8.1949; Ver Loren van Themaat, p. 157: De Wet, pp. 135–136; Pieterse, p. 89; Lombard, p. 64.
27. De Wet, pp. 135–136; TA, WO Acquisition, JPE 5: Staff Diary, Lines of Communication, 22.7.1900, p. 34; FA, Renier Collection 119.70: M.H. Wessels, 'Danie Theron en die Trein wat hulle gevang het', memoirs recorded 8.8.1949; TA, Acquisition 1250: D. de Witt, 'Die Trek naar die Bosveld', recorded by C.P. van der Merwe, p. 3.
28. FA, Renier Collection 119.70: M.H. Wessels, 'Danie Theron en die Trein wat hulle gevang het', memoirs recorded 8.8.1949; Ver Loren van Themaat, p. 158.
29. Van Schoor, 'Diaries of Jacob de Villiers', 23.7.1900, p. 18; De Wet, p. 136; Ver Loren van Themaat, p. 159; [Hintrager], p. 59; Lombard, p. 64; The *Natal Witness*, 5.9.1900: 'With De Wet: A Prisoner's Account'; TA, Acquisition 1250: D. de Witt, 'Die Trek naar die Bosveld', recorded by C.P. van der Merwe, p. 3.
30. Ver Loren van Themaat, pp. 158–159; Pieterse, p. 89.
31. TA, Leyds 730 (e): Telegram No. 46a, received 15.8.1900, De Wet – Transvaal government via Grobler.

32. H.C. Hopkins, *Maar Eén Soos Hy: Die Lewe van Kommandant C.A. van Niekerk*, p. 92.
33. De Wet, p. 136.
34. TA, LRP 39: Hart – Roberts, 20.7.1900, p. 96; compare PRO, WO 105, LRP 22 for the same source.
35. TA, SA Telegrams III: No. C2894, Roberts – OC, Heilbron, 20.7.1900, p. 80; compare PRO, WO 108/240 for the same source.
36. TA, SA Telegrams III: No. C2895, Roberts – Buller, 20.7.1900, p. 80; compare PRO, WO 108/240 for the same source.
37. TA, SA Telegrams III: No. C2896, Roberts – French, 20.7.1900, p. 81; compare PRO, WO 108/240 for the same source.
38. TA, SA Telegrams III: No. C2894, Roberts – Broadwood and Little via OC, Heilbron, 20.7.1900, p. 80; compare PRO, WO 108/240 for the same source.
39. TA, LRP 10: Broadwood, 'Chase of De Wet', 20.7.1900, p. 99; compare PRO, WO105, LRP 10 for the same source.
40. F. Wilkinson, *Australia at the Front: A Colonial View of the Boer War*, p. 268.
41. Howland, p. 130.
42. TA, LRP 39: No. B1227, GOC, Kroonstad – Military Secretary, Chief, Pretoria via Natal re telegram Broadwood, 22.7.1900, p. 19; compare PRO, WO 105, LRP 22 for the same source.
43. TA, LRP 10: Broadwood, 'Chase of De Wet', 20.7.1900, p. 99; compare PRO, WO105, LRP 10 for the same source.
44. TA, SA Telegrams III: No. C2855, Roberts – Broadwood and Little via GOC, Kroonstad and Bethlehem and OC, Heilbron, 12:30, 18.7.1900, p. 75; compare PRO, WO 108/240 for the same source.
45. Insufficient sources regarding these events preclude one from forming a final judgement.
46. TA, SA, Telegrams III: No. C2688, Roberts – Methuen via GOC, Kroonstad, 12.7.1900, p. 57. Compare TA, SA Telegrams III, No. C2721, Roberts – Barton, 13.7.1900, p. 61; compare PRO, WO 108/240 for both abovementioned sources.
47. H.M. Guest, *With Lord Methuen and the 1st Division*, p. 76.
48. Compare his telegram of 19.7.1900 to the 3rd Cavalry Brigade, in which he believed Gordon was still its commander.
49. TA, SA Telegrams III: No. C2896, Roberts – French, 20.7.1900, p. 81; compare PRO, WO 108/240 for the same source.
50. TA, LRP 38: No. 2011, GOC, Lines of Communication, Cape Town – Military Secretary, Chief, Pretoria via Natal re telegram no. 3858, Kelly-Kenny, 22.7.1900, p. 112; compare PRO, WO 105, LRP 19 for the same source.
51. The *Cape Times*, 17.8.1900: 'The Destroyed Train'; TA, Acquisition 1250: D. de Witt, 'Die Trek naar die Bosveld' recorded by C.P. van der Merwe, p. 3; Ver Loren van Themaat, p. 156.
52. Pieterse, p. 88.
53. FA, Renier Collection 119.70: M.H. Wessels, 'Danie Theron en die Trein wat hulle gevang het', memoirs recorded 8.8.1949; Preller, p. 135.
54. FA, Renier Collection 119.57: 'Danie Theron', memoirs of Dominee Naudé, recorded 12.9.1949.
55. [Hintrager], p. 59; Ver Loren van Themaat, p. 159; TA, Acquisition 1250: D. de Witt, 'Die Trek naar die Bosveld', recorded by C.P. van der Merwe, p. 4; FA, Renier Collection 119.57: 'Danie Theron', memoirs of Dominee Naude, recorded 12.9.1949; Pieterse, p. 89; Nierstrasz, II, Vol. 5, p. 1000.
56. [Hintrager], p. 60.

57. TA, Acquisition 1250: D. de Witt, 'Die Trek naar die Bosveld', recorded by C.P. van der Merwe, p. 4.
58. Van Schoor, 'Diaries of Jacob de Villiers', 23.7.1900, p. 18; Ver Loren van Themaat, p. 159; [Hintrager], p. 60; De Wet, p. 136; Nierstrasz, II, Vol. 5, p. 1000.
59. Lombard, p. 65; Ver Loren van Themaat, p. 160.
60. Van Schoor, 'Diaries of Jacob de Villiers', 23.7.1900, pp. 18–19; Ver Loren van Themaat, map facing p. 144; FA, Renier Collection 119.526: Oorlogsherinneringe van adj. C. du Preez, recorded by J.N. Brink, p. 26; A.M. de V. Esterhuysen, *Corneels Kanniedood,* p. 62.
61. Lombard, p. 65.
62. De Wet, p. 136.
63. Van Schoor, 'Diaries of Jacob de Villiers', 23.7.1900, p. 18; Lombard, p. 65.
64. De Wet, p. 136. The foundations of Mackenzie's mill can still be seen in Waterstraat in Vredefort – pointed out to author on 7.12.1972 by H. Wiegand, a burgher in the Heilbron commando.
65. De Wet, p. 136.

CHAPTER SIX

Give us this day our daily bread

WHEN BROADWOOD WOKE at Vaalkrans on the morning of Sunday 22 July, he had already decided on a change of course. The night before he sent a report to Honingspruit Station, south of Serfontein Siding, stating he would advance to Roodewal the next day. He requested his command to send ahead adequate provisions for 2 000 men and their mounts as the supplies being transported by the convoy plodding in his wake were all but depleted.[1] He also asked to be kept abreast of the Boer force's movements.[2] It was beginning to dawn on Broadwood that he had made a mistake and would have to set off in direct pursuit of the Boers.

On reaching Roodewal, Broadwood learned the Boers had been at Mahemspruit that morning, which as the crow flies was relatively close to Roodewal, and he immediately set about trying to reach them. But a series of impassable drifts and his shortage of supplies put paid to this plan. Broadwood was thus obliged to move further north to the Rhenoster River guard post at Koppies Station, commanded by Major-General Sir Herbert Chermside. That night a train carrying provisions for seven days steamed into Koppies;[3] it was Broadwood's first opportunity for replenishment since meeting Ewart's convoy on 18 July near Lindley.

By then Roberts, too, was aware of his mistake and set about devising a new strategy. On Sunday 22 July he at long last resumed contact with Broadwood, whom he ordered to pursue De Wet 'in what direction he may go'.[4] Roberts now believed that if the Boers forded the Vaal River, De Wet would probably make for Potchefstroom, which had but a small British garrison at its disposal. Thus at the earliest opportunity Methuen would be ordered to hasten from the Magaliesberg to Potchefstroom, which he was expected to reach before De Wet. But at that point the chief was not in touch with Methuen. He therefore stressed to Broadwood that it was vital to keep hard on De Wet's heels or capture him before he reached Potchefstroom. And this time Roberts was taking no chances with Broadwood: the 2nd Cavalry commander was instructed to keep him up to date with his movements by sending a daily report by messenger to Chermside's guard post at the Rhenoster River.[5] Potchefstroom's commanding officer, Major Allan Gough, was ordered to fortify his position 'and be prepared to hold out if attacked by De Wet's force' until Broadwood's cavalry came to the rescue.[6]

The next morning, Monday 23 July, Broadwood took his 2nd Cavalry and Ridley's mounted infantry,17 artillery horses and 40 mounted infantry horses supplied by Chermside, as well as supplies for seven days, and set off for Vredefort. The 4th Derbyshire Regiment (the 'Sherwood Foresters') and four guns were left behind at the guard post.[7] The presence of Boer patrols that day led Broadwood to deduce that 'the hare was not far ahead of the hounds.'[8] He was not far wrong, for Broadwood's bivouac that night, at a drift on the farm Shepstone, was but a short distance from Vredefort and the Boer laagers.[9] That Monday was of further significance because it marked the first time Broadwood communicated with Little since being ordered to work in tandem with the commander of the 3rd Cavalry five days previously.

Lieutenant-Colonel M.O. Little had found himself in an unenviable position since De Wet very nearly captured his brigade at Paardeplaats near Lindley on Thursday 19 July. With a force of around 700 men he was outnumbered threefold by the Boers, who, moreover, were far more familiar with the terrain. And despite the danger he faced, Roberts wanted Little to unite with Broadwood for a joint operation against De Wet. Little had in fact acknowledged Roberts' order midway through De Wet's assault, which would probably have ended in disaster for the 3rd Cavalry if Broadwood had not taken the heat off Little by surprising Piet de Wet further north at Karroospruit.[10]

Then there was the trouble with his supply convoy. When Little discovered Lindley was not in British hands he immediately heliographed his convoy, on its way from Kroonstad under a weak escort, to halt and take all possible precautions against an attack. That afternoon the convoy was about 25 km north-west of the battleground – and in the vicinity of a large Boer force. The next day, after Little's scouts had conducted a thorough search around Paardeplaats and found no sign of the enemy, the 3rd Cavalry hurriedly turned on its heels and hastened back the way it had come two days before to rescue the convoy which would resupply it.[11] Late that afternoon Little set up camp[12] and shortly thereafter his convoy arrived – a little shaken but otherwise unharmed.[13] It would appear as though the 3rd Cavalry Brigade set up camp at the same site as on the evening of 18 July while on their way to Lindley. If this is true, it meant that in both cases the brigade covered the distance in a matter of four hours – on the morning of 19 July between 08:00 and noon and on the afternoon of 20 July between noon and 16:00.

Roberts now offered to let Little off the hook. If the 3rd Cavalry commander could not get in touch with Broadwood or felt his small force would be no match for the Boers, he was permitted to withdraw either to Kroonstad or Heilbron.[14] But Little was determined to pursue the enemy[15] and early the next morning, on Saturday 21 July, his 17th Lancers took a pom-pom and raced north-west to see if there were any Boers in the vicinity. They were not disappointed. About 6 km later they ran into a patrol on the left flank of De Wet's rearguard, which they were able to drive off with their pom-pom. By late afternoon, while the Boers were fording Doornspruit and outspanning on its western bank before trekking over the railway, the rest of the brigade had reached the farm Welgelegen (the site of the present-day town Edenville). Here Little was forced to camp for the night to await the arrival of his supply convoy.[16]

The next morning, Sunday 22 July, he sent the 9th Lancers and 'A' Squadron to scout in the direction of the Rhenoster River. They spotted a few Boers who had apparently been cut off from their main force. The scouts later swung west to join the rest of the brigade, which for some reason had only left Welgelegen at 13:00,[17] and the British spent the night southwest of Roodewal, plagued by the same rain drenching the Boers at Wonderheuwel. On Monday 23 July, when Little was about 6 km from Roodewal, he received a cable from Broadwood[18] ordering him to advance to Chermside's guard post at the Rhenoster River and follow the 2nd Cavalry in pursuit of De Wet the next day.[19] Little arrived that evening and the following morning, 24 July, set off at a spanking pace toward Vredefort. Around noon he reached Broadwood,[20] who at that moment was engaging the Boers.

Broadwood had left Shepstone at dawn on 24 July and by 09:00 his advance guard rode into Vredefort – just as a couple of wagons were hastily leaving town, heading west.[21] Ridley immediately ordered Colonel N. Legge's mounted infantry of between 300 and 400 men on the left flank to head them off. Meanwhile, Broadwood led the rest of his force into Vredefort.[22]

Outside the town, the wagons raced hell-for-leather in the direction of the hills hugging the Vaal River. If they reached their destination in time they would probably make good their escape and be able to rely on the help of the rest of the Boer force further west. But the British had no intention of letting this happen. 'The chase grew most exciting,' reported the American journalist F.H. Howland, 'as the horsemen, taking snapshots now, drew nearer to the wagons, which in their turn were rapidly approaching their own goal.'[23] For a while it looked as though the Boers were getting away. But the commander of Kitchener's Horse, Major Cookson, made a determined sprint and succeeded in overtaking his quarry. After a gruelling 7 km chase, the Boers were beaten; 18 surrendered with their precious cargo, which should have been turned into bread and biscuits to feed De Wet's hungry commandos.[24]

When De Wet heard of the capture he immediately ordered the burghers at Klein-Bloemfontein to saddle up. Soon they were galloping toward the scene with De Wet in the lead, while the Boer artillery under Muller and Strydom was positioned on a hilltop.[25] The burghers and Theron's scouts in the main laager further west at Vlakkuil were also informed of the event. A Dutch volunteer fighting in Theron's scouts, Hendrik Ver Loren van Themaat, was preparing breakfast with some of his comrades when the order to saddle up resounded through the camp. The men immediately leapt into their saddles and galloped up the nearest hill. They now saw the British were in fact some distance away and apparently withdrawing. This spurred the Boers on to hasten to the aid of their comrades as fast as their mounts could carry them.[26]

The Boer 'front' consisted of 400 burghers[27] under De Wet, firing on the British troops, and who had just succeeded in capturing their wagons from behind a row of hills north and south of the Vredefort–Reitzburg road. Legge now applied a tactic which corresponded to Boer manoeuvres in previous skirmishes: the wagons and prisoners were hastily removed from the scene while his mounted infantry took up a rearguard position to check the Boer force.[28]

De Wet, who was under the impression that the enemy numbered between 500 and 600, resolved not to sacrifice the wagons without a fight. He ordered his men to charge from the hills.[29] Legge's failure to deploy his troops in the loose formation favoured by a Boer rearguard cost him dearly, for both his flanks were now under attack.[30] Not that the terrain really favoured an assault. 'It was an open plain,' De Wet recalled. 'There was no possible cover either for us or for the English. But we could not consider matters of that sort.'[31]

The British were amazed – in the light of previous events during the hunt, a Boer charge across an open plain was an unusual manoeuvre. Broadwood commended their bravery. 'The enemy showed great dash,' he cabled the Rhenoster River guard post, 'and at one moment commenced a vigorous counter attack.'[32] Hintrager, who accompanied the Boer artillery, was elated: 'It was a joy to behold the burghers storming the British today,' he enthused.[33]

Their Commander-in-Chief was equally impressed. 'The burghers charged magnificently,' De Wet remarked, 'and some even got to within two hundred paces of the enemy. They then dismounted and, lying flat upon the ground, opened a fierce fire. One of the hottest fights one can imagine followed.'[34] Halfway into the attack Muller and Strydom's artillery joined the fray from the right flank at a range of 4,65 km.[35] Legge, says Broadwood, 'speedily found himself under extremely heavy shell and rifle fire, which soon began to tell'.[36] It is difficult to determine precisely which Boer commandos took part in the heroic assault as the force had been scattered over Vlakkuil and Klein-Bloemfontein that morning and the burghers did not arrive at the battleground simultaneously.[37]

After fighting had raged for about an hour Broadwood, now in Vredefort, became aware of Legge's untenable position and ordered him to retire to a ridge a few kilometres to the rear.[38] De Wet was elated. 'I began to think that any moment the enemy might be put to rout,' he recalls. 'Then something happened which had happened very often before – a reinforcement appeared.' Broadwood's 2nd Cavalry and Ridley's mounted infantry had come to the rescue from Vredefort.[39]

Broadwood was in fact checked scarcely 4 km south-west of Vredefort by a fierce Boer attack. He now placed two guns in position to cover the withdrawal, obliging De Wet to retreat under the ensuing artillery barrage. According to Howland, most of the British casualties took place during this withdrawal.[40] At this point Little's 3rd Cavalry appeared on the scene. Little now fell under Broadwood's command and was ordered to support him on the left flank – the first time the cavalry commanders had joined forces since they had been ordered to do so six days before.[41] This delay probably gave De Wet more freedom of movement than he would otherwise have enjoyed, and allowed him to retain the initiative he had had since leaving Slabbert's Nek. As it turned out, the 3rd Cavalry did not have much to do that day and their guns merely fired the occasional shot at long range.[42] Almost an hour later a general retirement in the direction of Vredefort was ordered.

Casualties were high on both sides – the British counted 39 dead and wounded,[43] whereas De Wet reported five dead and 12 or 14 wounded on the Boer side.[44] But in relation to the number of combatants available to each side, Boer losses were far more significant. This setback can be ascribed largely to the fact that De Wet was not in a position to determine the time and terrain of the attack. For when the element of surprise was on his side he usually proved a near invincible opponent. When the British took the initiative, De Wet could still mete out far more than he received, but at a cost the Boers could ill afford – especially for the sake of five wagon-loads of flour.

The next day De Wet took his force behind the high hills north of Reitzburg to outspan on the farm Rhenosterpoort.[45] This would be the Boers' next mountainous stronghold and, like the Brandwater Basin, would gradually be turned into a trap, this time by Lord Kitchener himself.

Notes

1. Howland, p. 130.
2. TA, LRP 36: No. 2010, GOC, Lines of Communication, Cape Town – Military

Secretary, Chief, Pretoria via Natal re telegram from Broadwood received by Knox at Kroonstad, 22.7.1900, p. 114; compare PRO, WO 105, LRP 19 for the same source.
3. TA, LRP 10: Broadwood, 'Chase of De Wet', 20.7.1900, p. 99; compare PRO, WO 105, LRP 10 for the same source; TA LRP 37: No. C2982, Military Secretary, Chief, Pretoria – Roberts re telegram Chermside, 23.7.1900, p. 11; TA, SA Telegrams III: No. C2964, Roberts – Broadwood, Rhenoster guard post, 22.7.1900, p. 89; compare PRO, WO 108/240 for the same source.
4. TA, SA Telegrams III: No. C2964, Roberts – Broadwood, Rhenoster guard post, 22.7.1900, p. 89; compare PRO, WO 108/240 for the same source.
5. Ibid.
6. TA, SA Telegrams III: no number, Roberts – OC, Potchefstroom, 23.7.1900, p. 93; compare PRO, WO 108/240 for the same source.
7. TA, LRP 37: No. C2982, Military Secretary, Chief, Pretoria – Roberts re telegram Chermside, 23.7.1900, p. 11; TA, SA Telegrams III: no number, Military Secretary, Chief, Pretoria – GOC, Kroonstad, 23.7.1900, p. 93; compare PRO, WO 108/240 for the same source.
8. Howland, p. 131.
9. Amery (ed.), IV, p. 418.
10. TA, LRP 39: No. 1217, GOC, Kroonstad – Roberts re Little's report, 21.7.1900, p. 17; compare PRO, WO 105, LRP 22 for the same source.
11. Colvin and Gordon, p. 132.
12. TA, LRP 39: No. B1227, GOC, Kroonstad – Military Secretary, Chief, Pretoria via Natal re Little's report, 22.7.1900, pp. 22–23; compare PRO, WO 105, LRP 22 for the same source.
13. Colvin and Gordon, p. 132.
14. TA, SA Telegrams III: No. C2899, Roberts – Little via GOC, Kroonstad, 20.7.1900, p. 82; compare PRO, WO 108/240 for the same source.
15. TA, LRP 39: No. B1227, GOC, Kroonstad – Military Secretary, Chief, Pretoria via Natal re Little's report, 22.7.1900, p. 23; compare PRO, WO 105, LRP 22 for the same source.
16. Colvin and Gordon, p. 132.
17. Ibid., pp. 132–133.
18. TA, SA Telegrams III: No. C2855, Roberts – GOC, Kroonstad, and others, 12:30, 18.7.1900, p. 75; compare PRO, WO 108/240 for the same source.
19. Colvin and Gordon, p. 133.
20. Ibid.; TA, LRP 10: Broadwood, 'Chase of De Wet', 24.7.1900, p. 101; compare PRO, WO 105, LRP 10 for the same source.
21. Howland, p. 131; TA, LRP 10: Broadwood, 'Chase of De Wet', 24.7.1900, p. 100; compare PRO, WO 105, LRP 10 for the same source.
22. TA, LRP 10: Broadwood, 'Chase of De Wet', 24.7.1900, p. 100; compare PRO, WO 105, LRP 10 for the same source; Howland, pp. 131–133.
23. Howland, p. 133.
24. The incident probably took place on the farm Wonderfontein, just south of Stinkhoutboom on the Vredefort–Reitzburg road.
25. [Hintrager], p. 61.
26. Ver Loren van Themaat, p. 160.
27. De Wet, p. 137.
28. TA, LRP 10: Broadwood, 'Chase of De Wet', 24.7.1900, p. 100; compare PRO, WO 105, LRP 10 for the same source.
29. De Wet, p. 137.

30. TA, LRP 10: Broadwood, 'Chase of De Wet', 24.7.1900, p. 100; compare PRO, WO 105, LRP 10 for the same source.
31. De Wet, p. 137.
32. TA, LRP 38: no number, Broadwood – OC, Rhenoster guard post, 15:00, 24.7.1900, p. 94; compare PRO, WO 105, LRP 15 for the same source.
33. [Hintrager], p. 62.
34. De Wet, p. 137.
35. Howland, p. 133; [Hintrager], p. 61.
36. TA, LRP 10: Broadwood, 'Chase of De Wet', 24.7.1900, p. 100; compare PRO, WO 105, LRP 10 for the same source; Howland, p. 133 states that Legge's corps fired 23 000 rounds during this hour.
37. Ver Loren van Themaat, pp. 160–162.
38. TA, LRP 10: Broadwood, 'Chase of De Wet', 24.7.1900, pp. 100–101; compare PRO WO 105, LRP 10 for the same source; Howland, p. 133.
39. De Wet, p. 137; TA, LRP 38: no number, Broadwood – OC, Rhenoster guard post, 11:00, 24.7.1900, p. 94; compare PRO, WO 105, LRP 15 for the same source.
40. Howland, p. 134
41. TA, SA Telegrams III: No. C2855, Roberts – GOC, Kroonstad and others, 18.7.1900, p. 75; compare PRO, WO 108/240 for the same source
42. Colvin and Gordon, p. 133.
43. Amery (ed.), IV, p. 419n; Maurice and Grant, III, p. 326; Lombard, p. 65 claims, probably incorrectly, that there were 50 casualties in one place alone.
44. De Wet, p. 137.
45. Van Schoor, 'Diaries of Jacob de Villiers', 25 and 26.7.1900, p. 19; Lombard, p. 66; [Hintrager], p. 62; Ver Loren van Themaat, p. 164. The farm Rhenosterpoort belonged to Jan Botha, a former member of the *Volksraad*. His old farmstead still stands today at the foot of a hill in the valley formed by the Vaal River.

CHAPTER SEVEN

Pinned against the Vaal

FOUR DAYS HAD PASSED since 20 July when Roberts put in motion what he believed would be the final offensive against De Wet and his men: with Little and Broadwood breathing down their necks from the south; Clery waiting for them to appear at Greylingstad on their way to meet Kruger in the Eastern Transvaal; and French's cavalry at the ready (should they slip past), the troublesome Free Staters would soon be a distant if unpleasant memory. Now there were more pressing matters to attend to.

The drive against Botha's forces near Machadodorp, on the railway running through Portuguese East Africa to the Indian Ocean, could now gain momentum and Roberts prepared to move his headquarters nearer to the front to keep close tabs on developments there. As his departure date grew near, the signs for an end to the disturbances in the Free State began to look anything but auspicious. De Wet, as we have learned, refused to follow his assigned script. Instead of walking into the trap laid for him in the direction of Greylingstad in the east, the Free State commander crossed the railway west of Heilbron – capturing a train and 98 Welsh Fusiliers on the way – then reappeared near Vredefort at the Vaal River. For the moment Roberts was not too concerned. On Sunday 22 July he had finally resumed contact with Broadwood, who was hot on De Wet's heels; from now on the cavalry commander would be kept on a tighter leash. And two days later his two cavalry brigades in the Free State were at last acting in concert. Furthermore, on 23 July Roberts reached Methuen at Olifant's Nek just south of Rustenburg in the Western Transvaal. The commander of the 1st Division was informed De Wet was heading north-west toward the confluence of the Vaal and Rhenoster Rivers and ordered to race south toward Potchefstroom to head him off. 'Use every endeavour to deal with his force, which Steyn is accompanying,' Roberts added. 'If he and De Wet could be captured it would finish trouble in the Orange River Colony,' he concluded optimistically.[1]

Roberts left Pretoria on 24 July – the same day Little and Broadwood engaged De Wet outside Vredefort. After spending the night at Bronkhorstspruit, he continued on to Balmoral some 110 km east along the Delagoa Bay line.[2] But the very next morning Roberts took his headquarters straight back to Pretoria; there was still plenty of unfinished business closer to the Transvaal capital.

For a start, General Piet Liebenberg was becoming increasingly worrisome to the British in the Western Transvaal ever since his commandos had been sent to the region following De la Rey's victory at Silkaat's Nek on 11 July. First there was the unfortunate attack on a hospital train. On 19 July Liebenberg's men wrecked the railway near Bank Station northeast of Potchefstroom, then shelled an oncoming train which according to British sources was carrying wounded soldiers and flying the Red Cross flag; 35 prisoners were taken.[3] Five days later, while Roberts was on his way to the eastern front, Liebenberg entered Klerksdorp about 50 km south-west of Potchefstroom and forced Captain Lambert's garrison of 40 men of the Kimberley Mounted Corps to surrender.[4] Roberts told Baden-Powell later he believed it was a grave error 'to scatter small detachments about the country as they cannot hold their own and their easy capture encourages the enemy'.[5] Another disturbing report reached Roberts in Balmoral the next day. Boer prisoners and black informers had told Broadwood that De Wet planned to hole up in the hills around Reitzburg to launch raids on the railway line.[6] 'There is thus a considerable and continuous area in both the Orange River Colony and south-western Transvaal which has temporarily escaped from our control,' he cabled the British Colonial Secretary, Joseph Chamberlain.[7]

Roberts had long remained firmly convinced there was little hope the Transvalers would capitulate until the Free Staters had been subdued.[8] Capturing De Wet had become a priority and here at last was the perfect opportunity to finish him off once and for all. And his Chief of Staff, Lord Kitchener, would be sent with reinforcements to take over this crucial operation.

Roberts clarified his strategy a day after returning from Pretoria: De Wet should be forced into the Transvaal, where the Boers would run into Methuen's 1st Division. Furthermore, declared Roberts, 'many of his men would, it is believed, desert if he crossed the Vaal, whereas his numbers would assuredly increase if he is able to move in a southerly or easterly direction.'[9]

In this operation Broadwood would naturally play a key role. Not that he was anywhere near to being adequately equipped for the task. Bitter experience had taught the British that a force four times the size of Broadwood's would be needed to dislodge the Boers from their hilly stronghold.[10] Furthermore, the 2nd Cavalry's determined pursuit of De Wet had left the brigade in tatters. 'We were badly off for horses,' lamented a 9th Lancer on 23 July, 'and the men's clothes were in a terrible state.'[11]

Horses obviously played a crucial role in the hunt and concerns about

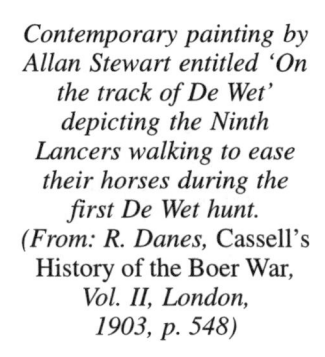

Contemporary painting by Allan Stewart entitled 'On the track of De Wet' depicting the Ninth Lancers walking to ease their horses during the first De Wet hunt. (From: R. Danes, Cassell's History of the Boer War, *Vol. II, London, 1903, p. 548)*

the shortcomings of the British cavalry had already been raised. A report published on 8 July under the chairmanship of the 3rd Cavalry's commanding officer, Brigadier-General J.P.R. Gordon, with the participation of Little (commander of the 9th Lancers before taking over from Gordon) and Major H. Lawrence (commander of the 16th Lancers), remarked that the average British remount was suitable for light cavalry such as the Hussars, but left much to be desired when used by the Lancers and Dragoons. Their mounts needed to be bred for size rather than quality.[12] At that stage only one Hussar regiment, as opposed to three Lancers, was engaged in the hunt for De Wet. The ideal mount would of course have been the largest type of Cape horse. As Major-General J.P. Brabazon aptly opined some months later in a report on the Imperial Yeomanry: 'The horse of the country is the horse for the country.'[13] But few such horses were actually obtainable. The British cavalry were by and large committed to small well-bred mounts. 'They can carry the necessary weight, can move quickly when required to do so and even when fatigued, if called upon for the effort of the charge will do their best and not give in,' Gordon's report stated.[14] However, even the best horses reached the limits of endurance and during the hunt British commanders continually had to send animals unfit for duty back to Kroonstad. These were infrequently replaced by fresh remounts.[15]

Brigadier-General R.G. Broadwood, commander of the 2nd Cavalry Brigade, who led the first Det Wet hunt in the Free State. He was unable to rob De Wet of the initiative, partly due to the fact that he had problems with the condition of his horses. (From: Black and White Budget, *4 August 1900, p. 567)*

The hunt had taken its toll on Broadwood's beasts of burden too. They were being used to ferry supplies from the Rhenoster River guard post and were virtually on their last legs. This meant the troops, already showing ample signs of wear and tear, had to be put on half rations. To make matters worse, and with the most punishing part of winter almost over, the heaven's opened their sluice gates to drench man and beast to the bone. For two nights it was all the men could do to stay dry, but with nowhere to shelter it was especially the horses, oxen and mules who bore the brunt of the icy conditions.[16]

Most of all, however, Broadwood needed reinforcements. If Methuen could control the Vaal crossing points from the north, Broadwood believed that with the help of an additional force of 2 000 infantry and 1 000 mounted infantry at Rhebokfontein in the south, he would be able to encircle De Wet. On 27 July he sent a request for these men to Roberts' Chief of Staff, Lord Kitchener, then set about deploying the forces at his disposal.[17] Ridley's mounted infantry were posted with 'P' Battery at Vleispruit near Vredefort; the 2nd Cavalry and 450 men from the 1st Battalion of the Derbyshire Regiment with two batteries Royal Horse Artillery and two 15-pounders were positioned further south just past Wonderheuwel; and Little's 3rd Cavalry some 3 km further south-west in the direction of Rhebokfontein.[18] With this 'thin line of khaki', in the words of the war correspondent Howland, which ran some 23 km, Broadwood hoped to prevent De Wet from doubling back south or heading east toward Greylingstad in the Transvaal.[19]

The Boers, meanwhile, had no intention of allowing the British to close in on them undisturbed. Just after Little's 3rd Cavalry crossed a tributary of the Rhenoster at Wonderheuwel on 27 July, Muller and Strydom's guns let rip at them from Witkoppies over 4 km away. The British replied with three guns and a pom-pom. The artillery duel that ensued continued until sunset without claiming any casualties.[20] During the next few days Boer and British gunners made a great show of sporadic exchanges of fire which never escalated to a full-scale skirmish, while the rest of the troops on either side remained idle.[21]

While Broadwood was thus engaged, Methuen was closing in on the Boers from the north. The commander of the 1st Infantry was swift in responding to Roberts' order of 23 July. Leaving Colonel R.G. Kekewich to hold Olifant's Nek with the 1st Battalion Loyal North Lancashires and two guns of the Bechuanaland Field Force, he set off for the Vaal. 'I move to Potchefstroom at once by Bank Station, where I obtain supplies,' he cabled Roberts the same day.[22]

Though Methuen's alacrity could only have been welcomed by Roberts, the chief was unimpressed by the want of detail in his reports. 'I should be much obliged if you would arrange to keep me more fully informed each day of your movements and dispositions,' he complained. 'For instance, what battalion, guns and supplies did you leave at Oliphant's Nek? What was the state of the country there and on your march to Bank? Have you any information about the force of the enemy in the Hekpoort neighbourhood [in the Magaliesberg]? On arrival in the vicinity of Potchefstroom, shall you be able to do anything in the direction of Klerksdorp which has been reoccupied by a small force of Boers?'[23] This would not be Methuen's last careless telegram, and was but the beginning of another round of frustrations for Roberts in his efforts to communicate with his commanders in the field.

Two days later, on Wednesday 25 July, Methuen reached Bank Station, but was forced to wait for his supplies to arrive from Krugersdorp.[24] It was only on Friday 27 July, while Broadwood was forming his 'thin line of khaki' south of the Vaal, that Methuen was finally ready to leave with a force of 3 000 men – the 3rd, 5th and 10th Imperial Yeomanry Battalions, the 1st Northumberland Fusiliers, the 2nd Northhamptonshires, the 4th and 20th Royal Field Artillery batteries, two Howitzers, two pom-poms, as well as the headquarters and Number One Section of the 11th Field Company Royal Engineers.[25] Smith-Dorrien and the rest of Methuen's division – 1 500 men comprising the 2nd Shropshire Light Infantry, the 1st Gordon Highlanders, a section of the 20th Battery Royal Field Artillery and of the 37th Howitzer Battery, and Section Two of the 11th Field Company Royal Engineers – were left behind at Bank Station to await the arrival of the City of London Imperial Volunteers, who would replace the Gordon Highlanders. Smith-Dorrien would then escort Methuen's supply convoy.[26]

That evening Methuen reached Wonderfontein north-east of Welverdiend Station and early the next morning, Saturday 28 July, he resumed his march south – right into the path of Liebenberg's commandos operating from the ideal shelter of the Gatsrand, a range of hills parallel to and 4 km south of the Bank–Frederikstad road. Commandant Douthwaite struck at 11:00 with 300 burghers, one artillery piece and a pom-pom. Methuen immediately launched an encircling movement to the left, then the right, forcing the Boers to retire to the west. By 16:00 they had been driven south across the Gatsrand and abandoned four supply wagons in their wake. Methuen gathered his force – four soldiers and a number of horses were wounded in the skirmish – and continued south-west, reaching Frederikstad before dark, having covered a distance of 30 km in oppressively humid weather and despite running into Boer resistance along the way.[27]

But the next morning, Sunday 29 July, the Transvalers continued to plague Methuen and he only advanced another 12 km along the railway before halting at Kolonieplaats. Now he decided to use the Royal Engineers to repair the railway damaged by the Boers in the area while waiting for his supplies to arrive with Smith-Dorrien. This he did instead of pressing on to Potchefstroom, apparently carrying out an earlier order from Roberts to establish order in the western districts of the Transvaal rather than focusing on the hunt for De Wet. Methuen sent a request to Major Gough, the commanding officer of Potchefstroom, to supply him with 150 railway sleepers. That evening a Dutch foreman, two sappers and four African workers were sent by trolley along with the sleepers, but they overshot the 1st Division in the dark and stumbled on another rail break 4 km from Frederikstad. And that is when disaster struck. Liebenberg's men started firing on the group and although the foreman somehow managed to reach Potchefstroom unscathed, three of his workers were killed and the fourth was injured.[28] While this was happening Methuen received a report – which would prove false – that De Wet had already crossed the Vaal River and was heading for Tygerfontein. It now dawned on Methuen that Roberts' order that he should do his utmost to stop De Wet 'would best be carried out by at once advancing on Potchefstroom'[29]. He managed to reach the town at noon the following day, on 30 July. But Methuen found himself almost immediately clashing with Liebenberg again; the Boer Pimpernel was nowhere to be seen. For a week Liebenberg's commandos would give Methuen no end of a headache, at precisely the time when the services of the 1st Division were sorely needed to prevent De Wet from slipping past his pursuers again.

In the meantime Broadwood's reinforcements were beginning to arrive south of the Vaal. On Wednesday 1 August, Major-General A.F. Hart, the most senior commander in the region, arrived at Koppie Alleen east of Rhebokfontein with the 5th Irish Brigade – the 2nd Battalion Royal Dublin Fusiliers, half of the 2nd Battalion Somerset Light Infantry, 200 Marshall's Horse, the 71st Company Imperial Yeomanry, 'G' Section pom-poms and a section of the 10th Ammunition Column. On the same day he was joined by about 900 men from the 2nd Battalion Northumberland Fusiliers sent from Bloemfontein.[30] That morning Major-General Sir C.E. Knox left Kroonstad taking the 17th Battery Royal Field Artillery and two pom-poms along with the 1st Battalion Oxfordshire Light Infantry, the 3rd Battalion Royal Scots, 250 men from the Royal Irish Regiment and Malta Mounted Infantry – a total of 2 000 men – reaching Hart two days later.[31] And on Thursday 2 August, two 4.7-inch guns from Captain C.R. Grant's Naval Brigade in Kroonstad were offloaded from a train near Koppies Station and trekked 25 km to Wonderheuwel, north of Koppie Alleen.

This great mass of troops and firepower being ranged against De Wet would be bolstered by Lieutenant-Colonel E.H. Dalgety's 1 000-strong mounted Colonial Division, hastening to the Vaal battle arena from the Brandwater Basin.[32] Since De Wet's departure from the basin on 15 July, the plan that the rest of the Boer forces should slip through the cordon Hunter was gradually tightening around them, had fallen into disarray. Dissention broke out among the Boer leadership and instead of abiding by the war council decision to evacuate the basin, most remained long enough for Hunter to occupy the exit passes. By the time Marthinus Prinsloo was elected Commander-in-Chief in dubious circumstances, the British were already upon them. On 30 July Prinsloo surrendered and within a few days about 4 400 Boers had laid down arms – half the Free Staters in the field.[33]

This spectacular capture must have convinced Roberts of the merits of pinning down De Wet instead of driving him over the Vaal River.[34] 'Our object', he cabled Broadwood on 2 August, 'is to hem De Wet in and prevent him from getting supplies.'[35] And two of Hunter's brigades at the Brandwater – Clements' 12th and Hector MacDonald's 3rd Highlanders – were now free to hasten north to tighten the cordon around De Wet south of the Vaal River.[36] Although Roberts' change of plan was probably a sound decision, it did contain one serious flaw: the success of the new strategy depended on the closely co-ordinated efforts of an ever-increasing number of commanders in the field, but communication foul-ups meant they were often unable to stay in touch with one another and their chief. This would provide De Wet with the very opening he needed to make good his escape.

Roberts now ordered his Chief of Staff, Lord Kitchener, to take over the operation.[37] Hart, Roberts felt, was not quite up to the task. 'Trying to surround them necessitated Hart being employed,' he wrote in a confidential telegram to British War Secretary, Lord Landsdowne, 'but as I did not feel confident of his ability to carry through the difficult business on hand I dispatched Kitchener to command.'[38] Now two of the most determined men in South Africa were pitted against each other.

Despite the overwhelming number of troops mobilised against him, De Wet seemed in no immediate danger of defeat. In fact, he was quite content to dig in his heels and allow his men to recuperate at his riverside sanctuary at Rhenosterpoort, which also served as a base camp from which to launch further raids on British supply lines to the south.

Notes

1. TA, SA Telegrams III: No. C2983, Roberts – Methuen, via Baden-Powell, Rustenburg, via OC, Elandsrivier, 23.7.1900, p. 92; compare PRO, WO 108/240 for the same source. Although Roberts had already made provision on 20 July for the possibility that Methuen would visit the south-western districts to neutralise the activities of the western border burghers (TA, SA Telegrams III: No. C2898, Roberts – Methuen, 20.7.1900, p. 81; compare PRO, WO 108/240 for the same source), it is clear that Methuen had been ordered emphatically as early as 23 July to focus his attention on De Wet, and not on 25 July, as indicated by Maurice and Grant, III, p. 342.
2. TA, Confidential Telegrams, No. 289: Roberts, Bronkhorstspruit – Secretary of State for War, London, 22:15, 24.7.1900, p. 186; PRO, WO 105, LRP 32: No. 917, Roberts – Proemial, London, 25.7.1900; TA, SA Telegrams III: No. C3006, Roberts – Buller, 24.7.1900, p. 95; compare PRO, WO 108/240 for the same source.
3. PRO, WO 105, LRP 27: No. 52, letter, Roberts – L. Botha, 5.8.1900; Maurice and Grant, III, pp. 246–247; compare L. Penning, *De Oorlog in Zuid-Afrika: De Strijd tusschen Engeland en de Verbonden Boeren Republieken Transvaal en Oranje-Vrystaat, in Zijn Verloop Geschetst*, III, p. 949.
4. Amery (ed.), IV, p. 362; Maurice and Grant, III, p. 247.
5. TA, SA Telegrams III: No. C3019, Roberts – Baden-Powell, via OC, Elands River guard post, 26.7.1900, p. 98; compare PRO, WO 108/240 for the same source.
6. TA, LRP 38: Broadwood – Roberts 25.7.1900, p. 97; compare PRO, WO 105, LRP 15 for the same source; Howland, p. 140.
7. PRO, CO 417/292: No. CO27256, Milner – Chamberlain, London, 1.8.1900, p. 614.
8. TA, SA Telegrams III: No. C2176, Roberts – Buller, 20.6.1900, p. 6; compare PRO, WO 108/240 for the same source; G. Arthur, *Life of Lord Kitchener*, I, p. 315.
9. TA, SA Telegrams III: No. C3024, Roberts – Kelly-Kenny, 27.7.1900, p. 99; compare PRO, WO 108/240 for the same source.
10. TA, SA Telegrams III: No. C3013, Roberts – Baden-Powell, 25.7.1900, p. 96; TA, SA Telegrams III: no number, Roberts – French, 25.7.1900, p. 97; compare PRO, WO 108/240 for the same source; Howland, p. 135.
11. Colvin and Gordon, p. 133.
12. PRO, WO 108/250: Organisation and Equipment of Cavalry, 8.7.1900, p. 6.
13. PRO, WO 108/263: Report on the Imperial Yeomanry, 16.10.1900, p. 6.

14. PRO, WO 108/250: Organisation and Equipment of Cavalry, 8.7.1900, p. 7.
15. Colvin and Gordon, pp. 130–136.
16. TA, LRP 44: Broadwood – Roberts (around 27.7.1900), p. 94; TA, LRP 38: Broadwood – Chief of Staff, 23.7.1900, p. 96; compare PRO, WO 105, LRP 15 for the same sources; Howland, p. 149; Colvin and Gordon, p. 113.
17. TA, LRP 38: Broadwood – Chief of Staff, 27.7.1900, p. 98; compare PRO, WO 105, LRP 15 for the same source.
18. Ibid.; TA, WO Acquisition JPE 5: Quarter-Master-General's Diary, 27.7.1900, pp. 41–42; F.F. Colvin and E.R. Gordon, p. 134; Amery (ed.), IV, p. 419.
19. Howland, p. 138.
20. TA, LRP 38: Broadwood – Chief of Staff, 27.7.1900, p. 98; compare PRO, WO 105, LRP 15 for the same source. Colvin and Gordon, p. 134; Van Schoor, 'Diaries of Jacob de Villiers', 28.7.1900; Lombard, p. 66.
21. Howland, p. 148.
22. Guest, p. 76; Amery (ed.), IV, p. 421.
23. TA, SA Telegrams III: No. C3029, Roberts – Methuen, 27.7.1900, p. 100; compare PRO, WO 108/240 for the same source.
24. TA, LRP 39: No. 602P, Barton – Roberts, 25.7.1900, p. 177; compare PRO, WO 105, LRP 22 for the same source; Maurice and Grant, III, p. 342; Amery (ed.), IV, pp. 421–422.
25. TA, LRP 35: No. A1166, Methuen, Bank – Roberts, 27.7.1900, p. 26; compare PRO, WO 105, LRP 14 for the same source; TA, LRP 40: No. B1, Methuen, Potchefstroom – Roberts, via Smith-Dorrien, Frederikstad and Barton, Krugersdorp, 6.8.1900, p. 6; compare PRO, WO 105, LRP 14 for the same source; TA, LRP 9: Methuen: 'Western Transvaal Report', 27.7.1900, p. 3; compare PRO, WO 105, LRP 10 for the same source; Amery (ed.), IV, p. 422; Maurice and Grant, III, p. 344 (which on p. 342 incorrectly gives Methuen's departure date from Bank as 28 July).
26. TA, LRP 39: No. 644P, Barton – Roberts, 27.7.1900, p. 184; compare PRO, WO 105, LRP 22 for the same source; PRO, WO 108/294: Guerrilla Warfare and Protection of Lines of Communication, p. 51; Maurice and Grant, III, p. 342.
27. TA, LRP 39: No. A1165, Methuen – Roberts, via Barton, Krugersdorp, 28.7.1900, p. 189; compare PRO, WO 105, LRP 14 for the same source. TA, LRP 9: Methuen, 'Western Transvaal Report', 28.7.1900, pp. 3–4; compare PRO, WO 105, LRP 10 for the same source. In the abovementioned telegram No. A1165 Methuen believed his adversary might be Liebenberg with 500 men, but in compiling the abovementioned report he apparently had information at his disposal that it was in fact Douthwaite with 300 men, which is why the author in this case accepts his report and not his telegram, as Maurice and Grant (III, p. 342) have apparently done.
28. TA, LRP 9: Methuen, 'Western Transvaal Report', 30.7.1900, p. 6; compare PRO, WO 105, LRP 10 for the same source.
29. TA, LRP 9: Methuen, 'Western Transvaal Report', 29.7.1900, p. 5; compare PRO, WO 105, LRP 10 for the same source.
30. TA, WO Acquisition, JPE 5: Quarter-Master-General's Diary, 27.7.1900, p. 42; TA, South African Dispatches II: Roberts' Account, 14 June to 10 October 1900, p. 10; compare PRO, WO 32/8000 for the same source; Amery (ed.), IV, p. 421.
31. TA, LRP 44: Kelly-Kenny, Kroonstad – Roberts, 3.8.1900 re Knox to Kelly-Kenny 2.8.1900, p. 100; TA LRP 44: Knox to Roberts, 2.8.1900, p. 213; compare PRO, WO 105, LRP 15 for the same sources.
32. TA, SA Telegrams III: No. C3027, Roberts – Hunter, 27.7.1900, p. 100; TA, SA Telegrams III: No. C3114, Roberts – Broadwood, 29.7.1900, p. 108; compare PRO, WO 108/240 for the same sources.

33. Maurice and Grant, III, p. 305.
34. TA, SA Telegrams III: No. C3027, Roberts – Broadwood, via Vredefort Road and Rhenoster guard post, 10:00, 27.7.1900, p. 99; compare PRO, WO 108/240 for the same source.
35. TA, SA Telegrams III: No. C3200, Roberts – Broadwood, Koppie Alleen, via Rhenoster guard post, 2.8.1900, p. 121; compare PRO, WO 108/240 for the same source.
36. TA, SA Telegrams III: No. C3212, Roberts – Hunter, 2.8.1900, p. 122; compare PRO, WO 108/240 for the same source; TA, Confidential Telegrams, No. 300: Roberts – Secretary of State for War, 6.8.1900, p. 190.
37. TA, SA Telegrams III: No. C3238, Roberts – Ian Hamilton, 3.8.1900, p. 124; compare PRO, WO 108/240 for the same source.
38. TA, Confidential Telegrams, No. 300: Roberts – Secretary of State for War, 6.8.1900, p. 190.

CHAPTER EIGHT

'Boer brigands of the veld'

THE BOERS, UNSURPRISINGLY, considered Rhenosterpoort an ideal base camp. The farm lies in a fertile valley west of Vredefort and north-west of Reitzburg on the Free State side of the Vaal – important for troop morale as most of the burghers were Free Staters. Nearby the river meanders through tall, densely wooded hills which – like the mountains of the Brandwater Basin – form a natural shelter, commanding the surrounding countryside from the west, past Reitzburg, through to Vredefort and Parys in the east. Access to the laager from the south was only possible from Reitzburg and some farms further east.[1] The closest Vaal crossing point was at Schoeman's Drift where the river forms a bulge to the south, due north of Reitzburg and about 40 km – or four-and-a-half hours on horseback – south-east of Potchefstroom. But the shallow ford is virtually surrounded by hills commanding miles of meadowland below. Crossings downstream included Scandinavia Drift about 15 km away and De Wet's Drift just west of the bulge, while upstream the Vaal could be crossed at Grobler's Drift opposite Parys and Lindeque's Drift further east – a distance of some 80 km from Scandinavia Drift along the winding footpaths hugging the river.

To guard against surprise attacks, De Wet posted sentries at strategic points in the hills on both sides of the Vaal River. Some were positioned as far south as Rhebokfontein on a rocky outcrop in a bulge formed by the Rhenoster River[2] – an excellent strategic choice as it commanded the fords on either side of the hill.[3] De Wet also continually sent out patrols to gather intelligence on British movements and bring horses into the laager from the surrounding countryside. British prisoners later described how each Boer possessed two or even three horses in excellent condition. For the burghers a spare horse was almost as indispensable as a mount, except while engaged in reconnaissance or other dangerous missions when mobility was paramount.[4] Thus Theron scout Wynand Malan's daring capture of about 100 horses was greeted with great enthusiasm.[5]

Most of the burghers, however, took the opportunity to recuperate after spending almost 10 days virtually glued to the saddle. Hintrager, the German artilleryman, who considered the surroundings 'particularly comely for South African highlands' and remarked that the Vaal looked as though it was 'made for swimming',[6] summed up the general languor of the camp: 'Everyone here is either sleeping or lazing about. Both man and beast really need the rest.'[7] Even food was plentiful: there was an abundant supply of wheat in the region and herds of cattle were continually driven into the laager.[8] De la Rey's comment six weeks earlier that in the Western Transvaal there was 'not only livestock available but as much grain as was needed' certainly proved true.[9] Furthermore, Liebenberg sent supplies to the laager almost every day from the Gatsrand. This was particularly appreciated by Hintrager and his cohorts, who had not received flour since crossing Slabbert's Nek.[10] But according to a British prisoner in the laager named Macdonald,[11] some burghers grumbled about the food, which is not at all surprising when one considers items such as sugar and salt were scarce or unobtainable luxuries.

De Wet, however, had no intention of letting Theron and his indefatigable scouts remain idle. A day after arriving at Rhenosterpoort, they were ordered to saddle up and head south under the cover of darkness. The next morning, Friday 27 July, the scouts reached Rhenosterkop,[12] which Theron intended to use as a lookout post to keep an eye on British movements and a base from which to attack the railway again.[13] That very evening they undertook their first raid, reaching the railway a few kilometres north of Kroonstad, near America Siding. The scouts' attempts at derailing a passing train failed because an effective method of blowing up the tracks beneath, or directly in front of, a train had not been fully developed by this stage in the war.[14] But their efforts did not go unrewarded. 'Near America – Rail points blown up, two rails removed, points damaged in 30 places,' read an official British report on the evening's activities.[15] The disruption in British rail traffic caused Roberts to order the commanding officer of Kroonstad to establish a guard post along the line consisting of 200 infantry, 30 mounted infantry and an artillery piece to protect the railway between Honingspruit and Kroonstad.[16]

North of the Vaal River, Liebenberg's men were enjoying similar successes wrecking the railway between Potchefstroom and Krugersdorp and disrupting British communication lines from their operational bases at the Gatsrand. Their most recent victim was the supply train accompanying Smith-Dorrien's columns following Methuen from Bank Station to Potchefstroom, which came horribly unstuck after smashing into a rail break down a hill near Frederikstad on 30 July. The locomotive was completely wrecked and the carriages near the front ploughed relentlessly into one another, leaving 14 Shropshire Light Infantrymen dead and 45 injured.[17]

This was not what Methuen wanted to hear. He had just arrived in Potchefstroom, intending to devote his energies to the hunt for De Wet. But Liebenberg clearly was not going to let him, as a cable Smith-Dorrien later sent to Roberts from Frederikstad eloquently underlined: 'The whole country is very much disturbed. Parties of the enemy are constantly crossing and re-crossing the line both north and south of this. All the railway telegraph instruments along this line are out of gear, and at this station completely broken down and a regular repair party should be sent along as all our efforts to get line to work have failed.' He further complained the area around Frederikstad was 'a hotbed of Boers', adding that if more troops were available 'the clearing of the Gatsrand and the closing down on De Wet from this side would be very effective'.[18] This was a forlorn hope.

Theron arrived back at Rhenosterkop on 28 July, the morning after his raid near America Siding.[19] But soon afterwards he departed again, five days later dealing the British the most serious blow during this period. In the meantime a detachment of scouts he left behind at Rhenosterkop continually attacked British supply lines. On 30 July this group blew up the railway at Leeuwspruit and the next day at Serfontein Siding, where the Boer laager had crossed but 10 days before. On 1 August the scouts struck again a little further south, destroying seven lengths of rail and pulling down two telegraph poles to cut the line. On the same day the railway bridge on the Wolwehoek Siding–Heilbron line was damaged.[20] The next day, Thursday 2 August, they ran into Lieutenant-Colonel C. Sitwell's mounted infantry – a section of General Knox's force sent from Kroonstad the day before to reinforce Broadwood – near Rhenosterkop. Sitwell succeeded in chasing the scouts north for some 6 km before being repulsed. The British managed to capture five wagons and the livestock the scouts had gathered in the last few days.[21] Two days later these scouts were back at the main Boer laager at Rhenosterpoort.[22] Further attacks on the railway did take place – one at Serfontein Siding again on 4 August and another 3 km north of Wolwehoek two days later[23] – but these were probably launched by another detachment of Theron's scouts.

On 2 August, the same day his scouts were being harassed by Sitwell, Theron set off on a sortie that would result in a sensational capture and unleash a storm of protest from the British. By now the number of attacks on the railway had made the British extremely cautious. The line was more heavily guarded and no trains ran north of Kroonstad at night. Undeterred, Theron elected to strike further south – a decidedly dangerous undertaking.

Theron chose a railway crossing about 30 km south of Kroonstad, near Holfontein Siding, where he booby-trapped the line with dynamite.[24] At 01:20 on 3 August a special goods train transporting British soldiers came steaming up from the south. When the locomotive hit the charge the blast derailed and overturned the first two carriages, killing three or four soldiers. Theron repeatedly demanded surrender, each time accompanied by a volley of Mauser fire. But there was no response. Eventually the scouts held their fire and approached the train. The British could do nothing but give in.

Now Theron made an interesting discovery: hitched to the back of the train was a saloon car occupied by the consul-general of the United States of America, Colonel J.S. Stowe, and his staff.[25] America's neutrality in this conflict prompted Theron to order the saloon to be uncoupled and pushed 300 m from the train so that the wounded – two soldiers, the engine driver and a member of Stowe's staff – could be attended to by Stowe's doctor. The rest of the British were released, except for four lieutenants.[26] Stowe later commended Theron for acting 'with all possible courtesy' toward him and his staff. After removing a large quantity of booty, including 10 sacks of mail, the train was torched and Theron and his scouts disappeared into the night.[27]

Painting by contemporary artist George Soper of Commandant Danie Theron and his men capturing a train near Holfontein, south of Kroonstad, on 3 August 1900. The attack was totally unexpected as the Boers were believed to be confined to the hills along the Vaal River near Reitzburg. (From: H.W. Wilson, After Pretoria: The Guerilla War, Vol. I, London, 1901, p. 77)

J.S. Stowe, consul-general of the United States of America in South Africa whose saloon car was attached to the train captured by Danie Theron near Holfontein on 3 August 1900. (From: Black and White Budget, *8 September 1900, p. 706)*

Word of the capture soon spread and before long British patrols from two guard posts nearby were pursuing the scouts: Holfontein guard post, a patrol commanded by Major M.J.R. Dundas; and at Ventersburg Station, 30 troops from the Malta Mounted Infantry under Captain J.E. Pine-Coffin. Early that morning, after a chase of some 15 km, the British caught up with their quarry. A brief but bloody skirmish ensued on an open plain.[28] According to British sources three scouts were killed, one of whom was recovered by his comrades, and eight to 10 were wounded, with one man captured in the confusion. A lack of Boer sources makes it difficult to establish the accuracy of these figures. J.E. Pine-Coffin, the British captain at the skirmish, said only one man on his side was wounded, while eight horses were shot dead because of insufficient cover.[29] The end of the engagement was typical of Boer rearguard actions: 'We followed them up for some distance when they broke up,' recalls Pine-Coffin. 'My horses being done up, I returned home.'[30] Theron and his train wreckers were back at Rhenosterpoort on Sunday 5 August.[31]

The derailment turned out to be a source of some controversy because Colonel Lord Algernon Gordon Lennox was also present in the diplomat's saloon car, carrying documents from the British High Commissioner in Cape Town, Sir Alfred Milner, destined for Lord Roberts.[32] According to *The Times History*, Theron had been led to believe Gordon Lennox was on Stowe's staff and had consequently left him in peace.[33] In a strongly worded objection to Roberts three

A contemporary sketch by Mortimer Menpes of Colonel Lord Algernon Gordon Lennox, who was on the train captured by Danie Theron near Holfontein on 3 August 1900, with documents from Sir Alfred Milner in Cape Town to Lord Roberts in Pretoria. His presence in the saloon car of the consul-general of the United States of America in South Africa turned out to be a source of some controversy.
(From: M. Menpes, War Impressions, *London, 1903, facing p. 136)*

days later, De Wet complained that all the statements he had heard from the Boer side, especially the testimony from the four captured lieutenants, indicated that Stowe had violated his neutrality. Upon being questioned by Theron, Stowe had apparently displayed his national flag and given his word of honour as consul-general of the United States of America that there was not a single person, document or item in the carriage that did not belong either to him or his staff.[34] De Wet's allegation is further substantiated by the fact that Stowe's visit to Pretoria took place in an atmosphere of cordial cooperation. The day before the capture, Milner had even expressed his desire that the train 'be pushed forward without delay'.[35] It thus appears that Gordon Lennox, with the documents for Roberts in his possession, was a member of Stowe's party, or had at least occupied the consul-general's carriage with the intention of passing himself off as a member of his staff.

The British, too, were outraged – but for different reasons. Roberts lodged a vehement protest with Louis Botha, calling the capture of trains 'acts of brigands, not of war',[36] and took steps to ensure the Bloemfontein–Pretoria line was only used between 04:00 and 20:00.[37] The Cape Colony broadsheet, the *Cape Argus,* also joined the fray, comparing Danie Theron to Dick Turpin and branding his men 'Boer brigands of the veld' in a leader article. With concern, the paper went on to say: 'The country is overrun by lawless bands of freebooters, whose sole idea is to do as much damage as possible and to perpetuate unrest and turmoil.'[38]

These public fulminations were if anything an indication of how successful De Wet had been in achieving one of his primary goals in heading for the hills around Vredefort after leaving the Brandwater Basin: British communication and supply lines were being attacked on two fronts. While Liebenberg's men were causing havoc along the Potchefstroom–Krugersdorp railway, his own scouts under Theron were able to exact a particularly heavy toll on Roberts' extended and vulnerable supply line running through the Free State.

Notes

1. CA, Map Collection, 2/1038: Map of Kroonstad, 1902.
2. T.T. Jeans (ed.), *Naval Brigades in the South African War, 1899–1900*, p. 163; Amery (ed.), IV, p. 419.
3. Amery (ed.), IV, p. 419; CA, Map Collection, 2/1038: Map of Kroonstad, 1902.
4. Ver Loren van Themaat, p. 164.
5. Pieterse, pp. 93–99.
6. [Hintrager], p. 62.
7. Ibid.
8. The *Natal Witness*, 5.9.1900: Statement by Trooper Harry Hastings.
9. TA, Leyds 754 (III): De la Rey – Botha, 18.6.1900, p. 670.
10. [Hintrager], p. 71.
11. TA, MGP 16: Statement by cavalryman Macdonald of French's Scouts, 16.8.1900, p. 149.
12. Preller, p. 137; Lombard, p. 66; TA, Acquisition 285, Danie Theron Collection: No. 45, Opsomming en Aantekening in verband met die Lewe van Danie Theron, 'Die Vaderland', 30.8.1935, 'Die Huisgenoot', December 1920.
13. TA, Acquisition 285, Danie Theron Collection: No. 28, letter, J. Versteeg, Parys – J.J. van Tonder, 26.3.1940.
14. Ver Loren van Themaat, p. 164; Preller, p. 137; TA, Acquisition 285, Danie Theron Collection: No. 45, Opsomming en Aantekening in verband met die Lewe van Danie Theron, 'Die Vaderland', 30.8.1935, 'Die Huisgenoot', December 1920; TA, WO Acquisition, History of the Railways, I, Appendix D, p. 131.
15. TA, WO Acquisition, History of the Railways, I, Appendix D, p. 131.
16. TA, LRP 37: No. F83, Chermside, Rhenoster guard post – Chief of Staff, Pretoria, 29.7.1900, p. 20; compare PRO, WO 105, LRP 17 for the same source; TA, LRP 36: No. DR176, Director of Railways, Johannesburg – Military Secretary, Chief, Pretoria, 28.7.1900, p. 96; compare PRO, WO 105, LRP 19 for the same source; TA, SA Telegrams III: No. C3078, Roberts – GOC, Kroonstad, 28.7.1900, p. 105; compare PRO, WO 108/240 for the same source.
17. Maurice and Grant, III, p. 342.
18. TA, LRP 44: No. Z88, Smith-Dorrien – Roberts, 6.8.1900, pp. 213–214; compare PRO, WO 105, LRP 15 for the same source.

19. Ver Loren van Themaat, p. 165; Preller, p. 138.
20. TA, WO Acquisition, History of the Railways, I, Appendix D, p. 131; TA, LRP 41: No. F153, Chermside, Serfontein – Chief of Staff, 2.8.1900, p. 176; compare PRO, WO 105, LRP 17 for the same source.
21. TA, LRP 44: no number, Knox – Roberts, 2.8.1900, p. 213; compare PRO, WO 105, LRP 15 for the same source.
22. Ver Loren van Themaat, p. 165.
23. TA, WO Acquisition, History of the Railways, I, Appendix D, p. 131; TA, LRP 41: No. F153, Chermside, Serfontein – Chief of Staff, 2.8.1900, p. 176; compare PRO, WO 105, LRP 17 for the same source.
24. Pieterse, p. 100; The *Natal Witness,* 23.8.1900: 'Held up by Boers' – told by Colonel Stowe; The *Natal Witness,* 14.8.1900: 'The Wrecked Train'.
25. TA, LRP 44: No. N620 Asst. Director of Railways, Bloemfontein – Chief of Staff, Pretoria, 2.8.1900, p. 213; TA, United States of America 5: Film A675, Vaughan, Cape Town – Stowe, 29.7.1900; The *Natal Witness,* 23.8.1900: 'Held up by Boers'.
26. Pieterse, p. 100; The Natal Witness, 23.8.1900: 'Held up by Boers'.
27. The Times, 12.2.1901: 'In Retreat with De Wet'; The Natal Witness, 23.8.1900: 'Held up by Boers'. Stowe states incorrectly that Theron only took one officer captive. Stowe and his staff were taken to Ventersburg Station later that morning by special train. From there they travelled on to Pretoria the following day without incident.
28. TA, LRP 9: Pine-Coffin, 'Ventersburg Road and Holfontein', 3.8.1900, pp. 14–16; compare PRO, WO 105, LRP 10 for the same source.
29. Ibid., PRO, WO 105, LRP 10: Maj. M.J.R. Dundas, 'Enemy Attack on Train at Holfontein Post', p. 1; *The Times,* 12.2.1901: 'In Retreat with De Wet.'
30. TA, LRP 9: Pine-Coffin, 'Ventersburg Road and Holfontein', 3.8.1900, p. 17; compare PRO, WO 105, LRP 10 for the same source.
31. Theron returned to Rhenosterpoort the day before the main laager crossed the Vaal (Ver Loren van Themaat, p. 166).
32. PRO, WO 105, LRP 32: No. 966, Roberts – Proemial, London, 3.8.1900; PRO, WO 105, LRP 34, No. C3256, Military Secretary, Chief, Pretoria – Military Secretary, Cape Town, 3.8.1900.
33. Amery (ed.), IV, p. 420.
34. WMC 155/42/1 (b): Letter, De Wet – Roberts, 6.8.1900. For further (subjective) Boer indignation, see Pieterse, pp. 102–103; Preller, p. 138; Ver Loren van Themaat, p. 165.
35. TA, LRP 44: No. N620, Asst. Director of Railways, Bloemfontein – Chief of Staff, Pretoria, 2.8.1900, p. 213.
36. PRO, WO 105, LRP 27: Letter, No. 52, Roberts – Botha, 5.8.1900.
37. TA, SA, Telegrams III: No. C3318, Roberts – Chermside, Rhenoster guard post, 5.8.1900, p. 133; compare PRO, WO 108/240 for the same source.
38. The *Cape Argus,* 16.8.1900: 'Freebooters of the Veld'.

CHAPTER NINE

'A just and sacred cause'

NOTWITHSTANDING THESE SUCCESSES, the time spent at Rhenosterpoort must have been a kind of test of faith for De Wet, who was a deeply religious man. The British were closing in on the Boers in overwhelming numbers, 'all trying their best to capture the government and me'.[1] And news from the Eastern Transvaal could hardly have been called encouraging: on 23 July a general British drive east had forced Botha to evacuate his headquarters at Balmoral and fall back beyond Middelburg right up to Machadodorp.[2] Botha now needed the services of the Free State commander's potential allies near Heidelberg. But the most crushing blow for De Wet at this time must undoubtedly have been the news that half the Free State forces had surrendered to the British at the end of July.

If these events weighed heavily on his mind, De Wet certainly did not show any outward signs of faltering. He tirelessly supervised posting pickets on the hills surrounding the laager to guard against surprise attacks, sent out patrols to keep an eye on enemy movements and to keep in touch with Liebenberg in the north, continued to hatch plans for joint operations with his Transvaal comrades-in-arms and kept trying to establish the safest route to escort Steyn to visit Kruger. 'He is indefatigable,' wrote Jacob de Villiers, who was present at Rhenosterpoort.[3]

Throughout De Wet managed to buoy the fighting spirit of his burghers both by his inspired leadership and a series of stirring and cunningly contrived addresses delivered to gatherings held outside his tent. Well aware of how fickle a creature Boer morale could be, he was always careful not to betray any doubts he himself may have had. Furthermore, De Wet was not afraid to bend the truth to restore flagging enthusiasm and ensure the compliance of recalcitrant burghers.

He would begin by sketching the war situation as though Roberts' biggest blunder was to march one step further than Bloemfontein, then entreat his men never to give up the struggle. 'If God wills it then we must fight until our children have grown up,' he exhorted in one such speech. 'I am the last to wish or believe it will take that long. But if God wills it, then that is how long we must fight. It is our sacred duty, because we are fighting for a just and sacred cause. Even if we lose everything, we are fighting for our children so that they may live in freedom in this land God granted us.'[4] Afterwards, to capitalise on the mood of his burghers, De Wet would get his secretary to read war reports of resounding Boer victories, embellishing these with his own remarks.[5] One report, sent by Louis Botha on 16 July sketching the situation on the eastern front, spoke of optimism and a firm faith that God would grant the Boers the necessary strength to fight the war to a successful conclusion. Botha said the Transvalers who had laid down arms were diligently enlisting again and he could thus confidently offer De Wet the following words of encouragement: 'Brother, remain steadfast and rely on me for real peace with honour or no peace at all.'[6] A young Boer in the crowd immediately cried: 'Long live Botha!' De Wet offered his burghers a final word of encouragement: 'Keep it up, fellow burghers! God will grant us victory. As in the Transvaal he is sending those who have laid down their weapons back to our ranks. God is with us.'[7] Before the meeting was dissolved an old burgher requested that the gathering sing the last verse of Hymn 20. Clutching their slouch hats to their chests, the Boers began to sing in their simple, nasal drawl:

> Come! let's forward now with cheerful tread,
> With steadfast faith in His word;
> The road may seem long and hard ahead,
> But our destination will surely be glorious.[8]

De Wet's style of delivery was certainly effective. 'He does not outwardly create the impression of a man of importance,' said one Transvaal burgher, 'but his voice is moving. He speaks from deep within his soul with a forcefulness no one can escape in a voice that carries for miles. De Wet is a born leader.'[9]

However, the British trooper Macdonald, a prisoner at Rhenosterpoort, believed De Wet held sway through coercion rather than his powers of persuasion or any genius for leadership. 'The Free Staters are sick of it,' he claimed, 'but De Wet is all powerful.'[10]

Given the Boers' legendary spirit of independence, it is unlikely they would have followed any leader unwillingly. This is further reinforced by the number of renegade burghers who kept joining De Wet's ranks. Since his escape from the Brandwater Basin, De Wet had sent patrols to visit the farms in the surrounding districts. Their brief, according to one of his men, was to 'see what the enemy had done to the burghers who had gone home, and to see what they had done to their homes and properties'.[11] The patrols were also ordered to notify the burghers that in terms of a proclamation issued by President Steyn on 19 July anyone who had laid down their weapons and sworn allegiance to the British crown should rejoin the commandos or face arrest.[12] As De Wet trekked north-west toward Vredefort, the presence of the Free State commander himself and his large fighting force did much to convince many renegade burghers in the area to take up arms again.[13] Word of his presence spread like wildfire. Just two days after the flour wagon skirmish near Vredefort, an English-speaking resident of Klerksdorp noted in his diary: 'The Boers are spreading rumours that General De Wet is in the Orange Free State not far from here.'[14] Thus De Wet was able to report to the Transvaal government on 25 July: 'On the Boer farms renegade burghers are joining up and seem determined to fight with renewed vigour,' claiming his fighting force had increased with 1 000 men since the flight from Brandwater.[15] This was an exaggeration, which no doubt served as an encouragement for the Transvalers. Nevertheless, most of the burghers who did return were armed because the Boers were in the habit of relinquishing only one of their weapons when surrendering to the British.[16]

The day after the Boers set up camp at Rhenosterpoort, about 200 renegade burghers from Bothaville rode into the laager.[17] De Wet immediately ordered an impromtu meeting in front of his tent. 'We found so many of them,' he told the gathering, pointing to the newcomers. 'But if you find just one more, drag him here by the hair. Everyone must join us in our struggle! But brothers,' he warned, 'each and every man who joins us again must remain with us to the end. A man must be reliable and true, and keep a clear conscience. If this is not encouragement enough I must warn you there is a proclamation that states that anyone who deserts again will be put to death. We have been merciful once, but will not be again. And I shall be the first to shoot such a man in cold blood. He who refuses to stay true must die. Because, brothers, we must persevere!'[18]

Burghers from surrounding farms kept arriving at Rhenosterpoort, swelling the force of 2 000 men, which had left the Brandwater Basin, to 2 500.[19] Among them were the Boshof burghers under Field-Cornet C.C.J. Badenhorst and the Kroonstad burghers under Commandant F. van Aard, who were cut off from their comrades during the skirmish at Paardeplaats on 19 July.[20] De Wet was elated to welcome them back, but his joy was short-lived. Badenhorst brought ill tidings: De Wet's own brother Piet de Wet had surrendered to the British.[21] Piet de Wet later wrote he had become convinced 'it would be better for our people to submit to God's will and in this way approach the future.'[22] De Wet, who must have been bitterly disappointed, certainly did not share his brother's interpretation of divine will.

He now turned his attention to launching joint military operations with the Transvaal generals. Although this had been one of his original intentions in trekking towards Vredefort, De Wet as usual had kept his cards close to his chest for fear of betraying his plans to the enemy.[23] At De Wet's funeral 22 years later, Dominee J.D. Kestell praised his ability to 'keep things to himself. Who could tell which course he would take next when his men dismounted in the evening.'[24] Nevertheless, during the trek the burghers were probably to some extent aware that military co-operation with the Transvalers was envisaged. And as a result of negligence or even treachery on the Boer side, it did not take long before the British had their suspicions too. Numerous rumours had been doing the rounds that commandos were heading for De Wet's riverside laager from the west and east, and that this was the destination of all the Boer wagon convoys in the district too.[25] The British, who during the hunt had learned to follow up on any information that came their way, were not about to dismiss the rumours out of hand.

The original plan for a combined operation involved General Piet Viljoen, who was supposed to trek toward Vereeniging from the Eastern Transvaal with the Heidelberg commando. This idea was put on hold when Buller occupied Greylingstad on 4 July; Viljoen now had more pressing matters to attend to closer to home. Although the Boer general still hoped to hasten to Vereeniging at the earliest opportunity to act in concert with De Wet and Liebenberg, it soon became apparent that Buller's force was too strong.[26] Soon the Standerton and Bethal commandos were sent to reinforce Viljoen and during the next few weeks he was tied up fighting Buller near Bethal.[27]

Meanwhile, the British offensive along the Delagoa Bay line was gaining momentum and Botha desperately needed reinforcements. On 25 July, on the same day De Wet reached Rhenosterpoort, Botha ordered Viljoen 'to advance with all possible haste to Machadodorp to help us keep the enemy at bay'.[28] Viljoen set off at once with 600 burghers,[29] thereby dashing De Wet's hopes that the Transvaal general would be able to participate in his plans. The news probably reached the Free State commander at Rhenosterpoort on 29 July.[30]

De Wet's envisaged operations with Liebenberg's men in the Western Transvaal now grew in significance. Like De Wet, Liebenberg kept recruiting burghers on his way south from the Magaliesberg, splitting his force into three under Snyman, Douthwaite and Du Toit, who, as we have learned, tirelessly attacked the enemy from their operational bases at the Gatsrand. General G. Barton, the British commanding officer at Krugersdorp, put their strength at less than 500 men, with two guns and a pom-pom. But, he added, 'they move in detached parties and separate laagers, therefore number and movements are most deceptive.'[31] About 30 Transvalers, most of them from Potchefstroom, who had joined De Wet's commandos in June and taken part in the trek from the Brandwater Basin now decided to push on from Rhenosterpoort to join Liebenberg. On 28 July they met up with Douthwaite, just as he was engaged in a skirmish with Methuen near Frederikstad.[32] A few days later they joined Liebenberg himself,[33] whose force now numbered 600.[34]

Although De Wet remained in touch with Liebenberg's forces, sending messengers and receiving food supplies from the Gatsrand,[35] the arrival of Methuen in the Western Transvaal with 4 500 men – who by this stage had two-thirds of his force under his personal command at Potchefstroom and a third under Smith-Dorrien at Frederikstad – posed a threat to any direct military co-operation. Liebenberg's occupation of Klerksdorp on 24 July thus in no way brought his commandos closer to De Wet. But as we have seen, this did not prevent the two Boer forces from attaining their common goal in isolation by independently disrupting British supply lines on two fronts. Furthermore, Liebenberg indirectly proved extremely useful to De Wet by constantly occupying Methuen's attention.

This respite also gave De Wet time to ponder the idea of bringing together the presidents of the two republics. The decision that Steyn should be taken to see Kruger was probably made at a war council held on 22 July, on the morning after the Boers crossed the Bloemfontein–Pretoria railway line at Serfontein Siding.[36] Now that the Free Staters found themselves on the bank of the Vaal at Rhenosterpoort, the visit became even more feasible. One morning De Wet called a heliographer named Philip Pienaar, a Transvaler, over to his tent and inquired about the best route to Louis Botha's headquarters at Balmoral.[37] From there it would be easy for Steyn to reach Kruger further east at Watervalonder near Machadodorp. The most direct route would be to head north-east to Parys and then on to Heidelberg, where Viljoen would be able to provide Steyn with an escort past Buller's forces. But De Wet soon learned that Louis Botha had vacated Balmoral for Machadodorp by then, and Viljoen had been sent to reinforce him against the major British offensive planned there. Another path would have to be found. As it turned out, the safest option was to head north past Potchefstroom and towards the Magaliesberg. It was true that the presence of Methuen and Smith-Dorrien between Potchefstroom and Frederikstad, of Barton at Krugersdorp and of Baden-Powell and Ian Hamilton at Rustenburg further north, would pose a grave threat to the president. But the appearance of Liebenberg's men at the Gatsrand and De la Rey's systematic re-establishment of Boer influence further north made this route a feasible choice.

Before the plan could be executed another event suddenly demanded De Wet's attention: on Wednesday 1 August he received a letter from Major-General Charles Knox. Marthinus Prinsloo, he was informed, had surrendered with his entire force at Fouriesburg.[38] If De Wet, 'a brave man and good general', followed suit, Knox 'could assure him of kind treatment'.[39] Now De Wet was in a quandary. Had Prinsloo indeed surrendered, or was this simply an attempt to dampen De Wet's fighting spirit. The next day he replied, telling Knox he distrusted the British general's information and was 'most surprised' by his suggestion that he surrender.

'I take umbrage at the gross insult and I therefore feel it beneath my dignity to reply to your excellency in this regard.'[40]

Knox's letter may have been inspired by a comment made by Piet de Wet, who had surrendered in Kroonstad a few days before Prinsloo. On 30 July the commanding officer of Kroonstad cabled Roberts in Pretoria, informing him that 'P. de Wet tells me if his brother knew Prinsloo had surrendered he would do so also.' But Piet de Wet was convinced his brother would not believe the news unless 'one of Prinsloo's men was sent to him'.[41] Consequently Roberts ordered Hunter, still at the Brandwater Basin, to send a Boer delegate accompanied by a British officer to see De Wet.[42] Broadwood then wrote to De Wet, asking him to guarantee that the messengers would be allowed to return unharmed. De Wet duly complied.

On 31 July an adjudant named Albert Grobler and a certain Major King left the Brandwater Basin bearing a letter from Prinsloo.[43] Three days later De Wet, Steyn and some of his councillors rode out to meet the delegation in a no-man's-land halfway between Broadwood's camp and Rhenosterpoort so as not to betray their position.[44]

Prinsloo's message was unambiguous. 'Sir, I have the honour to hereby inform you that I have been obliged, owing to the overwhelming forces of the enemy, to surrender unconditionally with all the Orange Free State commandos here.' It was signed 'M. Prinsloo, Commander-in-Chief'.[45]

De Wet slyly made no mention of the surrender in his reply, sent in an unsealed envelope, apparently refusing to respond to what may have been

Marthinus Prinsloo, who took advantage of the confusion among the Free Staters who were left behind by De Wet in the Brandwater Basin to take command. On 30 July 1900, he surrendered to General Hunter with more than 3 000 burghers, a figure that within a week was to rise to 4 400 men. On 3 August, whilst in the hills along the Vaal River near Reitzburg, De Wet received a letter from Prinsloo informing him of his action. (From: J. Malan, Die Boere-Offisiere van die Tweede Vryheidsoorlog 1899–1902, *Pretoria, 1990, p. 11)*

another attempt by the British to demoralise him. While waiting for Grobler, he had in fact received a letter from General Roux, informing him that although Prinsloo had assumed overall command, most of the commandos had already left the Brandwater Basin.[46] Instead, De Wet stressed the illegitimacy of the rank of the commander who had ordered the burghers to lay down arms.

'By what right do you usurp that title?' was his sharp retort. 'You were merely given temporary command over a few small sections which were to guard the passes. You have no right to act as Commander-in-Chief.' De Wet cheekily signed off: 'I have the honour to be – C.R. de Wet, Commander-in-Chief.'[47]

In reality De Wet was incensed by the surrender. 'It was nothing short of an act of murder', he wrote later, 'committed on the Government, the country and the nation. One could gnash one's teeth to think a nation should so readily rush to its own ruin!'[48]

Hunter now suggested General Roux be sent 'to inform him of the truth'.[49] This was rejected by Roberts, who realised De Wet could not be dissuaded from continuing the struggle.[50] Nevertheless, it must have been an extremely trying time for the Free State commander, who surely began to doubt whether he had chosen the right course of action. But his unshakable faith in God apparently saw him through this hour of need.[51]

A more detailed report of the surrender which reached De Wet a few days later from Christoffel Froneman must have helped too. Froneman told him not all the Boer commandos had accepted Prinsloo's surrender. About 1 600 burghers under the command of General Piet Fourie, with Froneman as his number two, had managed to escape through Golden Gate (the basin's eastern exit) in the direction of Harrismith. They included commandos under J.H. Olivier from Rouxville–Thaba 'Nchu, H.P.J. Pretorius from Jacobsdal, P.J. Visser from Fauresmith and Sarel Haasbroek from Winburg. The group had managed to salvage seven Krupps, one Armstrong, a Maxim-Nordenveldt, a smaller Maxim and six wagons loaded with ammunition. They were heading north and at that moment, on 3 August, stood at the bridge over the Cornelis River. Furthermore, about 800 burghers from Vrede and Harrismith under Acting-General Frik Hattingh and Commandant C.J. de Villiers had also rejected the surrender and were now in the region of Harrismith. According to Froneman, the Boer officers in his group all wished to join De Wet. He concluded by expressing the hope that 'in a few days we will be able to shake each other's hands and that the good Lord will bring us together so that we can speak face to face again'.[52]

This was good news indeed, and definitely did much to restore flagging spirits at Rhenosterpoort. De Wet immediately sent General (Judge) J.B.M. Hertzog to try to conduct the commandos to the Boer laager at the Vaal River.[53]

On the same day, Sunday 5 August, Theron and his scouts returned – and in the nick of time too, for by then Kitchener was drawing his cordon tight around the Boer laager. If the Free Staters tarried much longer they would be trapped. In fact, it was beginning to look as though every avenue of escape had already been sealed. Then some of De Wet's scouts arrived with welcome tidings: one escape hatch had been left open. The bad news was that a large British force was at that moment racing up to the Vaal to batten it down. There was no time to lose.

Notes

1. De Wet, p. 140.
2. Maurice and Grant, III, pp. 320–322.
3. Van Schoor, 'Diaries of Jacob de Villiers', 30.7.1900, p. 20.
4. Oberholster, pp. 92–93.
5. [Hintrager], pp. 65 and 68–69.
6. TA, Leyds 728 (h): Dispatch No. 8, Botha – De Wet, by dispatch rider, 16.7.1900; compare TA, Leyds 733: Dispatch, Botha – De Wet, by dispatch rider, 16.7.1900, p. 95.
7. Oberholster, p. 96; compare [Hintrager], p. 69.
8. Ibid.; compare Penning, III, p. 916.
9. *Leidsch Dagblad*, 18.8.1900, from *Rotterdamsch Nieuwsblad*. Although this report catered for a Dutch readership which slavishly supported the Boers, it can nevertheless serve as an example of a contemporary judgement of De Wet.
10. TA, MGP 16: Statement by Macdonald of French's Scouts, 16.8.1900, p. 149.
11. FA, Renier Collection 119.77: G.J. Joubert on General Piet de Wet.
12. Lombard, p. 62; Badenhorst, p. 53; TA, LRP 42: Hunter – Roberts, 11.8.1900, p. 59; compare PRO, WO 105, LRP 17 for the same source.
13. Compare Penning, III, pp. 914–915; Ver Loren van Themaat, p. 164.
14. TA, Acquisition 782: Diary of H. Bramley, a civilian, kept at Klerksdorp, 26.7.1900.
15. TA, Leyds 730 (e): Telegram No. 46a, received 15.8.1900, De Wet – Transvaal government, via Grobler, no date; compare TA, Leyds 751 (c): Telegram No. 27, received 15.8.1900 for the same source; compare TA, Leyds 734: Extra Oorlogsbericht, 21:00, 15.8.1900, p. 91.
16. [Hintrager], p. 63.
17. Ibid.; Nierstrasz, II, Vol. 5, p. 1004, who clearly uses Hintrager as a source.
18. Oberholster, pp. 92–93; compare [Hintrager], pp. 64–65.
19. Van Schoor, 'Diaries of Jacob de Villiers', 8.8.1900, p. 24.
20. Badenhorst, p. 45; Van Schoor, 'Diaries of Jacob de Villiers', 29.7.1900, p. 20.
21. Badenhorst, p. 44.
22. War Museum, Bloemfontein: Letter, P. de Wet – C.R. de Wet, 11.1.1901; compare *The Times*, 11.2.1901 for an English translation of the letter.
23. Pienaar, p. 145.
24. TA, G.S. Preller Collection 19: *Hollandsch-Zuid-Afrika*, 15.3.1922, funeral of General Christiaan de Wet, p. 8.
25. TA, LRP: No. B1227, GOC, Kroonstad – Military Secretary, Chief, Pretoria re tele-

gram Bullock, Honingspruit, 22.7.1900, p. 21; compare PRO, WO 105, LRP 22 for the same source.
26. TA, Leyds 750 (d): Telegram No. 4, P. Viljoen, Ras' farm – Botha, 10.7.1900.
27. TA, Leyds 750 (a): Telegram No. 16, Botha – Commandants Bethal and Standerton, 3.7.1900; TA, Leyds 750 (b): Telegram No. 17, Viljoen – Botha, 3.7.1900; TA, Leyds 750 (b): Telegram No. 12, received 5.7.1900, Viljoen – State President, sent 4.7.1900; TA, Leyds 750 (b): Telegram No. 68, received 5.7.1900 – State President, sent 4.7.1900; TA, Leyds 750 (d): Telegram No. 4, Viljoen – Botha, 10.7.1900; TA, Leyds 750 (d): Telegram No. 2, Viljoen – Botha, 15.7.1900.
28. TA, Leyds 750 (f): Telegram No. 13, Botha – Viljoen, via Magistrate, Bethal, 25.7.1900.
29. TA, Leyds 750 (f): Telegram No. 14, received 26.7.1900, Viljoen – Government, sent 25.7.1900.
30. Lombard, p. 66.
31. TA, LRP 39: No. 711P, Barton – Roberts, 1.8.1900, p. 107; compare PRO, WO 105, LRP 22 for the same source.
32. Pienaar, pp. 151–152; TA, LRP 9: Methuen, 'Western Transvaal Report', 28.7.1900, pp. 3–4; compare PRO, WO 105, LRP 10 for the same source.
33. Pienaar, pp. 151–152; TA, LRP 40: No. H621, Kitchener – Roberts, 7.8.1900, re intelligence report Methuen – Kitchener, 5.8.1900, p. 38; compare PRO, WO 105, LRP 16 for the same source.
34. TA, Leyds 759: Letter, Liebenberg, Sterkstroom – L. Botha, 17.8.1900, p. 57; Pienaar, pp. 151–152.
35. TA, SA Telegrams III: No. C3209, Roberts – Methuen, 2.8.1900, p. 121; TA, SA Telegrams III: No. C3090, Roberts – Kitchener, 28.7.1900, p. 106; compare PRO, WO 108/240 for the same sources; recounted to author by Mrs M. Malherbe (née Pienaar), Elandsfontein, 7.12.1972.
36. See Pretorius, 'Kommentaar op "Die Strategiese Oogmerke van Genl. C.R. de Wet"', pp. 23–24.
37. Pienaar, p. 145.
38. Van Schoor, 'Diaries of Jacob de Villiers', 2.8.1900, p. 21; compare FA, WMC 155/42/1 (b): Letter, De Wet, Veld near Vredefort – Knox, Kroonstad, 2.8.1900 re letter, Knox – De Wet, 30.7.1900; De Wet. p. 139; Nierstrasz, II, Vol. 5, p. 1009.
39. Van Schoor, 'Diaries of Jacob de Villiers', 2.8.1900, p. 21.
40. FA, WMC 155/42/1 (b): Letter, De Wet, Veld near Vredefort – Knox, Kroonstad, 2.8.1900.
41. TA, SA Telegrams III: No. C3154, Cowan, Pretoria – Hunter, Fouriesburg re telegram GOC, Kroonstad – Roberts, 30.7.1900, p. 113; compare PRO, WO 108/240 for the same source.
42. Ibid.
43. TA, LRP 37: No. A238, Hunter – Roberts, 08:50, 31.7.1900, p. 193; compare PRO, WO 10, LRP 17 for the same source. De Wet is clearly mistaken when he states in his memoirs (p. 138) that the delegate was Marthinus Prinsloo's secretary, Mr Kotzé. Jacob de Villiers' diary clears up any doubts (4.8.1900).
44. De Wet, p. 139; Van Schoor, 'Diaries of Jacob de Villiers', 4.8.1900, pp. 22–23. De Wet's memoirs contain a number of inaccuracies about the events which took place between 2 August and 6 August 1900, which has undoubtedly contributed to errors made by later researchers and writers.
45. De Wet, p. 139; FA, WMC 155/42/1 (a): Prinsloo – De Wet, 31.7.1900; compare Van Schoor, 'Diaries of Jacob de Villiers', 4.8.1900, p. 22.
46. Van Schoor, 'Diaries of Jacob de Villiers', 4.8.1900, p. 23.

47. De Wet, p. 139; FA, WMC 155/42/1 (b): De Wet – Prinsloo, 3.8.1900; also compare FA, WMC 155/42/1 (a): De Wet – Prinsloo, 3.8.1900 (copy); and Van Schoor, 'Diaries of Jacob de Villiers', 4.8.1900, p. 22.
48. De Wet, p. 131.
49. TA, LRP 42: No. A385, Hunter – Roberts, 8.8.1900, p. 261; compare PRO, WO 105, LRP 17 for the same source.
50. TA, SA Telegrams IV: No. C3420, Roberts – Hunter, 9.8.1900, p. 8; compare PRO, WO 108/241 for the same source.
51. Van Schoor, et al., *Christiaan Rudolph de Wet, 1854–1922,* p. 38.
52. FA, WMC 155/42/1 (a): Letter, Froneman, Cornelis River bridge – De Wet, 3.8.1900; compare F.A. Steytler, *Die Geskiedenis van Harrismith,* pp. 161–162.
53. De Wet, p. 140; De V. Esterhuysen, p. 63; FA, Renier Collection 119.526: Colonel Corneels du Preez, adjudant of President Steyn, recorded by J.N. Brink, p. 27; Nierstrasz, II, Vol. 5, p. 1028. C.H. Olivier, made a general later in the war and subsequently a member of the Executive Council of the Orange Free State, accompanied Hertzog in an attempt to 'salvage what could be salvaged' (TA, Acquisition 1250: D. de Witt, 'Die Trek naar die Bosveld', recorded by C.P. van der Merwe, p. 7). The British, however, realised that the commandos in the east would want to unite with De Wet and Louis Botha and keep a close watch on them. Commandant J.H. Olivier, who had in the meantime been separated from the rest of the commandos, was taken prisoner on 27 August near Winburg by Major-General Bruce Hamilton (TA, LRP 42: Hamilton – Roberts, 27.8.1900, p. 127.) The rest of the commandos under Piet Fourie were only able to unite with De Wet in September after the latter had returned from the Transvaal.

CHAPTER TEN

Wide open

KITCHENER JUMPED AT THE CHANCE to swap his desk job in Pretoria for active duty.[1] On the morning of Friday 3 August he arrived at Koppies north of Roodewal in an armoured train and set off for the front at once.[2] The Chief of Staff immediately made it clear to his generals that he was supreme commander in the field, angrily chiding Kelly-Kenny for issuing orders directly to Knox without consulting him.[3] And as usual he adopted a hands-on approach. Upon arrival at the front, he undertook the first of a series of regular inspection tours with Broadwood of the British positions, meeting Ridley further north near Vredefort that same afternoon. Kitchener's unfaltering energy and zeal, as well as his sheer professionalism and ability to focus unflinchingly on the task at hand, certainly boosted troop morale – especially among the officers who had been pursuing De Wet since the Brandwater Basin and believed by now that the campaign to trap the Boers was happening hopelessly too slowly.[4]

Like Hunter, Kitchener planned to tighten his cordon around the Boers before launching the final assault. First, however, he would have to establish the location of the Boer laager. On the day he arrived, Kitchener discovered that a number of Boers had dug themselves in at Witkoppies, south-east of Reitzburg.[5] It was only after speaking to Albert Grobler, the Boer delegate who had taken Prinsloo's letter to De Wet, that Kitchener was able to deduce that their main laager lay further north, near Schoeman's Drift.[6]

With reinforcements pouring in daily, Kitchener now had the means to flesh out that 'thin line of khaki' running from Vredefort east of the Boer laager to Koppie Alleen further south. However, his regular inspection tours of the front convinced him the terrain south-west of the Boers was more suited to his offensive. He would concentrate his forces at Winkel's Drift on the Rhenoster River[7] and send patrols up to Scandinavia Drift, blocking any escape route to the west. By pushing the British line forward, Kitchener's forces would surround De Wet from Parys in the east to Winkel's Drift in the south-west, with Methuen in Potchefstroom closing the cordon north-west of the Boers. The Pimpernel would be ensnared, and Kitchener could close in for the kill.

Early the next morning, Saturday 4 August, the British force went into action. Knox took 2 000 men and six guns along Honingspruit from Koppie Alleen toward Rhebokfontein – the Boers' most southern position. His right flank was covered by Little's 3rd Cavalry with 700 men and a further six guns. Before long Knox unleashed his artillery on the Boers in the koppies over the Rhenoster River, forcing them to retire without offering much resistance in the direction of the main laager under the heavy shellfire. It is unknown whether the Boers suffered any losses, but one of Knox's men was badly wounded during the exchange. Later that afternoon, the 3rd Cavalry withdrew to Koppie Alleen while Knox crossed the Rhenoster River to occupy Rhebokfontein and Rheboklaagte further north.[8]

The vanguard of Kitchener's thrust from the south-west would be Dalgety's Colonial Division. That evening his advance units arrived at Rhebokfontein and headed north-west along the Rhenoster River to Winkel's Drift, covered by Broadwood's 2nd Cavalry under Kitchener's personal command. The next morning Dalgety's patrols would be sent to the Vaal River.[9]

Methuen now became crucial to Kitchener's plan. On 4 August he sent a dispatch rider to the 1st Division commander with the order to send troops south from Potchefstroom to Scandinavia Drift, and from there to push on to Winkel's Drift south of the Vaal to close the western cordon. Furthermore, Methuen was ordered to make contact with the British guard posts near Parys in the east.[10] Had Kitchener known how dangerously thin Methuen's force was stretched and to what extent Liebenberg was wreaking havoc on his communication lines, the Chief of Staff would probably not have ordered him to further weaken his force on the northern cordon. This mistake would cost him dearly.

The next morning, Sunday 5 August, Little's 3rd Cavalry was sent back up toward Vredefort, bivouacking that evening a few kilometres south of the town at Paardekraal.[11] This freed Ridley to advance closer to the Vaal with his 2nd Mounted Infantry. Legge and De Lisle were sent ahead and the rest of the 2nd Mounted Infantry joined them at noon the next day on the summit of a hill on the farm Groot Eiland, abutting the Vaal River just west of Parys.[12] Kitchener had made a superb strategic choice. 'The Vaal, winding between thickly wooded banks, lay below us,' recalls Howland, who accompanied Ridley, 'and beyond it, and also on the higher side towards Vredefort, rose stately peaks and mountains, with one gorge which they sheltered, leading to the Boer position, plainly visible, and also another from which the gleaming river issued on its way to the distant sea. The road which the Boers would have to follow if they attempted to escape to the eastward lay below under our guns; and a splendid view of a large extent of country was to be obtained from Groot Eiland's commanding summit.'[13] The Royal Canadian infantry regiment, sent down

WIDE OPEN   113

BRITISH AND BOER POSITIONS ON THE VAAL RIVER, 6 AUGUST 1900

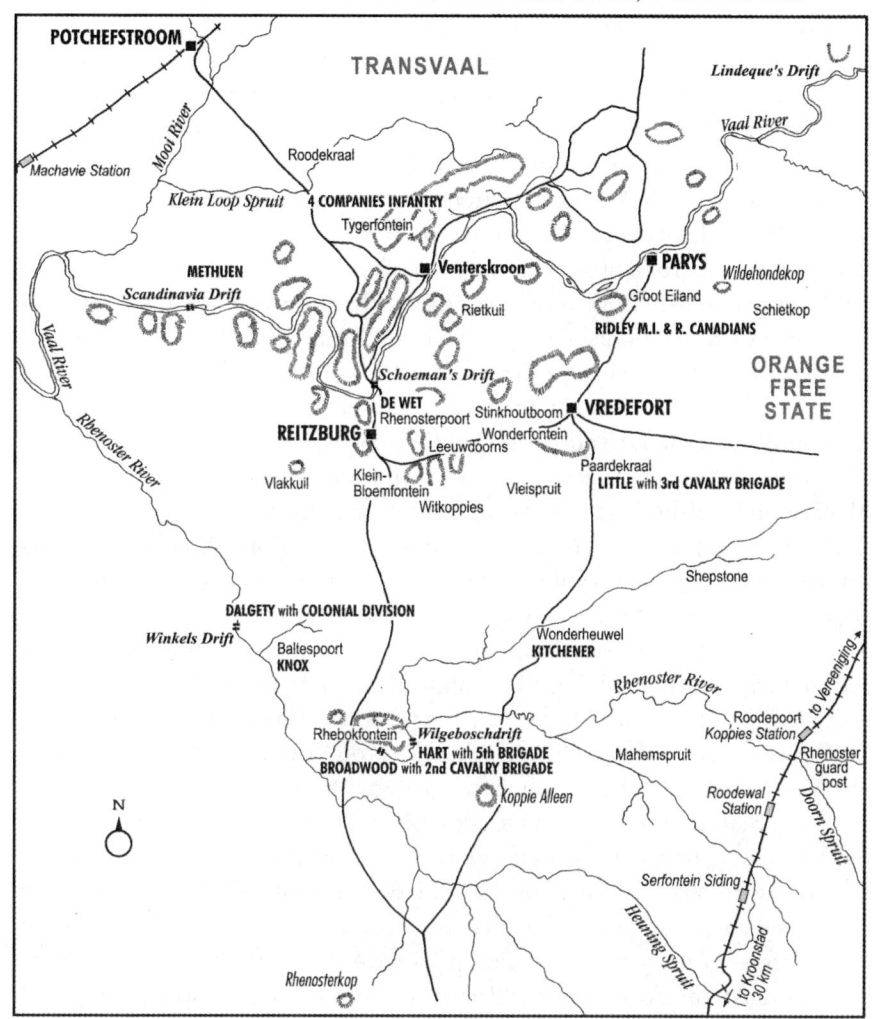

from Springs in the Transvaal, had arrived at Schietkop east of Parys the previous day.[14] The eastern exit was sealed.

Thus by Monday 6 August, Kitchener's cordon south of the Vaal was firmly in place. Ridley and the Canadians controlled the drifts around Parys; Little's 3rd Cavalry manned the eastern sector near Vredefort; and Hart's force along with the Northumberland Fusiliers occupied the line further south toward Rhebokfontein. Kitchener's headquarters were situated at Wonderheuwel, between the forces of Hart and Little. In the west, the British forces were deployed along the Rhenoster River, with Broadwood's 2nd Cavalry at Rhebokfontein, Knox further north at Baltespoort and Dalgety's Colonials closer to the Vaal at Winkel's Drift – 11 000 men[15] against De Wet's force less than a quarter that size. But Kitchener and Roberts believed a stronger force was needed.[16] Before the final assault, he would await the arrival of the 3rd Durhams, who would join the South Wales Borderers at Roodewal Station,[17] and the brigades of Clements and MacDonald on their way from the Brandwater Basin.

De Wet was well aware of his untenable position. According to his intelligence, Methuen's column from Potchefstroom and the force his scouts spotted on Sunday 5 August – which was in fact Ridley's mounted infantry racing for Groot Eiland – would be able to reach Van Vuuren's Kloof early on the morning of 6 August. This was halfway between Parys and De Wet's laager at Rhenosterpoort; his last exit would be blocked.

'We were forced now either to break through this cordon, or to cross the Vaal River into the South African Republic,' says De Wet. He knew the Free Staters would prefer to stay on their own soil, and could easily have done so had it not been for their wagon laager. But De Wet was keenly aware that the burghers would be unwilling to sacrifice all they possessed in order to break out in small mounted commandos.[18] There was nothing else for it but to take the wagon train with him and on Monday 6 August, the great laager at Rhenosterpoort struck camp and prepared to trek across the Vaal River.

But while Kitchener tightened the screws on De Wet south of the Vaal, Methuen found he was hardly in a position to apply the same pressure from the north; he had his hands full with Liebenberg's commandos. Since Methuen's arrival in Potchefstroom on 30 July, the western border burgers had given him no end of trouble. The first spot of bother was the news that Smith-Dorrien's supply train had been wrecked near Frederikstad on 30 July. At 06:00 the next morning Methuen sent ox and mule transport to fetch a further seven days' provisions from the derailed train.[19] According to Barton, the commanding officer of Krugersdorp, this would give Methuen sufficient supplies to last until 15 August.[20] At 08:00 Methuen heard artillery fire from the direction of Frederikstad and received a heliograph from Smith-Dorrien that Liebenberg had demanded his surrender an hour before with a force of 500 men and two guns. Soon afterwards Liebenberg actually attacked Smith-Dorrien from the south. Methuen now sent the Yeomanry, his artillery and half a battalion with supplies for one day to engage the Boers. In the ensuing skirmish two of his men were killed and seven were wounded. At 10:00 Methuen received a report that Liebenberg had retired north, in the direction of Ventersdorp. Methuen recalled his infantry and supplies to Potchefstroom and pursued the Boers with the Yeomanry on the Ventersdorp road. Just before noon they caught up with Liebenberg's rearguard. After an exchange of artillery fire and a chase which lasted some two hours, the Boer commando escaped.[21]

Methuen now had no choice but to divide up his force again. Smith-Dorrien would be reinforced with two guns and 120 men from the Imperial Yeomanry. He was to remain at Frederikstad and keep the railway to Krugersdorp clear.[22] Meanwhile, one-and-a-half Yeomanry battalions were sent west to Machavie Station to patrol the railway up to Klerksdorp and the area near Scandinavia Drift where the Mooi River meets the Vaal.[23] The result was that Methuen had even fewer men at his disposal to devote to the operation against De Wet. On 31 July he sent a report to Roberts that Liebenberg's activities meant his force would only be united on 2 August for the drive against De Wet.[24] But two days after that date he was forced to report a further delay. 'I shall of course carry out your orders as soon as my force is collected here, which cannot be before August 7th,' he told Roberts.[25] Liebenberg had thus severely curtailed Methuen's ability to devote himself to the operation against De Wet, which certainly influenced later events.

Furthermore, Liebenberg's presence caused the British endless communication headaches at a time they could least afford them, emphasising just how vulnerable communication lines had become in this new mobile warfare being waged by the Boers. Methuen felt particularly isolated. In his report to Roberts on 31 July he wrote: 'I can neither send nor obtain information except by signal because the Boers are shooting my natives as well as their own and have terrified my black boys not unnaturally.'[26] With the telegraph line between Krugersdorp and Bank Station down since 28 July,[27] Methuen was forced to heliograph messages to Smith-Dorrien at Frederikstad, who in turn sent cyclists to Barton in Krugersdorp who were in danger of being captured or shot by Liebenberg's commandos. From there messages could be relayed by telegraph to Roberts in Pretoria.[28] However, the Boer heliographers soon deciphered the British code and could thus easily keep tabs on the enemy's movements from their refuge among the hills along the Vaal River.[29] Methuen only became aware of the problem on 2 August, after a British prisoner escaped from the Boer laager,[30] but by then the damage had been done. It is difficult to explain why Methuen did not cotton on sooner, or at least take the likelihood into account. To make matters worse, Barton was only able to send him a new code on 6 August.[31] The telegraph line to Pretoria was finally restored on 7 August, but only as far as Welverdiend, 46 km north-east of Potchefstroom.[32] And by then it was too late.

Roberts meanwhile had been badgering Barton for any news from Methuen, but in vain. The last time he had heard from the 1st Division commander was on 28 July – when Methuen ran into Liebenberg's commandos operating from the Gatsrand – and his patience was wearing thin.[33] When on 3 August Methuen's cyclists at last succeeded in reaching Krugersdorp with three messages, Roberts showed little sympathy for his dilemma. 'I must ask you to give me fuller and more frequent accounts of your proceedings or it will be impossible for me to arrange for you to co-operate with other forces now in the field,' he immediately cabled back, reminding Methuen that no military plan could be crowned with success if the commanders involved in a campaign were not kept fully up to date with one another's positions and circumstances.[34] His words were to prove prophetic.

Methuen replied two days later, on 5 August. 'I hear some of my messages have not reached you. I reported my presence here on July 30th to Chief of Staff at Krugersdorp and since then I have reported daily, but very difficult to get messages through as bearers were sometimes stopped, sometimes killed.'[35] In other words, Methuen had done his best under extremely trying conditions. On the other hand, the messages which did get through to Roberts were, as usual, far too sketchy. Furthermore, in Roberts' telegram of 3 August the chief had expressly ordered Methuen to inform him which of his messages the 1st Division commander had in fact received. In his reply to Roberts on 5 August,[36] Methuen had failed to comply. In these two respects at least Roberts' anger was entirely justified.

Roberts, directly responsible for devising the overall strategy for capturing De Wet and communicating his plans to his commanders in the field, was beset by his own set of problems in trying to reach Methuen. Since Methuen had advanced into the teeth of Liebenberg's commandos past Bank Station, Roberts, too, had been forced to rely on cyclists relaying messages from Krugersdorp and Frederikstad through enemy controlled territory.[37] Roberts therefore tried to reach Methuen via Kitchener south of the Vaal River. On 2 August Kitchener was ordered to relay the chief's orders to Methuen regarding the 1st Division commander's role in the operation against De Wet.[38] Thus Kitchener, who arrived at the front the next morning, in effect assumed overall command of the entire campaign on both sides of the Vaal River.

Roberts' orders to Methuen were if anything highly unrealistic. As unaware as Kitchener of how weak and fragmented Methuen's force had

Lord Methuen who, according to The Times History, *was the heart and soul of the first De Wet hunt. Boer operations on the Potchefstroom–Johannesburg railway line and communication problems, ensured that his advance towards the Vaal River was slow enough to give De Wet that small opening which he needed to slip away. (Transvaal Archives Depot, Pretoria)*

become,[39] Roberts instructed him to prevent supplies from reaching De Wet from the Gatsrand at all costs. Methuen was also ordered to supply Smith-Dorrien at Frederikstad with sufficient troops to restore the rail link to Krugersdorp and thus eliminate supply problems. Finally, he was told to take his main force to a suitable location near the Vaal to be able to control the drifts across the river[40] – an extremely daunting task, because he was thereby assigned no less than 12 fords between Scandinavia Drift and Lindeque's Drift.[41] Methuen made no attempt to hide his frustration in his reply to Roberts' orders: 'Bank station to Potchefstroom very weak force considering activity and numbers of the enemy. Have to use large portion on convoy duty. My force is therefore also very weak for duty assigned.'[42]

This order, issued on 3 August, did not get through to Methuen until 5 August as Kitchener found it no less of a challenge than Roberts to reach the 1st Division commander. Heliographs were out of the question and messengers thus had to be sent – an extremely unreliable method of conveying orders because of the obvious hazards involved. And according to Broadwood, De Wet's men had gained control of the banks of the Vaal as early as 27 July, blocking the passage of British patrols. Kitchener nevertheless sent two messengers to Methuen on 4 August and another the following day, but on 6 August was obliged to reported to Roberts: 'My messengers did not get through to Methuen. They found the Vaal drifts all occupied.'[43]

The supreme irony is that one of Kitchener's messengers did in fact succeed in reaching Methuen on 5 August – with the order he had issued on 4 August instructing the 1st Division commander to march south from Potchefstroom to Scandinavia Drift. The next morning Methuen launched an ill-considered attempt to cut off De Wet from the north. He sent four companies of infantry, artillery and a squadron of Imperial Yeomanry south-east in the direction of Parys to Klein Loopspruit, while he himself took a small force and set off due south for Scandinavia Drift at the Vaal River.[44] From that moment the route through Schoeman's Drift across the Vaal River was left wide open for De Wet.

Notes

1. Arthur, I, p. 315.
2. TA, LRP 40: Kitchener – Roberts, 3.8.1900, p. 25; compare PRO, WO 105, LRP 16 for the same source. This and Kitchener's following telegrams to Roberts prove that the latter stated incorrectly in his report dated 10.10.1900 that Kitchener left Pretoria on 4 August and arrived at Wonderheuwel on the following day (TA, South African Dispatches II: Roberts' Account, 14 June to 10 October 1900, p. 10; compare PRO, WO 32/8000 for the same source). Sources supporting Kitchener's telegram are: TA, WO Acquisition, JPE 5: Staff Diary, 5th Brigade, 3.8.1900, p. 63; Howland, p. 148; The *Natal Witness*, 13.10.1900: F.H. Howland, 'The Chase of De Wet'. Writers using Roberts' dates include Maurice and Grant, II, p. 343; Nierstrasz, II, Vol. 5, p. 1013; Arthur, I, p. 315; Penning, III, p. 917.
3. TA, LRP 40: No. H589, Kitchener – Roberts, 21:30, 3.8.1900, p. 26; TA LRP 40: No. H593, Kitchener – Roberts, 10:15, 4.8.1900, p. 30; TA LRP 40: No. H597, Kitchener – Roberts, 20:55, 4.8.1900, p. 33; compare PRO, WO 105, LRP 16 for the same source.
4. Howland, p. 148.
5. TA, LRP 40: Kitchener – Roberts, 3.8.1900, p. 28; compare PRO, WO 105, LRP 16 for the same source.
6. TA, LRP 40: No. H597, Kitchener – Roberts, 4.8.1900, p. 33; compare PRO, WO 105, LRP 16 for the same source.
7. TA, LRP 40: No. H608, Kitchener – Roberts, 5.8.1900, p. 36; compare PRO, WO 105, LRP 16 for the same source.
8. TA, LRP 40: No. H597, Kitchener – Roberts, 4.8.1900, p. 31; compare PRO, WO 105, LRP 16 for the same source; Colvin and Gordon, p. 136; Amery (ed.), IV, p. 420.
9. TA, LRP 40: No. H608, Kitchener – Roberts, 5.8.1900, p. 36; compare PRO, WO 105, LRP 16 for the same source; Colvin and Gordon, p. 136; TA, SA Dispatches II: Roberts' Account, 14 June to 10 October 1900, p. 10; compare PRO WO 32/8000 for the same source.

10. TA, LRP 40: No. H597, Kitchener – Roberts, re telegram Kitchener – Methuen, 20:55, 4.8.1900, p. 31; compare PRO, WO 105, LRP 16 for the same source.
11. Colvin and Gordon, p. 136; TA, LRP 40: No. H597, Kitchener – Roberts, 4.8.1900, p. 32; compare PRO, WO 105, LRP 16 for the same source.
12. TA, LRP 40: No. H614, Kitchener – Roberts, 6.8.1900, p. 37; compare PRO, WO 105, LRP 16 for the same source; Howland, p. 171; Amery (ed.), IV, p. 421.
13. Howland, pp. 171–172; compare TA, LRP 40: No. H614, Kitchener – Roberts, 6.8.1900, p. 37; compare PRO, WO 105, LRP 16 for the same source.
14. TA, LRP 40: No. H597, Kitchener – Roberts, 4.8.1900, p. 32; compare PRO, WO 105, LRP 16 for the same source; W.S. Evans, *The Canadian Contingents and Canadian Imperialism: A Story and a Study*, pp. 216–218; Amery (ed.), IV, p. 421.
15. Amery (ed.), IV, p. 421; Arthur, I, pp. 315–316.
16. TA, LRP 40: No. H608, Kitchener – Roberts, 5.8.1900, p. 36; compare PRO, WO 105, LRP 16 for the same source; TA, SA Telegrams III: No. C3326, Roberts – Kitchener, 21:00, 5.8.1900, p. 135; compare PRO, WO 108/240 for the same source.
17. TA, LRP 40: No. H614, Kitchener – Roberts, 6.8.1900, p. 37; compare PRO, WO 105, LRP 16 for the same source.
18. De Wet, p. 138.
19. TA, LRP 9: Methuen, 'Western Transvaal Report', 31.7.1900, pp. 6–7; compare PRO, WO 105, LRP 10 for the same source; Maurice and Grant, III, pp. 342–343.
20. TA, LRP 45: No. 729P, Barton, Krugersdorp – Roberts, 3.8.1900, p. 111; compare PRO, WO 105, LRP 22 for the same source.
21. TA, LRP 9: Methuen, 'Western Transvaal Report', 31.7.1900, pp. 6–7; compare PRO, WO 105, LRP 10 for the same source; Maurice and Grant, III, pp. 342–343.
22. TA, LRP 40: No. A1179, Methuen – Roberts, 1.8.1900, p. 2; compare PRO, WO 105, LRP 14 for the same source; Maurice and Grant, III, p. 343; Amery (ed.), IV, p. 422n. However, both abovementioned sources supply the date 2 August.
23. TA, LRP 40: No. A1182, Methuen – Roberts, 2.8.1900, p. 3; compare PRO, WO 105, LRP 14 for the same source; Maurice and Grant, III, p. 343.
24. TA, LRP 35: No. A1177, Methuen – Chief of Staff, Pretoria, 31.7.1900, p. 28; compare PRO, WO 105, LRP 14 for the same source; TA, LRP 40: No. 729P, Barton – Roberts, 3.8.1900, p. 111; compare PRO, WO 105, LRP 22 for the same source.
25. TA, LRP 45: No. A1197, Methuen – Roberts, 4.8.1900, p. 122; compare PRO, WO 105, LRP 14 for the same source.
26. TA, LRP 9: Methuen, 'Western Transvaal Report', 31.7.1900, p. 8; compare PRO, WO 105, LRP 10 for the same source.
27. TA, LRP 36: No. 711P, Barton – Roberts, 28.7.1900, p. 138; compare PRO, WO 105, LRP 22 for the same source.
28. TA, LRP 40: No. A1179, Methuen – Roberts, 1.8.1900, p. 2; compare PRO, WO 105, LRP 14 for the same source; TA, LRP 45: No. 766P, Barton – Roberts, 5.8.1900, p. 120; compare PRO, WO 105, LRP 22 for the same source.
29. Lombard, pp. 66–68; Pienaar, pp. 145–146.
30. TA, LRP 40: No. A1183, Methuen – Chief of Staff, 2.8.1900, p. 4; compare PRO, WO 105, LRP 14 for the same source.
31. TA, LRP 45: No. 772P, Barton – Roberts, 6.8.1900, p. 122; compare PRO, WO 105, LRP 22 for the same source.
32. TA, LRP 45: No. 796P, Barton – Roberts, 15:00, 7.8.1900, p. 125; compare PRO, WO 105, LRP 22 for the same source.
33. PRO, WO 105, LRP 37: No. C3179, Military Secretary, Chief, Pretoria – Barton,

1.8.1900; TA, SA Telegrams III, No. C3209, Roberts – Methuen via Barton, Krugersdorp, 2.8.1900, p. 121; compare PRO, WO 108/240 for the same source.
34. TA, SA Telegrams III: No. C3264, Roberts – Methuen, 3.8.1900, p. 128; compare PRO, WO 108/240 for the same source.
35. TA, LRP 40: No. 1215, Methuen – Roberts, 5.8.1900, p. 5; compare PRO, WO 105, LRP 14 for the same source.
36. Ibid.
37. TA, LRP 39: No. 707P, Barton – Roberts, 1.8.1900, p. 106; TA, LRP 39: No. 711P, Barton – Roberts, 1.8.1900, p. 107; compare PRO, WO, LRP 22 for the same sources.
38. TA, SA Telegrams III: No. C3236, Roberts – Kitchener, Rhenoster guard post, 2.8.1900, p. 124; compare PRO, WO 108/240 for the same source.
39. SA Telegrams III: No. C3326, Roberts – Kitchener, 5.8.1900, p. 135; compare PRO, WO 108/240 for the same source; PRO, CO 417/292: No. CO 27256, Milner – Chamberlain, London, 1.8.1900, p. 614.
40. TA, SA Telegrams III: Nos. C3264 and C3266, Roberts – Methuen, via Kitchener, Rhenoster guard post and Barton, Krugersdorp, 3.8.1900, p. 128; compare PRO, WO 108/240 for the same sources.
41. Amery (ed.), IV, p. 422.
42. TA, LRP 40: No. B1, Methuen, Potchefstroom – Roberts, via Smith-Dorrien, Frederikstad and Barton, Krugersdorp, 6.8.1900, p. 6; compare PRO, WO 105, LRP 14 for the same source.
43. TA, LRP 40: No. H614, Kitchener – Roberts, 6.8.1900, p. 37; compare PRO, WO 105, LRP 16 for the same source.
44. TA, LRP 40: No. H614, Kitchener – Roberts, 6.8.1900, re telegram Methuen – Kitchener, 5.8.1900, p. 38; compare PRO, WO 105, LRP 16 for the same source; TA, LRP 40: No. A1215, Methuen – Roberts, 5.8.1900, p. 5; compare PRO, WO 105, LRP 14 for the same source; TA, LRP 10: Methuen, 'Chase of De Wet', 5 and 6.8.1900, pp. 27–28; compare PRO, WO 105, LRP 10 for the same source.

CHAPTER ELEVEN
Across the Vaal

ON THE EVENING of Sunday 5 August, De Wet called a meeting outside his tent. What he had to tell his burghers was grim news indeed: Kitchener would attack the next day. He ordered his artillery and commandos to position themselves along the hills south of Rhenosterpoort early the next morning. The laager would be defended.[1]

Before sunrise on Monday 6 August, the men were ready to saddle up and head off. Some artillerymen decided to rouse De Wet and ask for further instructions. They were told to go on ahead – De Wet would catch up later.[2] In good faith the burghers positioned themselves in the hills and waited for the British to launch their offensive.[3] But nothing happened. No matter how often they scanned the horizon with their field glasses, there was no sign of the British attack. Finally an order from Rhenosterpoort arrived: they were to return to the laager. For some reason the artillery did not receive the instruction, but on seeing the commandos abandon their positions, they decided to follow suit. When the burghers collected back at Rhenosterpoort that afternoon a strange sight greeted them: the campsite was virtually empty. The reason soon became clear – the wagons had crossed the Vaal River that morning at Schoeman's Drift.

It turned out that Kitchener's 'attack' had been an elaborate ruse cooked up by De Wet for the benefit of any burghers unwilling to leave their homeland. No sooner had they left the laager than De Wet ordered the wagon drivers to inspan. A short while later the immense convoy began to cross the Vaal. 'Now the entire laager with all our baggage and supplies was on the opposite bank,' wrote the German artilleryman Oskar Hintrager. There was nothing left to do but follow.[4]

Theron scout Ver Loren van Themaat 'sat and watched the extraordinary spectacle' for a long time. 'The kaffirs, who were completely naked, uttered tremendous cries to urge on the oxen. The Boers stripped down too, walking over the stones in the drift as though the soles of their feet were made of leather. The wagons trundled jerkily across the river, the water so low it hardly reached their axles, whereas the light carts crossed much quicker, cheerfully bumping over the stones while the horses carrying Boers wielding whips kicked up plumes of spray. The drivers were as

THE HUNT CONTINUES IN THE TRANSVAAL, 6–11 AUGUST 1900

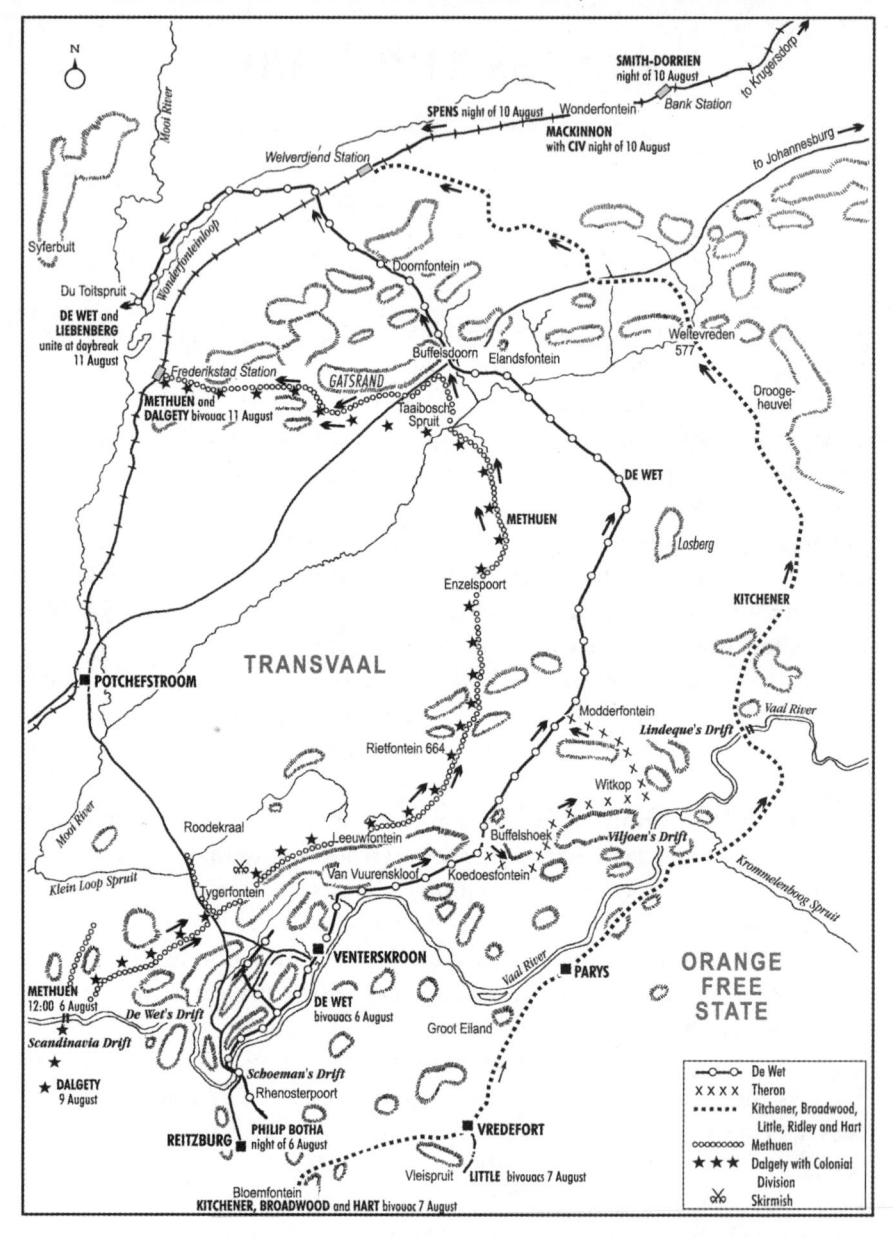

varied a lot as the loads carried by their wagons and carts – anything from young bucks to old codgers, poor bywoners to wealthy farmers.'[5]

Once in the Transvaal, the convoy set off for Venterskroon barely 10 km north-east of Schoeman's Drift on a narrow dusty track which ran hard against the Vaal River in the lee of a long range of steep, densely wooded hills – the first of three parallel ranges. De Wet, Steyn and his entourage rode ahead.[6] By early evening a number of burghers and the Boer artillery had crossed the river too, joining the advance guard to bivouac for the night around Venterskroon.[7] Theron, who had crossed the river the same day, remained about an hour's ride behind with 40 scouts as a rearguard.[8]

The same morning, 6 August, after a week of uninterrupted action against Liebenberg, Methuen was finally able to devote his full attention to the operation against De Wet, launching what would turn into a dramatic nine-day hunt with several thousand troops mustered against the elusive Pimpernel. At 06:00 he set off for Scandinavia Drift with the 5th and 10th Battalions Imperial Yeomanry, half of the 1st Battalion Northumberland Fusiliers, half the Northampton Battalion, two sections of the 4th Battery Royal Field Artillery and two Howitzers.[9] An hour later four infantry companies – two Scots and two Welsh Fusiliers – as well as one section 78th Battery RFA and an Imperial Yeomanry squadron left Potchefstroom for Klein Loopspruit on the farm Roodekraal.

After a rapid five-hour march from Potchefstroom, Methuen reached Scandinavia Drift. There he was joined by Colonel Younghusband, who had been sent to Machavie Station on 2 August with the 3rd Battalion Imperial Yeomanry, the rest of the Northamptons, two guns and two pom-poms. But before the troops got the chance to have a meal, Methuen received word that De Wet was busy crossing the Vaal at Schoeman's Drift, a mere 15 km further east. The Yeomanry were immediately ordered to saddle up again. Half an hour later Methuen set off north-east to head off De Wet with his force of mounted men and the artillery. The infantry were told to follow, while the Northumberland Fusiliers, two guns and a squadron of the Imperial Yeomanry under Colonel C.G.C. Money were sent south of the Vaal to Winkel's Drift. This would reduce the size of Methuen's already dangerously small force, but he had no way of knowing if the report of De Wet's crossing was not yet another false rumour. Besides, Kitchener's original orders were for Methuen to take his force south to close the western cordon, a mistake which had already cost Methuen valuable time.

The terrain he now had to cross was extremely inhospitable, and by nightfall his force had only reached a position 11 km north-east of Scandinavia Drift, in the region of Tygerfontein on the road to Potchefstroom. As his supply column had been left behind, Methuen and the Yeomanry, who had not eaten since breakfast, were left to snuggle into their coats for the night without food or blankets and hardly a drop of water to drink.[10] The sacrifice seemed worthwhile. For together with the infantry who were spending the night at Klein Loopspruit nearby, Methuen was virtually in position to secure the exit to the bulge in the Vaal in which Schoeman's Drift lay. De Wet would surely be walking into a trap. What Methuen did not realise was that three parallel ranges of hills lay between his position and the Vaal River, and that De Wet might be able to slip out of the bulge's northern exit at Venterskroon, which had been left unguarded.

The infantry and a convoy under Major-General C.W.H. Douglas marched all night from Scandinavia Drift, reaching Methuen the next morning, Tuesday 7 August, just as he was about to leave. Methuen now advanced cautiously as the difficult terrain offered excellent cover for any Boer snipers who might be in the vicinity, while the infantry companies at Klein Loopspruit set off for Tygerfontein.[11] At 09:25 Methuen made contact with the Boers in the foothills of Tygerfontein.[12]

Early that morning De Wet's scouts informed him of Methuen's advance, warning that part of his force could be heading for Van Vuuren's Kloof. This was worrying news, because the track along the Vaal River which the convoy had taken crossed a neck to the kloof. There was a very real danger that the British could cut them off.[13] Furthermore, De Wet possessed only a small force as most of the burghers had not yet crossed the Vaal. De Wet immediately ordered the laager to inspan and hasten to the neck. He now split the burghers at his disposal in two. The first group of 500 was to race ahead to secure the road, while the second group would position themselves in the third set of hills parallel to and furthest away from the Vaal facing Tygerfontein to cover the convoy's north-western flank.[14]

De Wet now raced back along the Vaal from Venterskroon toward Schoeman's Drift, on the way ordering his burghers to saddle up and join the effort to balk the enemy on the north-western flank.[15] Among those who followed him were 40 men from Griqualand West under Field-Cornet J.A. van Zyl and the artillery commanded by Strydom, Borslap and De Bruyn (Muller was still south of the Vaal). Halfway to Schoeman's Drift, De Wet veered right through the first range of riverside hills, taking another track past the second parallel range. Then he turned right again, continuing between the second and third parallel range in the direction of Tygerfontein. His detachment had now completed a full horseshoe since leaving Venterskroon, along the way encountering several small commandos well hidden by the boulders and thornbushes dotting the slopes. 'If their horses weren't standing at the bottom of the hills one would scarcely have noticed them,' observed Hintrager, who accompanied the artillery with De Wet.[16] A little further along they ran into the heat of battle.

By then the Boers sent earlier to the third range of hills from the Vaal

Field-Cornet J.A. van Zyl, who responded with his 40 Griqualand West rebels to De Wet's call for reinforcements during the skirmish at Tygerfontein on 7 August 1900. (From: J. Malan, Die Boere-Offisiere van die Tweede Vryheidsoorlog 1899–1902, *Pretoria, 1990, p. 55)*

River at Tygerfontein, which commanded the road running from Schoeman's Drift to Potchefstroom, had run into Methuen's force and been driven back to the second parallel range. The British now occupied the position the Boers had vacated, thus controlling the road. But the Boers' new position afforded them a good view of the enemy across a narrow ravine about 800 m across, watered by a small stream, which offered excellent cover in the intricate series of folds and gullies cut into the wooded slopes. This was brought home to the British with the Yeomanry's first attempt to dislodge the enemy, and Methuen thus resorted to a violent short-range artillery bombardment with four 15-pounders, two Howitzers and the pom-poms.[17] One lyddite shell after another pounded the Boer positions. 'It is terrifying (or must be to the Boers) to hear it in the air,' was how H.M. Gaskell described the lyddite bombardment in his war memoirs. 'The shell makes a regular puffing noise, like a train going out of a station, and the roar of the Howitzer is awful. But when the shell bursts . . . it sounds as loud as the gun itself, and kicks up dust and rocks and stuff and a cloud as big as a house.'[18]

This was the scene that greeted De Wet and the burghers he had collected along the way when they arrived at the battleground, probably about half an hour after Methuen had launched his assault. The Boer artillery followed hard on his heels, but the enemy's effective small calibre shell-fire soon forced De Wet to order the guns to be withdrawn before they could be used. Fortunately for the Boers, Methuen was unable to range any of his guns against the Boer artillery in time.[19] The Boer gunners now fell back along the track they had taken and galloped up toward Venterskroon between the first and second range of hills without being hit,[20] while De Wet raced back to the advance guard, now beyond Venterskroon, to secure the road to Van Vuuren's Kloof. But no sooner had the Boer guns reached the hills west of Venterskroon on the range nearest the Vaal, than they again came under ferocious British artillery and small arms fire because by then the British were overwhelming the Boer positions on the second range of hills. Strydom decided the guns should be withdrawn to safety again, probably before they could be brought into action.[21] But before he could carry out his plan, the British barrage forced him to abandon the guns on the hill and they would have been lost if it was not for the timely arrival of Theron and his scouts.

That morning after breakfast Danie Theron, blissfully unaware of the attack Methuen had launched at 09:25, ordered his 40 rearguard scouts to saddle up and head in the direction of Venterskroon on the narrow track along the Vaal River to join De Wet. But after continuing at a leisurely pace for half an hour, they suddenly ran into some dispatch riders sent to inform them De Wet was busy retiring ahead of the enemy and that the scouts were in danger of being cut off themselves. Now there was no time to lose, and the scouts galloped ahead. But half an hour later they were stopped again, this time by a Free State artillery officer (according to Hintrager it was Strydom) reporting that 'De Wet was fleeing and that his two Maxims [and a pom-pom] were still on top of the mountain because De Wet couldn't get them down.'[22]

With the Boer artillery in danger, Theron immediately called 'TVK!' and, followed by his 40 men, charged for the hill. On reaching the ridge closest to the Vaal, Theron found the enemy occupying the northern crest of the same hill, and a heavy small arms exchange ensued. After offering stubborn resistance, the British were eventually driven back and about 20 Boers were able to advance in the direction of the three guns. Once the Boers had secured their positions and the guns were safely in their possession, the horses at the bottom of the valley had to be made ready. Now some method had to be found of getting the guns down the slope. The burgher Henri Slegtkamp recounts the event: 'It was a tricky operation, because the guns had been brought up on the enemy side and now had to be brought over to our side down an extremely rugged kloof of 300 m. A rope was fastened to the back of the Maxims, and that was how we let them down. Sometimes we were unable to hold on and the gun slid rapidly down the slope until it came to rest against a tree. Then, with a united and determined effort, we had to pull it free before it could be lowered again. All the while the rest of the scouts covered us by returning enemy fire. After a sustained effort we succeeded in getting both Maxims [and De Bruyn's pom-pom] down the mountain, whereupon the horses were immediately spanned in and we set off at a wild gallop.'[23]

The rescue mission lasted about an hour, during which two Boers were killed and removed from the battlefield, as was customary. Another two men were wounded and a few horses were either killed or wounded; an ammunition cart which the artilleryman De Bruyn had allowed to roll down the hill was also captured by the British.[24]

Before long the British occupied the range of hills closest to the Vaal River and the gunners and scouts now had to run the gauntlet along the narrow riverside track under a merciless barrage of rifle fire from a range of between 400 m and 500 m. Miraculously, only one of Strydom's men was shot – through the hand. When they at last reached the first houses of Venterskroon after crossing a small tributary of the Vaal, the Boers were temporarily out of danger and could enjoy a brief respite.[25]

In the meantime, while the artillery were being pushed from pillar to post, the burghers De Wet had left on the second range of hills to protect the Boers' north-western flank continued to offer resistance to Methuen's artillery and rifle barrage. The British now decided to try to encircle these burghers with 500 Yeomanry supported by two pom-poms, but when this attempt failed Methuen changed tactics. While the artillery continued to bombard the Boers, three companies of Welsh Fusiliers who had joined Methuen from Klein Loopspruit were ordered to storm the koppie in the middle of the range of three hills ahead of them – the key to the position – while a company of Scots Fusiliers and the Yeomanry followed hard upon them on their left.[26] 'The enemy held on with great tenacity and I have seen nothing finer in this campaign than the dash shown by the Fusiliers in this attack,' Methuen remarked afterwards.[27]

By noon, after two hours of fierce fighting, the infantry and Yeomanry had succeeded in conquering the second range of hills and forced the Boers to fall back yet again, all the while subjected mercilessly to heavy rifle fire.[28] But the Boers were not the only ones smarting under the British barrage that day. Every now and then lyddite shells exploded among a troop of baboons in the hills, causing untold consternation among the poor animals. One burgher, Corneels du Preez, even went as far as surmising the British had mistaken the baboons for a Boer commando. Needless to say, the incident provoked no end of pithy remarks from the Boers.[29]

The Boers now took up their third position, which was north-west of Venterskroon on the same range of hills where Strydom's guns had retired to earlier. If they could hold out here long enough, the wagon convoy as well as the burghers still to cross the Vaal would be able to reach the safety of Van Vuuren's Kloof in time. The Boers offered stubborn resistance against an attack launched by the Welsh and Scots Fusiliers on the middle and the right flanks, and the dismounted Yeomanry on the left. But the British gradually gained ground by deploying detachments of three or four men to storm ahead for a few metres, then take cover in the grass or behind rocks while the next wave of infantry advanced behind them. Because the Boers had positioned themselves across a broad front in the hills, the British gunners found it difficult to locate their positions among the trees and boulders dotting the slopes. Methuen was thus unable to cover the infantry charge with his artillery. But the Scots and Welshmen nevertheless finally succeeded in driving off the Boers, although a few burghers stayed behind to loose off a round or two before racing after their comrades in the direction of Van Vuuren's Kloof. Once the Boers began to fall back, the British brought a section of the 4th Battery into play from a range of 800 m, but neither the retreating burghers nor their wagon convoy further off was hit. Still, by 14:00 all the Boers had left the hills and the British had conquered the last range of hills before the Vaal River and Venterskroon. An hour later Methuen and his force returned to Tygerfontein and set up camp.[30]

Most of the British casualties took place during this last skirmish. Methuen puts the total for the day at two dead and 15 wounded, including six officers, but the British War Office Collection lists three killed and 19 wounded, with another missing in action.[31] De Wet, on the other hand, claims more than 100 British were killed or wounded,[32] though this is obviously an inaccurate estimate.

Apart from the loss of an ammunition cart and the casualties suffered by the Theron scouts, heliographer P.S. Lombard claimed the Boers only lost two more men that day – one from the Bethlehem commando and the other a Heilbronner.[33]

These sacrifices not only bought the wagon laager enough time to reach safer ground, but allowed the rest of the burghers who had not yet forded the Vaal, including Theron's remaining scouts, to cross Schoeman's Drift and emerge unscathed past Venterskroon.[34] Not that the burghers racing down the riverside track were entirely out of danger. The deafening din of shelling up ahead served as a constant reminder that they ran the risk of being cut off, or could at any moment find themselves in the line of fire if the British occupied the first range of hills now sheltering them. Apparently the last of Theron's scouts to cross the Vaal River raced past the hill where the Boer artillery was stranded just as their commander was salvaging the guns. Luckily, at that point the British were too far from the nearest ridge to inflict much harm, firing from a range of about 1 800 m.

Ver Loren van Themaat was full of admiration for the calm and considered behaviour of the burghers; the panic and confusion of a rout were nowhere in evidence. This he ascribed to a handful of burghers with authority, who despite coming under fire, regarded it their duty to stand fast and keep the men in tolerable order by holding back anyone who wanted to jump the queue. These men, said Ver Loren van Themaat, were willing to expose themselves to personal danger for the sake of the common good, an example of 'a strong sense of community and responsibility which only great men possess in an undisciplined army'.[35]

The group apparently reached Venterskroon without incurring any casualties. A short while later Theron and the artillery he had salvaged joined them.[36] After sunset they were back in the saddle, now veering away from the Vaal River in the direction of Van Vuuren's Kloof to join the other burghers already outspanned for the night in an extended line from Van Vuuren's Kloof right up to Koedoesfontein further east.[37] The group Muller was with, which had found Schoeman's Drift occupied by the British and been forced to cross the Vaal at De Wet's Drift a few kilometres further west, also joined the laager with his gun.[38]

By that evening, De Wet found himself occupying a relatively secure position in the mountainous region of Van Vuuren's Kloof. For now, Kitchener and his forces south of the Vaal posed no threat, while north of the river he only had to contend with Methuen, who now controlled a triangle extending from Schoeman's Drift up to Tygerfontein, then down to Venterskroon. Because Liebenberg's commandos had kept Methuen occupied for a full week, he had been unable to send a detachment to Parys in time to head off the Boers in the east. Furthermore, he had only received this order on 5 August, and by then it was too late.

Notes

1. [Hintrager]. p. 77.
2. Ibid.
3. Compare Colvin and Gordon, p. 136.
4. [Hintrager], p. 77.
5. Ver Loren van Themaat, p. 166.
6. TA, Acquisition 235 (II): Slegtkamp's manuscript, p. 145; D. Mostert, *Slegtkamp van Spioenkop: Oorlogsherinneringe van Kapt. Slegtkamp Saamgestel uit sy Dagboek,* p. 105.
7. [Hintrager], p. 77; FA, WMC 155/82/1: Kriegs-Tagebuch, Dr O. Hintrager, map, p. 165; De Wet, p. 140; Lombard, p. 68; Badenhorst, pp. 45–46; De V. Esterhuysen, p. 64; FA, Renier Collection 119.526: 'Kol. Corneels du Preez, adj. van pres. Steyn', recorded by J.N. Brink, p. 28.
8. TA, Acquisition 235 (II): Slegtkamp's manuscript, pp. 145–147; Mostert, pp. 105–106; TA, Acquisition 285: Danie Theron Collection, No. 33, statement H.F. Slegtkamp. 7.12.1936.
9. TA, LRP 10: Methuen, 'Chase of De Wet', 6.8.1900, pp. 28–29; compare PRO, WO 105, LRP 10 for the same source; TA, WO Acquisition, JPE 5: Staff Diary, 1st Division, 6.8.1900, p. 58; H.M. Gaskell, *With Lord Methuen in South Africa, February 1900 – June 1901,* p. 177; Guest, pp. 76–77.
10. TA, LRP 10: Methuen, 'Chase of De Wet', 6.8.1900, p. 28; compare PRO, WO 105,

LRP 10 for the same source; TA, LRP 40: no number, Methuen – Roberts, 6.8.1900, p. 7; compare PRO, WO 105, LRP 14 for the same source; Gaskell, p. 177.
11. TA, LRP 10: Methuen, 'Chase of De Wet', 7.8.1900, p. 30; compare PRO, WO 105, LRP 10 for the same source; Gaskell, pp. 177–178; TA, LRP 40: no number, Methuen – Roberts, no date (probably 7.8.1900), p. 9; compare PRO, WO 105, LRP 14 for the same source.
12. TA, LRP 40: no number, Kitchener, Wonderheuwel – Roberts, 10:25, 7.8.1900, p. 41; compare PRO, WO 105, LRP 16 for the same source; Gaskell, pp. 177–178; TA, LRP 10: Methuen, 'Chase of De Wet', 7.8.1900, p. 30; compare PRO, WO 105, LRP 10 for the same source.
13. De Wet, p. 141.
14. Ibid.; TA, LRP 40: no number, Methuen – Roberts, no date, p. 9; compare PRO, WO 105, LRP 14 for the same source.
15. [Hintrager], p. 78; Van Schoor, 'Diaries of Jacob de Villiers', 8.8.1900, pp. 23–24. Compare De Wet's memoirs (p. 141), where he creates the false impression that he had been leading the advance guard to Van Vuuren's Kloof from the start.
16. [Hintrager], p. 78.
17. Ibid., pp. 78–79; FA, WMC 155/82/1: Kriegs-Tagebuch, Dr O. Hintrager, map, p. 165; TA, LRP 10: Methuen, 'Chase of De Wet', 7.8.1900, pp. 30 and 57; compare PRO, WO 105, LRP 10 for the same source.
18. Gaskell, p. 178.
19. [Hintrager], p. 79; TA, LRP 10: Methuen, 'Chase of De Wet', 7.8.1900, p. 31; compare PRO, WO 105, LRP 10 for the same source; *The Times,* 26.9.1900: 'Lord Methuen's Chase after De Wet'.
20. [Hintrager], p. 79; FA, WMC 155/82/1: Kriegs-Tagebuch, Dr O. Hintrager, map, p. 165.
21. [Hintrager], p. 79; TA, WO Acquisition, JPE 5: Staff Diary, 1st Division, 7.8.1900, p. 58.
22. TA, Acquisition 235 (II): Slegtkamp's manuscript, p. 148; compare Mostert, p. 106 and [Hintrager], p. 80.
23. TA, Acquisition 235 (II): Slegtkamp's manuscript, p. 149; compare [Hintrager] pp. 79–81.
24. [Hintrager], p. 80; TA, LRP 10: Methuen, 'Chase of De Wet', 7.8.1900, p. 33; compare PRO, WO 105, LRP 10 for the same source.
25. [Hintrager], pp. 79 and 81; TA, Acquisition 235 (II): Slegtkamp's manuscript, pp. 148–149; Mostert, p. 107.
26. TA, LRP 10: Methuen, 'Chase of De Wet', 7.8.1900, p. 31; compare PRO, WO 105, LRP 10 for the same source; TA, WO Acquisition, JPE 5: Staff Diary, 1st Division, 7.8.1900, p. 58; R. Danes, *Cassell's (Illustrated) History of the Boer War 1899–1901,* p. 1323.
27. TA, LRP 10: Methuen, 'Chase of De Wet', 7.8.1900, p. 31; compare PRO, WO 105, LRP 10 for the same source.
28. TA, WO Acquisition, JPE 5: Staff Diary, 1st Division, 7.8.1900, p. 58; TA, LRP 10: Methuen, 'Chase of De Wet', 7.8.1900, p. 31; compare PRO, WO 105, LRP 10 for the same source; *The Times,* 26.9.1900: 'Lord Methuen's Chase after De Wet'.
29. De V. Esterhuysen, pp. 64–65; FA, Renier Collection 119.526: 'Kol. Corneels du Preez, adj. van pres. Steyn', recorded by J.N. Brink, p. 28; De Wet, p. 141.
30. TA, LRP 10: Methuen, 'Chase of De Wet', 7.8.1900, pp. 31–33; compare PRO, WO 105, LRP 10 for the same source; TA, WO Acquisition JPE 5: Staff Diary, 1st Division, 7.8.1900, p. 58; TA, LRP 40: no number, Methuen – Roberts, no date,

p. 9; compare PRO, WO 105, LRP 14 for the same source; Gaskell, p. 179; *The Times*, 26.9.1900: 'Lord Methuen's Chase after De Wet'; [Hintrager], p. 80.
31. TA, LRP 10: Methuen, 'Chase of De Wet', 7.8.1900, p. 33; compare PRO, WO 105, LRP 10 for the same source; PRO, WO 108/231: Telegram, Roberts – State Secretary, London, No. 991, 8.8.1900, p. 234; No. 7541, 9.8.1900, p. 245; No. 7667C, 15.8.1900, p. 312; No. 7738A, 19.8.1900, p. 344; No. 7738C, 19.8.1900, p. 351; No. 8007D, 2.9.1900, p. 540; TA, Transvaal Publications 159(3), pp. 43 and 58.
32. De Wet, p. 141.
33. Lombard, p. 68.
34. De Wet, p. 141; Van Schoor, 'Diaries of Jacob de Villiers', 8.8.1900, p. 24.
35. Ver Loren van Themaat, pp. 168–169.
36. Ibid., p. 168; [Hintrager], p. 81.
37. TA, Acquisition 1250: D. de Witt, 'Die Trek naar die Bosveld', recorded by C.P. van der Merwe, p. 6; FA, Renier Collection 119.1098: Letter of J.J. van Deventer in connection with events during the Anglo-Boer War; Lombard, p. 68; Ver Loren van Themaat, p. 169; Badenhorst, p. 46; TA, LRP 40: No. A1217, Methuen – Roberts, 8.8.1900, p. 8; compare PRO, WO 105, LRP 14 for the same source; Amery (ed.), IV, p. 424.
38. Ver Loren van Themaat, p. 169; [Hintrager], p. 82.

CHAPTER TWELVE

Surprised!

ON WEDNESDAY 8 AUGUST, the Boers took the opportunity to recuperate and take stock of the situation and the near disaster that had befallen them the day before. Although it has been argued that De Wet's famous flight past Venterskroon was made possible by the way Theron and his scouts covered the rear,[1] this is highly unlikely. For apart from Theron's heroic rescue of the Boer artillery, his scouts did not take part in the skirmish at all.[2] The likely reason for this is that De Wet expected Methuen to advance along the road to Schoeman's Drift and thus positioned Theron as a rearguard near this crossing. Methuen's surprise attack further north at Tygerfontein had found the scouts in the wrong place. Whether Theron would have been able to get wind of Methuen's advance and alert De Wet in time is difficult to establish. Nevertheless, despite his valour, Theron was obliged to appear before a war council convened on 8 August because 'his spies did not warn the laager in time', according to a burgher named Dirk de Witt, who received the information later from Commandant A. de Kock of Frankfort.[3] 'The ears and the eyes of De Wet', as Theron had become known,[4] were on this occasion not as sharp as was to be expected. Furthermore, De Witt claims Theron blamed himself for the débâcle and that henceforth De Wet increasingly relied on the services of Gideon Scheepers.

Captain Gideon Scheepers, who with his scouting corps and that of Commandant Danie Theron, was the eyes and ears of De Wet during his journey through the Free State and Western Tranvaal in July–August 1900. (From: G.S. Preller, Scheepers se Dagboek en die Stryd in Kaapland, *Cape Town, 1938, facing p. 42)*

133

Another item on the agenda was the great wagon train which still hung like an albatross around De Wet's neck. By then it consisted of 262 Cape carts and 130 wagons[5] stretching some 5–10 km.[6] The tense flight past Venterskroon once again emphasised the need to scale it down. Although the burghers were familiar with De Wet's views on the subject, he found it necessary to tell the council he now regarded the laager as nothing but a curse.[7] To his great relief a decision was taken 'to send away everything that was not strictly necessary so that only a few carts would accompany us'[8] – which meant transport for the government as well as one wagon for every 25 burghers.[9]

As usual, that evening De Wet separated the commandos and the laager for the night,[10] this time with the intention of sending away most of the wagons and carts the next morning. The convoy was arranged in a horseshoe formed by a fork in the road on the border between Koedoesfontein and Buffelshoek. Most of the wagons were placed on the right-hand fork, evidently with the intention of allowing them to trek back into the Free State over Lindeque's Drift further east. The remainder were positioned on the road winding north-east toward Losberg between two prominent outcrops. The three parallel ranges along the Vaal converged and ran up to the western outcrop, which meant De Wet commanded a strong strategic position. Theron's scouts, now united, spent the night 1,5 km behind the laager to serve as a rearguard in case Methuen launched an attack through Van Vuuren's Kloof.[11]

On the morning of 8 August, while the Boers tarried at Van Vuuren's Kloof, Methuen was in fact ready to advance on De Wet from his encampment at Tygerfontein. But the 1st Division commander had received two conflicting reports, both false, as it turned out. Methuen was first informed that the Boers had left for Leeuwfontein beyond Van Vuuren's Kloof. Then an English shopkeeper told him De Wet had crossed the Vaal River back into the Free State at Venterskroon and Rensburg Drift. Methuen decided to await reliable intelligence. Furthermore, he apparently felt his horses needed time to recuperate. This would also give his detachments from Winkel's Drift and Scandinavia Drift time to catch up. They arrived at 20:30 that evening after a gruelling 34 km march over difficult terrain. In the meantime, he had reliably learned that the Boers were encamped around Koedoesfontein.[12] With a larger force now at his disposal he was ready to attack. That night Methuen also received a report on Kitchener's movements south of the Vaal, brought by a certain Captain Cheyne who had walked past the Boer positions in the dark.

The news that De Wet had slipped through the net so painstakingly prepared for him only reached Kitchener at 03:30 on Tuesday 7 August – that is almost a full day after the Boer laager had begun to cross Schoeman's Drift. The source of this intelligence was not Methuen, still unable to communicate with Roberts, Kitchener or virtually anyone else for that matter, but a Welsh Fusilier previously captured by the Boers who had managed to escape and reach one of Little's advance posts near Vredefort. The Welsh Fusilier also reported that De Wet was planning to move between Potchefstroom and Krugersdorp to the area north of Pretoria. Kitchener immediately made arrangements to launch a determined pursuit of De Wet.[13] Later that day Roberts cabled Kitchener, warning him the Boers would undoubtedly try to delay him with their artillery and a rearguard action. He added that should Kitchener succeed in crossing the Vaal and capturing a few Boer wagons, the Free Staters' resistance would crumble.[14] This comment illustrates just how far Roberts underestimated De Wet's resilience and tenacity; it is unlikely Methuen would have been half as sanguine at this stage.

Kitchener now ordered Ridley, who was at Groot Eiland, to send a patrol over the Vaal River at Parys. Broadwood was ordered to advance from Rhebokfontein, followed by Hart from Wilgebosch Drift, while Kitchener decided to move his headquarters from Wonderheuwel to De Wet's Drift west of Schoeman's Drift. Little was told to reconnoitre in the direction of Reitzburg, close to the positions occupied by Philip Botha's forces, including Muller's artillery. Knox was ordered to cross the Rhenoster River at Baltespoort and head for Doornhoek further west. Dalgety and his Colonials would advance to Scandinavia Drift and cross the Vaal River in the west. While Kitchener was making these arrangements he could hear Methuen's guns pounding the Boer left flank at Tygerfontein, but at this crucial juncture he was unable to reach the 1st Division commander. Kitchener now suspected that instead of heading north as expected, De Wet was digging in his heels opposite Schoeman's Drift.[15]

Hart and Broadwood, accompanied by Kitchener and his headquarters, now slowly advanced north-west and by nightfall had only progressed as far as the farm Bloemfontein. Hart's 'B' and 'G' section pom-poms started out 8 km behind the rest of the force, experiencing transport problems along the way; they only arrived at the bivouac at 21:00.[16] In the west, Dalgety and his Colonial Division moved toward Scandinavia Drift, followed by Knox.[17] That evening Ridley's patrols returned with the news that the Boers were trekking north at Buffelshoek with their wagon convoy and a force of 3 000 men.[18] In the meantime, Little's scouts, the 16th Lancers, had run into Philip Botha's burghers in the hills near Reitzburg. The scouts were subjected to heavy Mauser and artillery fire and forced to fall back, spending the night at Vleispruit further east.[19]

Kitchener's leisurely deployment, which came at a time when Methuen could have done with some help fast, was exacerbated by false intelligence he received from some Africans, who told him De Wet had been forced back against the Vaal.[20] This news did have the advantage of turning Kitchener's thoughts to shifting most of his force east to cross at Lindeque's Drift and to encircle De Wet from the east and north-east and pin him down in the bulges of the Vaal. But the manoeuvre was to cost Kitchener two whole days, because to execute it his columns would first have to advance along the Vaal parallel to De Wet. This would leave the Boers relatively unmolested on the opposite bank.

The next day, Wednesday 8 August, while the Boers were recuperating and Methuen was resting his horses and waiting for reinforcements, Kitchener put his new plan into operation. Ridley was ordered to cross the Vaal not at Parys where he was stationed and where the Boers could have been confronted immediately and delayed, but 30 km further east at Lindeque's Drift – a notoriously difficult crossing.[21] At 09:20 Kitchener left the farm Bloemfontein and, along with Broadwood and Hart's forces and two 4.7 inch naval guns, followed Ridley north-east, uniting with Little east of Vredefort later that day. Then, after a long and arduous trek along the Vaal River, this combined force set up camp at sunset in the valley between Groot Eiland and Parys.[22] The Colonials, Kitchener decided, should continue to march on Scandinavia Drift in the west, while Roberts ordered Knox to stay behind near Reitzburg to ensure that 'none of the enemy who have gone north return to the Free State'.[23]

The Boers woke on Thursday 9 August expecting an orderly departure, but for a second time that week De Wet would suffer the misfortune of receiving vital information too late, allowing Methuen to foil his plans yet again.[24] De Wet had taken the precaution of sending Captain Gideon Scheepers north-west to keep an eye on Methuen's movements. But that morning he and six of his scouts had a brush with a 30-strong enemy detachment near Rietfontein. Fighting raged for almost an hour before British reinforcements arrived – two infantry companies and artillery sent from Potchefstroom. Scheepers was forced to beat a hasty retreat. On his way back to Van Vuuren's Kloof he spotted Methuen's columns advancing on the laager from Tygerfontein.

Methuen had set off with his united force at 07:00. He had managed to get in touch with Dalgety at Scandinavia Drift and the Colonials were ordered to follow. Methuen now advanced north-east, beneath Tygerfontein's northern slopes, arriving at Leeuwfontein just after 10:00. His scouts reported that De Wet's laager was barely 5 km ahead and preparing to leave. Methuen immediately ordered the Imperial Yeomanry, commanded by Lord Chesham, and the artillery to advance with all possible haste; the infantry would follow.

Scheepers managed to slip past the Yeomanry by the skin of his teeth, arriving at the Boer camp some 3 km ahead of the enemy to report their imminent arrival to De Wet.[25] By then he need hardly have bothered, for the British had already started firing on the Boers and pounding them with their artillery.[26] In the meantime De Wet had probably learned that Ridley's Mounted Infantry south of the Vaal was on its way from Parys to Lindeque's Drift – precisely the route the wagons should have taken back to the Free State.

De Wet immediately sprang into action, exhibiting his legendary prowess under pressure. Amid shellfire bursting over the laager, he ordered the commandos and artillery to position themselves behind every available hill and koppie, using the tried and tested method of delaying the enemy long enough with a rearguard action for the laager to make good its escape. Now the Boers' ability to strike camp at lightning speed came into play and in a remarkably short space of time the wagons had been spanned in. The burghers in charge of the wagons had been ordered to depart in two different directions[27] and soon, as shells began to burst overhead, one convoy was heading east and the other north-east.

A quarter of an hour after Methuen reached Leeuwfontein, the smaller laager which was supposed to remain with De Wet came into view as it raced north-east on the Losberg road and climbed a pass at Buffelshoek. Aware that the Boers had positioned themselves in an extended line along the koppies ahead, Methuen sent the 3rd Battalion Yeomanry under Younghusband to the right flank to take a key hill west of the Losberg road. The fleeing laager could then be blocked from the rear. The 5th and 10th Yeomanries, the latter commanded by Chesham, were ordered to gallop to the left to cut the laager off north of Buffelshoek, while the British artillery bombarded it from the centre at a range of 3 km.[28]

Meanwhile, Younghusband's 3rd Yeomanry were making good progress on the right flank. Under a hail of bullets they progressively drove back 300 burghers mustered against them to a high, strategically important koppie. The burghers hastily constructed stone breastworks. Younghusband ordered his men to storm the position while two pom-poms and the 4th Battery RFA unleashed a lethal barrage on the Boers from the rear. Fierce fighting ensued, but when Lieutenant Knowles stormed the summit at the head of his squadron, the Boers were forced to fall back. The Yeomanry paid dearly for the victory, incurring a number of casualties. Younghusband himself was wounded and replaced by Major Gascoigne, while Knowles' heroic charge cost him his life. Now Gascoigne pursued the retreating Boers. Although he was unable to catch his quarry, he did manage to come within striking distance of the rear wagons on the Losberg road, subjecting these to such an intense barrage that four were abandoned by their drivers. Meanwhile, the British had also moved their artillery ahead of the positions held earlier by the 3rd Yeomanry. The mounted Boers and wagons were subjected to heavy shelling and another driver was forced to relinquish his wagon.[29]

In an admirable charge elsewhere (it was not possible to establish the exact location), Sergeant Fox and 20 Yeomanry leapt from their mounts under heavy fire and stormed a heavily manned hill while firing continuously. Scarcely 100 m from the summit they unsheathed their bayonets and bore down on the Boers. According to a British source, the Yeomanry were outnumbered by the Boers, who nevertheless considered it prudent to retreat ahead of the bayonets.[30]

In the meantime, the main wagon laager veering east from Koedoesfontein with Theron was not being let off lightly either. Although this convoy was supposed to separate from the commandos following the previous day's war council decision, there was no question of carrying out this directive now. With Theron's scouts covering the rear, and the first shells bursting overhead, the convoy raced toward Witkop and Lindeque's Drift, probably with the intention of rejoining the rest of the Boer force later.

A vivid account of the nightmarish wagon flight is provided by a British prisoner forced to accompany the trek: 'Away we went helter-skelter up the steep slopes of the hills, aiming for the most impossible-looking pass, strewn with gigantic boulders and small stones. We had just reached the pass when three wagons toppled over and fell down the gorge and every moment we expected the same fate. The pass selected was an inconceivable place for vehicles to get through, but the Boers have a happy knack of negotiating difficult country. Over the neck we went bumping and thumping through the boulders and directly we showed on the other side we were greeted with shell as British artillery had gained a position covering our exit. Shell after shell came whizzing over our heads; one struck ten yards on the right of our cart, another shaved our left, a third whizzed close by my head, causing a deafening sensation on my ears, and a fourth plumped right down in front of our leading horses, killing both. A crash, and over went the cart, flying us through the air in company with mailbags, Mausers and cushions, landing among a pile of boulders. With great difficulty the Boers righted the cart, pulled the hood down as being too conspicuous a mark, and putting in two horses we dashed off.'[31]

The shelling was halted temporarily because the British could distinguish figures which looked like British POWs, but was soon resumed with renewed vigour.[32] While the rest of the Boer force was racing north-east on the Losberg road, the main convoy headed for the bulge the Vaal River forms around Parys – only to come within range of Kitchener's guns south of the Vaal.

Kitchener's forces had heard the reveille shortly before sunrise after one of the coldest nights that winter and immediately struck north-east across difficult mountainous terrain. At about 14:00, Broadwood and Little's cavalry brigades had crossed Kromellenboogspruit, a tributary of the Vaal. A short while later they caught sight of the tail end of the main wagon

A dramatic contemporary painting by J. Finnemore of an incident during Methuen's surprise attack on De Wet on 9 August 1900 north of the Vaal River. A British prisoner who was with the wagon laager near Koedoesfontein described the incident: 'Shell after shell came whizzing over our heads . . . a fourth plumped right down in front of our leading horses, killing both. A crash, and over went the cart, flying us through the air. . .' (From: H.W. Wilson, After Pretoria: The Guerilla War, *Vol. I, London, 1901, p. 43)*

convoy, as well as Boers in 'scattered parties'. At that point Methuen was a mere 10 km from Kitchener, but the two commanders were still unable to communicate with one another. Nevertheless, Broadwood's artillery opened fire on the wagons within range, but without causing much damage. The Boer rearguard swiftly retaliated, killing one man and wounding another, both from the 12th Lancers.[33] This exchange did not last long because the Boer rearguard was soon out of range. The British watched them racing to catch up with the convoy, which now swung north-west on the farm Witkop to join the group with De Wet, which had already covered 12 km on the Losberg road since the surprise attack that morning.[34] 'Dashing on', continued the British POW, 'we caught up their main body, a mass of Cape carts and guns, yelling and shrieking drivers, flogging their oxen and urging them on while the rattle of Mausers and boom of guns showed that a fierce rearguard action was in progress.'[35]

Methuen's bombardment gradually began to subside as the Boer rearguard abandoned their positions. By 16:30 the Yeomanry had given up the chase. Methuen, who spent the night on the battlefield near Rietfontein, declared the day 'trying to both men and animals'.[36] Though De Wet was still at large, in some respects the engagement had been successful. The British booty was large: it included six Boer wagons, two of which were loaded with ammunition, as well as 350 sheep and 1 000 oxen. A doctor, A.E.R. Ramsbottom, who had accompanied the Boers and become separated from their main force, also fell into British hands, along with three ambulance wagons.[37] But these successes had come at a price: the British counted eight wounded and four dead at the end of the day.[38]

Despite the heroism shown by Methuen's troops, his strategic choices were less praiseworthy. On 8 August, the day before the engagement, his scouts had reported that the Boer laager was in the region of Leeuwfontein – a stone's throw from the British camp at Tygerfontein. By using his Yeomanry to launch an encircling movement from the north, Methuen would have been able to block the Boers' exit from the bulge the Vaal River forms at Parys. Yet he chose not to take up the chase. This was partly because of the conflicting intelligence he had received that day. He was also waiting for his infantry reinforcements to arrive from Scandinavia Drift and Winkel's Drift, probably because they had proved so effective at Tygerfontein on 7 August. His cavalry would not have fared as well in the mountainous terrain. But by relying on his infantry, Methuen had sacrificed mobility – a fatal error when up against De Wet and a clear indication that he had learned little from his previous encounters with the Boer commander. Finally, Methuen's excuse that his horses needed rest cannot be accepted at face value, precisely because his infantry had played a leading role at Tygerfontein.

On the Boer side, the rearguard in particular bore the brunt of Methuen's attack on 9 August because Scheepers' report had only reached the laager at the last minute. Although it is unclear from available sources what role De Wet himself played in the skirmish, given his conduct during similar crises it is likely he remained in the thick of things to urge the rearguard to hold their positions for as long as possible and probably thereby prevented further losses. De Wet himself claims Boer casualties amounted to only one man killed and one wounded.[39] The contemporary British writer R. Danes, referring to the day's events, praised the Boers as 'well-armed sharpshooters, commanded by a general who in this particular line of tactics had nothing to learn from any general in the world'.[40]

Notes

1. Breytenbach, pp. 202–203.
2. Compare TA, Acquisition 235 (III): Slegtkamp's manuscript, pp. 148–150; Ver Loren van Themaat, pp. 166–169; *The Times,* 12.2.1901: 'In Retreat with De Wet'.

3. Van Schoor, 'Diaries of Jacob de Villiers', 8.8.1900, p. 24; TA, Acquisition 1250: D. de Witt, 'Die Trek naar die Bosveld', recorded by C.P. van der Merwe; p. 7; Badenhorst, p. 46; Grobler, p. 59.
4. Rompel, p. 44.
5. Van Schoor, 'Diaries of Jacob de Villiers', 9.8.1900, p. 24.
6. The *Cape Times,* 17.8.1900: 'De Wet's Army: A Convoy 3 Miles Long'; Pienaar, p. 139.
7. Van Schoor, 'Diaries of Jacob de Villiers', 9.8.1900, p. 24.
8. Badenhorst, p. 46; compare Van Schoor, 'Diaries of Jacob de Villiers', 8.8.1900, p. 24.
9. Van Schoor, 'Diaries of Jacob de Villiers', 9.8.1900, p. 24.
10. Lombard, p. 69.
11. *The Times,* 12.2.1901: 'In Retreat with De Wet'; TA, MGP 16: Statement by cavalryman Macdonald of French's Scouts, 16.8.1900, p. 149.
12. TA, LRP 10: Methuen, 'Chase of De Wet', 8.8.1900, pp. 34–35; compare PRO, WO 105, LRP 10 for the same source; TA, LRP 40: No. A1217, Methuen – Roberts, 8.8.1900, p. 8; compare PRO, WO, LRP 14 for the same source; TA, WO Acquisition JPE 5: Staff Diary, 1st Division, 9.8.1900, p. 61; *The Times,* 26.9.1900: 'Lord Methuen's Chase after De Wet'.
13. TA, LRP 40: No. H, Kitchener, Wonderheuwel – Roberts, 09:00, 7.8.1900, p. 39; compare PRO, WO 105, LRP 16 for the same source; Colvin and Gordon, p. 136; TA, SA Telegrams III: No. C3358, Roberts – Methuen, 7.8.1900, p. 142; compare PRO, WO 108/240 for the same source; TA, Leyds 730 (f): Telegram 73, Representative, Lourenço Marques – HTD, Machadodorp, 14.8.1900.
14. TA, SA Telegrams III: No. C3359, Roberts – Kitchener, Wonderheuwel, 11:00, 7.8.1900, p. 142; compare PRO, WO 108/240 for the same source.
15. TA, LRP 40: No. H624, Kitchener – Roberts, 10:10, 7.8.1900, p. 42; compare PRO, WO 105, LRP 16 for the same source; TA, LRP 40: no number, Kitchener – Roberts, 10:25, 7.8.1900, p. 41; compare PRO, WO 105, LRP 16 for the same source; Arthur, I, p. 316.
16. TA, LRP 40: No. H627, Kitchener – Roberts, 18:40, 7.8.1900, p. 44; compare PRO, WO 105, LRP 16 for the same source; C.F. Romer and A.E. Mainwaring, *The Second Battalion Royal Dublin Fusiliers in the South African War,* p. 131; Jeans (ed.), p. 164.
17. The *Natal Witness,* 9.10.1900: 'When De Wet Escaped: A Colonial's Story'; Amery (ed.), IV, p. 424.
18. TA, LRP 40: No. S634, Kitchener – Roberts, 07:30, 8.8.1900, p. 46; compare PRO, WO 105, LRP 16 for the same source.
19. TA, LRP 40: No. H628, Kitchener – Roberts, 19:05, 7.8.1900, p. 45; compare PRO, WO 105, LRP 16 for the same source; Colvin and Gordon, p. 136; Amery (ed.), IV, p. 424.
20. TA, LRP 40: No. H627, Kitchener – Roberts, 18:40, 7.8.1900, p. 44; compare PRO, WO 105, LRP 16 for the same source.
21. TA, LRP 40: No. S634, Kitchener – Roberts, 07:30, 8.8.1900, p. 46; compare PRO, WO 105, LRP 16 for the same source.
22. TA, LRP 40: No. H635, Kitchener – Roberts, 09:20, 8.8.1900, p. 47; TA, LRP 40: no number, Kitchener – Roberts, 07:25, 9.8.1900, p. 48; compare PRO, WO 105, LRP 16 for the same sources; Colvin and Gordon, p. 136; W. Wood, *The Northumberland Fusiliers,* p. 195; Romer and Mainwaring, pp. 131–132.
23. TA, SA Telegrams IV: No. C3519, Roberts – Knox, via OC, Vredefort Road, 12.8.1900, p. 22; compare TA, SA Telegrams III: no number, Roberts – Kelly-Kenny, Kroonstad, 2.8.1900, p. 121; TA, SA Telegrams III: No. C3359, Roberts – Kitchener, 7.8.1900, p. 142; and PRO, WO 108/240 and 108/241 for the three

abovementioned sources; TA, LRP 40: No. S634, Kitchener – Roberts, 8.8.1900, p. 46; compare PRO, WO 105, LRP 16 for the same source.
24. Badenhorst, p. 46.
25. De Wet, p. 142; TA, LRP 10: Methuen, 'Chase of De Wet', 8.8.1900, p. 34; compare PRO, WO 105, LRP 10 for the same source.
26. De Wet, p. 142.
27. The Times, 12.2.1901: 'In Retreat with De Wet'.
28. TA, LRP 10: Methuen, 'Chase of De Wet', 9.8.1900, p. 36; compare PRO, WO 105, LRP 10 for the same source; TA, WO Acquisition JPE 5: Staff Diary 1st Division, 9.8.1900, p. 61; The Times, 26.9.1900: 'Lord Methuen's Chase after De Wet'; Danes, p. 1323; Amery (ed.), IV, p. 424.
29. TA, LRP 10: Methuen, 'Chase of De Wet', 9.8.1900, pp. 36–37 and 55; compare PRO, WO 105, LRP 10 for the same source; TA, WO Acquisition, JPE 5: Staff Diary, 1st Division, 9.8.1900, p. 61; Danes, pp. 1323–1324.
30. TA, LRP 10: Methuen, 'Chase of De Wet', 9.8.1900, p. 56; compare PRO, WO 105, LRP 10 for the same source; Danes, p. 1324.
31. The Times, 12.2.1901: 'In Retreat with De Wet'.
32. The Times, 26.9.1900: 'Lord Methuen's Chase After De Wet'; The Times, 12.2.1901: 'In Retreat with De Wet'; TA, WO Acquisition JPE 5: Staff Diary, 1st Division, 9.8.1900, p. 61.
33. TA, LRP 10: Methuen, 'Chase of De Wet', 9.8.1900, p. 37; compare PRO, WO 105, LRP 10 for the same source; TA, LRP 40: no number, Kitchener – Roberts, 9.8.1900, p. 50; TA, LRP 40: no number, Kitchener – Roberts, 10.8.1900, p. 57; compare PRO, WO 105, LRP 16 for the same sources; Colvin and Gordon, p. 137.
34. TA, LRP 40: no number, Kitchener – Roberts, 14:30, 9.8.1900, p. 50; compare PRO, WO 105, LRP 16 for the same source; Ver Loren van Themaat, p. 170.
35. The Times, 12.2.1901: 'In Retreat with De Wet'.
36. TA, LRP 10: Methuen, 'Chase of De Wet', 9.8.1900, p. 37; compare PRO, WO 105, LRP 10 for the same source.
37. TA, LRP 10: Methuen, 'Chase of De Wet', 9.8.1900, p. 37; compare PRO, WO 105, LRP 10 for the same source; TA, LRP 40: No. 871P, Barton – Roberts, 11.8.1900 re telegram Kitchener – Roberts, 10.8.1900, p. 56; compare PRO, WO 105, LRP 22 for the same source; Van Schoor, 'Diaries of Jacob de Villiers', 13.8.1900, p. 27.
38. TA, LRP 10: Methuen, 'Chase of De Wet', 9.8.1900, p. 37; compare PRO, WO 105, LRP 10 for the same source; The Times, 26.9.1900: 'Lord Methuen's Chase after De Wet'; TA, LRP 40: Kitchener – Roberts re telegram Methuen – Roberts, 9.8.1900, pp. 55–56; compare PRO, WO 105, LRP 16 for the same source; Maurice and Grant, III, p. 347.
39. De Wet, p. 142.
40. Danes, p. 1325.

CHAPTER THIRTEEN

No sign of the Boers

NOTHING HAD COME of Roberts' hope that Methuen would check De Wet until Kitchener could attack him from the rear. A new strategy was called for. Roberts expected that De Wet would join forces with the Transvaal general De la Rey, at this stage operating 56 km west of Rustenburg at Elands River,[1] and then join Botha on the eastern front. General Ian Hamilton would have to be drawn into the hunt from the north.

Hamilton was escorting Baden-Powell from Rustenburg to Pretoria along the northern slopes of the Magaliesberg and at that moment was about 10 km west of Commando Nek. Roberts assumed that once De Wet had become aware of Hamilton's presence the Boer commander would move further west to Olifant's Nek. On 8 August, when the chief heard De Wet was heading north-east from Schoeman's Drift, he ordered Hamilton to cross the Magaliesberg and advance to Hekpoort, about halfway between the two necks on the southern slopes. Baden-Powell would stay behind to occupy Commando Nek. From Hekpoort Hamilton should determine where the enemy was heading. In the meantime Kitchener, Broadwood and Little would do everything in their power to catch up with De Wet from the rear. But the Free State commander was moving so rapidly this would only be possible if he was held up by Hamilton. Roberts stressed that De Wet must on no account be allowed to cross the Magaliesberg: 'If he escapes you he will assuredly join Botha, while if you can stop him the war will practically be over,' he concluded.[2]

For the execution of Roberts' plan the British had the following troops lined up in the Western Transvaal: at Krugersdorp General G. Barton formed a supply base with a garrison of 3 000 men ready to support any British force within reach. Ian Hamilton and Baden-Powell together had 9 500 men in the Magaliesberg west of Pretoria and Lieutenant-General Sir F. Carrington with the Rhodesia Field Force had 2 500 men near Zeerust.[3] Nearer the Vaal, Smith-Dorrien, the commander of the 19th Brigade (1 500 men), was ordered to move east from Frederikstad to Welverdiend, and then on to Bank Station 'with a view to head De Wet should he go north'.[4] Thus, after De Wet outwitted Methuen's force of 3 000, there were still 16 500 British troops waiting for him further north.

DE WET ESCAPES OVER OLIFANT'S NEK, 11–14 AUGUST 1900

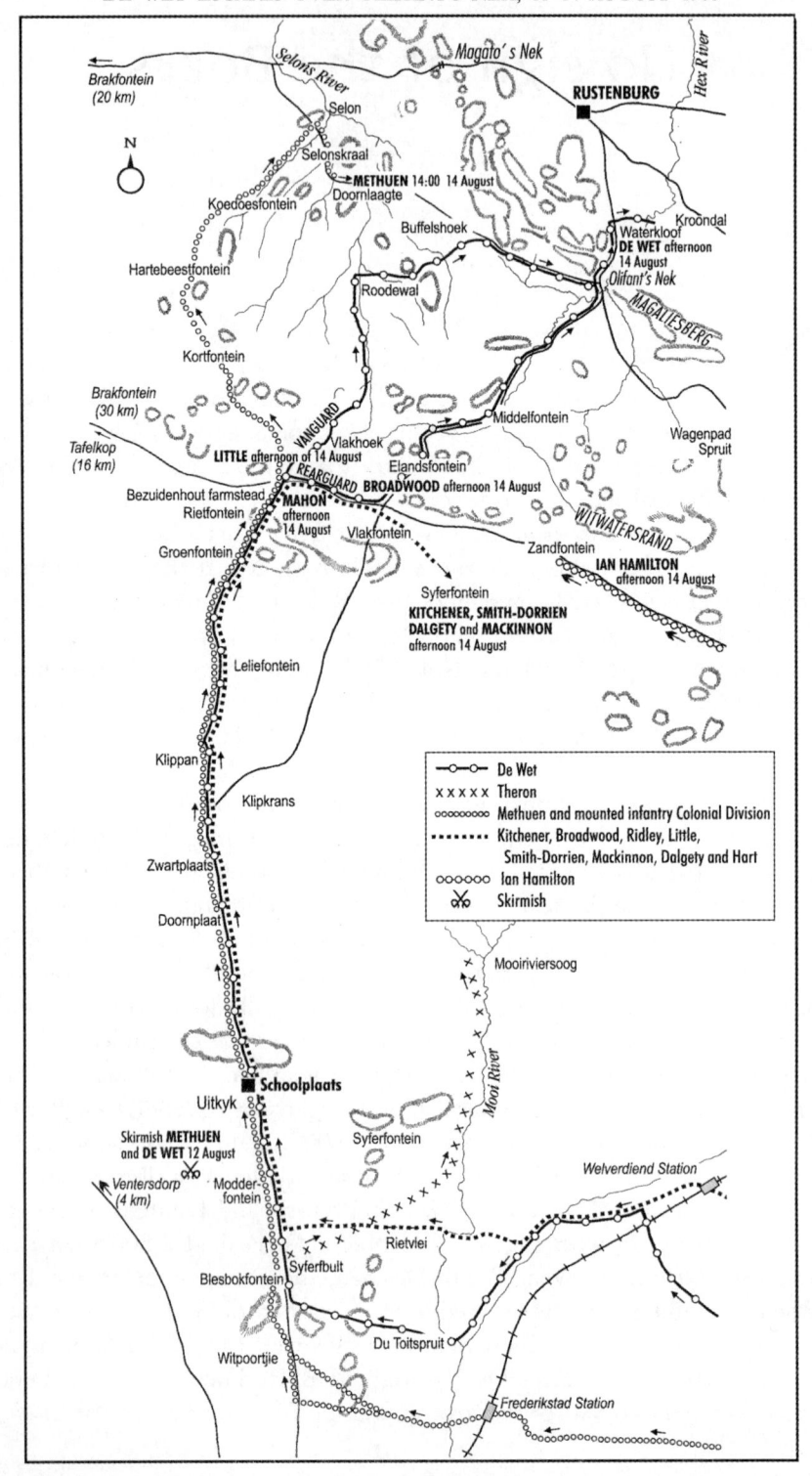

On the evening of Thursday 9 August, while De Wet and his entourage struck deep into the Transvaal, Kitchener and the two cavalry brigades at last set up camp at Lindeque's Drift. Ridley had crossed at the same ford earlier that day. Kitchener now mounted guard outposts across the Vaal River, while Hart's infantry brigade bivouacked 8 km further back at Kromellenboogspruit.[5] The next morning Kitchener's combined force of 8 000 men launched a determined pursuit of De Wet on the right flank. Methuen, joined by 1 000 men from the Colonial Division, took up the chase again on the left flank. He now had a combined force of 4 000. South of the Vaal, Knox stayed behind with 2 000 men to keep an eye on the fords.

Methuen set off at 06:15 am on Friday 10 August, heading due north from Rietfontein.[6] But barely 2 km later the column halted. The Boers, according to two Africans, were manning a broad ridge up ahead. Methuen sent out some scouts but it turned out to be a false alarm; there was no sign of the enemy. One British soldier was convinced the whole episode was a delaying tactic orchestrated by the Boers.[7] And so the hunt for the elusive Pimpernel continued. 'The British columns now hot on the trail, now missing it and cutting off corners in the attempt to find it again, kept stolidly trudging along, with now and then a brief interval,' is how *The Times History* described it. 'Not so much for repose as to take their bearings or to wait for the necessary supplies. Occasionally an obstinate rearguard or a glimpse of the last wagons of the Boer convoy seemed to give them the longed-for chance of having a blow at the inscrutable enemy, but ... after an inconclusive skirmish the stolid trudging would begin all over again, until at last the men began to feel that life was one stupid, almost ceaseless march.'[8]

After covering another 15 km, Methuen reached Enzelspoort and heard that De Wet had spent the previous night at Losberg further east with his united laager, then veered north-west with the intention of crossing the Gatsrand. Methuen took up the chase with renewed vigour; he was on the right track at last. Later that afternoon, shortly before reaching Taaiboschspruit at the foot of the Gatsrand, his efforts were rewarded: 'All at once, hanging in a thick, motionless cloud over the line of hills a mile or so ahead, we saw what we had been looking for all day, the dust of De Wet's convoy,'[9] was how Gaskell greeted the sight.

In the event, De Wet had spent but an hour at sunset west of Losberg to reunite and reorganise his forces before tacking north-west under the cover of darkness. The Kroonstad and Bethlehem commandos protected the laager from the rear,[10] while Theron's scouts remained at Losberg as a rearguard to reconnoitre the area further back in small groups.[11] Once beyond Losberg, the laager halted for a few hours.[12] De Wet sent two scouts to the farm Elandsfontein at the foot of the Gatsrand to inform the owner,

Piet Pienaar, that he would be passing through with a large force the next morning and would need replenishments. Before dawn on Friday 10 August, the burghers began to arrive at the farmstead to feed their exhausted mounts and oxen. Those unable to be catered for continued to another farm over the Gatsrand.[13]

After a repose of a few hours, De Wet ordered the trek to resume, warning his burghers the British forces had united in a determined effort to pursue and destroy them.[14] Informed by his scouts that Smith-Dorrien was lying in wait further north at Bank Station, De Wet swung west to cross the Gatsrand on a small track at Buffelsdoorn. A crossing of almost 400 wagons undoubtedly took a good few hours and at 15:00, when enemy signals were spotted in the distance, it became clear the British were hard on their heels.[15] A short while later the British caught sight of the wagon convoy; Methuen had finally caught up.[16]

De Wet immediately ordered the artillery and the Kroonstad burghers, commanded by Philip Botha, to take up positions behind the ridges at the crossing point to cover the laager's departure. Soon Boer shells were raining on Methuen's forces near Taaiboschspruit. The 1st Division commander lost no time in replying – just as Theron and his scouts appeared on the scene. Theron's men had remained around Losberg until 22:00, but when the British made no move to launch a night march they regrouped to follow the main force. Around midnight the scouts halted again for two hours to see if the enemy was following, then rode until 10:00 to outspan south of the Gatsrand.[17] They had spent 17 of the previous 24 hours in the saddle and covered a distance of 60 km while constantly looking over their shoulders for their pursuers. That afternoon the scouts saddled up again to join the rest of the burghers at the summit of the Gatsrand, only to walk straight into the artillery duel.[18]

The setting sun soon put a stop to the shelling and after 15 minutes the Boer rearguard was able to descend the northern slopes of the Gatsrand to rejoin the laager due south of Welverdiend Station.[19] The hills of Doornfontein now protected the Boers from Smith-Dorrien's view.[20] During the artillery exchange only a few horses were killed on either side.[21] De Wet's next objective was to cross the Potchefstroom–Krugersdorp railway without betraying his presence to Smith-Dorrien or a British force at that moment heading toward Welverdiend Station.

Methuen set up camp at Taaiboschspruit, about 800 m south of Gatsrand, apparently convinced the Boers would spend the night just over the hill. He would attack the next morning.[22] Dalgety, meanwhile, had been plodding along behind Methuen since leaving Scandinavia Drift on 7 August. The Colonials, who had not engaged the Boers, for some reason progressed as slowly as the 1st Division. But on 10 August Dalgety left his supply convoy behind and raced ahead with his mounted troops. That night the Colonials bivouacked at Enzelspoort, a short distance behind Methuen.[23]

At 05:00 that same morning, Kitchener began to cross the Vaal River at Lindeque's Drift with more than 7 000 troops. Broadwood and Little's cavalry brigades took the lead, followed by Hart's infantry and the various supply convoys. The difficult crossing took over six hours to accomplish, and it was well after noon before the two naval guns were finally pulled ashore on the Vaal's northern bank. Then, after marching out against a long hill, a great uninterrupted plain stretched before the troops, virtually right up to the Gatsrand.[24] Kitchener believed De Wet was probably on his way to Bank Station and would not reach the railway before Saturday 11 August.[25] He set off due north in pursuit.

Kitchener's columns marched all day, the cavalry brigades racing ahead in the hope of catching sight of the enemy. But, as befell Methuen earlier that day, their efforts went unrewarded – for the simple reason that Kitchener was on the wrong track. De Wet had in fact passed their present position a good distance further west the day before. At that point he was already crossing the Gatsrand, where Methuen would spot him a short while later.

Nevertheless, by nightfall Kitchener's force had covered a respectable distance since crossing the Vaal River. Up ahead, Broadwood's 2nd Cavalry, Little's 3rd and Ridley's mounted infantry had advanced about 35 km to set up camp at the foot of the Gatsrand at Weltevreden. There the British scouts informed their commanders the Gatsrand was poorly guarded and that the Boers had crossed further west near Elandsfontein.[26] Kitchener and his headquarters followed slowly in the cavalry's tracks, with the infantry, naval guns and supply convoys bringing up the rear. The column eventually bivouacked after sunset on the southern spur of Droogeheuvel near Tweefontein. Hart, who had set out 8 km behind Kitchener that morning, fared particularly well by covering a distance of about 35 km. 'If it had not been for the bad drift at Lindeque,' Kitchener pointed out to Roberts, 'we could have got further today.' Exhausted after a long day's march, the troops warmed themselves at veldfires while waiting for their dinner and blankets. At 22:00 on Friday 10 August, after a strenuous slog, the supply convoy at last arrived at the campsite.[27]

10 August was of further significance because by that evening communication among the various British commanders chasing De Wet was restored for the first time since Kitchener had taken charge of the operation south of the Vaal River on 3 August. Methuen had contacted Kitchener and Broadwood by heliograph late that afternoon, which meant the two flanks were now aware of each other's respective positions. Methuen had sent two more messages that day. The first was an instruction to Dalgety at Enzelspoort to leave for Frederikstad at dawn, but the commander of

the Colonials unaccountably never received the order.[28] Methuen and Broadwood also sent a message to Smith-Dorrien to keep him up to date with the latest developments in the hunt. Smith-Dorrien clearly received the information too late, because when Broadwood's dispatch rider reached him at 01:00 on 11 August with the news that the 'Boer convoy began crossing the Gatsrand above Wolvaardt at 7 pm',[29] the Boers were already over the railway. In fact, only a rearguard had remained at the Gatsrand to keep abreast of British movements. Despite the elaborate precautions taken, De Wet had somehow managed to slip past Smith-Dorrien.

To understand this feat we need to examine Smith-Dorrien's movements up to 10 August. Before being ordered from Frederikstad to Bank Station it was Smith-Dorrien, not Methuen, who had borne the brunt of Liebenberg's activities around the Gatsrand which were causing severe disruptions along the railway between Krugersdorp and Potchefstroom. On 6 August Smith-Dorrien therefore sent a detachment under Colonel J. Spens from Frederikstad to Welverdiend Station further east to secure the line against attacks. 'Spens can thus move along escorting trains of supplies and endeavouring to keep telegraph in order,' he explained to Roberts. Spens arrived at Welverdiend the same day.[30]

For the next two days Smith-Dorrien had his hands full getting supplies railed down from Krugersdorp to Frederikstad amid Boer attacks on the line.[31] Then, on 8 August, Roberts received a report from Methuen that De Wet had crossed the Vaal River and been driven from Tygerfontein.[32] The chief was convinced De Wet was heading north-east to Commando Nek and ordered Smith-Dorrien to hasten east to Bank Station and lie in wait there for the Free Staters. This meant Frederikstad would no longer be in British hands, as Roberts made plain to Methuen.[33] Smith-Dorrien also took the precaution of reporting his movements to Methuen, leaving it up to the 1st Division commander to keep an eye on the railway near Frederikstad.[34] But Methuen apparently never received the message.

A train which Smith-Dorrien had sent toward Potchefstroom with supplies for Methuen arrived at Frederikstad at 19:00 on 8 August. Two hours later the 19th Brigade set off for Welvderdiend, reaching their destination in the early hours of 9 August after a 23 km march.[35] Colonel Spens had in the meantime left Welverdiend, reaching Bank Station at 06:30 the same morning.[36] At this point Smith-Dorrien felt it prudent to inform Roberts by cable that by pressing on to Bank Station, he would leave a gap open for De Wet in the west. But Roberts failed to reply and at 09:00, after shutting down the telegraph post at Welverdiend, Smith-Dorrien set off for Bank.[37] At 15:00 that afternoon he arrived, along with the City of London Imperial Volunteers (the CIV) and the Yeomanry, followed three hours later by the Shropshires and an ox-wagon convoy. Roberts praised them for their rapid march.[38] The same afternoon a battalion of West

Yorkshires under Major Fry arrived by train from Krugersdorp with two Howitzers. Smith-Dorrien thus had a force of 2 000 infantry, 200 Yeomanry, two sections RFA and two Howitzers at his disposal. That night transport and provisions for 14 days arrived from Barton's supply depot in Krugersdorp.[39]

As the railway controlled the northern slopes of Gatsrand, Barton spelled out Smith-Dorrien's role as follows: he was to pin the Boers against the Gatsrand to give the columns pursuing De Wet from the rear the chance to fall on their prey.[40] For this purpose Smith-Dorrien asked Roberts if he would be permitted to keep a train which had just arrived from Potchefstroom. 'My infantry will be in a splendid position if I have a train to move them,' he assured the chief, adding that this would enable him to control the railway up to 32 km further west. Roberts readily consented.[41] Barton, too, stressed the importance of the train: 'Smith-Dorrien is better able to hold De Wet and it is undoubtedly the safest and best way for him to give time for the pursuing columns to come up.'[42]

In order to be thoroughly equipped, Smith-Dorrien further requested a 6-inch gun: 'If De Wet crosses anywhere on this open piece of country about here or Welverdiend a six-inch gun on a truck ... would be very useful ... on account of its long range,' he explained.[43] Roberts immediately agreed[44] and the gun arrived the same day.[45]

Smith-Dorrien was painfully aware that his evacuation of Frederikstad had left the western exit wide open for De Wet. Furthermore, he had also received intelligence that Liebenberg's men – who at this stage were at Syferbult, a short distance north-west of Frederikstad – were intending to unite with the Free Staters.[46] He cabled Roberts on the afternoon of 10 August to assure him 'no large force can pass between this and two miles west of Welverdiend', but added significantly: 'Beyond that I cannot extend.'[47] Roberts replied that De Wet was apparently on his way to Bank Station after all. Smith-Dorrien was not convinced.[48] His secret fear was that if he conducted a westward drive, De Wet would be forced to make for the unguarded terrain further down the line at Frederikstad. He thus decided to leave the railway further west unguarded until after dark, with only a few empty tents pitched along the line in the hope of delaying the enemy.[49] 'By midnight Welverdiend and an intermediate post halfway between that and here will be occupied each by two guns, a Battalion and a squadron with the same here [at Bank Station] under me,' he informed Roberts at 17:00 on 10 August.[50]

Although Smith-Dorrien's patrols had noticed the presence of Boer scouts in the Gatsrand since 9 August,[51] he did not expect the Free Staters to reach the railway before the morning of 11 August. Then, at 17:00 on 10 August, he received a report that about 100 Boers had been spotted south of the Gatsrand, heading toward Frederikstad in small groups. But a short while later Smith-Dorrien heard the artillery duel between Methuen and De Wet from the same direction. He now assumed the 1st Division commander would probably be in a position to prevent the Boers from escaping at Frederikstad. The following morning he and Methuen would be able to march on Frederikstad from two directions to pin De Wet against the railway.[52]

After sunset on 10 August, Colonel Spens left by train for Welverdiend with the Shropshires, two guns and 90 horsemen. This was the same force De Wet's scouts had spotted as the Boers were preparing to cross the railway. Another detachment under Colonel W.H. MacKinnon comprising the CIV, two Howitzers, the 86th Battery RFA of Captain Woodcock and 50 horsemen marched in the same direction for 11 km until they reached Wonderfontein (later Oberholzer Station). Both Spens and MacKinnon used signal lamps to keep in touch with Smith-Dorrien.[53]

That same night, contrary to the expectations of Spens, MacKinnon and especially Smith-Dorrien and Methuen, the Boers set off for the railway as soon as it was dark. De Wet arranged the convoy in a similar formation as used to leave the Brandwater Basin. At 19:00, under a clear moonlit sky, the Free State commander, Botha, President Steyn and his councillors crossed the line scarcely 5 km west of Welverdiend and 2 km beyond Smith-Dorrien's reach. They were followed by their personal wagons, the artillery and the rest of the wagon train. The commandos covered the flanks, while Theron's scouts formed the rearguard as usual. The scouts were also ordered to wreck the railway, which by 21:00 had been blown up in eight different places. A culvert scarcely 2 km from Welverdiend was also destroyed. Smith-Dorrien heard the explosions from Bank Station 25 km away, but only discovered the cause the following day.[54] Henri Slegtkamp offered an interesting explanation for the blasts. He claimed a number of burghers refused to saddle up because 'their poor horses were on their last legs'. De Wet therefore decided a few well-timed explosions would convince them they were being shelled by the enemy. 'It worked,' concluded Slegtkamp. 'The burghers fled with renewed vigour and all made it safely over the rails.'[55]

Now the convoy veered west south-west and continued virtually parallel to the railway. De Wet intended to rendezvous with Liebenberg's men, who had been ordered to gather in the region of Syferbult, west of the Mooi River and less than 20 km north-west of Frederikstad.[56] The long-cherished goal of joint action between the western border burghers and the Free Staters would finally be realised.

The trek continued through the night, with the burghers bunched together in small groups. By then man and beast must have been close to utter exhaustion, especially the oxen pulling the artillery. The animals would not be able to continue the next day without being given a chance to rest.

Major-General H.L. Smith-Dorrien who, with part of Methuen's 1st Division, was unable to prevent De Wet from crossing the Potchefstroom–Johannesburg railway line. (From: H.W. Wilson, With the Flag to Pretoria, *Vol. II, London, 1901, p. 413)*

Thankfully the enemy was nowhere in sight and the convoy advanced unhindered, with Theron's scouts and a number of Bethlehemers under Commandant Michael Prinsloo covering the rear. 'Endless plains stretched before us in the colourless moonlight,' recalled Ver Loren van Themaat, 'and the horsemen and ox wagons plodded on as though the journey would never end, without a fixed point in sight against which to measure progress. Nowhere, not even in the hazy distance, could we see the long wished-for ridge behind which we would be able unsaddle safely, out of sight of the enemy. We rode on in small isolated groups, stopping after a long stretch to take our saddles off our horses and let them wander about for a while. Then it was back in the saddle again.'[57] After crossing a small muddy drift on the Mooi River[58] (Smith-Dorrien had blown up all the bridges a few days before),[59] the scouts finally reached the wagon laager outspanned at Du Toitspruit scarcely 6 km north-west of Frederikstad.[60] Towards daybreak the Free Staters encountered the first parties of Liebenberg's advance guard. Half an hour later the general himself appeared with his laager and commando to join De Wet.[61] The Boer scouts spotted on 9 August by British patrols on the Gatsrand passes[62] had done a good job keeping De Wet up to date about enemy deployments; the area around Frederikstad was safe for now.[63]

The Boer generals took the opportunity to take stock of the situation. Within a month Liebenberg had doubled his force to 600 men,[64] as well as being saddled with a laager of some 200 wagons and carts.[65] He had been able to inflict considerable damage to the Potchefstroom–Krugersdorp railway with only Methuen and Smith-Dorrien stationed in the Western Transvaal. But now that De Wet had drawn a large number of

General Piet Liebenberg, whose presence in the Western Transvaal assisted De Wet in his endeavours to elude the British columns. (From: P.H.S. van Zyl, Die Helde-Album, Johannesburg, 1944, p. 102)

British troops into the area, the western border burgers would obviously come under tremendous pressure.[66] This, together with the fact that Liebenberg's horses were in a poor state and many of his new recruits had no weapons, ruled out the possibility of any further operations. Liebenberg and De Wet therefore decided to travel to Rustenburg together, with the intention of uniting with General De la Rey.[67]

The Free Staters and their oxen were given almost five hours to recuperate from their gruelling trek. That afternoon the order was given to span in once more. 'The sturdy figure of De Wet sits atop his snow white mount,' wrote a Transvaal burgher. 'Majestic and proud, he swiftly takes stock of his men, then leads out his commando.'[68]

The united Boer force now headed north-west in the direction of Ventersdorp. The Free Staters led the procession, followed by Liebenberg's men. Theron's scouts crossed the Mooi River again to form the rearguard.[69] The ride that day was made extremely unpleasant by a fierce Western Transvaal sand storm. Howling winds whipped up swirling dust clouds, making it difficult to see even a few feet ahead.[70] Fortunately the burghers had only departed that afternoon and managed to miss most of the storm. The trek continued into the night until De Wet eventually called a halt among a series of ridges 18 km east of Ventersdorp.[71] For the first time since 8 August the march did not continue until dawn and the burghers were able to enjoy a good night's rest.

The next morning, Sunday 12 August, Danie Theron decided to split from the main party.[72] Since the trek out of the Brandwater Basin the scouts had consistently undertaken the most arduous and dangerous work. Their commander probably believed now that Liebenberg's commando was escorting the Free Staters, De Wet would be able to do without his services. It also appears as though there was some friction between the two men, possibly because Theron was summoned to appear before the war council of 8 August when his scouts allegedly failed to warn De Wet of Methuen's attack the day before.[73] De Wet was unhappy with Theron's decision,[74] but Steyn supported the TVK leader, arguing that his crack corps would be able to inflict more damage by operating independently.[75] Theron thus bade farewell and took his men north to Mooiriviersoog, a densely wooded area with numerous ridges behind which to shelter. Here his men would be able to shake off the tensions of a sustained pursuit and give their exhausted mounts the opportunity to recuperate.[76]

Meanwhile, 18 hours previously, while De Wet and his wagon train were still tacking south-west to meet Liebenberg beyond Mooi River, Smith-Dorrien finally received Broadwood's message that the Boers had crossed the Gatsrand. Unlike Roberts, Smith-Dorrien still believed De Wet was heading toward Frederikstad. He now suggested that Broadwood shift his right flank closer to Bank Station and ordered Spens and MacKinnon to join forces at Doornfontein at the foot of the Gatsrand and about 10 km south of Welverdiend. Smith-Dorrien himself would take half his infantry and cavalry west toward Welverdiend.[77] These measures, he believed, would completely block the Boers' attempts to reach Frederikstad.

Early on the morning of 11 August, when De Wet was already about 6 km north of Frederikstad, the British sprang into action – only to embark on a series of hit and misses. One of MacKinnon's patrols came across a group of 50 Boers north of the railway at Welverdiend, and drove them off with shellfire. The intelligence officer of Krugersdorp thus reported to Pretoria that De Wet had tried to cross the line at Welverdiend that morning, but that Smith-Dorrien was attacking him.[78] This faulty information, like previous and subsequent errors, would cause strategic decisions taken by the British commanders to bear little fruit. For more often than not, as in this case, what was thought to be De Wet's main force was nothing more than a small rearguard detachment.

Then, upon arriving at Doornfontein further south, MacKinnon had to hear from Spens that the Boers had already passed through the area ahead of them and crossed the line, blowing up a culvert and the rails in various places. The two colonels immediately decided to return to Welverdiend. Smith-Dorrien himself began his westward advance with supplies for his own force and Methuen's shortly before 06:00 on 11 August – only to be told the same news 6 km from Welverdiend by an African: De Wet's commandos and laager were already over the line, having crossed 5 km beyond the station.[79]

Now tragedy turned to farce. The 19th Battalion commander heard a few rounds of shelling from the direction of Gatsrand. Smith-Dorrien now assumed a large part of the Boer force had yet to cross the Gatsrand,

and Methuen was engaging them at that moment. At least Smith-Dorrien would be ready for this force. The forlorn truth only came to light later. It turned out that Methuen's Yeomanry were scouring the hills for any sign of the Boers. 'Every now and then two pom-poms let off a few rounds at likely places,' one Yeomanryman recalled, 'but received no reply.'[80]

Faulty intelligence was of course in no small measure to blame for the dismal British performance. If Smith-Dorrien had known earlier that the Boers had crossed the Gatsrand and were racing for the railway, he could have occupied Welverdiend on the afternoon of 10 August and undoubtedly made it much more difficult for De Wet to cross there. What was more, Smith-Dorrien assumed Methuen would be able to guard the line near Frederikstad. But the 1st Division commander was in fact pursuing De Wet much further south and had therefore not received Smith-Dorrien's request that he secure Frederikstad.

De Wet's success can also be attributed to his own sound strategic choices: by staying put and remaining well out of Smith-Dorrien's sight after crossing the Gatsrand, then under the cover of darkness making for a crossing point his scouts had first established was unguarded, De Wet was able to move well beyond the enemy's reach by the morning of 11 August. Smith-Dorrien, who was ordered to concentrate his forces at Welverdiend, later wrote the only hope that remained 'was to block the passes through the Magaliesberg range'.[81]

On the morning of Saturday 11 August, Kitchener was still south of the Gatsrand. He had not yet learned of De Wet's escape. At first light his cavalry brigades set off, followed by the infantry and supply convoys. This time, however, Kitchener and his staff joined the cavalry. Before noon, now over the Gatsrand, Kitchener heard the Boers had moved westward toward Frederikstad and accordingly changed course, hoping to replenish his supplies and receive remounts at Welverdiend on the way.[82] Veldfires now turned the march into torture, a strong headwind flung dust mixed with fine ash and burning cinders into the faces of the advancing troops.[83] 'These soon filled eyes, ears, nostrils, throats and lungs, until breathing became well-nigh impossible, and the agony caused by their penetration into our eyes almost intolerable,' a Dublin Fusilier recalled.[84]

Toward sunset on Saturday 11 August, after a march of more than 40 km, the cavalry reached Welverdiend, with Kitchener and the commanding officers riding at the head of the column.[85] They were joined by their transport at 21:30, led by drivers who by now were virtually frost bitten. Hart's infantry set up camp some way back at 16:30 after a slow march.[86] It had been a disheartening trek; all day Kitchener had seen no sign of the Boers. Then, on arrival at Welverdiend, the news greeted him that De Wet had slipped through after all – a mere 5 km from where he stood and a full 24 hours before his arrival.

Notes

1. TA, SA Telegrams III: No. C3359, Roberts – Kitchener, 7.8.1900, p. 142; compare PRO, WO 108/240 for the same source.
2. TA, SA Telegrams IV: No. C3403, Roberts – Hamilton, 8.8.1900, p. 6; compare PRO, WO 108/241 for the same source; also Maurice and Grant, III, pp. 348–349; TA, SA Dispatches II: Roberts' Account 14 June to 10 October 1900, p. 10; compare PRO WO 32/8000 for the same source.
3. Amery (ed.), IV, p. 422; TA, LRP 43: No. B270, Hamilton – Roberts, 9.8.1900, p. 176; compare PRO, WO 105, LRP 16 for the same source.
4. TA, SA Telegrams IV: No. C3421A, Roberts – Methuen via Potchefstroom, 9.8.1900, p. 9; compare PRO, WO 108/241 for the same source.
5. TA, LRP 40: no number, Kitchener – Roberts, 14:30, 9.8.1900, p. 50; TA, LRP 40: no number, Kitchener – Roberts, 18:00, 9.8.1900, p. 51; TA, LRP 40: no number, Kitchener – Roberts, 10.8.1900, p. 57; compare PRO, WO 105, LRP 16 for the same sources; Colvin and Gordon, pp. 136–137; Romer and Mainwaring, p. 132; PRO, WO 108/231: No. 7588C, GOC, Lines of Communication – Secretary of State for War, 11.8.1900, p. 276; TA, South African Dispatches II: Roberts' Account, 14 June to 10 October 1900, p. 10; compare PRO, WO 32/8000 for the same source; Maurice and Grant, III, pp. 347–348; Amery (ed.), IV, pp. 424–425.
6. TA, LRP 10: Methuen, 'Chase of De Wet', 10.8.1900, p. 38; compare PRO, WO 105, LRP 10 for the same source.
7. Gaskell, pp. 188–189.
8. Amery (ed.), IV, p. 425.
9. Gaskell, p. 190.
10. Grobler, p. 59.
11. Ver Loren van Themaat, p. 170; [Hintrager], p. 83; *The Times*, 12.2.1901: 'In Retreat with De Wet'; Nierstrasz, II, Vol. 5, p. 1016; TA, LRP 40: no number, Kitchener – Roberts, 18:00, 9.8.1900, p. 51; compare PRO, WO 105, LRP 16 for the same source.
12. TA, LRP 10: Methuen, 'Chase of De Wet', 10.8.1900, p. 38; compare PRO, WO 105, LRP 10 for the same source; TA, WO Acquisition, JPE 5: Staff Diary, 1st Division, 11.8.1900, p. 66; Maurice and Grant, III, p. 349.
13. Recounted to the author by Mrs M. Malherbe (née Pienaar), Elandsfontein, 7.12.1972. Pienaar's farmstead still stands, a few kilometres east of Fochville, near the neck where the Johannesburg–Potchefstroom road crosses the Gatsrand and directly behind the Danie Theron monument. Compare [Hintrager], p. 83; Lombard, p. 69; De Wet p. 142; Nierstrasz, II, Vol. 5, p. 1016.
14. De Wet, p. 142; compare [Hintrager], p. 83.
15. Lombard, p. 69; [Hintrager], p. 83.
16. TA, LRP 10: Methuen, 'Chase of De Wet', 10.8.1900, p. 38; compare PRO, WO 105, LRP 10 for the same source.
17. *The Times*, 12.2.1901: 'In Retreat with De Wet'; Ver Loren van Themaat, p. 170.
18. *The Times*, 12.2.1901: 'In Retreat with De Wet'.
19. Ver Loren van Themaat, p. 171.
20. CA, Map Collection, 2/184: Farm Surveys, Potchefstroom, 1905.
21. Van Schoor, 'Diaries of Jacob de Villiers', 13.8.1900, p. 27; Lombard, p. 69; [Hintrager], p. 84; Gaskell, pp. 192–193.
22. TA, LRP 10: Methuen, 'Chase of De Wet', 10.8.1900, p. 38; compare PRO, WO 105, LRP 10 for the same source; TA, LRP 44: No. Z127, Smith-Dorrien – Roberts re telegram Broadwood, 11.8.1900, p. 22; compare PRO, WO 105, LRP 15 for the same source.

23. TA, LRP 10: Methuen, 'Chase of De Wet', 10.8.1900, p. 38; compare PRO, WO 105, LRP 10 for the same source, and the accompanying map not recorded in the TA; The *Natal Witness*, 9.10.1900: 'When De Wet Escaped: A Colonial's Story'; TA, LRP 40: no number, Kitchener – Roberts re Broadwood – Kitchener, 10.8.1900, p. 55; compare PRO, WO 105, LRP 16 for the same source.
24. Colvin and Gordon, p. 137; Romer and Mainwaring, pp. 132–133; Jeans (ed.), p. 165.
25. TA, LRP 40: no number, Kitchener – Roberts, 9.8.1900, p. 51; compare PRO, WO 105, LRP 16 for the same source.
26. TA, LRP 44: No. Z127, Smith-Dorrien, Bank – Roberts re statement Broadwood, 11.8.1900, pp. 22 and 191; compare PRO, WO 105, LRP 15 for the same source; TA, LRP 40: No. 871P, Barton – Roberts re telegram Kitchener, 10.8.1900, pp. 53–54; compare PRO, WO 105, LRP 22 for the same source; CA, Map Collection, 2/184: Farm Surveys, Potchefstroom, 1905.
27. TA, LRP: No. 871P, Barton – Roberts re telegram Kitchener, 10.8.1900, pp. 53–58; compare PRO, WO 105, LRP 22 for the same source; Colvin and Gordon, p. 137; Romer and Mainwaring, pp. 132–133; Jeans (ed.), p. 165; CA, Map Collection, 2/184: Farm Surveys, Potchefstroom, 1905.
28. TA, LRP 10: Methuen, 'Chase of De Wet', 10.8.1900, pp. 38–39; compare PRO, WO 105, LRP 10 for the same source; TA, LRP 40: no number, Kitchener – Roberts, 11.8.1900, pp. 60–61; compare PRO, WO 105, LRP 16 for the same source.
29. TA, LRP 10: Methuen, 'Chase of De Wet', 10.8.1900, p. 39; compare PRO, WO 105, LRP 10 for the same source; TA, LRP 40: No. 871P, Barton – Roberts re telegram Kitchener, 10.8.1900, p. 55; compare PRO, WO 105, LRP 22 for the same source; TA, LRP 44: No. Z123, Smith-Dorrien – Roberts, 10.8.1900, p. 20; compare PRO, WO 105, LRP 15 for the same source; TA, LRP 40: no number, Kitchener – Roberts, 11.8.1900, pp. 60–61; compare PRO, WO 105, LRP 16 for the same source.
30. TA, LRP 44: No. Z88, Smith-Dorrien – Roberts, 6.8.1900, p. 2; compare PRO, WO 105, LRP 15 for the same source; TA, LRP 45: No. 789P, Barton – Roberts, 6.8.1900, p. 124; compare PRO, WO 105, LRP 22 for the same source; H.L. Smith-Dorrien, *Memories of Forty Eight Years' Service*, p. 230.
31. TA, LRP 45: No. 799P, Barton – Roberts, 6.8.1900, p. 124; compare PRO, WO, LRP 22 for the same source; Smith-Dorrien, p. 230.
32. TA, LRP 44: No. Z98, Smith-Dorrien – Roberts, 10:31, 8.8.1900, p. 9; compare PRO, WO 105, LRP 15 for the same source; Smith-Dorrien, p. 230.
33. TA, SA Telegrams IV: No. C3403, Roberts – Hamilton, 8.8.1900, p. 6; TA, SA Telegrams IV: No. C3421A, Roberts – Methuen, 9.8.1900, p. 9; compare PRO, WO 108/241 for the same sources; Smith-Dorrien, p. 230.
34. TA, LRP 44: No. Z109, Smith-Dorrien – Roberts, 9.8.1900, p. 9; compare PRO, WO 105, LRP 15 for the same source.
35. Smith-Dorrien, pp. 230–231; PRO, WO 108/294: Royal Engineers XIII, Guerrilla Warfare, p. 51; Maurice and Grant, III, p. 342.
36. TA, LRP 45: No. 823P, Barton – Roberts, 9.8.1900, p. 130; compare PRO, WO 105, LRP 22 for the same source.
37. TA, LRP 44: No. Z101, Smith-Dorrien – Roberts, 8.8.1900, p. 6; TA, LRP 44: No. Z112, Smith-Dorrien – Roberts, 9.8.1900, p. 8; compare PRO, WO 105, LRP 15 for the same sources; Smith-Dorrien, pp. 230–231.
38. The Shropshires covered 69 km in 32 hours and the rest of the force 48 km in 17 hours (TA, LRP 44: No. Z112, Smith-Dorrien – Roberts, 9.8.1900, p. 11; TA, LRP 44: No. Z122, Smith-Dorrien – Roberts, 10.8.1900, p. 19; compare PRO WO 105,

LRP 15 for both sources; Smith-Dorrien, p. 321; W.H. MacKinnon, *The Journal of the CIV in South Africa*, p. 156; TA, SA, Telegrams IV: No. C3441, Roberts – Smith-Dorrien 10.8.1900, p. 12; compare PRO WO 108/241 for the same source).
39. TA, LRP 44: No. Z113, Smith-Dorrien – Roberts, 9.8.1900, p. 12; compare PRO, WO 105, LRP 15 for the same source; TA, LRP 45: No. 832P, Barton – Roberts, 9.8.1900, p. 132; compare PRO, WO 105, LRP 22 for the same source; Smith-Dorrien, p. 231.
40. TA, LRP 45: No. 838P, Barton – Roberts, 10:15, 10.8.1900, p. 133; compare PRO, WO 105, LRP 22 for the same source.
41. TA, SA Telegrams IV: No. C3437, Roberts – Smith-Dorrien, 10.8.1900, p. 12; compare PRO, WO 108/241 for the same source.
42. TA, LRP 45: No. 840P, Barton – Roberts, 10.8.1900, pp. 135 and 137; compare PRO, WO 105, LRP 22 for the same source.
43. TA, LRP 44: No. Z115, Smith-Dorrien – Roberts, 10.8.1900, p. 15; compare TA, LRP 44: No. Z120, Smith-Dorrien – Roberts, 10.8.1900, p. 16; compare PRO, WO 105, LRP 15 for the same sources.
44. TA, SA Telegrams IV: No. C3451, Roberts – Smith-Dorrien et al., 10.8.1900, p. 13; compare PRO, WO 108/241 for the same source.
45. Smith-Dorrien, p. 232.
46. TA, LRP 44: No. Z105, Smith-Dorrien – Roberts, 8.8.1900, p. 7; compare PRO, WO 105, LRP 15 for the same source.
47. TA, LRP 44: No. Z121, Smith-Dorrien – Roberts, 10.8.1900, p. 17; compare PRO, WO 105, LRP 15 for the same source.
48. TA, LRP 44: No. Z123, Smith-Dorrien – Roberts, 10.8.1900, p. 20; compare PRO, WO 105, LRP 15 for the same source; Smith-Dorrien, pp. 231–232.
49. Smith-Dorrien, p. 233.
50. TA, LRP 44: No. Z123, Smith-Dorrien – Roberts, 10.8.1900, p. 20; compare PRO, WO 105, LRP 15 for the same source.
51. TA, LRP 44: No. Z112, Smith-Dorrien – Roberts, 9.8.1900, p. 11; compare PRO, WO 105, LRP 15 for the same source; TA, LRP 45: No. 826P, Barton – Roberts, 9.8.1900, p. 131; compare PRO, WO 105, LRP 22 for the same source.
52. TA, LRP 44: No. Z123, Smith-Dorrien – Roberts, 10.8.1900, p. 20; compare PRO, WO 105, LRP 15 for the same source.
53. Smith-Dorrien, p. 232; MacKinnon, p. 157; TA, LRP 44: No. Z127, Smith-Dorrien – Roberts, 11.8.1900, pp. 22–23; compare PRO, WO 105, LRP 15 for the same source.
54. [Hintrager], p. 84; *The Times*, 12.2.1901: 'In Retreat with De Wet'; The *Natal Witness*, 5.9.1900: 'With De Wet: A Prisoner's Account'; TA, LRP 44: No. Z127, Smith-Dorrien – Roberts, 11.8.1900, p. 22; compare PRO, WO 105, LRP 15 for the same source; Smith-Dorrien, pp. 232–233; MacKinnon, p. 158.
55. TA, Acquisition 235 (II): Slegtkamp's manuscript, p. 151.
56. J.H. Meyer, *Kommando-Jare: 'n Oudstryder se Persoonlike Relaas van die Tweede Vryheidsoorlog*, p. 148; Pienaar, p. 159; TA, LRP 44: No. Z119, Smith-Dorrien – Roberts, 11.8.1900, p. 21; compare PRO, WO 105, LRP 15 for the same source; *The Times*, 26.9.1900: 'Lord Methuen's Chase after De Wet'.
57. Ver Loren van Themaat, p. 172.
58. TA, Acquisition 1250: D. de Witt, 'Die Trek naar die Bosveld', recorded by C.P. van der Merwe, p. 7.
59. TA, LRP 44: No. Z105, Smith-Dorrien – Roberts, 8.8.1900, p. 7; compare PRO, WO 105, LRP 15 for the same source.

60. Lombard, p. 70; Ver Loren van Themaat, p. 172; CA, Map Collection, 2/184: Farm Surveys, Potchefstroom, 1905; CA, Map Collection, 3/34: Ventersdorp and surrounding areas, October 1900.
61. Meyer, pp. 148–149; De Wet, p. 143; Pienaar, p. 161; Lombard, p. 70; [Hintrager], p. 85.
62. TA, LRP 44: No. Z112, Smith-Dorrien, Bank – Roberts, 9.8.1900, p. 10; compare PRO, WO 105, LRP 15 for the same source; TA, LRP 45: No. P9, Barton, Krugersdorp – Roberts re Smith-Dorrien – Roberts, 9.8.1900, p. 131; compare PRO, WO 105, LRP 22 for the same source.
63. In the spirit of cordial co-operation of the previous weeks, it would thus appear that De Wet had deliberately changed direction from the railway line to unite with Liebenberg's forces and that their meeting was not a chance meeting as has been suggested. That is why Badenhorst – a field-cornet at the time – was probably incorrect in asserting that it was very doubtful whether the unification of forces was in line with De Wet's aims (C.C.J. Badenhorst, p. 47, as quoted by Pretorius, 'Die Eerste Dryfjag op Genl. De Wet', *Historia*, September 1972, 17(3), p. 186).
64. TA, Leyds 759: Letter, Liebenberg – L. Botha, 17.8.1900, p. 57. Two British POWs who accompanied the TVK at the rearguard, an officer and a soldier named Hastings, provide the figures 1 500 and 2 300 respectively for the number of western border burghers (*The Times*, 12.2.1901: 'In Retreat with De Wet'; The *Natal Witness*, 5.9.1900: 'With De Wet: A Prisoner's Account').
65. Pienaar, pp. 161–162.
66. [Hintrager], p. 85; De Wet, p. 143; Preller, p. 142.
67. TA, Leyds 759: Letter, Liebenberg – L. Botha, 17.8.1900, p. 57.
68. Meyer, p. 149.
69. Grobler, p. 61; Ver Loren van Themaat, p. 172; Nierstrasz, II, Vol. 5, p. 1018; [Hintrager], p. 85, incorrectly states the direction was north-east.
70. Ver Loren van Themaat, p. 172; [Hintrager], pp. 84–85.
71. TA, LRP 40: No. H678, Kitchener – Roberts, 12.8.1900, p. 68; compare WO 105, LRP 16 for the same source; TA, LRP 10: Methuen, 'Chase of De Wet', 12.8.1900, p. 42; compare PRO, WO 105, LRP 10 for the same source; Meyer, p. 149; De Wet, p. 143; Maurice and Grant, III, p. 350.
72. TA, Acquisition 285, Danie Theron Collection: No. 28, Letter, J. Versteeg – J.J. van Tonder, 26.3.1940; Ver Loren van Themaat, p. 173; Pieterse, p. 108; Breytenbach, p. 204; Preller, p. 142; Van Everdingen, p. 76; The *Cape Times*, 20.8.1900: 'De Wet's Army: A Convoy Three Miles Long'. In the abovementioned Boer memoirs and literature, the date for Theron's departure is stated incorrectly. It appears as though Theron parted from De Wet on the same day Methuen engaged with De Wet northwest of Frederikstad – which was 12 August. The cavalryman Macdonald, a POW in the Boer laager, escaped on the afternoon of 12 August. He writes that Theron 'was with us on Sunday 12th, but left that day in a NE direction' (TA, MGP 16: Statement by cavalryman MacDonald, 16.8.1900, p. 149).
73. TA, Acquisition 1250: D. de Witt, 'Die Trek naar die Bosveld', recorded by C.P. van der Merwe, p. 7.
74. TA, Acquisition 285, Danie Theron Collection: No. 39, Statement by General Enslin, as reported by J.H. Breytenbach, p. 204; compare Preller, p. 143.
75. Preller, p. 143.
76. Breytenbach, p. 205; compare TA, Acquisition 285, Danie Theron Collection: No. 28, Letter, J. Versteeg – J.J. van Tonder, 26.3.1940 and No. 41, statement by J. Versteeg, 28.8.1939. A week later the TVK moved to the farm Elandsfontein to renew raids on the enemy.

77. TA, LRP 44: No. Z127, Smith-Dorrien – Roberts, 11.8.1900, pp. 22–23; compare PRO, WO 105, LRP 15 for the same source; Smith-Dorrien, p. 232; MacKinnon, pp. 157–158.
78. TA, LRP 45: No. 465, Intelligence, Krugersdorp – Director of Military Intelligence, 11.8.1900, p. 139.
79. TA, LRP 44: No. Z119, Smith-Dorrien – Roberts, 11.8.1900, p. 21; compare PRO, WO 105, LRP 15 for the same source; Smith-Dorrien, p. 232; MacKinnon, pp. 157–158.
80. Gaskell, p. 194.
81. Smith-Dorrien, p. 232.
82. TA, LRP 40: no number, Kitchener – Roberts, 11:00, 11.8.1900, p. 60; compare PRO, WO 105, LRP 16 for the same source.
83. Colvin and Gordon, p. 137; Romer and Mainwaring, p. 134; Jeans (ed.), p. 165; Wood, p. 196.
84. Romer and Mainwaring, p. 134.
85. TA, LRP 40: no number, Kitchener – Roberts, 16:50, 11.8.1900, p. 64; compare PRO, WO 105, LRP 16 for the same source.
86. Wood, p. 196; Jeans (ed.), p. 165; compare Romer and Mainwaring, p. 134, which states the camp was on Orange Grove near Bank Station.

CHAPTER FOURTEEN

Scorched earth

IN THE END, Methuen's 1st Division was the only British force pursuing De Wet from the rear that had stood a chance of capturing him before he crossed the railway line. But instead of pressing home the advantage, Methuen had spent the night of 10 August south of the Gatsrand at Taaiboschspruit, believing the Boers were camped just over the hill. De Wet, of course, had set off for the railway just after sunset. At 06:30 on Saturday 11 August, Methuen prepared to attack, sending his Yeomanry up the ridge with two pom-poms. Unsurprisingly, there was no sign of the enemy. Upon reaching the summit, the Yeomanry swung west to comb the area along the ridge, firing the very same shots Smith-Dorrien had heard further north, while the infantry followed a parallel course in the valley below. Before long it dawned on Methuen that De Wet had miraculously slipped the net yet again.[1]

Methuen now decided to try to cut the Boers off on the left flank, and hastened west to Frederikstad. Kitchener would be able to cover the right flank. Late on Saturday 11 August, after a march of 27 km, the 1st Division reached its destination,[2] joined by Dalgety and the Colonials, who had set off from Enzelspoort that morning.[3] For the first time since they began to pursue De Wet on 7 August, the two commanders were able to join forces.[4]

Colonel E.H. Dalgety, commander of the Colonial Division, who was unable to join hands with Methuen's 1st Division until late on 11 August 1900. (From: L.S. Amery, The Times History of the War in South Africa, *Vol. IV, London, 1906, facing p. 220)*

161

That evening Methuen heard Liebenberg's burghers had collected at Syferbult intending to unite with the Free Staters.[5] Later that night Kitchener informed him that De Wet himself had made his appearance too.[6] Methuen was back on his trail; all that remained was to force him up against Olifant's Nek, 'which I believed, it went without saying, must be occupied [by Ian Hamilton's troops]', Methuen was to report later.[7] He now shifted his transport from mule carts to ox wagons, left it behind with his infantry and at 03:00 on Sunday 12 August departed with 600 Yeomanry, 600 Colonials, four 15-pounder guns, two sections 4th Battery RFA, one section 78th Battery, a section of Howitzers and three pom-poms.[8] Although the Colonials only possessed enough fodder for one day because their supply convoy from Kroonstad was a full eight days behind, the Yeomanry's feed could last them more than two days and would probably be shared. The infantry would follow with provisions for the troops themselves.[9]

Methuen now headed west from Frederikstad to execute a flanking manoeuvre to the left around the presumed position of the Boer force, crossing the Mooi River bridge, which the Royal Engineers had repaired during the night. By 05:30 he was less than 10 km from Syferbult.[10] Dawn on Sunday 12 August brought relief from the icy winter's night[11] and Methuen headed to Witpoortjie while a detachment was sent to scout north.[12] At 08:00 he received a report that the Boer laager was just north of Syferbult. The pursuers were given half an hour to rest before taking up the chase again.[13] Less than four hours later their efforts were rewarded when the advance guard spotted a number of Boer scouts.[14] Then the Boer laager suddenly came into view 6 km ahead, racing hell for leather for the horizon.

In the meantime, Kitchener was delayed at Welverdiend Station. He had finally arrived there on the evening of Saturday 11 August after an exhausting march, and was in no position to attack the Boers from the east as he had suggested to Methuen[15] – a move which would certainly have put De Wet under enormous pressure. His horses were spent, the men dressed in rags and he was short of supplies. Early that morning Broadwood had in fact asked the commanding officer at Bank Station if the provisions and remounts Kitchener had requested for his large force had arrived yet.[16] From Pretoria, Roberts also asked Barton in Krugersdorp to ensure that the troops following De Wet received provisions for a full 14 days, since they were likely to be operating some distance from the railway.[17] The supplies Smith-Dorrien had brought with him from Bank Station were nowhere near sufficient.[18] Furthermore, Kitchener cabled his headquarters in Pretoria with an urgent request for uniforms.[19] But while Methuen was racing toward Frederikstad in the early hours of Sunday morning, Kitchener had still seen no trace of his supply train.

By daybreak on Sunday 12 August, Kitchener's patience had snapped. After sending a telegram to Roberts – asking him to see that the assistant-director of railways in Johannesburg did everything in his power to ensure the trains from Krugersdorp reached Welverdiend – he prepared to take up the chase again.[20]

In reply to Kitchener's complaints, Roberts cabled Barton in Krugersdorp, stressing the importance of getting a supply train through to Kitchener immediately.[21] Barton replied that the delay had certainly not been caused by any neglect of duty on his part. He had kept two supply trains at the ready for Kitchener, but until shortly before midnight on 11 August he had not had any locomotives available. He complained that in the last two weeks he had sent six locomotives toward Potchefstroom but that two had been captured by Liebenberg. Barton said he had repeatedly urged Methuen and Smith-Dorrien to return the remaining locomotives, but received no response. In the event, Barton had in fact sent two supply trains down to Kitchener – one at 23:30 on 11 August and another the following morning at 11:00. But as it turned out, both arrived too late. The situation was exacerbated, he informed the chief, by blunders and poor administration along the railway. For example, the assistant director of railways had withdrawn the station master at Bank, who also served as a telegraphist. Furthermore, Smith-Dorrien had departed from the same station before the trains with supplies and remounts had arrived.[22]

Kitchener had one important task to perform before he departed: to conclude the hunt for De Wet successfully he must have a secure supply line, as Roberts had put it to him.[23] In other words, there ought to be no disruptions or delays in receiving troops and especially supplies and telegrams. Although Kitchener knew the British sweep had driven the Boer commandos out of the region,[24] he took the precaution of leaving 400 men under the command of Major Wilmot at Welverdiend and half the CIV as well as 150 mounted infantry at Bank Station. Frederikstad was already guarded by 500 mounted Colonials.[25]

At 10:06 on Sunday 12 August, acting on intelligence he had received from an African, Kitchener set off due west from Welverdiend for Syferbult 27 km away, taking Broadwood and Little's cavalry brigades, Ridley's mounted infantry and Smith-Dorrien's infantry.[26] At 12:05 Kitchener's first supply train steamed into Welverdiend – two hours too late.

Further west, meanwhile, Methuen's advance guard had already caught up with the Boers. Just after Theron and his scouts had separated from the laager, De Wet had received a report from his remaining scouts that 'the English are coming, covering the length and breadth of the earth.'[27] The Boers were exhausted, and in no state to engage the British on an open plain.[28] But if they hesitated now they ran the risk of losing their wagons and carts, or falling into the hands of the enemy themselves. The order was immediately given to saddle up. 'In a flash the calm scene was transformed into a hive of activity. The wagons were spanned in, horses saddled up, rifles snatched and guns unlimbered. Food and utensils were hurriedly snatched up and we were on our way,' was how one burgher described the scene.[29] As usual a rearguard was formed with the artillery, while the laager raced north past Ventersdorp. De Wet hoped his pursuers would be exhausted before they could catch up.[30]

Suddenly a thick whirling cloud appeared in the distance. Methuen's 5th Imperial Yeomanry were charging in close formation for a low rise at Blesbokfontein, west of Syferbult. If they took the position, the Boer retreat would be in jeopardy.[31] But De Wet's rearguard beat them to it, unleashing a hail of Mauser and artillery fire.[32] The Boer gunners were so successful that soon the gun furthest back was brought forward to cover the flanks of the laager.[33] The Yeomanry were checked at a range of about 4 km, where they dismounted and advanced on foot, dropping to the ground at intervals to let rip at the Boers with their Lee Enfields. It soon became apparent to Methuen that he would have to await the arrival of his own guns, giving the laager more time to make good its escape. When the British artillery were finally brought in line with the Yeomanry, their horses drenched in sweat, the cavalry remounted and charged until forced to halt again. Then the process was repeated all over again.[34]

At one point the Yeomanry dashed ahead to execute a brilliant flanking manoeuvre to the left. Although their formation had been all but abandoned, they managed to put enormous pressure on the Boer rearguard, which allowed the 78th Battery – who were following hard on the cavalry's heels – to fire on the enemy at a range of 1 400 m. Borslap's 15-pounder was the first casualty, when a shrapnel shell from Captain Powell's gun burst over the horses that were attempting to pull it to safety. This incident took place on the farm Modderfontein. Five of the six horses were killed and the gun was overturned. Although a few burghers tried in vain to cut their corpses loose and save the gun, Borslap was forced to abandon it and flee with his comrades.[35] De Wet said later that if the 15-pounder had not remained in position for as long as it did, the Boer laager would probably have fallen into the hands of the enemy.[36] In any event, a Yeomanry squadron swiftly galloped up to take possession of the gun,[37] which turned out to be the same 15-pounder captured from Major-General Sir W.F. Gatacre's 77th Battery at Stormberg during the infamous Black Week.[38] By now it only had five shells left,[39] but was not damaged in any way. The British immediately hitched on some horses and by 14:00 its shells were raining on the Boers.[40]

The capture fired up the British forces and the 3rd and 5th Imperial Yeomanry now galloped hard for the left flank with pom-poms blazing, while the 10th Yeomanry advanced in the centre with Captain Powell's battery. The Colonials took the right flank.[41] The Boers were forced to abandon one position after another while their pursuers surged forward relentlessly. 'The fresh gun wheel tracks of the Boers lay on the veld before us,' Gaskell recalls. 'Here and there a piece of limber, corn, boxes and other impedimenta lay on the track where they had been dropped.'[42]

This contemporary painting by J.H. Thornely depicts the moment during the running skirmish between Methuen and De Wet on Modderfontein on 12 August 1900 when a British shrapnel shell burst over a Boer gun team, killing five horses and overturning the gun. Gunner Borslap was forced to abandon the gun and flee with his comrades. It turned out to be the same 15-pounder captured from Major-General Sir W.F. Gatacre's 77th Battery at Stormberg on 10 December 1899. (From: H.W. Wilson, After Pretoria: The Guerilla War, *Vol. I. London, 1901, p. 47)*

The open terrain on the farm Modderfontein certainly did not favour the Boers and it became clear that the rearguard did not have much fight in them.[43] The last wagons of the fleeing convoy took a terrible pounding, and later that afternoon nine containing food and ammunition were abandoned. This served to spur on the Yeomanry, although by now the pursuers and their quarry were both on their last legs, the Boer mules dropping dead in their tracks. Their oxen somehow managed to fare better, and the British later remarked that the Boers were particularly successful in getting the animals to trot at a brisk pace.[44] Throughout, the British continued to pound the tail-end of the laager and a number of oxen were slaughtered by shrapnel fire, forcing the Boers to torch another five ammunition wagons.[45]

Then De Wet came up with an ingenious plan. To check his pursuers and rob their animals of pasturage, he ordered his burghers to set alight the dry winter grass which covered the plain – De Wet's own version of the British scorched earth policy. Soon, with the help of a north wind, the entire veld was ablaze and the British found themselves advancing over a charred and blackened landscape.[46] But they showed no sign of giving up the chase.

A short while later the British shelling freed about 80 POWs, most of whom had been captured on 21 July when Theron seized a train while the Boer laager was crossing the Bloemfontein–Pretoria railway at Serfontein Siding. These prisoners were always transported at the rear of the convoy, whereas the four lieutenants Theron captured at Holfontein rode up ahead in a Cape cart. Until Theron's departure that morning, all these prisoners were guarded by his scouts. Now some Free Staters had taken over. Suddenly a shell burst near one of the wagons at the rear, wounding three POWs. In the ensuing confusion the Boer guards took to their heels. Most of the prisoners then leaped off the wagons and began to run back toward the British lines. A young burgher on horseback nearby raised his Mauser to finish them off, but a grizzly old veteran persuaded him to let them be. It was also felt this was a good opportunity to be rid of them.[47]

To the Yeomanry's great surprise they suddenly saw four British soldiers in a dreadful state running toward them.[48] The prisoners recounted their experiences at the hands of the Boers to Methuen. Steyn, they claimed, had instructed the guards to treat them well, but his request had fallen on deaf ears. Initially they were forced to accompany the laager on foot and were sjambokked if too exhausted to continue. Later they were allowed to ride on the wagons at the rear of the convoy. They complained of being badly fed and forced to subsist on a meagre diet of meat and mealies.

The prisoners naturally had a wealth of information of military importance to impart to their commanders. The Boers, they said, had five guns and although one POW had been told by a German doctor that their force numbered 7 500 in total, 'a very intelligent Australian escaped prisoner' counted the burghers at their last outspan and arrived at a figure of 4 000 men after Liebenberg joined the Free Staters. The Boers possessed plenty of Mauser ammunition, but felt their artillery should be abandoned because they were short of shells. The Boer horses were in excellent condition and each burgher possessed a spare mount. The burgers, the prisoners claimed, were all despondent, but De Wet ruled them with an iron hand. He was always in the thick of things, ever vigilant and brave in any circumstances. But he continually fed his burghers lies. One rumour he encouraged was that Louis Botha had ré-conquered Pretoria and taken 40 000 prisoners, including Lord Roberts. Steyn, on the other hand, appeared very ill, though reasonably cheerful. He never left the laager and was constantly under guard. The prisoners praised the Boer scouts, whom they constantly saw entering and leaving the laager, mostly clad in khaki. They informed Methuen that Theron and his scouts, whom they considered De Wet's best men, had formed the rearguard that morning, then departed from the laager in a different direction. From conversations with their captors, the prisoners firmly believed De Wet was heading north via Marico to join Louis Botha on the eastern front.[49]

But the most important information they imparted to Methuen was that De Wet was under enormous pressure and his oxen were virtually spent. If the pursuers could persevere, the entire Boer force would undoubtedly fall into their hands.[50] By now, however, the British horses too had reached the limits of endurance, and those pulling the artillery were about to collapse.[51] What was more, it was pitch dark already. Time to call it a day. Methuen gave the order to dismount and his force gratefully settled in for the night on the farm Doornplaat, 21 km north-east of Ventersdorp.

Kitchener had in the meantime reached a virtually impassable drift through the Mooi River on the farm Rietvlei. This caused a lengthy delay, with Smith-Dorrien and MacKinnon's infantry only completing the passage by noon the next day,[52] thus rendering them incapable of posing a threat to De Wet. But the cavalry brigades surged forward and that afternoon they heard Methuen's guns booming up ahead.[53]

Kitchener now managed to heliograph Methuen and was kept up to date with how the battle was progressing. By then, however, a joint offensive was out of the question: Kitchener had moved too far west to launch a flank attack from the east. Had the Chief of Staff been able to reach Methuen earlier at Rietvlei, he could have advanced north via Syferfontein and Uitkyk to surprise De Wet on his right flank or head off the fleeing laager.

Kitchener remained in the saddle until dark with Broadwood, Ridley and Little to set up camp at Schoolplaats on the farm Uitkyk, some distance behind Methuen's cavalry camp. His supply wagons only trundled in at 06:00 the next morning.[54] By then Hart's infantry was too far behind to be involved in the hunt any longer.

The battlefield where Methuen's cavalry bivouacked now provided a tranquil yet strangely compelling nocturnal spectacle. Here and there flames licked at stranded groups of wagons while the fire lines of the burning veld spread out into the distance. From time to time an ammunition cart exploded, lighting up the night sky with a shower of fireworks.[55] But the beauty of this scene could do little to allay the hunger and cold gnawing at the troops. 'We were camped in the middle of a level sea of black burned veldt with not a blade of grass for the horses,' recalled a Yeomanryman, 'far away from water, and with the convoy, with our food, drink and blankets, miles away in the darkness behind us.'[56] One officer from the Colonials settled in for the night next to a burning Boer wagon.[57]

Methuen's columns had been on De Wet's trail since 03:00, and despite engaging the enemy for the last six hours had covered more than 50 km.[58] At 23:00 the supply convoys finally arrived to offer succour to the exhausted troops.[59] Another infantry column, the 9th Brigade under Major-General Douglas, had set off from Frederikstad at noon, leaving 21 wagons behind to await supplies and follow later, while two companies with 130 wagons and the rest of the Colonials followed immediately. That evening this force only made it as far as Witpoortjie, south of Blesbokfontein – miles from De Wet and his immediate pursuers.[60]

Methuen was justifiably satisfied with the day's events. He had captured a few Boers, 16 wagons and one gun, which was now pressed back into Her Majesty's service after being AWOL for eight months. Furthermore, the only casualties on the British side occurred when one of their shells exploded near the wagons transporting the POWs. Methuen's tactic of sending his cavalry ahead and allowing the supplies and infantry to catch up later had paid off handsomely again. But his rapid advance also bore testimony to his unflinching dedication and extraordinary powers of endurance. After a hellish chase of over 50 km, braving an icy winter's night, then being flayed by the harsh South African sun, his troops had delivered an exemplary performance during a long and taxing battle. Only utter exhaustion prevented them from taking another step further.

However, the skirmish at Modderfontein was substantially different from Methuen's previous two encounters with De Wet: this time the outcome was decided on an open plain. This meant the artillery – in which the British vastly outnumbered the Boers – could be deployed more effectively as range and distance are much easier to calculate when a target is clearly visible. The disadvantage was of course that the Boers could see the attack coming and take evasive action in time, which explains why only one burgher was slightly wounded during the fierce skirmish.[61]

In some ways De Wet had played into Methuen's hands too. If he had not veered south-west to meet Liebenberg after crossing the railway, he would probably have maintained his lead on the British columns pursuing him. The detour added to the exhaustion of his men and animals, as well as putting him within striking distance of the enemy. But as we have seen, Liebenberg and his burghers had been staunch allies of the Free Staters, both by sending them supplies from the Gatsrand to their sanctuary at the Vaal and by keeping Methuen and Smith-Dorrien at bay. It would thus have been churlish and imprudent of De Wet to abandon them to their fate now that large British columns were sweeping across the countryside.

Notes

1. Gaskell, pp. 193–194.
2. TA, LRP 10: Methuen, 'Chase of De Wet', 11.8.1900, p. 40; compare PRO, WO 105, LRP 10 for the same source; *The Times,* 16.9.1900: 'Lord Methuen's Chase after De Wet'.
3. The *Natal Witness,* 9.10.1900: 'When De Wet Escaped: A Colonial's Story'.
4. TA, LRP 10: Methuen, 'Chase of De Wet', 7–11.8.1900, pp. 30–40; compare PRO, WO 105, LRP 10 for the same source; The *Natal Witness,* 9.10.1900: 'When De Wet Escaped: A Colonial's Story'. Sources such as Maurice and Grant, III, p. 350; Amery (ed.), IV, p. 426; Nierstrasz, II, Vol. 5, p. 1018, incorrectly state Methuen and the Colonial Division united on the evening of 10 August.
5. *The Times,* 26.9.1900: 'Lord Methuen's Chase After De Wet'.
6. TA, LRP 10: Methuen, 'Chase of De Wet', 12.8.1900, p. 42; compare PRO, WO 105, LRP 10 for the same source.
7. TA, LRP 10: Methuen, 'Chase of De Wet', 11.8.1900, p. 40; compare PRO, WO 105, LRP 10 for the same source.
8. TA, LRP 10: Methuen, 'Chase of De Wet', 11 and 12.8.1900, pp. 40–42; compare PRO, WO 105, LRP 10 for the same source; H.W. Wilson, *After Pretoria: The Guerilla War,* I, pp. 46–47; Maurice and Grant, III, pp. 350–351; The *Natal Witness,* 9.10.1900: 'When De Wet Escaped: A Colonial's Story'; Guest, p. 77; TA, WO Acquisition, JPE 5: Staff Diary, 1st Division, 11.8.1900, p. 66.
9. Maurice and Grant, III, p. 351; TA, LRP 10: Methuen, 'Chase of De Wet', 11.8.1900, p. 41; compare PRO, WO 105, LRP 10 for the same source.
10. TA, LRP 10: Methuen, 'Chase of De Wet', 12.8.1900, p. 42; compare PRO, WO 105, LRP 10 for the same source; Maurice and Grant, III, p. 351; CA, Map Collection, 3/34: Ventersdorp and surrounding areas, October 1905; CA, Map Collection 2/184: Farm Surveys, Potchefstroom, 1905. Any place names that do not appear in the sources consulted regarding the skirmishes of 12 August have been deduced by the author by surveying the terrain and consulting the abovementioned maps.
11. Gaskell, p. 195.
12. TA, LRP 10: Methuen, 'Chase of De Wet', 12.8.1900, p. 42; compare PRO, WO 105, LRP 10 for the same source.
13. Ibid; The *Natal Witness,* 9.10.1900: 'When De Wet Escaped: A Colonial's Story'.
14. TA, LRP 10: Methuen, 'Chase of De Wet', 12.8.1900, p. 42; compare PRO, WO 105, LRP 10 for the same source; Wilson, *After Pretoria,* I, p. 47; *The Times,* 26.9.1900: 'Lord Methuen's Chase After De Wet'; Gaskell, p. 196.

15. TA, LRP 40: No. H670, Kitchener – Roberts, 22:50, 11.8.1900, p. 65; compare PRO, WO 105, LRP 16 for the same source.
16. TA, LRP 44: no number, OC, West Yorks, Bank – Roberts, 10:20, 11.8.1900 re report Broadwood, p. 94; compare PRO, WO 105, LRP 15 for the same source.
17. TA, SA Telegrams IV: No. C3497, Roberts – Barton, 11.8.1900, p. 19; compare PRO, WO 108/241 for the same source.
18. TA, LRP 40: No. H400, Kitchener – Roberts, 04:00, 12.8.1900, p. 66; compare PRO, WO 105, LRP 16 for the same source.
19. TA, LRP 40: No. H676, Kitchener – Col. H.S. Rawlinson, 12.8.1900, p. 67; compare PRO, WO 105, LRP 16 for the same source.
20. TA, LRP 40: No. H678, Kitchener – Roberts, 10:00, 12.8.1900, p. 68; compare PRO, WO 105, LRP 16 for the same source.
21. TA, SA Telegrams IV: No. C3504, Roberts – Barton, Krugersdorp, 12.8.1900, p. 20; TA, SA Telegrams IV: No. C3510, Roberts – Kitchener, 12.8.1900, p. 20; compare PRO, WO 108/241 for the same sources.
22. TA, LRP 45: No. 919P, Barton, Krugersdorp – Roberts, 12:00, 12.8.1900, pp. 143–148; TA, LRP 45: No. 925P, Barton – Roberts, 13:40, 12.8.1900, p. 149; TA, LRP 45: No. 942P, Barton – Roberts, 13.8.1900, p. 159; compare PRO, WO 105, LRP 22 for the same sources.
23. TA, SA Telegrams IV: No. C3510, Roberts – Kitchener, 12.8.1900, p. 20; compare PRO, WO 108/241 for the same source.
24. TA, LRP 40: no number, Kitchener – Roberts, 13.8.1900, p. 74; compare PRO, WO 105, LRP 16 for the same source.
25. TA, LRP 40: no number, Kitchener – Roberts, 13.8.1900, p. 73; compare PRO, WO 105, LRP 16 for the same source; MacKinnon, p. 160.
26. TA, LRP 40: No. H678, Kitchener – Roberts, 10:00, 12.8.1900, p. 68; compare PRO, WO 105, LRP 16 for the same source; MacKinnon, p. 160; Smith-Dorrien, p. 233; Colvin and Gordon, p. 137.
27. Translator's note: Translated from original Dutch, De Wet, *De Strijd tusschen Boer en Brit,* p. 194. Compare De Wet, p. 143.
28. [Hintrager], p. 86.
29. Meyer, p. 149.
30. De Wet, p. 143.
31. Meyer, p. 150; [Hintrager], p. 85.
32. Wilson, *After Pretoria,* I, p. 47; *The Times,* 26.9.1900: 'Lord Methuen's Chase After De Wet'.
33. Meyer, p. 150; [Hintrager], pp. 85–86.
34. *The Times,* 26.9.1900: 'Lord Methuen's Chase After De Wet'; Gaskell pp. 196–197; Wilson, *After Pretoria,* I, p. 47; Danes, p. 1326; Van Schoor, 'Diaries of Jacob de Villiers', 13.8.1900, p. 28; [Hintrager], p. 86.
35. TA, LRP 10: Methuen, 'Chase of De Wet', 12.8.1900, pp. 42–43 and 58; compare PRO, WO 105, LRP 10 for the same source; *The Times,* 26.9.1900: 'Lord Methuen's Chase After De Wet'; *The Times,* 12.2.1901: 'In Retreat with De Wet'; Wilson, *After Pretoria,* I, p. 47; Gaskell, pp. 197–198; A. Conan Doyle, *The Great Boer War,* p. 488; Danes, pp. 1326–1327; Lombard, p. 70; De Wet, p. 144; TA, Acquisition 1250: D. de Witt, 'Die Trek naar die Bosveld', recorded by C.P. van der Merwe, p. 8; [Hintrager], p. 86.
36. De Wet, p. 144.
37. TA, LRP 10: Methuen, 'Chase of De Wet', 12.8.1900, p. 43; compare PRO, WO 105, LRP 10 for the same source. Maurice and Grant, III, p. 351 incorrectly claims the 10th Imperial Yeomanry took the gun.

38. TA, LRP 10: Methuen, 'Chase of De Wet', 12.8.1900, p. 43; compare PRO, WO 105, LRP 10 for the same source; Maurice and Grant, III, p. 351; TA, WO Acquisition, JPE 5: Staff Diary, 1st Division, 12.8.1900, p. 66; *The Times,* 26.9.1900: 'Lord Methuen's Chase after De Wet'; Wilson, *After Pretoria,* I, p. 47; Gaskell, p. 198; Amery (ed.), IV, p. 427; Doyle, p. 488; Danes, pp. 1326–1327; De Wet (p. 144) incorrectly stated it was a Krupp.
39. FA, WMC 155/82/1: Kriegs-Tagebuch, Dr O. Hintrager, p. 170; compare Oberholster, p. 109.
40. Danes, p. 1327; FA, WMC 155/82/1: Kriegs-Tagebuch, Dr O. Hintrager, p. 170; compare Oberholster, p. 109.
41. *The Times,* 26.9.1900: 'Lord Methuen's Chase After De Wet'; The *Natal Witness,* 9.10.1900: 'When De Wet Escaped: A Colonial's Story'; Wilson, *After Pretoria,* I, p. 47.
42. Gaskell, p. 197.
43. [Hintrager], p. 86.
44. Danes, p. 1327; *The Times,* 26.9.1900: 'Lord Methuen's Chase After De Wet'; Maurice and Grant, III, p. 351.
45. TA, LRP 10: Methuen, 'Chase of De Wet', 12.8.1900, p. 43; compare PRO, WO 105, LRP 10 for the same source; TA, LRP 40: No. H679, Kitchener – Roberts, 08:00 13.8.1900, p. 75; compare PRO, WO 105, LRP 16 for the same source; TA, SA Telegrams IV: No. C3542, Roberts – Ian Hamilton, 13.8.1900, p. 25; compare PRO, WO 108/241 for the same source; *The Times,* 26.9.1900, 'Lord Methuen's Chase After De Wet'; The *Natal Witness,* 9.10.1900: 'When De Wet Escaped: A Colonial's Story'; Wilson, *After Pretoria,* I, p. 47; Danes, p. 1327; TA, Leyds 730 (f): Telegram No. 102, Pott, Lourenço Marques – HTD, Machadodorp, 15.8.1900.
46. De Wet, p. 196; TA, Acquisition 1250: D. de Witt, 'Die Trek naar die Bosveld', recorded by C.P. van der Merwe, p. 8; Meyer, p. 151; Gaskell, p. 198.
47. [Hintrager], p. 86; *The Times,* 12.2.1901: 'In Retreat With De Wet'; TA, LRP 40: No. H679, Kitchener – Roberts, 08:00, 13.8.1900, pp. 75–76; compare PRO, WO 105, LRP 16 for the same source; TA, SA Telegrams IV: No. C3542, Roberts – Ian Hamilton, 13.8.1900, p. 25; compare PRO, WO 108/241 for the same source; Wilson, *After Pretoria,* I, p. 47; Gaskell, p. 201; Maurice and Grant, III, p. 351; compare De Wet, p. 144, who falsely implies he released the prisoners of his own free will.
48. Gaskell, p. 201.
49. TA, LRP 40: No. H679, Kitchener – Roberts, 13.8.1900, pp. 75–77; compare PRO, WO 105, LRP 16 for the same source; TA, MGP 16: Statement by cavalryman MacDonald, 16.8.1900, p. 149; The *Natal Witness,* 5.9.1900: 'With De Wet: A Prisoner's Account'; The *Cape Times,* 20.8.1900: 'De Wet's Army: A convoy 3 miles long'; Gaskell, p. 201. The prisoners had a lot of contact with their captors, who probably told them their open secrets.
50. Gaskell, p. 201.
51. Ibid., p. 199.
52. TA, LRP 40: no number, Kitchener – Roberts, 12.8.1900, p. 69; compare PRO, WO 105, LRP 16 for the same source; Smith-Dorrien, p. 233; MacKinnon, p. 161.
53. Colvin and Gordon, p. 137; Smith-Dorrien, p. 233.
54. TA, LRP 40: No. H679, Kitchener, Schoolplaats – Roberts, 08:00, 13.8.1900, pp. 75–76; compare PRO, WO 105, LRP 16 for the same source; Colvin and Gordon, p. 138.
55. Gaskell, p. 201; *The Times,* 26.9.1900: 'Lord Methuen's Chase After De Wet'; Wilson, *After Pretoria,* I, p. 47.

56. Gaskell, pp. 201–202; compare TA, LRP 10: Methuen, 'Chase of De Wet', 12.8.1900, p. 44; compare PRO, WO 105, LRP 10 for the same source; also compare The *Natal Witness,* 9.10.1900: 'When De Wet Escaped: A Colonial's Story'; Wilson, *After Pretoria,* I, p. 47; and Danes, p. 1327.
57. The *Natal Witness,* 9.10.1900: 'When De Wet Escaped: A Colonial's Story'.
58. TA, LRP 10: Methuen, 'Chase of De Wet', 12.8.1900, p. 44; compare PRO, WO 105, LRP 10 for the same source; The *Natal Witness,* 9.10.1900: 'When De Wet Escaped: A Colonial's Story'; Wilson, *After Pretoria,* I, p. 47; Gaskell, pp. 201–202; Danes, p. 1327.
59. TA, LRP 10: Methuen, 'Chase of De Wet', 12.8.1900, p. 44; compare PRO, WO 105, LRP 10 for the same source; Gaskell, p. 202; Danes, p. 1328.
60. TA, LRP 10: Methuen, 'Chase of De Wet', 12.8.1900, p. 44; compare PRO, WO 105, LRP 10 for the same source; Maurice and Grant, III, p. 351.
61. Lombard, p. 70.

CHAPTER FIFTEEN

Over the neck

METHUEN'S RELENTLESS PURSUIT from Modderfontein on 12 August certainly took its toll on the Boers: 16 wagons and 30 exhausted horses were abandoned on the battlefield that day.[1] Nightfall soon put a stop to the shelling, but otherwise offered the Boers little respite. De Wet now realised it was imperative to put as much distance as possible between himself and his pursuers to avoid another surprise attack. Not that the burghers themselves necessarily shared his sense of urgency. They had been on the run from large British columns since escaping from the Brandwater Basin – and engaged in rearguard actions virtually every step of the way. Now that they had crossed the Vaal River, the hunt had simply intensified. It is therefore small wonder that the burghers ran the risk of becoming apathetic or careless. 'Where are we going now?' or 'Whence are we retiring now?' were questions De Wet was continually plagued by, and on one occasion he replied tersely: 'To a place where you'll jump into the lion's mouth on one side and British shells on the other if you retire.'[2] By then it probably dawned on everyone they would have to shake off their pursuers at all costs.

With De Wet, Steyn and his councillors riding up ahead, the battle-weary burghers continued to trek north after their wagon convoy – the Witwatersrand now stretching before them. The advance guard remained in the saddle until they reached the farm Leliefontein at 22:00.[3] When the order was given to halt, men, horses, mules and oxen simply dropped to the ground where they stood, huddling together in one exhausted mass to snatch a few hours' sleep before being forced back on their feet.

Further back, the rearguard, including Liebenberg's Transvalers, followed in their footsteps, still torching the grass as they advanced. The artillery, which was probably at the tail-end of this group, only reached Leliefontein an hour after the advance guard had departed.[4] An hour later they too were back in the saddle, now veering right, then swinging north again to cross the Witwatersrand east of the main force on the road from Vlakfontein to Olifant's Nek.[5] From Leliefontein, the artillery hitched their guns to teams of 12 oxen, allowing their exhausted horses to canter alongside. It was a bitterly cold night and here and there small groups of

173

President Steyn, second from left, with an escort on the move during the first De Wet hunt, trying to keep out the winter cold. (From: L. Penning, De Oorlog in Zuid-Afrika, *Vol. 3, Rotterdam, 1903, p. 866)*

burghers could be seen warming themselves around the fires that dotted the countryside.[6] At sunrise on Monday 13 August, the rearguard outspanned for a few hours before setting off again. That evening, after a gruelling march, they reached a valley on the farm Middelfontein.[7] With the Witwatersrand behind them and the Magaliesberg looming up ahead, the Boers settled in for night.

In the meantime, the rearguard's change of course had caused great consternation among the Free Staters up ahead. Without the Transvalers to guide them, they left Leliefontein and continued north for another four hours to the farm Rietfontein, which belonged to the widow Bezuidenhout. Here De Wet and his burghers remained until after dawn before crossing the Witwatersrand,[8] continuing north along the Selons River to outspan on the afternoon of 13 August on the farm Roodewal, 20 km north-west of the rearguard and about the same distance west of Olifant's Nek.[9] By now man and beast were truly on their last legs. It was with great relief that the burghers threw off their clothes and leapt into the river to wash away the dust and grime which had accumulated during the long march, then slumped down exhausted next to their horses. 'I am now enjoying the first bit of rest I have had for many a day,' Jacob de Villiers noted in his diary.[10]

Ahead of the Boers, the Magaliesberg rose out of the Highveld and the bushveld beyond like a giant horseshoe of knotted cliffs and crowns running west from Pretoria parallel to the Witwatersrand for 120 km, then curving north-west around Rustenburg. With peaks reaching an altitude of 1 670 m and towering 430 m above the surrounding countryside, the range offered an ideal shelter from the enemy – provided a suitable crossing could be found. There were four principal passes – Silkaat's Nek and Commando Nek in the east near Pretoria, Magato's Nek north-west of Rustenburg and Olifant's Nek due south of the town. Of these, Olifant's Nek was of great strategic significance because for the next 60 km east – that is, until Commando Nek – there was no way of crossing the Magaliesberg. It was this pass which De Wet was heading for; if the British left it unoccupied he would be home and dry.

At the same time, tension was mounting in the camps of De Wet's pursuers. By the evening of Sunday 12 August, with the Witwatersrand and Magaliesberg up ahead, it looked as though the end of the hunt was finally in sight. By all accounts De Wet's oxen had been driven to the brink of extinction. And Methuen was still breathing down his neck, followed closely by Kitchener. If the British could force the Boer leader up against Olifant's Nek it would all be over. The night before, Roberts had assured Kitchener that Baden-Powell had been left behind at Commando Nek and that Ian Hamilton would 'occupy Olifant's Nek with a sufficient force, and be prepared to move with the rest wherever he may be required'.[11] At 14:00 Kitchener heliographed this information to Methuen.[12] De Wet was walking into a trap.

With this in mind,[13] Methuen took his mounted troops and artillery and set off with renewed vigour for Olifant's Nek at 03:00 on 13 August, as usual leaving the infantry and supply convoy behind. But first they had to find water; the men and their mounts had spent the night without so much as a drop to drink. Two-and-a-half hours later they were able to slake their thirst south of Leliefontein.[14] When it became light the pursuers noticed the veld was strewn with the baggage the Boers had tossed from their wagons like ballast dropped from an air balloon. Anything that could slow them down had been abandoned.[15] 'Here were cases of ammunition that had been wrenched open and out of which the Boers had taken a few cartridges. There were bundles of forage, with a few bites taken out of them; there were cases of shells; there were half-burnt camp fires, and broken-down waggons charred where their late owners had tried to fire them.'[16] From Leliefontein, Methuen chose the route De Wet and the advance guard had taken, unaware that they had parted company with the rearguard here. At noon, after covering 32 km in nine hours, the British dismounted at Rietfontein at the foot of the Witwatersrand for a well-earned rest[17] – just in time to see the Boer rearguard making a beeline for Olifant's Nek on the road from Vlakfontein.[18]

Further back at Uitkyk, Kitchener also set off at 03:00 on Monday 13

Lord Kitchener, Roberts' Chief of Staff, who took charge of the British forces encircling De Wet in the hills along the Vaal River. His command of the hunt in the Transvaal was unimpressive and produced few successes, save putting enormous pressure on De Wet with the large force at his disposal. (Transvaal Archives Depot, Pretoria)

August, taking Broadwood, Ridley and Little's mounted troops.[19] Their supplies were left behind. Methuen, fearful that De Wet might change direction if he felt he was being put under too much pressure, had requested that only Smith-Dorrien's columns and the 9th Brigade under Douglas should follow in the 1st Division's footsteps to Rietfontein. The rest of Kitchener's troops should be kept east of De Wet's trail. For some reason Kitchener refused to comply and by the afternoon of 13 August all his troops halted directly behind Methuen: Broadwood, Ridley and Little at Grootfontein, a farm south of Rietfontein,[20] and Smith-Dorrien and MacKinnon at Zwartplaats and Klippan.[21] Hart's infantry brigade set up camp further back.[22]

Methuen now faced two options. He could either set off in hot pursuit of the Boers he had just spotted, or choose a course that would close any other openings De Wet might find.[23] Methuen chose the latter for three reasons. Firstly, Kitchener's columns coincidentally found themselves in a position to block De Wet should he cunningly contrive to double back. The second, more significant reason was that Methuen was convinced Hamilton would be waiting for the Boers at Olifant's Nek. Thirdly, the British strongly suspected De Wet would veer west and head toward Brakfontein on the Eland's River,[24] where De la Rey with a number of Western Transvaal commandos had besieged Lieutenant-Colonel C.O. Hore's guard post of 300 Rhodesians and Australian Bushmen for more than a week. Methuen thus resolved to launch a night march to Buffelshoek southwest of Rustenburg to 'cut off De Wet from the western road, and enable the other columns to close in on him near Olifant's Nek'.[25]

At 01:00 on Tuesday 14 August, a clear moonlit night, Methuen's mounted troops set off at a brisk pace from Rietfontein with half a day's rations,[26] cheerfully anticipating De Wet's demise. 'This was positively his last appearance,' said one soldier. 'We were much elated and forgot how tired we were. De Wet caught, the war would be over, and *we* should have ended it! Our march of a week's continuous trekking at full speed, with little food and less sleep, would not have been wasted, and would go down to posterity as *the* march of the war. The general [Methuen] would be the hero of the hour, and well he deserved to be.'[27] The horsemen advanced along faint footpaths that crossed densely wooded hills or wound tortuously through nigh impenetrable valleys, but by now no feat of endurance could temper their triumph, which they knew was imminent. 'Every mile seemed to seal more certainly the fate of De Wet, who was dropping so many horses and oxen on the road that it was plain that his powers of flight were fast diminishing.' [28]

Shortly before dawn, some British scouts came across two Boers and took them prisoner; the enemy must be close by.[29] At 05:00 Methuen called a halt to establish his position. An hour later he received a report that the Boer laager was camped west of Olifant's Nek on a farm on the banks of the Selons River – Roodewal, as it turned out. Methuen now sent a messenger to Broadwood to inform the cavalry commander of his plans and point out the position of the Boer laager. He was ordered to push on to Olifant's Nek.[30] Broadwood heliographed back at 08:00 from Vlakfontein. He could see a long column of dust trekking past Buffelshoek, and had engaged De Wet's rearguard[31] further south near Elandsfontein. During the short skirmish Lieutenant-Colonel De Lisle and two British soldiers were slightly wounded.[32]

Still firmly convinced Olifant's Nek was in any case occupied by Hamilton, Methuen now kept to his chosen course. It was an oppressively hot morning as his column of horsemen crossed the high hills and dense winter grass of Kortfontein and Hartebeestfontein, following a broad curve to the west, then swinging north-east towards Selonskraal on the Selons River.[33] At 11:00 the British spotted a dust cloud near Buffelshoek through the smoke caused by De Wet's veldfires. This encouraged Methuen to continue north-east and at 13:00 he reached a position west of Doornlaagte. The road leading west from the foothills of the Magaliesberg was now blocked. But there was still no sign of the Boers. Methuen continued west through the dense bushveld until he reached Doornlaagte on the Selons. By 14:00 he controlled a number of westward routes;[34] it was just a matter of time before De Wet was driven into his arms and crushed. But at Doornlaagte some alarming rumours reached Methuen, confirmed a short while later and causing him to curse the day he decided to pin his hopes on Hamilton.

Hamilton, as we have seen, was drawn into the hunt for De Wet on 8 August while escorting Baden-Powell from Rustenburg to Pretoria. In July Baden-Powell, commanding a force of 2 200,[35] had suggested to Roberts that he allow himself to be besieged in Rustenburg.[36] But the chief was not in favour of the idea.[37] Methuen was sent to clear the road to Rustenburg in mid-July. Then, on 23 July, he raced south toward Potchefstroom to join the efforts to pin De Wet against the Vaal River, leaving behind a force of 1 300 men under Kekewich to hold Olifant's Nek. Now Hamilton was sent to accompany Baden-Powell back to headquarters with a large force of 6 000 men.[38] On the evening of 6 August, Kekewhich evacuated Olifant's Nek[39] and the following morning the combined force of 9 500 men under Hamilton's command left Rustenburg for Pretoria.[40] Roberts hoped this force would be able to block De Wet in the region of Commando Nek or the Crocodile River in the Magaliesberg should the Boer leader manage to slip past Methuen at the Vaal.[41]

At the same time, in keeping with Roberts' policy not to man small, isolated posts,[42] Lieutenant-General Sir F. Carrington was ordered to evacuate his troops from Zeerust and Ottoshoop and move them to Mafeking.[43] Roberts obviously wanted to concentrate his forces on the eastern front, but these measures served to substantially weaken the British position in the Western Transvaal. For now the Magaliesberg west of Commando Nek, including Rustenburg, as well as Zeerust and Ottoshoop further west and Klerksdorp and Potchefstroom further south, were no longer in British hands.

On 8 August Hamilton set up camp at Bokfontein on the northern slopes of the Magaliesberg near Commando Nek.[44] There he received Roberts' telegram outlining De Wet's movements further south at the Vaal, and the order to cross the Magaliesberg and double back along the southern slopes as far as Hekpoort. From there De Wet should be delayed at all costs until Kitchener and Methuen could finish him off from the rear.

The next morning, Thursday 9 August, Hamilton's war machine rolled into action. First he sent Colonel T.E. Hickman and part of his column – 400 men and a section of pom-poms – over Commando Nek to fetch supplies from Wesfort outside Pretoria.[45] Then Hamilton himself trekked over the neck with the rest of his columns – the 1st Battalion King's own Scottish Borderers, 1st Battalion Border Regiment, 2nd Battalion Royal Berkshire Regiment, 1st Battalion Argyll and Sutherland Highlanders, 22nd Field Hospital, half the 6th Brigade Bearer Company, two 5-inch guns, two 6-inch Howitzers and the Royal Canadian Artillery's 'D' Battery[46] – to bivouac at Grootplaats.[47] Baden-Powell also crossed the neck but advanced to Rietfontein, closer to Pretoria.[48]

9 August was a day of great uncertainty for Roberts. After Methuen engaged De Wet at Leeuwfontein, it looked at one stage as though the

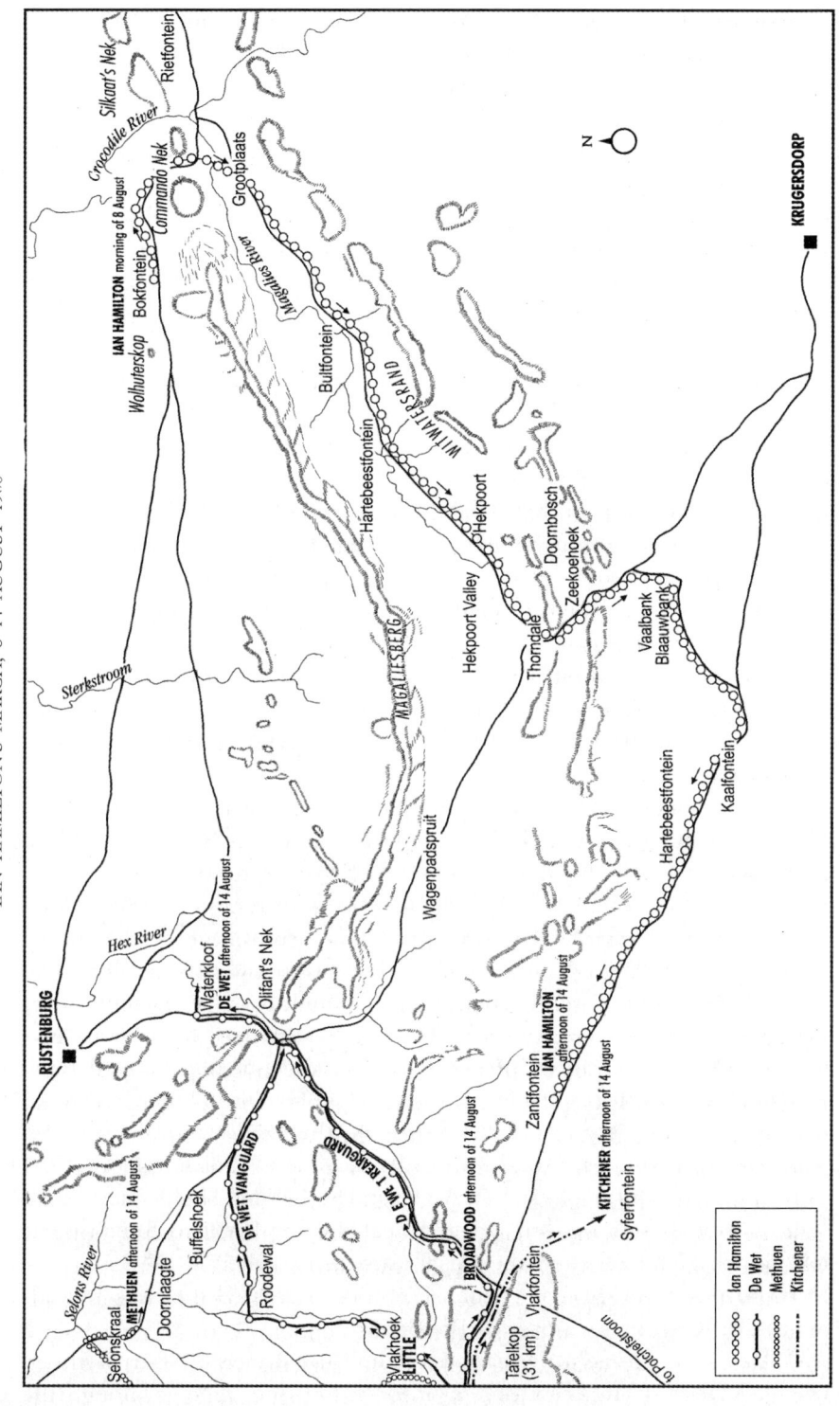

OVER THE NECK 179

Boers wanted to cross back into the Free State at Lindeque's Drift. Then they were seen heading north-east in the direction of Krugersdorp and Commando Nek. Roberts thought they might even try to cross to the eastern front, taking a route south of Johannesburg.[49] He therefore ordered Hamilton to remain where he was until further intelligence was received. In any case, Hamilton was not planning on going anywhere until his supply convoy arrived from Wesfort.[50] The next day Roberts was still in the dark. De Wet's pursuers seemed to be chasing phantoms across the veld and Hamilton was again told to stay put.[51] These unavoidable delays would cost the British dearly when dealing with the mercurial De Wet.

Then, at 09:45 on Saturday 11 August, Hamilton received his first solid piece of intelligence in days: De Wet was heading north, probably towards Olifant's Nek. 'We require troops in that direction, and you should move to the westward at once towards Hekpoort,' Roberts cabled him. 'To-morrow you will probably be at Zeekoehoek, where the road from Krugersdorp passes through the Witwatersberg. Barton will be instructed to meet you at that point to-morrow afternoon or Monday morning. A cable cart will accompany them to enable you to communicate freely with us. The Hekpoort valley is full of supplies and you should help yourself freely from the well-stocked farms. Baden-Powell's force with the battalion that Methuen left at Olifant's Nek should remain for the present at Commando Nek.'[52] Any mention of the urgency of occupying Olifant's Nek was conspicuously lacking.

An hour later, Hamilton – accompanied by Brigadier-General B.T. Mahon and his cavalry and Kekewich with his Loyal North Lancashire Regiment – set off for the Hekpoort valley, leaving the 1st Border Regiment behind at Commando Nek.[53] The 400 fresh remount mules which had arrived the previous day were a welcome acquisition for the supply and baggage cart drivers,[54] but Hamilton's convoy now uncoiled for some 11 km.[55] This undoubtedly caused a substantial loss of mobility. Soft sand and a number of small drifts also greatly hampered his advance and by sunset his column had only progressed 21 km to set up camp at Bultfontein. Mahon's cavalry scouted up ahead in the direction of Hartebeestfontein, every now and then driving off sharpshooters who sniped at them from the Magaliesberg.[56] The supply convoy only trundled into camp later that night.[57]

Roberts sent two more telegrams to Hamilton that Saturday, both of which encouraged him to act on his own initiative. In the first he was instructed to 'send on such a force as you think sufficient to occupy Oliphant's Nek' as soon as he reached Zeekoehoek, 'with as many days' supplies as you can spare. You will then be available to move about with the remainder of your troops in any direction that may be required. It is important that we should prevent De Wet from moving north of the Magaliesberg, and if he can be delayed anywhere for a couple of days Methuen and Kitchener should close in upon him.'[58] 'Will do my best,' came Hamilton's curt reply.[59]

The second telegram informed Hamilton that De Wet had crossed the Krugersdorp–Potchefstroom railway at 08:30 that morning near Welverdiend. 'Your force should just be in the right place to-morrow to head him should he go north and prevent him going north-east, or to follow him should he go west,' he assured Hamilton.[60] Since Roberts had no way of knowing for certain that De Wet was indeed making a beeline for Olifant's Nek, he naturally left it up to Hamilton to decide on the most appropriate course of action in the field. The result was that Hamilton failed to appreciate the urgency implicit in Roberts' orders. Furthermore, the chief's report concerning De Wet's movements served to put Hamilton's mind at ease. But the information turned out to be false. As we have learned, De Wet's main force had in fact crossed the line more than 12 hours earlier; the Boers spotted near Welverdiend that morning were merely a small group of burghers at the tail-end of the rearguard. Hamilton's biggest blunder, however, was not to take Roberts' previous order to occupy Olifant's Nek seriously enough. 'If I have to go west,' he replied to the chief, 'I propose not to lose time by occupying Olifant's Nek, as my westward movement would cover that pass, which is sure to be held [by Boers], and is now strongly fortified.'[61] There was therefore a weak link in Roberts' strategy even before Hamilton's departure from Grootplaats in the direction of Olifant's Nek. What made matters worse was the fact that the British generals pursuing the Boers from the south – Kitchener, Broadwood, Methuen and Smith-Dorrien – were under the impression, created by Roberts' second telegram, that Hamilton 'will occupy Olifant's Nek with a sufficient force, and be prepared to move with the rest to wherever he may be required'.[62] Their subsequent movements thus rested on this supposition.

At 08:30 on Sunday 12 August, Hamilton continued his ponderous advance.[63] Some Africans had told him that the Boers of the Hekpoort valley were preparing to fight the British further ahead at Vaalbank. But when Hamilton's column appeared, a force of some 300 burghers fled to the north and west,[64] although a number of snipers remained in the mountains and farmhouses nearby, wounding and killing a few British soldiers.[65] This invisible enemy did not impede the British advance, but their presence posed a continual threat to the soldiers on the march.

The Hekpoort valley is particularly fertile and there was no shortage of water,[66] but Hamilton used his supplies sparingly and the troops were put on three-quarter rations that day[67] – a decision which did not endear him to his men. 'Reduction of rations has a weakening effect on a man morally as well as physically,' a soldier from the King's Own Scottish Borderers remarked. At 16:00 the column set up camp in the region of Doornbosch and Thorndale, while Mahon's brigade advanced some distance further up to Zeekoehoek.[68]

That night Hamilton had to choose between two possible routes further west. The first led directly to Olifant's Nek 42 km away via Wagenpadspruit along the southern slopes of the Magaliesberg. The disadvantage here was that the troops would be hemmed in between the Magaliesberg and the Witwatersberg. This would limit their view. Hamilton chose the second route – south over the Witwatersberg, then west toward Tafelkop along the road to Mafeking, which Jameson had used for his abortive raid almost five years before. This road offered an unimpeded view to the west and to some degree controlled the three roads leading to Olifant's Nek from the south.[69] Of more significance was the fact that Roberts believed De Wet might head north-west to Eland's River, where Hore's garrison was still under siege.[70] The report Hamilton received that De Wet had crossed the railway at Welverdiend and was continuing north-west seemed to confirm this.[71] Furthermore, Hamilton was firmly convinced Olifant's Nek was securely in the hands of the Western Transvalers and that a westward advance to Tafelkop would automatically head off De Wet.[72]

At 08:30 on Monday 13 August, Hamilton's cavalry set off, first negotiating a difficult crossing over the Witwatersberg,[73] then veering west toward Tafelkop. Mahon's cavalry had been sent ahead and were now racing down 'Jameson's road' to cut off De Wet,[74] unaware that the Boer leader was already beyond their reach. Later that afternoon Mahon halted a short distance west of Hartebeestfontein, still some way from Tafelkop. And by then the burghers were bathing in the cool waters of the Selons River some 20 km from Olifant's Nek.

At 15:00 that afternoon, Hamilton halted further back at Kaalfontein with the main force, awaiting the arrival of Barton's supply convoy, without which he was apparently unable to proceed.[75] Early that morning Hamilton had sent Kekewich and his battalion toward Krugersdorp to escort the convoy back to base. They were accompanied by 200 mounted infantry, a section of pom-poms and a section of the RFA's 75th Battery.[76] The convoy had left the town at 05:00 with provisions for eight days, biscuits for five, bully beef for one and oats for the horses and mules for two days. Kekewich intercepted the wagon train at 13:00 and led it back to Kaalfontein.

Throughout these proceedings, communication between Hamilton and his chief in Pretoria and Barton in Krugersdorp left much to be desired. While Hamilton was advancing down the Hekpoort valley, Roberts was able to keep in touch with him by sending telegraphs to Baden-Powell at

Field-Marshal Lord Roberts, who had to co-ordinate the first De Wet hunt from his headquarters in Pretoria with information that was often more than 24 hours old. The chase of De Wet delayed his eastern offensive along the Pretoria–Delagoa Bay railway line. (Transvaal Archives Depot, Pretoria)

Rietfontein, where a cable station had been established on 9 August,[77] and these were passed on by messenger.[78] But because Hamilton was behind the Witwatersberg, he could not be reached by Barton.[79] Once Hamilton crossed the Witwatersberg, the situation was reversed; Barton could reach him but Baden-Powell could not. Now Roberts was obliged to communicate with Hamilton via Krugersdorp, and Barton was ordered to send him a cable cart.[80] The problem was that the information Roberts received from De Wet's pursuers was in most cases 24 hours or even two days old, which often rendered his orders to Hamilton obsolete.[81] For some reason Hamilton failed to take this into account.

That day, 13 August, Roberts sent Hamilton a telegram informing him De Wet was still on his way to Tafelkop.[82] This was encouraging news; it showed he had anticipated the chief's plans in using his own initiative to head in the same direction.[83]

At 07:00 the next morning, Tuesday 14 August, Hamilton informed Roberts that his main force was moving toward Zandfontein and that Mahon's brigade would probably reach Tafelkop later that afternoon.[84] The degree to which Olifant's Nek had become of secondary importance to Roberts is further illustrated by a telegram he sent Hamilton the same day: 'Information received from Hore at Elands River, dated the 10th instant, shows that he was still holding out ... it is essential that you should reach Elands River post in sufficient strength, and as speedily as possible, to ensure Hore's relief. This operation will exactly fit in with the object you have hitherto had in view, namely to prevent De Wet from reaching Elands River post before you.'[85] Hamilton apparently did receive intelligence which led him to reconsider his strategy. For that very morning he had cabled Roberts to suggest that Baden-Powell should march along the

Olifant's Nek in the Magaliesberg mountain range, from the south – the focal point of both Boer and British attention in the dramatic closing stages of the first De Wet hunt. The neck was free of British troops and the Boer Pimpernel eluded his pursuers yet again, and would live to fight another day.

northern slopes of the Magaliesberg toward Rustenburg and close in on Olifant's Nek from the north. But the telegram only reached Pretoria at 16:30, and by then it was already too late.[86]

De Wet must have been pleased when his scouts returned to his camp on the Selon's River on Monday 13 August with the news that the British had kindly left Olifant's Nek in Boer hands. At midnight his convoy left Roodewal and headed east.[87] After a slow march, the advance guard finally reached the foot of the Magaliesberg at 07:00 on Tuesday 14 August. There they were joined by the members of the rearguard who had set out from their camp at Middelfontein at midnight.[88] Jacob de Villiers recorded the event in his diary: 'At daybreak I saw one of the finest pictures I had seen for many a day. It was a crisp moonlight night and we halted to allow the waggons to catch up with us. Next to the road there was a patch of long grass. Here man and horse sank down and slept. Men were lying down next to horses, one sleeping mass of confusion. X [De Wet] was amongst them with his horse in his hand, while Louis[89] was lying with his boyish face upturned to the moon together with two others, all in a bunch.'[90]

That afternoon the Boers saddled up and crossed the neck, where a commando of Pretorians led by Commandant K. Boshoff was stationed to see the Free Staters safely over.[91] The Transvalers were greeted by an impressive spectacle. 'One long laager crossed over Olifant's Nek,' recalled one. 'With all its wagons, carts and oxen it was the largest commando I had ever laid eyes on.'[92] While Boshoff's commando rode back toward Middelfontein to meet the furthest wagons and escort them to safety,[93] the advance guard forded the Hex River to outspan on President Kruger's farm Waterkloof.[94] De Wet had eluded his pursuers yet again, and would live to fight another day.

In the British camp, the news of De Wet's umpteenth miraculous escape was met with profound disappointment, sheer disbelief and outright anger – especially among Methuen's men, who for more than a week had borne the brunt of the hunt. 'When it became apparent that the pass to which they had hunted their quarry was undefended, the rage and vexation of officers and men was unrestrained, loud and long,' was how H.M. Guest, who accompanied the 1st Division, described the general mood.[95]

Lieutenant-General Ian Hamilton, whose lack-lustre performance south of and parallel to the Magaliesberg mountain range gave De Wet the opportunity to escape over Olifant's Nek on 14 August 1900, causing the hunt to fail in its closing stages. (From: H.W. Wilson, With the Flag to Pretoria, *Vol. II, p. 509)*

Methuen could not hide his disappointment either. 'I could see the column of dust showing the last wagons going over the pass,' he wrote in his report. 'De Wet had escaped through the one outlet which I felt sure was occupied and which I forced De Wet to make for.'[96] For Kitchener and his troops these were equally bitter tidings.[97]

Although Roberts, and especially Hamilton, were clearly responsible for the débâcle, Hamilton tried to shift the blame onto Methuen and Kitchener in his report two days later: 'I have ascertained beyond doubt that De Wet went through Magato Pass and occupied Olifant's Nek yesterday from the north-east,'[98] he claimed a day after admitting that De Wet had in fact escaped over Olifant's Nek.[99] Roberts, too, tried to exonerate himself. 'I share your great disappointment that De Wet has given us the slip, and deeply regret that Olifant's Nek was not closed,' he wrote to Kitchener on 16 August. 'I told Ian Hamilton to send troops there for this purpose, but he seemed to think it unnecessary. It is most unfortunate.'[100] Most unfortunate indeed.

Notes

1. TA, LRP 40: No. H679, Kitchener – Roberts, 13.8.1900, p. 75; compare PRO, WO 105, LRP 16 for the same source.
2. Oberholster, p. 114.
3. De Wet, p. 144; Nierstrasz, II, Vol. 6, p. 1019.
4. [Hintrager], pp. 86–87.
5. TA, Acquisition 235 (I): Memoirs of Johannes P. Botha, recorded 23.8.1945, p. 39; TA, LRP 10: Methuen, 'Chase of De Wet', 13.8.1900, p. 45; compare PRO, WO 105, LRP 10 for the same source.
6. [Hintrager], pp. 86–87.
7. Ibid.; TA, Acquisition 235 (I): P. Botha, p. 39.
8. Van Schoor, 'Diaries of Jacob de Villiers', 13.8.1900, p. 28.
9. Ibid.; CA, Map Collection, 3/26: Rustenburg and surrounding areas, Jackson Map, October 1905; CA, Map Collection, 2/547: Rustenburg, Jackson Map, 1903. De Villiers confuses the Eland's River with its tributary, the Selons River.
10. Van Schoor, 'Diaries of Jacob de Villiers', 13.8.1900, p. 28.
11. TA, SA Telegrams IV: No. C3482, Roberts – Smith-Dorrien, Broadwood et al. 11.8.1900, p. 17; compare PRO, WO 108/241 for the same source.
12. TA, LRP 40: no number, Kitchener – Roberts, 23:15, 12.8.1900, p. 70; compare PRO, WO 105, LRP 16 for the same source; Smith-Dorrien, p. 233; compare *The Times*, 26.9.1900: 'Lord Methuen's Chase After De Wet'.
13. TA, LRP 10: Methuen, 'Chase of De Wet', 11.8.1900, p. 40 and 13.8.1900, p. 45 and 14.8.1900, p. 48; compare PRO, WO 105, LRP 10 for the same source.
14. TA, LRP 10: Methuen, 'Chase of De Wet', 13.8.1900, p. 45; compare PRO, WO 105, LRP for the same source; *The Times*, 26.9.1900: 'Lord Methuen's Chase After De Wet'; Danes, p. 1328; Guest, p. 77; Gaskell, p. 203.
15. Gaskell, p. 203.
16. Danes, p. 1328.

17. TA, LRP 10: Methuen, 'Chase of De Wet', 13.8.1900, p. 45; compare PRO, WO 105, LRP 10 for the same source; *The Times,* 26.9.1900: 'Lord Methuen's Chase After De Wet'; Gaskell, p. 204; Danes, p. 1328; Wilson, *After Pretoria,* I, p. 48; Maurice and Grant, III, p. 352.
18. TA, LRP 10: Methuen, 'Chase of De Wet', 13.8.1900, p. 45; compare PRO, WO 105, LRP 10 for the same source; *The Times,* 26.9.1900: 'Lord Methuen's Chase After De Wet'.
19. TA, LRP 40: no number, Kitchener – Roberts, 23:15, 12.8.1900, p. 71; compare PRO, WO 105, LRP 16 for the same source; Smith-Dorrien, p. 234; Maurice and Grant, III, p. 352.
20. TA, LRP 40: No. H680, Kitchener – Roberts, 05:00, 14.8.1900, p. 78; compare PRO, WO 105, LRP 16 for the same source; Colvin and Gordon, p. 138.
21. Smith-Dorrien, p. 234; MacKinnon, p. 161.
22. Romer and Mainwaring, pp. 135–136.
23. Danes, p. 1328.
24. TA, LRP 40: no number, Kitchener – Roberts, 12.8.1900, p. 70; compare WO 105, LRP 16 for the same source.
25. TA, LRP 10: Methuen, 'Chase of De Wet', 13.8.1900, p. 46; compare PRO, WO 105, LRP 10 for the same source.
26. TA, LRP 10: Methuen, 'Chase of De Wet', 14.8.1900, p. 47; compare PRO, WO 105, LRP 10 for the same source; *The Times,* 26.9.1900: 'Lord Methuen's Chase After De Wet'; Guest, p. 77; Danes, p. 1328.
27. Gaskell, pp. 206–207.
28. Maurice and Grant, III, pp. 352–353.
29. Danes, p. 1328.
30. TA, LRP 10: Methuen, 'Chase of De Wet', 14.8.1900, p. 47; compare PRO, WO 105, LRP 10 for the same source.
31. TA, LRP 10: Methuen, 'Chase of De Wet', 14.8.1900, p. 48; compare PRO, WO 105, LRP 10 for the same source; Colvin and Gordon, p. 138.
32. TA, LRP 40: No. H683, Kitchener – Roberts, 15.8.1900, p. 83; compare PRO, WO 105, LRP 16 for the same source; TA, LRP 10: Broadwood, 'Chase of De Wet', 15.8.1900, p. 102; compare PRO, WO 105, LRP 10 for the same source. Broadwood incorrectly states the events took place on the 15th instead of the 14th.
33. Compare Methuen's own map in PRO, WO 105, LRP 10: Methuen, 'Chase of De Wet'.
34. TA, LRP 10: Methuen, 'Chase of De Wet', 14.8.1900, pp. 47–48; compare PRO, WO 105, LRP 10 for the same source.
35. TA, LRP 43: No. B270, Ian Hamilton – Roberts, 9.8.1900, p. 176; compare PRO, WO 105, LRP 16 for the same source.
36. TA, LRP 36: No. 39K, Baden-Powell, Rustenburg – Roberts, 2.7.1900, p. 258; compare PRO, WO 105, LRP 15 for the same source; TA, SA Telegrams III: No. C3136, Roberts – Baden-Powell, 31.7.1900, p. 115; compare PRO, WO 108/240 for the same source.
37. TA, SA Telegrams III: No. C3280, Roberts – Carrington, Zeerust, 4.8.1900, p. 131; compare PRO, WO 108/240 for the same source.
38. TA, SA Telegrams III: No. C3341, Roberts – Hamilton, 6.8.1900, p. 138; compare PRO, WO 108/240 for the same source.
39. Maurice and Grant, III, p. 141.
40. TA, LRP 43: No. 966, Hamilton – Roberts, 6.8.1900, p. 154; compare PRO, WO 105, LRP 16 for the same source; E.H. Collen, *Diary and Sketches of the South African War,* p. 92.

41. TA, SA Telegrams III: No. C3359, Roberts – Kitchener, 11:00, 7.8.1900, p. 142; compare PRO, WO 108/240 for the same source.
42. TA, SA Telegrams III: No. C3280, Roberts – Carrington, Zeerust, 4.8.1900, p. 131; compare PRO, WO 108/240 for the same source.
43. Amery (ed.), IV, p. 360.
44. Collen, p. 93; CA, Map Collection, 2/547: Rustenburg, Jackson Map, 1903; terrain visited by author.
45. TA, LRP 43: No. 992, Hamilton – Roberts, 13:20, 9.8.1900, p. 179; TA, LRP 43: No. 993, Hamilton – Roberts, 16:30, 9.8.1900, p. 180; TA, LRP 43: No. 1002, Hamilton – Roberts, 11:00, 10.8.1900, p. 182; compare PRO, WO 105, LRP 16 for the same sources.
46. Amery (ed.), IV, p. 394.
47. W. Home, *With the Border Volunteers to Pretoria*, p. 134; Collen, p. 93.
48. Maurice and Grant, III, p. 349.
49. TA, SA Telegrams IV: No. C3411, Roberts – Hamilton, 10:00, 9.8.1900, p. 7; compare PRO, WO 108/241 for the same source.
50. TA, LRP 43: No. B270, Hamilton – Roberts, 07:10, 9.8.1900, p. 176; compare PRO, WO 105, LRP 16 for the same source.
51. TA, SA Telegrams IV: No. C3434, Roberts – Hamilton, 10.8.1900, p. 11; compare PRO, WO 108/241 for the same source.
52. TA, SA Telegrams IV: No. C3471, Roberts – Hamilton, 07:45, 11.8.1900, pp. 15–16; compare PRO, WO 108/241 for the same source.
53. TA, LRP 43: No. 1012, Hamilton – Roberts, 11:05, 11.8.1900, p. 161; compare PRO, WO 105, LRP 16 for the same source.
54. Collen, p. 94.
55. TA, LRP 43: no number, Hamilton – Roberts, 12.8.1900, p. 169; compare PRO, WO 105, LRP 16 for the same source.
56. TA, LRP 43: No. 1016, Hamilton – Roberts, 16:30, 11.8.1900, p. 165; compare PRO, WO 105, LRP 16 for the same source; TA, LRP 41: No. 7, Baden-Powell, Rietfontein – Roberts, 21:00, 11.8.1900, p. 31; compare PRO, WO 105, LRP 15 for the same source; Collen, p. 94; Home, p. 134; CA, Map Collection, 2/547: Rustenburg, Jackson Map, 1903.
57. TA, LRP 43: no number, Hamilton – Roberts, 12.8.1900, p. 169; compare PRO, WO 105, LRP 16 for the same source; Collen, p. 94.
58. TA, SA Telegrams IV: No. C3476, Roberts – Hamilton, 11.8.1900, p. 16; compare PRO, WO 108/241 for the same source; Maurice and Grant, III, p. 354.
59. TA, LRP 43: No. 1014, Hamilton – Roberts, 11.8.1900, p. 163; compare PRO, WO 105, LRP 16 for the same source.
60. TA, SA Telegrams IV: No. C3483, Roberts – Hamilton, 11.8.1900, p. 17; compare PRO, WO 108/241 for the same source; Maurice and Grant, III, p. 355.
61. TA, LRP 43: No. 1015, Hamilton – Roberts, 11.8.1900, p. 164; compare PRO, WO 105, LRP 16 for the same source.
62. TA, SA Telegrams IV: No. C3482, Roberts – Smith-Dorrien, Broadwood and others, 11.8.1900, p. 17; compare PRO, WO 108/241 for the same source; also compare TA, LRP 10: Methuen, 'Chase of De Wet', 13.8.1900, p. 45; compare PRO, WO 105, LRP 10 for the same source as last mentioned; and H.L. Smith-Dorrien, p. 233.
63. Collen, p. 94; Home, p. 136.
64. TA, LRP 43: No. 30, Hamilton – Roberts, 12:05, 12.8.1900, p. 167; compare PRO, WO 105, LRP 16 for the same source.
65. Home, pp. 135–136; Collen, p. 94.

66. Collen, p. 94; Home, p. 136.
67. Home, p. 134.
68. TA, LRP 43: no number, Hamilton – Roberts, 12.8.1900, p. 169; compare PRO, WO 105, LRP 16 for the same source; Collen, p. 94.
69. Maurice and Grant, III, p. 356; CA, Map Collection, 2/931: Acquisition E 69, Jeppe Sheet 4, Map of the Transvaal, 1899. The Witwatersberg, south of and parallel to the Magaliesberg, should not be confused with the Witwatersrand further south.
70. TA, SA Telegrams III: No. C3359, Roberts – Kitchener, 7.8.1900, p. 142; compare PRO, WO 108/240 for the same source.
71. TA, SA Telegrams IV: No. C3483, Roberts – Hamilton, 11.8.1900, p. 17; compare PRO, WO 108/241 for the same source.
72. TA, LRP 43: No. 1015, Hamilton – Roberts, 11.8.1900, p. 164; compare PRO, WO 105, LRP 16 for the same source.
73. Collen, pp. 94–95.
74. TA, LRP 43: No. 1018, Hamilton – Roberts, 09:30, 13.8.1900, p. 170; compare PRO, WO 105, LRP 16 for the same source.
75. TA, LRP 43: No. 1020, Hamilton – Roberts, 19:00, 13.8.1900, p. 171; compare PRO, WO 105, LRP 16 for the same source.
76. TA, LRP 43: No. 1018, Hamilton – Roberts, 09:30, 13.8.1900, p. 170; compare PRO, WO 105, LRP 16 for the same source.
77. R.L. Hippisley, *History of the Telegraphic Operations during the War in South Africa*, p. 64.
78. TA, SA Telegrams IV: No. C3551, Roberts – Baden-Powell, 13.8.1900, p. 27; compare PRO, WO 108/241 for the same source.
79. TA, LRP 45: No. 933P, GOC, Krugersdorp – Roberts, 12.8.1900, p. 154; TA, LRP 45: No. 948P, GOC, Krugersdorp – Roberts, 13.8.1900, p. 161; compare PRO, WO 105, LRP 22 for the same sources.
80. TA, LRP 45: No. 930P, GOC, Krugersdorp – Roberts, 12.8.1900, p. 153; compare PRO, WO 105, LRP 22 for the same source; TA, SA Telegrams IV: No. C3551, Roberts – Baden-Powell, 13.8.1900, p. 27; compare PRO, WO 108/241 for the same source.
81. For example, compare TA, SA Telegrams IV: No. C3403, Roberts – Hamilton, 8.8.1900, p. 6; TA, SA Telegrams IV: No. C3483, Roberts – Hamilton, 11.8.1900, p. 17; TA, SA Telegrams IV: No. C3542, Roberts – Hamilton, 13.8.1900, p. 25; compare PRO, WO 108/241 for the same sources.
82. TA, SA Telegrams IV: No. C4542, Roberts – Hamilton, 13.8.1900, p. 25; compare PRO, WO 108/241 for the same source.
83. TA, LRP 43: No. 1024, Hamilton – Roberts, 10:00, 14.8.1900, p. 173; compare PRO, WO 105, LRP 16 for the same source.
84. TA, LRP 43: No. 1027, Hamilton – Roberts, 07:00, 14.8.1900, p. 171a; compare PRO, WO 105, LRP 16 for the same source.
85. TA, SA Telegrams IV: No. Q3563, Roberts – Hamilton, 14.8.1900, p. 29; compare PRO, WO 108/241 for the same source; also compare Collen, p. 95.
86. TA, LRP 43: No. 1027, Hamilton – Roberts, 11:20, 14.8.1900, p. 174; compare PRO, WO 105, LRP 16 for the same source.
87. Van Schoor, 'Diaries of Jacob de Villiers', 13.8.1900, p. 28.
88. [Hintrager], p. 89.
89. Probably Louis Botha, son of Assistant Chief Commandant Philip Botha.
90. Van Schoor, 'Diaries of Jacob de Villiers', 13.8.1900, p. 28.
91. TA, Acquisition 235 (I): Memoirs of Johannes P. Botha, 23.8.1945, p. 39; D.S. van Warmelo, *Mijn Commando en Guerilla Commando-Leven*, pp. 77–78.

92. Van Warmelo, p. 78.
93. TA, Acquisition 235 (I): Memoirs of Johannes P. Botha, 23.8.1945, p. 39.
94. Van Schoor, 'Diaries of Jacob de Villiers', 13.8.1900, p. 28; J.H.C. Penzhorn, 'Lebenslauf und Erinnerungen aus dem Leben von Johannes Heinrich Carl Penzhorn', p. 22. The laager site according to Penzhorn's description was pointed out to the author by Mr E.E. Penzhorn from Waldstille, Kroondal. De Wet, p. 145; Lombard, p. 70 and some later writers incorrectly name the river as the Crocodile River.
95. Guest, p. 78.
96. TA, LRP 10: Methuen, 'Chase of De Wet', 14.9.1900, p. 48; compare PRO, WO 105, LRP 10 for the same source.
97. TA, LRP 40: No. H683, Kitchener – Roberts, 15.8.1900, p. 81; compare PRO, WO 105, LRP 16 for the same source; TA, LRP 10: Broadwood, 'Chase of De Wet', 15.8.1900, p. 102; compare PRO, WO 105, LRP 10 for the same source; Colvin and Gordon, p. 138; MacKinnon, p. 164; Romer and Mainwaring, pp. 137–140; Smith-Dorrien, p. 234.
98. TA, WO Acquisition, JPE 5: Staff Diary, Hamilton's Force, 16.8.1900, p. 74.
99. TA, LRP 43: No. 1031, Hamilton – Roberts, 15:00, 15.8.1900, p. 184; compare PRO, WO 105, LRP 16 for the same source.
100. TA, SA Telegrams IV: No. Q3617, Roberts – Kitchener, 16.8.1900, p. 37; compare PRO, WO 108/241 for the same source.

CHAPTER SIXTEEN

Wandering about the bush

DE WET AND HIS BURGHERS now found themselves in another natural fortress – the mountains curving north around Rustenburg forming a protected valley with Magato's Nek in the west and Olifant's Nek to the south as the only access routes. Although sustained mobility had saved De Wet's bacon, he realised his men and animals needed a decent rest before going to war again.[1] But the danger existed that fresh troops would be sent against him from Pretoria and he was forced to take precautions against a surprise attack.

On Wednesday 15 August he sent the burghers with the weakest horses – a force of 1 200 and a good number of Cape carts commanded by Commandant Stefanus 'Rooi Faans' van Vuuren of Heilbron – north into the bushveld 'to provide the horses with better grazing and rest'.[2] He also ordered the artillery to position themselves on Olifant's Nek with three guns and a pom-pom to keep an eye on enemy movements, while Liebenberg's men covered Magato's Nek.[3] The rest of the Free Staters remained on Kruger's farm to enjoy the rest they so sorely needed. Throughout Steyn did his best to boost his burghers' morale. 'Our president is here,' Philip Botha reported to his brother Louis Botha. 'He is remarkably cheerful and a constant source of encouragement to our burghers, even joining them in their perils.'[4] Nonetheless, De Wet and Steyn fully appreciated their predicament: it would be extremely difficult to find their way back to the Free State when beyond the necks the countryside was crawling with the enemy. Furthermore, a report reached them on the morning of Thursday 16 August that Silkaat's Nek further east was now also in British hands, which meant the plan to visit Kruger might have to be abandoned.[5]

On the afternoon of Tuesday 14 August, the British pursuers ground to a halt in a semi-circle around the Boers: Ian Hamilton was camped at Zandfontein, 24 km due south of Olifant's Nek, while Mahon had halted near Rietfontein, about 30 km south-west of the neck. Methuen and his mounted troops remained at Doornlaagte, 20 km north-west of the Boers, while his infantry commanded by Douglas was on its way from the south. Kitchener, Smith-Dorrien's infantry, Dalgety's Colonials and MacKinnon's

CIV bivouacked near Mahon at Syferfontein, about 30 km from Olifant's Nek, with Broadwood and Little's cavalry brigades further west. Hart, with his infantry brigade, was at Groenfontein, furthest away to the south.[6]

Though the hunt had left their troops and horses utterly exhausted, the British were not given a moment's respite. Hore was still holding out with 300 men against the Western Transvalers at Eland's River and Roberts ordered Methuen and Little to relieve him.[7] At 06:00 on Wednesday 15 August, Kitchener, who had taken over from Methuen, headed west with Broadwood, Little and Ridley, while Smith-Dorrien and MacKinnon's infantry brought up the rear. With the appearance of the vast British columns, the Western Transvalers soon fled, raising a siege Hore had endured for almost two weeks,[8] suffering 67 casualties, including 12 killed.[9]

In the meantime, Methuen decided to go after De Wet again, this time with Hamilton's help. On Thursday 16 August he launched a furious assault on Magato's Nek with his 1st Division and the Colonials.[10] Liebenberg's men were no match for this force and fled in disarray, retiring to Rustenburg that afternoon. De Wet now decided Kruger's farm was no longer safe and ordered his burghers to inspan and saddle up before the animals had been given sufficient time to rest. By sunset on 16 August, a column of 1 200 Free Staters set off along the road running from Rustenburg to Pretoria north of and parallel to the Magaliesberg.[11] Liebenberg and his burghers followed, using a parallel road further north.[12] As a decoy, De Wet left a small Griqualand-West commando led by Field-Cornet J.A. van Zyl at the neck with the Free State artillery.[13] It worked, because by the time Hamilton took Olifant's Nek on the afternoon of Friday 17 August after a cautious advance,[14] the Free Staters had already emerged much further east, near Commando Nek.[15]

Methuen had intended to hasten east after De Wet, but unbeknown to him Kitchener had hijacked his supply convoy for his own troops. This left Methuen with a mere four days' provisions for his men and two-and-a-half days for his animals from 15 August. He thus considered his capture of Magato's Nek as his last action in the hunt for De Wet and on Friday 17 August headed west for Zeerust, arriving virtually without supplies.[16]

De Wet now planned to cross the Magaliesberg again over Commando Nek and return to the Free State,[17] but the moment he appeared near the neck, Baden-Powell raised the alarm. Roberts, who assumed De Wet and Steyn were heading for the eastern front, immediately grasped the Free Staters' unenviable position[18] and set about hatching plans to pin them against the Pretoria–Pietersburg railway with the help of Hickman, Paget and Baden-Powell.[19] Ian Hamilton and Mahon were to advance post haste from the west with their mounted troops and do their utmost to delay De Wet from behind. But the British forces soon proved unsuited to waging war in the bushveld and for a number of days Hamilton and Mahon un-

Commandant Lukas Steenekamp of the Heilbron commando. When De Wet returned to the Free State from north of the Magaliesberg, Steenekamp was ordered to take the Free Staters and their wagons deep into the Transvaal bushveld. Once their horses and oxen had recovered they were to return to the Free State. (From: P.H.S. van Zyl, Die Helde-Album, *Johannesburg, 1944, p. 140)*

successfully tried to surprise the Free Staters from the west, and Paget from the south.[20]

As it happened, when De Wet's scouts reported that Commando Nek was occupied, he was obliged to abandon his plan[21] to cross the Magaliesberg there. Early on Saturday 18 August, he swung due north to outspan a few hours later at the Crocodile River,[22] at the site of the present day town of Brits. A war council was convened to take stock of the situation and decide on a course of action. The result was that General Liebenberg, who along with his burghers had accompanied the Free Staters since 11 August, returned to the area around Magato's Nek.[23] The Free State force was split into three groups. Steyn and his councillors would leave the same day with a small escort to meet Kruger at Watervalonder,[24] while De Wet himself would take a small force and return to the Free State. This would serve to draw attention from Steyn and the rest of the Free Staters, who would remain in the bushveld. They numbered about 900 men, now led by Commandant L. Steenekamp of Heilbron. He had been ordered to take the burghers and their wagons deep into the bushveld, as far north as the area around Warmbaths and Nylstroom, to allow their horses and oxen to rest.[25] Once the animals had recovered they were to return to the Free State. 'Rooi Faans' van Vuuren received the same orders further back near Rustenberg.[26]

But more importantly, De Wet felt the time was ripe for the new mobile warfare, of which he and Danie Theron had become such outstanding exponents, to be organised in his homeland.

On Monday 20 August, De Wet took 246 horsemen – including his staff, Philip Botha of the Vrede commando, Michael Prinsloo of Bethlehem and Alex Ross of Frankfort, a number of their burghers, as well as

Captain Gideon Scheepers and his scouts – and set off southward, leaving the rest of the Free Staters behind at Zoutpan.[27]

The following day, Tuesday 21 August, De Wet approached the Magaliesberg near Commando Nek again, but it soon became apparent his commando was hemmed in from all sides. To his west, Kitchener's vanguard, on its way to Pretoria after relieving Hore, was approaching Wolhuter's Kop, where Brigadier-General Ridley was encamped with 500 mounted infantry.[28] From the east, at Silkaat's Nek, Major Urmston of the Sutherland Highlanders was heading in his direction with a convoy for Hamilton, who was now north-east of De Wet.[29] And Commando Nek, where De Wet had hoped to break through to the south, was now guarded by Colonel Barter with a large force and artillery. It appeared as though he was well and truly trapped in a semi-circle against the Magaliesberg.

There was one escape route: directly ahead of the Boers, 8 km to the west of Commando Nek, a steep goat track led over the mountain. De Wet asked an African if the path was ever used. Seldom by people, came the reply, but baboons often crossed there. De Wet needed no more encouragement and soon his commando was scrambling over the rugged footpath.[30]

On its arrival at Wolhuter's Kop, Kitchener's vanguard did in fact spot a row of horsemen notched against the skyline,[31] but only discovered their identity when it was too late. That night De Wet and his small following were safely south of the Magaliesberg and the next morning set off for home, leaving the chimney stacks and mine dumps of the Witwatersrand far behind.

Roberts only learned the next day, 22 August, that De Wet had split from the main force and slipped through his fingers again.[32] The futility of the operation in the bushveld gradually began to dawn on him. 'It is only a waste of men and power wandering about the bush after an enemy who will never be captured,' he fumed to Kitchener. On 27 August Roberts withdrew his forces,[33] thus officially calling off the first De Wet hunt – six days after the Boer Pimpernel had bolted.

Notes
1. De Wet, p. 144.
2. Ibid.
3. [Hintrager], p. 91; Badenhorst, p. 47; TA, Leyds 759: Letter, Liebenberg – L. Botha, 17.8.1900, pp. 57–58; Maurice and Grant, III, p. 357.
4. TA, Leyds 758 (a): Telegram, no number, P. Botha, Kruger's Magaliesberg farm – L. Botha, no date.

WANDERING ABOUT THE BUSH 195

5. Van Schoor, 'Diaries of Jacob de Villiers', 16.8.1900, p. 29.
6. TA, LRP 43: No. 1021, Hamilton – Roberts, 14.8.1900, p. 171a; compare PRO, WO 105, LRP 16 for the same source; TA, LRP 10: Methuen, 'Chase of De Wet', 14.8.1900, p. 48; compare PRO, WO 105, LRP 10 for the same source; Collen, p. 95; Smith-Dorrien, p. 234; MacKinnon, p. 163; Colvin and Gordon, p. 138; Maurice and Grant, III, p. 351. Hart at that point was north of Leliefontein on Groenfontein with his infantry brigade.
7. TA, SA Telegrams IV: No. Q3588, Roberts – Kitchener, Hamilton and Methuen via Barton, Krugersdorp, 15.8.1900, p. 33; compare PRO, WO 108/241 for the same source.
8. Colvin and Gordon, p. 138; Smith-Dorrien, p. 234; MacKinnon, p. 163; Amery (ed.), IV, pp. 428–429.
9. PRO, WO 105, LRP 10: Report, Lt-Col. C.O. Hore, Defence of Eland's River and Advance from Mafeking, casualty list.
10. TA, LRP 10: Methuen, 'Chase of De Wet', 15 and 16 August, pp. 51–52; compare PRO, WO 105; LRP 10 for the same source; Maurice and Grant, III, p. 360.
11. Van Schoor, 'Diaries of Jacob de Villiers', 17.8.1900, p. 29; De Wet, p. 145; [Hintrager], p. 92.
12. TA, Leyds 759: Letter, Liebenberg – L. Botha, 17.8.1900, p. 58.
13. C.C.J. Badenhorst, p. 47; TA, LRP 43: No. 1040, Hamilton – Roberts, 18.8.1900, p. 187; compare PRO, WO 105, LRP 16 for the same source.
14. TA, LRP 43: No. 1040, Hamilton – Roberts, 18.8.1900, p. 187; compare PRO, WO 105, LRP 16 for the same source; Collen, p. 96; Home, pp. 142–143; Maurice and Grant, III, p. 360; Badenhorst, p. 47.
15. Van Schoor, 'Diaries of Jacob de Villiers', 18.8.1900; Meyer, p. 152; Van Warmelo, p. 79.
16. TA, LRP 10: Methuen, 'Chase of De Wet', 15 and 17.8.1900, pp. 50 and 53; compare PRO, WO 105, LRP 10 for the same source; TA, South African Dispatches II: Roberts' Account, 14 June to 10 October 1900, p. 10; compare PRO, WO 32/8000 for the same source.
17. De Wet, p. 145; Van Schoor, 'Diaries of Jacob de Villiers', 17.8.1900, p. 29.
18. TA, SA Telegrams IV: No. C3659, Roberts – Hamilton via Barton, Krugersdorp, 18.8.1900, p. 42; compare PRO, WO 108/241 for the same source.
19. TA, SA Telegrams IV: by telephone, No. 400, Roberts – Hickman near Hornsnek via Wesfort and heliograph, 10:00, 18.8.1900, p. 42; TA, SA Telegrams IV: by telephone, No. 401, Roberts – Paget, Doornpoort via Wonderboomfort and heliograph, 10:00, 18.8.1900, p. 42; TA, SA Telegrams IV: No. C3679, Robert – Baden-Powell, 19:15, 18.8.1900, p. 44; compare PRO, WO 108/241 for the same sources; TA, WO Acquistion: History of the Railways During the War in South Africa, I, p. 44.
20. Compare for example TA, South African Dispatches II: Roberts' Account, 14 June to 10 October 1900, p. 11; compare PRO, WO 32/8000 for the same source; TA, LRP 13: Report of Movement of Maj.-General Baden-Powell's Column, 17–27 August, 1900, pp. 58–64.
21. De Wet, p. 145.
22. Van Schoor, 'Diaries of Jacob de Villiers', 18.8.1900, p. 30; Van Warmelo, p. 80; Lombard, p. 71; [Hintrager], p. 97, incorrectly claims that the trek took place that afternoon; CA, Map Collection, 2/547: Rustenburg, Jackson Map, 1903; terrain visited by author.
23. Meyer, p. 153; also compare General De la Rey's order in this regard to General Liebenberg (TA, De la Rey Collection 7: Letter, Ferreira pro De la Rey, Brakkloof – Liebenberg, 21.8.1900, p. 20).

24. TA, Leyds 731 (d): Telegram no. 87, Wilkens, Machadodorp – Editor, *Leydenburger*, 25.8.1900; Van Schoor, 'Diaries of Jacob de Villiers', 18–27.8.1900, pp. 30–33; [Hintrager], pp. 96–121; Lombard, pp. 72–74.
25. De Wet, p. 146; TA, G.S. Preller Collection 81: Die Oranje-Vrystaat-kommando's 1858–1915, Frankfort-kommando, p. 2; Nierstrasz, II, Vol. 6, p. 1028.
26. TA, Leyds 73 (e): Telegram No. 114, Steyn, Watervalonder – Van Vuuren, district Rustenburg, 27.8.1900.
27. De Wet, pp. 146–147; TA, LRP 43: no number, Paget, Klipdrif – Roberts, 21.8.1900, p. 33; compare PRO, WO 105, LRP 21 for the same source; Nierstrasz, II, Vol. 6, p. 1032; TA, G.S. Preller Collection 81: Die Oranje-Vrystaat-kommando's 1858–1915, Frankfort-kommando, p. 2.
28. TA, LRP 43: no number, Kitchener – Roberts via Barter, Rietfontein, 21.8.1900, p. 215; compare PRO, WO 105, LRP 16 for the same source; Penzhorn, p. 23; Smith-Dorrien, p. 236; MacKinnon, p. 170; Nierstrasz, II, Vol. 6, p. 1033.
29. TA, LRP 43: no number, Barter, Rietfontein – Chief of Staff, 20.8.1900, p. 206; TA, LRP 43: no number, Barter – Chief of Staff, 21.8.1900, p. 209.
30. De Wet, p. 147; Maurice and Grant, III, p. 363.
31. TA, LRP 43: no number, OC, Commando Nek – Roberts re information by Captain Legge, 20:45, 21.8.1900, pp. 215–216; Smith-Dorrien, p. 236; Penzhorn, p. 23.
32. TA, LRP 43: No. C109, Paget – Roberts, 22.8.1900, p. 42; compare PRO, WO 105, LRP 21 for the same source; TA, South African Dispatches II: Roberts' Account, 14 June to 10 October 1900, p. 11; compare PRO, WO 32/8000 for the same source.
33. TA, SA Telegrams IV: No. C3953, Roberts, Belfast – Kitchener, 27.8.1900, p. 76; compare PRO, WO 108/241 for the same source.

EPILOGUE

The most spectacular guerrilla warfare modern times have seen

BY LEADING THE FREE STATE FORCES, President Marthinus Steyn and his councillors over Olifant's Nek with a large wagon convoy in tow on 14 August 1900, Christiaan de Wet had successfully thwarted the first concerted attempt by the British to hunt him down. Lord Roberts was thereby robbed of the opportunity, as he saw it, to bring the war to a speedy conclusion.

De Wet was successful in two further respects. Firstly, during his sojourn at the Vaal River he realised the primary objective of the trek out of the Brandwater Basin, namely to renew raids on British supply and communication lines. Although General Piet Viljoen was prevented from leading his commando south-west toward Vereeniging to embark on joint offensives with De Wet, General Piet Liebenberg did manage to collaborate with Danie Theron and his scouts by attacking the Potchefstroom–Krugersdorp railway line while the TVK simultaneously wreaked havoc on the rail connection between Bloemfontein and Pretoria. Roberts' extended supply line through the Free State was particularly hard hit. Secondly, Steyn was able to keep the promise he made three months earlier to visit President Paul Kruger. The two leaders eventually met on 25 August at Watervalonder in the Eastern Transvaal.

Since the hunt and surrounding events have been accounted for in the preceding chapters, it is now possible to highlight certain aspects of this watershed period in the Anglo-Boer War in an attempt to explain De Wet's success.

A striking feature of the British campaign was defective communication – a serious handicap in dealing with a foe as swift as De Wet. Each and every commander in the field should have known precisely where and when supplies and co-operation could be expected, and been informed immediately of De Wet movements. In reality, these requirements were seldom met. In fact, shortcomings in this regard often assumed absurd

197

proportions and on numerous occasions De Wet was granted freedom of movement at a critical stage. The wily Boer commander exploited each opportunity to the full. As the hunt progressed from the rolling veld of the Free State to the high hills hugging the Vaal River at Vredefort and the smouldering winter grass of the Western Transvaal, an increasing number of British columns took up the chase. Sooner or later each of their commanders caused, or fell prey to, communication foul-ups, leading to delayed or plainly inappropriate tactics. At a crucial stage of the chase and as a result of poor communications, the columns under Kitchener pursuing the Boer Pimpernel from the south were led to believe that Olifant's Nek was occupied by Ian Hamilton – when in fact both Hamilton and Roberts had lost sight of that precious goal. By the time De Wet was safely over Olifant's Nek, the British communication system was in disarray. C.M. Bakkes correctly includes uninterrupted contact among commanders in the field in his list of requirements for a successful campaign.[1]

Another characteristic of the hunt, closely related to faulty communication, was a British scouting system which was not up to scratch. Unreliable communication meant British commanders were forced to depend on their own reconnaissance efforts to determine the movements of the enemy. But even when the scouts succeeded, their information often failed to reach the other commanders in the field. It is true that De Wet's pursuers managed to find his trail again even when they were thrown completely off course. But *The Times History* justly criticises the British for lacking an organised scouting system.[2] Furthermore, British soldiers had little or no scouting experience, whereas the Boers had more often than not learned the ropes from an early age on the South African veld. As De Wet[3] and Jacob de Villiers[4] remarked, British scouting methods left much to be desired and created the impression that scant heed was paid to the need for caution or the art of remaining invisible to the enemy.

The Boer reconnaissance system was a different kettle of fish. While it is true that lax scouting occasionally caused the Boers to be taken by surprise, De Wet could generally expect consistently outstanding work from his scouts. Furthermore, sympathetic local farmers made his task easier. The highly capable Gideon Scheepers and his corps of about 30 scouts were apparently always posted at the vanguard to determine the safest route through the British columns lying in wait for the Boers. As the American war correspondent Howland noted: 'The British would learn his [De Wet's] direction and station a column across his path, only to find out later that De Wet's watchful and extraordinary efficient scouts had given ample warning to enable their commander so to change his direction as to make necessary a new disposition of the forces seeking to check him.'[5] On two occasions the Boers successfully crossed British-controlled railway lines thanks to efficient scouting, mainly by Scheepers and his corps.

Commandant Danie Theron, the 'ears and eyes of De Wet', also contributed a great deal to Boer successes during the hunt. The task of the Theron Verkenningskorps was primarily to protect the Boer force from the rear and perform reconnaissance work in the direction of their pursuers. With the odd exception, they acquitted themselves of their task admirably throughout. In fact a characteristic of the hunt, and the reason De Wet was able to evade the columns sent to capture him with relatively minor losses, was the protection afforded by Theron's rearguard actions. As soon as the enemy attacked, the Boer rearguard was placed in Theron's capable hands while the wagon convoy and most of the burghers hastily departed. Whenever possible, Theron divided his corps and the remaining burghers into groups of 12, positioned almost 1 km apart to confront the enemy in a long chain that could not easily be driven into a corner by artillery fire. The Boers' extended battle line also meant the flank attacks commonly used by the British cavalry were difficult to execute successfully. Furthermore, because the Boers fired in volleys where possible, it was hard to establish their strength at any given point. Then, as soon as the enemy fire grew too fierce, the Boer rearguard simply fell back a short distance to offer resistance from their new positions. When Theron finally judged that the laager was out of danger, he would order a general withdrawal after the wagons. Theron himself would usually stay behind with a handful of scouts to keep an eye on the enemy's movements. This group would rejoin the main force as soon as everything was safe. The TVK also ensured De Wet's most important objective in leaving the Brandwater Basin was met by repeatedly wrecking the Bloemfontein–Pretoria railway and disrupting British communications, during the period when the Boer forces tarried at the Vaal River for two weeks. The train captures at Serfontein Siding and Holfontein Siding were two highlights of this period.

Supply problems experienced by the British also contributed to De Wet's success. The columns converging on the Free State commander were constantly plagued by difficulties in feeding and equipping their troops – from the time Clements' concern over supplies prevented Hunter from tightening his cordon around the Boers at Brandwater in time, to Kitchener's delay at Welverdiend Station while waiting for provisions to arrive from Krugersdorp. This repeatedly robbed the pursuers of precious time. De Wet, unsurprisingly, capitalised on these delays. Then, to crown it all, supply problems obliged Methuen to call off the hunt at precisely the point when the British intended to marshal their forces in one last attempt to pounce on their exhausted prey. These difficulties were compounded by having a large army move across the vast African veld where railways, which could have been used to bring up the necessary supplies, were often sorely lacking. Indeed, whenever the British were in fact able to rely on rail traffic, Boer operations along the line simply exacerbated the problem.

It must be said that the British commanders and their troops were certainly not short of courage and perseverance. Nevertheless, their plans were no match for the masterful De Wet. Clements chose the wrong moment to prioritise the acquisition of supplies, while Paget was guilty of neglecting to send out patrols or post sentries. Although Hunter was the victim of unenviable circumstances, he nevertheless delivered an exemplary performance. But Broadwood, who led the hunt in the Free State, was unable to rob De Wet of the initiative. It must, however, be taken into account that his horses were not always in fine fettle. Kitchener, who took over the hunt at the Vaal, also failed in this respect. Furthermore, his command of the hunt in the Transvaal was unimpressive and produced few successes, save putting enormous pressure on De Wet with the large force at his disposal. Smith-Dorrien did not possess De Wet's gift of putting himself in his opponent's shoes, while the supreme commander Lord Roberts could hardly be said to have put his stamp on the hunt from his headquarters in Pretoria, with one or two exceptions. Admittedly, this was caused by communication problems.

The most lack-lustre performance of the hunt was delivered by Ian Hamilton. His actions gave De Wet the opportunity to escape over Olifant's Nek, causing the hunt to fail in its closing stages. Roberts probably put too much faith in Hamilton, whom he regarded one of the most promising officers in the British Army.[6] Not even his failure at Olifant's Nek led to a fall from grace. On the contrary, a year later Roberts recommended to Kitchener, who by then was the supreme commander of the British forces in South Africa, that Hamilton be appointed his Chief of Staff. Kitchener readily complied. [7]

Howland unfairly branded Methuen's actions during the hunt 'failures in the field'.[8] By contrast *The Times History* regarded the 1st Division commander as the heart and soul of the campaign: 'Often disappointed, he made few mistakes and never for a moment would he let his quarry go.' The smallest successes were ascribed to Methuen's 'dogged tenacity'.[9] Although greatly hampered by faulty communication, in which he too played a part, Methuen put his stamp on the hunt across the grey and wintery Western Transvaal. It was the stamp of resolution and indefatigable effort. In nine days, with only one day's rest, his troops covered 250 km while engaging the enemy on three occasions. The last 130 km were completed in 57 hours, during which time the important skirmish on 12 August took place. Methuen's infantry also managed to complete the last 107 km in 66 hours.[10] Methuen praised his troops to Roberts, expressing the hope that 'the distance marched under very trying conditions may show we endeavoured to the best of our power to carry out your orders to capture

Commandant De Wet'.[11] In this he must be given his due. It must, however, be borne in mind that his slow advance towards the Vaal River gave De Wet that small opening which he needed to slip away.

But at the end of the day, the successes De Wet enjoyed during the hunt can primarily be ascribed to his own personality. His powerful leadership made great demands on his burghers, yet inspired fierce loyalty. 'He rarely told them what he meant them to do,' declares *The Times History*, 'they simply had to follow.'[12] His sheer determination – 'in any great undertaking, the first requirement is: must!'[13] – undoubtedly gripped the imagination of his followers. Furthermore, he was able to win their trust through his own actions, clear insights and calm demeanour. De Wet was also a master strategist. His ability to exploit mistakes made by the enemy, swiftly sum up any situation and turn it to his own advantage, and his habit of surfacing or attacking when and where his enemies least expected, ensured continued success. His remarkable mobility, despite the encumbrance of a large wagon laager, and brilliant scouting conducted by De Wet himself and his scouts, certainly contributed.

Furthermore, the safety of his burghers was precious to De Wet, and night and day he would use his formidable knowledge of the veld to ensure they came to no harm.[14] De Wet was also gifted with a kind of premonition which allowed him to pre-empt the enemy, thereby winning the trust of his burghers. C.M. Bakkes considers this another prerequisite for success in the field.[15] On a number of occasions De Wet responded to British manoeuvres just at the right moment and was able to lead his followers to safety. As he himself remarked: 'A Boer only becomes a formidable foe when one succeeds in surrounding him.'[16] But above all, as a result of the abovementioned qualities, De Wet managed to keep the initiative throughout the hunt – another prerequisite for achieving success in the field.[17] Methuen, and to a far lesser degree Broadwood, on occasion threatened to rob De Wet of the initiative, but he stubbornly refused to relinquish it. This not only allowed De Wet to set the tone for the hunt, obliging the British commanders to plan their operations around his movements, but also put him in a position to fend off the enemy and cross Olifant's Nek with virtually his entire force intact. De Wet did not consider his success a personal achievement. That his burghers had placed their trust in him was enough reward. For the Boer leader was deeply religious, and regarded himself an instrument in the hands of God,[18] without whom he would have been unable to continue the struggle.[19]

The hunt was a turning point in the war – a watershed in Boer strategy. Henceforth the conventional warfare of set-piece battles became a thing of the past and the Boer commanders committed themselves whole-heartedly to mobile and guerrilla warfare. When Roberts swept through the Free State to capture the Transvaal capital on 5 June 1900, he unwittingly set the pattern for the rest of the war. His rapid advance rendered the most important British rail and telegraph connection – the line between Bloemfontein and Pretoria – as well as small isolated British units far from the railway, extremely vulnerable. This situation did not escape the ever-vigilant De Wet. He realised the British were dependent on the railway line for communication, for rapid troop deployment and for the transport of supplies. He therefore set himself the task of continually disrupting British rail and telegraph connections and attacking the small, isolated detachments. From 31 May 1900, De Wet and his fellow Free State commanders achieved numerous successes in the execution of this plan. The large booty captured at Roodewal in the Free State on 7 June was a highlight of this period. With the realisation that De Wet stood in the way of a speedy British victory, Roberts sent a number of mobile columns in hot pursuit, trapping De Wet and the Free State forces in the Brandwater Basin. But De Wet had no intention of allowing a British cordon to strangle the Boers and decided the Free State forces should trek out of the basin in three groups to renew raids on the railway. This led both to the first De Wet hunt and the surrender of Marthinus Prinsloo with half the Free State forces. With this disheartening news, De Wet was saddled with the important task of inspiring his burghers to take up the struggle anew. In this he succeeded admirably. He not only achieved the primary goal of the trek out of the Brandwater Basin by repeatedly launching attacks on the Bloemfontien–Pretoria railway toward the end of July and the beginning of August, but also demonstrated to his burghers how a mobile war could be waged while the enemy controlled the greater part of their country.

After an absence of almost three weeks, De Wet reappeared at Van Vuuren's Kloof at the Vaal River on 25 August.[20] Three weeks later he met the Free State commandos who had managed to escape from the Brandwater Basin led by Acting Chief Commandant Piet Fourie when Prinsloo surrendered.[21] That September, the Free Staters who had been left behind north of the Magaliesberg also made their way back to their homeland in small groups. 'In many cases,' recalled De Wet, 'the oxen had been so exhausted that the waggons had to be left behind, the burghers returning on horseback, or even on foot.'[22]

This, along with the hard lessons learned during the hunt and from Prinsloo's surrender, meant De Wet was finally able to convince his burghers to get rid of their burdensome wagon laagers.[23] 'It was now that I conceived the great plan of bringing under arms all the burghers who had laid down their weapons, and taken the oath of neutrality, and of sending them to operate in every part of the [Free] State.'[24] Henceforth highly mobile guerrilla warfare would be the order of the day. With this in mind De Wet set to work, dividing his force into six assistant cheif commandsantships.[25]

De Wet on Fleur with some of his men in front of the Landdrost and Post and Telegraph Offices in Potchefstroom on 27 August 1900, less than two weeks after he had successfully escaped from his pursuers. (Transvaal Archives Depot, Pretoria)

With his men behind him, De Wet (raising his hand) addresses the Boer inhabitants of Potchefstroom on 27 August 1900. His powerful and stirring speeches during the war were a source of inspiration to many a burgher. (Transvaal Archives Depot, Pretoria)

Probably the most famous photograph of Christiaan de Wet – taken on 27 August 1900 in Potchefstroom, shortly after the end of the first De Wet hunt. The Boer inhabitants of the town repaired a number of rifles destroyed by the British authorities, and De Wet was so impressed with their handiwork that he had this picture taken of himself with the two hundredth Mauser that had been repaired. (Transvaal Archives Depot, Pretoria)

The war followed the same pattern in the Transvaal. On 25 August, Steyn reached Kruger at Watervalonder. Not far off the Transvaal forces under Louis Botha were engaged in the Battle of Dalmanutha (or Bergendal). Two days later, on 27 August, General Buller made a breakthrough and the Boers were forced to fall back. That evening Kruger cabled Botha and urged him to carry out his proposed plan to organise a guerrilla war.[26] Botha agreed and Dalmanutha became the last set-piece battle of the war. Then, on 28 August, the two republics held a joint executive council meeting, where Steyn recommended that the 74-year-old Kruger should be granted six months' leave. As his age prevented him from remaining with his burghers in the field, he was sent to Europe to further the Boer cause there.[27] Steyn remained in the Eastern Transvaal and on his way back to the Free State via Pietersburg and Rustenburg he succeeded in stoking the flames of resistance wherever he went.[28] On 1 November he met De Wet near Ventersdorp and returned to his beloved Free State.[29]

These positive consequences of the hunt for the Boers obviously confounded Roberts' attempts to bring the war to a speedy conclusion. A more direct effect on British operations was to delay the advance along the Pretoria–Delagoa Bay railway. Roberts had intended to launch this offensive after occupying Pretoria on 5 June and driving the Transvaal government and forces east along the line. But De Wet's operations along the Bloemfontein–Pretoria railway and the ensuing hunt assumed far greater proportions than Roberts had ever envisaged. He was therefore not only obliged to deploy a number of columns to pursue De Wet – troops who could have come in handy on the eastern front – but was

THE MOST SPECTACULAR GUERRILLA WARFARE

After De Wet returned to the Free State at the end of August 1900 he reorganised his forces and started drumming up support for his plan to invade the Cape Colony, as is illustrated in this painting by D. Dyer-Davies entitled 'De Wet addressing the burghers on the scheme for invading the Cape Colony'. (Transvaal Archives Depot, Pretoria)

also forced to devote a great deal of attention to these unexpected developments. For example, orders issued to commanders in the Eastern Transvaal were interrupted between 6–9 August, at the same time that columns led by Smith-Dorrien and Ian Hamilton were being drawn into the hunt.[30] The hunt for De Wet therefore undoubtedly delayed Roberts' eastern offensive along the Pretoria–Delagoa Bay line. On 13 July the chief believed 'it is not desirable to defer that move any longer.'[31] But in his report he set out the situation as follows: 'As soon as the troops engaged in the pursuit of De Wet became available for operations elsewhere, I redistributed the field army with the object, first, of advancing along the Delagoa Bay Railway to Komati Poort, and, secondly, of forming flying columns to pursue and disperse the scattered Boer Commandos which were carrying on a guerrilla warfare both in the Transvaal and the Orange River Colony.' [32]

Nevertheless, the hunt did have a direct positive result for the British: the fruitless pursuit of De Wet over Olifant's Nek put Kitchener in a position to take his columns west on 15 August and relieve Hore at Eland's River the following day. This served to temper to some extent the British disappointment at their failure to capture De Wet.

And that's how the hunt came to an end for Boer and Brit. In an outstanding display of military wizardry, De Wet's force of 2 000 – reinforced

THE FIRST DE WET HUNT, 15 JULY – 14 AUGUST 1900

by 500 burghers at the Vaal – managed to evade a British force of several columns amounting to more than 50 000 men, all told.[33] Between 15 July and 14 August the Boer force covered a distance of some 480 km from the Brandwater Basin to hard upon Roberts' headquarters in Pretoria, with two weeks spent at the Vaal River.[34] In more ways than one, the hunt became an epic saga in which De Wet emerged as an excellent strategist and the blunders of his opponents were mercilessly exposed. Furthermore, the hunt not only took place at a significant stage of the war; it also had far-reaching consequences.

By the end of the hunt, Howland observed, 'De Wet was still at large, and possessed of renewed resources that enabled him to go on roaming at will over South Africa, cutting lines of communication, swooping down on detached forces and posts, and generally conducting the most spectacular guerrilla warfare that modern times have seen. The chase had ended in a fizzle.'[35]

Notes

1. C.M. Bakkes, 'Die Militêre Situasie aan die Benede-Tugela op die Vooraand van die Britse Deurbraak by Pietershoogte (26 Februarie 1900)' in *Argiefjaarboek vir Suid-Afrikaanse Geskiedenis,* 1967, I, p. 49.
2. Amery (ed.), IV, pp. 432–433.
3. De Wet, p. 124.
4. Van Schoor, 'Diaries of Jacob de Villiers', 23.8.1900, p. 18.
5. Howland, p. 180.
6. TA, SA Telegrams III: Confidential letter, Roberts – Milner, Cape Town, 4.7.1900, p. 41; compare PRO, WO 108/240 for the same source.
7. Arthur, II, p. 52.
8. Howland, p. 198.
9. Amery (ed.), IV, p. 432.
10. TA, LRP 40: No. A1244, Methuen – Roberts, 26.8.1900, p. 15; compare PRO, WO 105, LRP 14 for the same source.
11. TA, LRP 10: Methuen, 'Chase of De Wet', 25.8.1900, p. 26; compare PRO, WO 105, LRP 10 for the same source.
12. Amery (ed.), IV, p. 261.
13. Van Everdingen, p. vii.
14. Van Schoor et al., *Christiaan Rudolph de Wet 1854–1922,* pp. 43–44; FA, Renier Collection 119.737: J.D. Kestell, 'Generaal de Wet', p. 3.
15. Bakkes, p. 50.
16. Van Everdingen, p. 232.
17. Bakkes, p. 52; Montgomery of Alamein, *A History of Warfare,* p. 21 (as quoted by W.L. v R. Scholtz, 'Die Slag van Bakenlaagte, 30 Oktober 1901' in *Historia,* May 1974, 19(1), p. 74.
18. FA, WMC 155/13/1(g): G. Boldingh, 'De Guerilla in den OVS', p. 11.
19. FA, Renier Collection 119.737: J.D. Kestell, 'Generaal De Wet', p. 7.
20. TA, G.S. Preller Collection 81: Die Oranje-Vrystaat-kommando's 1858–1915,

Frankfort-kommando, p. 2; Nierstrasz, II, Vol. 6, p. 1040. De Wet, p. 152, incorrectly supplies the date 21 August.
21. De Wet, p. 157; FA, WMC 155/13/1 (g): G. Boldingh, 'De Guerilla in den OVS', p. 11.
22. De Wet, p. 157.
23. FA, Renier Collection 119.513: Papers of Captain H. Muller, Free State Artillery. Minutes of meeting at Lindequesfontein 3.9.1900; Private collection: Memoirs of P.J. Meyer, recorded by H.J.W. Dafel, Babanango, 1936; FA, Renier collection 119.463: Memoirs of B.B. Bresler, recorded 10.11.1952; TA, G.S. Preller Collection 19: Newspaper clippings, p. 140; TA, Acquisition 1250: D. de Witt, 'Die Trek naar die Bosveld', recorded by C.P. van der Merwe.
24. De Wet, p. 157.
25. Ibid., pp. 157–158.
26. TA, Leyds 739: wire conversation, Kruger – Botha, 20:00, 27.8.1900; compare TA, Leyds 757, p. 457 for the same source.
27. TA, Leyds 681 (II): Executive Council Decision, Article 142, 28.8.1900, p. 542; TA, G.S. Preller Collection 36: Letter, M.T. Steyn, Roossenekal – All commandants and officers of the Transvaal, 3.10.1900, p. 18; N.J. van der Merwe, *Marthinus Theunis Steyn: 'n Lewensbeskrywing*, II, p. 64.
28. TA, Leyds 758 (c): no number, Steyn, Nelspruit – L. Botha, Watervalonder, 29.8.1900; TA, Leyds 758 (c): no number, Kruger, Nelspruit – L. Botha, Lydenburg, 30.8.1900; TA, G.S. Preller Collection 36: Letter, M.T. Steyn, Roossenekal – All commandants and officers of the Transvaal, 3.10.1900, pp. 18–19; TA, G.S. Preller Collection 209: Historical Information files, p. 191; TA, Acquisition 1150: President Steyn's Address, 17.10.1900; TA, Frederik Rompel Collection 7: Appendix B, No. 10, President Steyn's Address, pp. 10–12; TA, Acquisition W 21 (d) Vol. 8: Telegram, M.T. Steyn – Van Reede, Pronker Paris, et al., 28.8.1900; The *Cape Argus*, 1.10.1900: 'Kruger blames Steyn'; The *Transvaal Leader*, 10.9.1903; O.T. de Villiers, *Met de Wet en Steyn in het Veld*, p. 35; J.F. Naudé, *Vechten en Vluchten van Beyers en Kemp 'bokant' de Wet*, p. 182; Van Warmelo, p. 78; R.W. Schikkerling, *Hoe ry die Boere*, p. 47; W.J. de Kock, 'Pres. M.T. Steyn en die Siel van die Vryheidstryd' in J.H. Breytenback (ed.), *Gedenkalbum van die Tweede Vryheidsoorlog*, p. 252; Amery (ed.), IV, p. 474.
29. J.P. Brits, *Diary of a National Scout: P.J. du Toit 1900–1902*, 1.11.1900, p. 21.
30. Compare Roberts' original telegram in PRO, WO 105, LRP 37: Telegrams to General Officers Commanding, 6–10 August 1900; also TA, SA Telegrams III and IV: 6–10 August 1900; compare PRO, WO 108/240 for the same sources.
31. TA, SA Telegrams III: No. C2720, Roberts – Buller, Standerton, 13.7.1900, p. 61; compare SA Telegrams III, No. C2717, Roberts – Baden-Powell, Rustenburg 13.7.1900, p. 61; compare PRO, WO 108/240 for the same sources.
32. TA, South African Despatches II: Roberts' Account, 14 June to 10 October 1900, p. 12; compare PRO, WO 32/8000 for the same source.
33. Hunter's cordon around the Brandwater Basin, with the exception of Broadwood and Ridley (approximately): 20 000; Broadwood and Ridley: 3 000; Little: 700; Kitchener's cordon south of the Vaal, excluding Broadwood, Ridley and Little: 7 300; Methuen: 3 000; Smith-Dorrien: 2 200; Ian Hamilton and Baden-Powell: 9 500; Carrington: 2 500; Barton: 3 000 (a total of 51 200).
34. Maps: South Africa 1: 500 000, Kroonstad SE 29/26 Topographical Issue, 1969; South Africa 1: 500 000, Johannesburg SE 27/26 Topographical Issue, 1974; South Africa 1:250 000, Kroonstad 2726 Topographical surface, 1974; South Africa 1:250 000, West Rand 2626 Topo-cadastral surface, 1974; South Africa 1: 250 000, Rustenburg 2526 Topographic surface, 1972. The following maps are from the CA,

Map Collection – 1/51: Map of the Orange River Colony, 1907; 2/26: Bethlehem, 1905; 2/184: Farm Survey, Potchefstroom, 1905; 2/525: ORC, Frankfort, 1901; 2/547: Rustenburg, Jackson Map, 1903; 2/1038: Kroonstad, 1902; 3/34: Ventersdorp and surrounding areas, October 1900.
35. Howland, pp. 174–175.

Bibliography

I. ARCHIVAL SOURCES

UNPUBLISHED SOURCES

A. TRANSVAAL ARCHIVES DEPOT

1. **Dr W.J. Leyds Archives**

   Volumes
   - 94   Legation, ZAR, Correspondence, Reports from and to the ZAR during the Anglo-Boer War, 1899–1902, Vols. I–III.
   - 191   News Reports and News Paper Cuttings Received from Irish Secret Correspondent, 1899–1902.
   - 474   Consulate, ZAR, Consul-General, ZAR, at Lourenço Marques (George Pott), War Telegrams, Vol. IV, May – September 1900.
   - 726(a)–732(g)   Collected War Telegrams, 25 May – 17 September 1900.
   - 733   Register: Incoming War Telegrams, June – September 1900.
   - 734   Buitengewone Staatscourant en Oorlogsberichten te Velde, Printed, 7 June – 14 September 1900.
   - 739   Wire Communications Between Pres. Kruger and Generals, May – August 1900.
   - 748(f)–751(f)   Gen. Louis Botha, War Telegrams, 23 May – 3 September 1900.
   - 753   Gen. Louis Botha, Telegram Copy Book, Vol. III, 1899–1900.
   - 757   Gen. Louis Botha, Copies of War Telegrams, April – September 1900.
   - 758   Gen. Louis Botha, War Telegrams (From Jonkheer Sandberg), April – Sept. 1900.
   - 759   Gen. Louis Botha, Incoming Documents, March – September 1900.
   - 765   Lt. L.W.J.K. Thomson, Collected Papers, Anglo-Boer War, Vol. I.
   - 766–776   Nierstrasz, P.A., La Guerre Sud-Africaine, 1899–1902: Der Süd-Afrikanische Krieg, 1899–1902, Unpublished Manuscript in 19 Volumes, 's- Gravenhage, 1905.

2. **N.J. de Wet Collection (W2)**

   - 2   War Council Minutes.
   - 13   Incoming Telegrams, 19 May – 4 June 1900.

3. **Transvaal Museum Collection (W21)**

    War Reports.

4. **Frederik Rompel Collection (W213)**

    7 Appendix B, No. 10, Pres. Steyn's Address, October 1900.

5. **F.V. Engelenburg Collection (A140)**

    22 Anglo-Boer War. Manuscript by M.P.C. Valter, 'Botha contra De Wet'.

6. **Col. D. Reitz Collection (A148)**

    11–14 Copies of War Telegrams, 12 July – 15 September 1900.

7. **Anglo-Boer War Accession (A235)**

    I Reminiscences of Johannes P. Botha, Potchefstroom, Tweede Vryheidsoorlog, 1899–1902, Compiled by Himself 1938 and 1945.
    II Manuscript by Capt. Henri F. Slegtkamp, Tweede Vryheidsoorlog, Vol. I.

8. **Danie Theron Collection (A285)**

9. **J.H. de la Rey Collection (A313)**

    3 War Correspondence, 1899–1902.
    7 Letter Copy Book, 13 August – 11 October 1900.
    9 Letter Copy Book, 17 August 1900 – 20 April 1901.
    17 Reminiscences of Gen. J.H. de la Rey, 1899–1901 (Unfinished Manuscript).

10. **H.C. Bredell Collection (A413)**

    2 Tweede Vryheidsoorlog, Proclamations and War Reports, 2 June 1900 – 7 August 1901, Tweede Vryheidsoorlog, War Telegrams, 13 June – September 1900.

11. **Mrs H.B. Bramley Accession (A782)**

    Diary of H. Bramley, Kept in Klerksdorp during the Anglo-Boer War.

12. **Dr G.S. Preller Collection (A787)**

    1 Gen. Louis Botha, Incoming Letters and Reports, 1899–1901.
    19 Gen. C.R. de Wet, Correspondence (Funeral of De Wet).

    36   Documents of Gens. J.C. Emmett, D. Erasmus and P.J. Liebenberg, 1899–1902.
    80   L.E. Krause, Correspondence on Gen. Louis Botha.
    81   Commando Histories, Orange Free State Commandos, 1858–1915.
    134   Papers of J. de Villiers, 1899–1919.
    209   Historical Information Files, Pres. M.T. Steyn, 1893–1929.

13. Collection of the Archivist for Source Research in the United Kingdom (A1016)

News Cuttings – The South African War: A Daily Record of the Boer War and After in South Africa, Compiled and Arranged from The *Daily Telegraph*, Vol. II, 31 May 1900 – 21 September 1901.

14. H. Olivier Accession (A1237)

Reminiscences of Henning Olivier, son of Gen. J.H. Olivier, Bloemfontein, 1940.

15. C.P. van der Merwe Accession (A1250)

    I   (i) Dirk de Witt, 'Die Trek naar die Bosveld'.
        (ii) Gert Scheepers, Reminiscences.

16. Archives of the Intelligence Officer, Pretoria, 1900–1902

    23   Correspondence, Copy (Memorandum) Books. Capt. Hughes, June – December 1900.

17. Archives of the Military Governor, Pretoria, 1900–1902

    16   Incoming Correspondence, July – August 1900.

18. Transvaal Publications, 1900–1910 (T93)

    154   Anglo-Boer War, Surrendered Burghers of the South African Republic.
    159   List of Casualties in the South African Field Forces, 1 August – 31 December 1900.

19. Milner Papers (Photo Copies)

1204–1205   Correspondence, Lord Roberts, 1900.

20. Lord Roberts Papers (A1643)

Public Record Office, War Office Accession. Despatches and Reports of Operations in South Africa, 1899–1900.

    7   Capt. E.B. Bailey, 'Roodewal Affair', 21 June 1900.

8   Maj.-Gen. Sir A.H. Paget, 'Report on Engagement at Witklip, 16th July 1900', 18 July 1900.
9   Lt.-Gen. Lord Methuen, 'Western Transvaal Report, July 25 to August 3, 1900', 3 August 1900.
    Lt.-Gen. Sir A. Hunter, 'July Prinsloo's Surrender, Report, 10th to 31st July 1900', 4 August 1900.
    Capt. J.E. Pine-Coffin, 'Ventersburg Road and Holfontein, Capture of Train, Report, August 3, 1900', 3 August 1900.
10 Lt.-Gen. Lord Methuen, 'Operations against De Wet, Report, 5th to 17th August, 1900', 25 August 1900.
    Brig.-Gen. R.G. Broadwood, 'De Wet, Operations Report, 15th July to 15th August, 1900', 31 August 1900.
11 Capt. A.G.W. Grant, 'Roodewal Station, Report, 7th June, 1900', 21 September 1900.
12 Field-Marshal Lord Roberts, 'Account, June 14 to October 10, 1900', 10 October 1900.
13 Maj.-Gen. Sir A.H. Paget, 'North of Pretoria, Report, 16th August to 22nd September 1900', 17 October 1900.
18 Gen. Sir R. Buller, Commanding Natal Field Force, Telegrams, 22 June – 30 July 1900.
31 Maj.-Gen. R.S.S. Baden-Powell, Telegrams, 25 November 1899 – 28 May 1900.
33 Lt.-Gen. Lord Kitchener, Telegrams, June 1900.
    Lt.-Gen. Lord Methuen, Telegrams, June 1900.
35 Lt.-Gen. Lord Methuen, Telegrams, July 1900.
    Maj.-Gen. G.T. Pretyman, Telegrams, June 1900.
36 Maj.-Gen. R.S.S. Baden-Powell, Telegrams, July 1900.
    Lt.-Col. E.P.C. Girouard, Director of Railways, Telegrams, July 1900.
    Lt.-Gen. Lord Kitchener, Telegrams, July 1900.
    General Officer Commanding, Lines of Communications, Cape Town, Telegrams, August 1900.
37 Maj.-Gen. Sir H. Chermside, Telegrams, July 1900.
    Lt.-Gen. Sir A. Hunter, Telegrams, July 1900.
38 Brig.-Gen. R.G. Broadwood, Telegrams, July 1900.
    Maj.-Gen. R.A.P. Clements, Telegrams, July 1900.
    Lt.-Col. R.L. Hippisley, Director of Telegraphs, Telegrams, July 1900.
    Lt.-Gen. Sir T. Kelly-Kenny, Commanding Lines of Communications, Orange River Colony, Telegrams, July 1900.
    Sir Godfrey Lagden, Resident Commissioner, Basutoland, Telegrams, July 1900.
    Maj.-Gen. Sir A.H. Paget, Telegrams, July 1900.
39 Maj.-Gen. G. Barton, Telegrams, July 1900.
    General Officer Commanding, Kroonstad, Telegrams, July 1900.
    Maj.-Gen. A.F. Hart, Telegrams, July 1900.
40 Lt.-Gen. Lord Kitchener, Telegrams, August 1900.
    Lt.-Gen. Lord Methuen, Telegrams, August 1900.
41 Maj.-Gen. R.S.S. Baden-Powell, Telegrams, August 1900.
    Maj.-Gen. Sir H. Chermside, Telegrams, August 1900.

Maj.-Gen. Sir G.H. Marshall, Commanding Forts at Pretoria, Telegrams, August 1900.
42   Lt.-Gen. Sir A. Hunter, Telegrams, August 1900.
General Officer Commanding, Lines of Communications, Cape Town, Telegrams, August 1900.
43   Lt.-Gen. Sir Ian Hamilton, Telegrams, August 1900.
Maj.-Gen. Sir A.H. Paget, Telegrams, August 1900.
44   Brig.-Gen. R.G. Broadwood, Telegrams, August 1900.
Lt.-Col. E.P.C. Girouard, Director of Railways, Telegrams, August 1900.
General Officer Commanding, Kroonstad, Telegrams, August 1900.
Lt.-Gen. Sir T. Kelly-Kenny, Telegrams, August 1900.
Maj.-Gen. Sir C.E. Knox, Telegrams, August 1900.
Maj.-Gen. G.T. Pretyman, Telegrams, August 1900.
Maj.-Gen. H.L. Smith-Dorrien, Telegrams, August 1900.
45   Maj.-Gen. G. Barton, Telegrams, August 1900.
50   Lt.-Gen. Lord Kitchener, Telegrams, September 1900.
62   Sir A. Milner, High Commissioner, South Africa, Telegrams, August 1900.

B. PUBLIC RECORD OFFICE, LONDON

1. War Office (WO) 32

7998   Report by Lt.-Gen. Sir A. Hunter on Operations in Eastern Districts of Orange River Colony, 25 June – 1 August 1900.
8000   Account by Field-Marshal Lord Roberts of Operations in Orange River Colony and Transvaal, 14 June – 10 October 1900.

2. War Office (WO) 105 – Lord Roberts Papers

Despatches and Reports of Operations in South Africa, 1899–1902, by Commander-in-Chief and Commanders in the Field.

Box
8   Capt. W.P. Anderson, 'Roodewal Station', 7 June 1900.
Capt. E.B. Bailey, 'Roodewal and Rhenoster River', 21 June 1900.
9   Maj.-Gen. Sir A.H. Paget, 'Witklip near Slabbert's Nek', 18 July 1900.
10   Lt.-Gen. Lord Methuen, 'Wonderfontein, Welverdiend Station, Frederikstad and Tygerfontein', 3 August 1900.
Lt.-Gen. Sir A. Hunter, 'Operations Resulting in Capture of Generals Prinsloo and Crowther with their Forces at Brandwater Basin', 4 August 1900.
Maj. M.J.R. Dundas, 'Enemy Attack on Train at Holfontein Post', 9 August 1900.
Field-Marshal Lord Roberts, 'Operations from 14th May to 13th June, 1900', 14 June 1900.

Lt.-Gen. Lord Methuen, 'Potchefstroom to Magato Pass', 25 August 1900.
Maj.-Gen. Bruce Hamilton, 'Despatch', 29 August 1900.
Brig.-Gen. R.G. Broadwood, 'Senekal, Witklip, Kopjes and Rhenoster Poort', 31 August 1900.

11 Capt. A.G.W. Grant, 'Roodeval Station', 21 September 1900.
Field-Marshal Lord Roberts, 'Account from 14 June to 10 October 1900', 10 October 1900.
Maj.-Gen. Sir A.H. Paget, 'Operations from 16 August to 22 September 1900', 17 October 1900.

Telegrams and Reports between Lord Roberts and Commanders in the Field

14 Lord Methuen, June – November 1900.
15 Maj.-Gen. H.L. Smith-Dorrien, July – August 1900.
    Maj.-Gen. Sir C.E. Knox, June – December 1900.
    Brig.-Gen. R.G. Broadwood, July – August 1900.
    Col. T.E. Hickman, August 1900.
    Maj.-Gen. R.S.S. Baden-Powell, June – August 1900.
16 Lt.-Gen. Sir Ian Hamilton, July – August 1900.
    Lt.-Gen. Lord Kitchener, February – December 1900.
17 Maj.-Gen. Sir H. Chermside, April – August 1900.
    Maj.-Gen. R.A.P. Clements, July – August 1900.
    Lt.-Gen. Sir L. Rundle, April – August 1900.
    Lt.-Gen. Sir. A. Hunter, April – August 1900.
18 Sir G. Lagden, March – December 1900.
19 Lt.-Col. E.P.C. Girouard, February – September 1900.
    Lt.-Col. R.L. Hippisley, March – September 1900.
20 Sir A. Milner, February – December 1900.
    Lt.-Gen. Sir T. Kelly-Kenny, July – August 1900.
21 Maj.-Gen. Sir A.H. Paget, July – August 1900.
    Maj.-Gen. G.T. Pretyman, May – August 1900.
22 General Officer Commanding, Kroonstad, July – August 1900.
    Maj.-Gen. A.F. Hart, April – August 1900.
    Maj.-Gen. G. Barton, July – August 1900.

Miscellaneous

27 Confidential Papers, Nos. 51–84, 1900.
28 Confidential Papers, Nos. 85–109, 1900.
29 Index Register, Nos. 110–166, 1900.
32 Telegrams from Secretary of State for War and Chief of Staff, Index Nos. 1–1269, July – September 1900.
33 Telegrams to Secretary of State for War, February – December 1900.
34 Telegrams Despatched to the High Commissioner, Sir Alfred Milner, Index Nos. 1–184, April – August 1900.
36 Telegrams to General Officers Commanding, May – July 1900.
37 Telegrams to General Officers Commanding, August – September 1900.

3. War Office (WO) 108, South African War – Papers

85–88 Weekly Returns – Statement of Strength of Forces in South Africa – Expected Arrivals, and Casualties, October 1899 – December 1901.
91 Nominal Rolls of Casualties of Colonial Contingents, 1900.
231–232 Deputy Adjudant General's Department, Miscellaneous Subjects including Transport, Casualties by Regiments, Battles, etc., 6 June – 4 December 1900.

Telegrams and Letters Despatched by Field-Marshal Lord Roberts

239 Vol. II – Nos. C.1216 – C.2146, 20 April – 18 June 1900.
Vol. III – Nos. C.2149 – C.3376, 19 June – 7 August 1900.
Vol. IV – Nos. C.3378 – C.4599, 8 August – 13 September 1900.

Reports to the Field-Marshal, Commander-in-Chief, from Officers Commanding Units

250 Organisation and Equipment of Cavalry, June – November 1900.
263 Imperial Yeomanry, October 1900.
283–298 Royal Engineers, Field Companies, 'A' Troop, Telegraph, Balloon, Steam and Transport Sections – Role Played by Them in the Operations, 1899–1902.
302–308 Maps, Sketches, etc., in Connection with Royal Engineer Services, Bridging, etc., 1899–1900.

4. Colonial Office (CO) 417

Original Correspondence, High Commissioner

292 Despatches: South African Republic, 9 July – 6 August 1900.
293 Despatches: South African Republic, 7 August – 12 September 1900.

C. FREE STATE ARCHIVES DEPOT

1. War Museum Collection (A155)

155/13/1 Miss A. Boldingh, Haarlem, Holland, Papers of Lt. G. Boldingh:
(a) Part of a Commando Diary.
(f) G. Boldingh, 'Het Verraad van Genl. Prinsloo'.
(g) G. Boldingh, 'De Guerilla in den O.V.S.'.
(h) Report by Keulemans Adding to Boldingh's Letter (See (f)).
155/41/12 Deutschen Buren Centrale, Munich. File Containing Communications and Press Reports:
(a) War Reports Compiled by the D.B.C.

(b) Communications by Dr Hintrager and Böhmer.
155/42/1 Mr Justice Jacob de Villiers, File with Papers:
(a) Incoming Correspondence of Gen. C.R. de Wet, 27 June – 3 August 1900.
(b) Outgoing Correspondence of Gen. C.R. de Wet, 14 June – 6 August 1900.
155/82/1 Dr Oskar Hintrager, 'Kriegs-Tagebuch'.
155/109/2 Dr W.J. Leyds, Loose Newspapers, *De Zoutpansberg Wachter*, 24 August 1900.
155/110/1 W.J.M. Liernur, *Eerste Bulletin van Het Vaderland*.
155/115/2 J. Lugten, 'De Oorlog in Zuid-Afrika'. Four Scrap-Books with Newspaper Cuttings on the War – *Rotterdamsch Nieuwsblad*.
155/163/2 Dr S.L.C. Schouten, Newspapers, *Op! Voor Transvaal. Weekblad Verschijnende tijdens den Onafhankelijkheidsoorlog der Zuid-Afrikaansche Boeren-Republieken* (Amsterdam), 8 July – 28 October 1900.
155/241/3 *Nieuwe Rotterdamsche Courant*, 1 July – 29 September 1900.

2. **President M.T. Steyn Collection (A156)**
156/6/141 T.P. Tresling, 'De Generaals Botha, De Wet en De la Rey' (From: *Mannen en Vrouwen van Beteekenis in Onze Dagen*, Haarlem, 1903).

3. **National Museum Collection (A2)**

2/10 The *Bloemfontein Post*, 5 June – 23 October 1900.

4. **Senator D.J. Malan Collection (A60)**

94 War Diary, 15 January – 29 December 1900 (60.23).
95 War Diary, n.d. (60.22).

5. **FAK Collection (A90)**

90.22–90.36 Correspondence, 1900.

6. **Renier Collection (A119)**

Incoming Letters, Mr G. Joubert, *Die Volksblad*, Bloemfontein.

7. **C.R. de Wet Gedenkboek en -Fees Collection (A201)**

D. WAR MUSEUM OF THE BOER REPUBLICS, BLOEMFONTEIN

Loose File: Letter, Piet de Wet, Lindley – C.R. de Wet, 11.1.1901.

E. CENTRAL ARCHIVES DEPOT, PRETORIA

1. J.B.M. Hertzog Collection (A32)

    1   Personal Correspondence, Anglo-Boer War, 1899–1902.
  95 Reminiscences and Diaries, 1899–1902.

2. Map Collection

  1/110 Jeppe's Map of the Transvaal, 1899.
  2/26 Bethlehem, 1905.
  2/184 Farm Surveys, Potchefstroom, 1905.
  2/525 Frankfort, Orange River Colony, 1901.
  2/546 Pretoria, Jackson's Map, 1903.
  2/547 Rustenburg, Jackson's Map, 1903.
  2/931 Accession E69, Jeppe's Map of The Transvaal, Sheet 4, 1899 (Allegedly in possession of Lord Methuen when he was captured at Tweebosch).
  3/17 Transvaal and OFS, Kroonstad and area between Bothaville and Heilbron, 1899.
  3/34 Ventersdorp and surrounding areas, October 1900.
  3/88 Fouriesburg, 1907–1920.
  3/89 Fouriesburg, 1908–1913.
  3/506 Kroonstad (Shews Reitzburg near Vredefort), March 1900.
  3/515 Krugersdorp, March 1900.
  3/1420 Map of Transvaal showing the position of Welverdiend, 1913.
  3/1425 Map of the ORC showing position of Heilbron, March 1909.
  3/1438 Map of the ORC, Vredefort, October 1908.
  4/32 Frankfort, September 1905.

F. DEEDS OFFICE, PRETORIA

  DB/81 Leliefontein (344).
  DB443/29 Leliefontein (344).
  DB396 Map, Folio 1, Leliefontein (344).

G. PRIVATE COLLECTIONS

1. Diary of Jacob de Villiers (Mrs H. Reitz, Durban).

2. J.H.C. Penzhorn, 'Lebenslauf und Erinnerungen aus dem Leben von Johannes Heinrich Carl Penzhorn' (Copy in Possession of Mr E.E. Penzhorn, Kroondal).

3. Reminiscneces of P.J. Meyer (Recorded by Mrs H.J.W. Pretorius, née Dafel, Pretoria).

PUBLISHED SOURCES

Governmment Publications

1. British Blue Books

    Cd. 426   Proclamations Issued by Field-Marshal Lord Roberts in South Africa, London, 1900.

    Cd. 1790–1791   Minutes of Evidence taken before the Royal Commission on the War in South Africa, Vols. I and II, London, 1903.

    Cd. 1792   Appendices to the Minutes of Evidence taken before the Royal Commission on the War in South Africa, London, 1903.

2. Other Government Publications in the Transvaal Archives Depot

(a) Buitengewone Staatscourant der Zuid-Afrikaansche Republiek, Machadodorp 7 Junie – Nelspruit 5 September 1900 (Deel XX, No. 1121–1147) benevens de Ambtelijke Oorlogsberichten, Telegrammen, Circulair Telegrammen, Gouvernements Kennisgevingen, Proclamatiën ens. Uitgevaardigd tusschen 9 Junie 1900 en 10 September 1900. Algemeen Nederlandsche Verbond, Dordrecht, 1902.

(b) War Office Records – Accessions of the Transvaal Archives Depot from the Public Record Office, London:
  (i) Girouard, Lt.-Col. E.P.C., *History of the Railways in the South African War, 1899–1902*, London, 1903.
  (ii) Hippisley, Lt.-Col. R.L., *History of the Telegraphic Operations during the War in South Africa, 1899–1902*, London, 1903.
  (iii) *Journal of the Principal Events Connected with South Africa*, Vol. 5 (Secret), London, 1900.
  (iv) *South African Despatches*, Vol. II, London, 1901.
  (v) *South African Telegrams and Letters Sent by Field-Marshal Lord Roberts, December 1899 – December 1900*, London, 1901.
  (vi) *South African War: Confidential Telegrams*, London, 1900.

II. PERIODICALS

1. Newspapers

Het *Algemeen Handelsblad* (Amsterdam), 13 July – 4 September 1900.
The *Bloemfontein Post*, 5 June – 23 October 1900.
The *Cape Argus*, 5 June – 31 December 1900.
The *Cape Times*, 5 June – 29 December 1900.
The *Daily Telegraph* (London), 31 May – 31 December 1900.
Die Eiche, Beilage 4 (Munich), 1949.
Het *Leidsch Dagblad* (Leiden), 1 July – 3 October 1900.
The *Natal Witness*, 5 June – 18 December 1900.
Nieuwe Rotterdamsche Courant, 1 July – 3 December 1900.
Op! Voor Transvaal (Amsterdam), 8 July – 28 October 1900.
Rotterdamsch Nieuwsblad, 12 July – 9 October 1900.
The *Times* (London), 13 July 1900 – 4 March 1901.

Wereldkroniek. Geïllustreerd Weekblad voor Iedereen (Rotterdam), 7(2), 18 August 1900, 7(21), 25 August 1900, and 8(1), April 1901.
De Zoutpansberg Wachter, 24 August 1900.

III. PUBLISHED DIARIES, REMINISCENCES, ETC.

Badenhorst, C.C.J., *Uit den Boeren-Oorlog, 1899–1902*, Amsterdam, 1903.
Boldingh, G., *Een Hollandsch Officier in Zuid-Afrika*, Rotterdam,1903.
Brink, J.N., *Oorlog en Ballingskap*, Cape Town, 1940.
Brits, J.P., *Diary of a National Scout: P.J. du Toit 1900–1902*, Pretoria, 1974.
Childers, E., *In the Ranks of the CIV*, London, 1900.
Collen, E.H., *Diary and Sketches of the South African War*, Calcutta, 1901.
Colvin, F.F. and Gordon, E.R., *Diary of the Ninth (QR) Lancers during the South African Campaign, 1899–1902*, London, 1904.
Crum, F.M., *With the MI in South Africa: Being Sidelights on the Boer Campaign 1899–1902*, Cambridge, 1903.
De Souza, C.W.L., *No Charge for Delivery*, Cape Town, 1969.
De Wet, C.R., *Three Years War (October 1899 – June 1902)*, Reprint, Johannesburg, 1986.
Esterhuysen, A.M. de V., *Corneels Kanniedood*, Johannesburg, 1953.
Evans, W.S., *The Canadian Contingents and Canadian Imperialism: A Story and a Study*, London, 1901.
Gaskell, H.M., *With Lord Methuen in South Africa, February 1900 – June 1901*, London, 1906.
Grobler, M.J., *Met die Vrystaters onder die Wapen: Generaal Prinsloo en die Bethlehem-Kommando*, Bloemfontein, 1937.
Guest, H.M., *With Lord Methuen and the 1st Division*, Klerksdorp, 1902.
Hales, A.G., *Campaign Pictures of the War in South Africa, 1899–1900*, London, 1900.
Hiley, A.R.I. and Hassell, J.A., *The Mobile Boer: Being the Record of the Observations of Two Burgher Officers*, New York, 1902.
[Hintrager, O.], *Steijn, De Wet und die Oranje-Freistaater, Tagebuchblätter aus dem Süd-Afrikanischen Kriege*, Tübingen, 1902.
Hippisley, R.L., *History of the Telegraphic Operations during the War in South Africa*, London, 1903.
Home, W., *With the Border Volunteers to Pretoria*, Hawick, 1901.
Hopkins, H.C., *Maar Eén Soos Hy: Die Lewe van Kommandant C.A. van Niekerk*, Cape Town, 1963.
Howland, F.H., *The Chase of De Wet and Other Later Phases of the Boer War as Seen by an American Correspondent*, Providence, 1901.
Jeans, T.T. (ed.), *Naval Brigades in the South African War, 1899–1900*, London, 1901.
Kestell, J.D., *Through Shot and Flame*, London, 1903.
Leyds, W.J., *Correspondentie: Tweede Verzameling (1899–1900)*, 3 Vols. and *Derde Verzameling (1900)*, 2 Vols., 's-Gravenhage, 1930–1931.
Lombard, P.S., *Uit die Dagboek van 'n Wildeboer*, Johannesburg, 1939.
MacKinnon, W.H., *The Journal of the CIV in South Africa*, London, 1901.
Maritz, M., *My Lewe en Strewe*, Johannesburg, 1939.
Meyer, J.H., *Kommando-Jare: 'n Oudstryder se Persoonlike Relaas van die Tweede Vryheidsoorlog*, Cape Town, 1971.
Miller, M. and Miller, H.R., *A Captain of the Gordons*, London, 1909.
Moeller, B., *Two Years at the Front with the Mounted Infantry*, London, 1903.
Mostert, D., *Slegtkamp van Spioenkop: Oorlogsherinneringe van Kapt. Slegtkamp Saamgestel uit sy Dagboek*, Cape Town, 1935.

Naudé, J.F., *Vechten en Vluchten van Beyers en Kemp 'bôkant' de Wet*, Rotterdam, 1903.
Oberholster, J.J., 'Dagboek van Oskar Hintrager – Saam met Christiaan de Wet, Mei tot September 1900', in *Christiaan de Wet-Annale*, 2, Bloemfontein, 1973.
Pienaar, P., *With Steyn and De Wet*, London, 1902.
Pieterse, H.J.C., *Oorlogsavonture van Genl. Wynand Malan*, Cape Town, 1941.
Romer, C.F. and Mainwaring, A.E., *The Second Battalion Royal Dublin Fusiliers in the South African War*, London, 1908.
Ross, P.T., *A Yeoman's Letters*, London, 1901.
Schikkerling, R.W., *Hoe ry die Boere ('n Kommando-dagboek)*, Johannesburg, 1964.
Smith-Dorrien, H.L., *Memories of Forty Eight Years' Service*, London, 1925.
Spurgin, K.B., *On Active Service with the Northumberland and Durham Yeomanry, Under Lord Methuen (South Africa, 1900–1901)*, London, n.d.
Van Warmelo, D.S., *Mijn Commando en Guerilla Commando-Leven*, Amsterdam, 1901.
Ver Loren van Themaat, H., *Twee Jaren in den Boeren Oorlog*, Haarlem, 1903.
Wilkinson, F., *Australia at the Front: A Colonial View of the Boer War*, London, 1901.
Williams, B., and Childers, E., *The HAC in South Africa*, London, 1903.
Wood, W., *The Northumberland Fusiliers*, London, n.d.

IV. SECONDARY SOURCES

Amery, L.S. (ed.), *The Times History of the War in South Africa, 1899–1902*, 7 Vols., London, 1900–1909.
Andriessen, W.F., *Gedenkboek van den Oorlog in Zuid-Afrika*, Amsterdam, 1904.
Arthur, G., *Life of Lord Kitchener*, 3 Vols., London, 1920.
Aus dem Süd-Afrikanische Kriege 1899 bis 1902. Kriegsgeschichtliche Enzelschriften herausgegeben vom Grossen Generalstabe, 3 Vols., Berlin, 1903–1905.
Bakkes, C.M., 'Die Militêre Situasie aan die Benede–Tugela op die Vooraand van die Britse Deurbraak by Pietershoogte (26 Februarie 1900)', in *Argiefjaarboek vir Suid-Afrikaanse Geskiedenis*, Vol. I, Pretoria, 1967.
Barnard, C.J., *Generaal Louis Botha op die Natalse Front 1899–1900*, Cape Town, 1970.
Barnard, C.J., 'Studies in the Generalship of the Boer Commanders' in *Military History Journal*, 2(5), June 1973.
Birch, J.H., *History of the War in South Africa*, Sydney, n.d.
Bodenstein, H.D.J., *Was Generaal Botha in 1900 'n Verrader?*, Amsterdam, 1916.
Boon, N.J., *De Oorlog in Zuid-Afrika*, Amsterdam, 1900.
Breytenbach, J.H. (ed.), *Gedenkalbum van die Tweede Vryheidsoorlog*, Cape Town, 1949.
Breytenbach, J.H., *Die Geskiedenis van die Tweede Vryheidsoorlog in Suid-Afrika, 1899–1902*, Vol. I, Pretoria, 1969.
Breytenbach, J.H., *Komdt. Danie Theron: Baasverkenner van die Tweede Vryheidsoorlog*, Cape Town, 1950.
Creswicke, L., *South Africa and the Transvaal War*, 8 Vols., London, n.d.
Danes, R., *Cassell's (Illustrated) History of the Boer War 1899–1901*, London, 1901.
Davitt, M., *The Boer Fight for Freedom*, New York, 1902.
De Bloch, J., *Lord Roberts's Campaign and its Consequences*, London, n.d.
De Villiers, O.T., *Met de Wet en Steyn in het Veld*, Amsterdam, 1903.
Delport, P.J., *Die Rol van Genl. Marthinus Prinsloo gedurende die Tweede Vryheidsoorlog*, Unpublished MA dissertation, UOFS, Bloemfontein, 1972.
De Watteville, H., *Lord Kitchener*, London, 1939.
De Wet, C.R., *De Strijd tusschen Boer en Brit*, Amsterdam, 1902.
Dooner, M.G., *The 'Last Post', being a Roll of All Officers (Naval, Military or Colonial) who gave*

BIBLIOGRAPHY

their lives for the Queen, King and Country, in the South African War, 1899–1902, London, 1903.

Doyle, A. Conan, *The Great Boer War*, London, 1900.

Du Cane, H., *The War in South Africa: The Advance to Pretoria After Paardeberg, the Upper Tugela Campaign, etc. Prepared in the History Section of the Great General Staff*, Berlin, London, 1906. Also known as: *The German Official Account of the War in South Africa*.

Fletcher, J.S., *Roberts of Pretoria: The Story of His Life*, London, 1900.

Forrest, G., *The Life of Lord Roberts, K.G., V.C.*, London, 1914.

Gronum, M.A., *Die Engelse Oorlog, 1899–1902: Die Gevegsmetodes waarmee die Boere-Republieke Verower is*, Cape Town, 1972.

Hall, D., *The Hall Handbook of the Anglo-Boer War*, Pietermaritzburg, 1999.

Hamilton, I.B.M., *The Happy Warrior: A Life of General Sir Ian Hamilton – by his Nephew*, London, 1966.

A Handbook of the Boer War, London, 1910.

Holt, E., *The Boer War*, London, 1958.

James, D., *Lord Roberts*, London, 1954.

Kepper, L., *De Zuid-Afrikaansche Oorlog: Historisch Gedenkboek*, Leiden, n.d.

Kestell, J.D., *Christiaan de Wet: 'n Lewensbeskrywing*, Cape Town, 1920.

Klinck-Lütetsburg, C., *Christiaan de Wet: De Held van Zuid-Afrika*, Zutphen, 1902.

Krüger, D.W., *Paul Kruger*, 2 Vols., Johannesburg, 1961–1963.

Kruger, C.J.H., *Militêre Bewind in die Oranje-Vrystaat, Maart 1900 – Januarie 1901*, Unpublished MA dissertation, UP, Pretoria, 1958.

Kruger, R., *Good-Bye Dolly Gray: The Story of the Boer War*, 5th edition, London, 1965.

Magnus, P., *Kitchener: Portrait of an Imperialist*, London, 1958.

Malan, J., *Die Boere-Offisiere van die Tweede Vryheidsoorlog 1899–1902*, Pretoria, 1990.

Maurice, F. and Grant, M.H., *History of the War in South Africa, 1899–1902*, 8 Vols., London, 1906–1910. Also known as: *Official History of the War in South Africa, 1899–1902*.

Nasson, B., *The South African War 1899–1902*, London, 1999.

Nierstrasz, P.A., *La Guerre Sud-Africaine, 1899–1902: Der Süd-Afrikanische Krieg, 1899–1902*, Unpublished Manuscript in 19 Vols.

Oosthuizen, J., *Jacobus Herculas de la Rey en die Tweede Vryheidsoorlog*, Unpublished DLitt thesis, PU for CHE, Potchefstroom, 1949.

Pakenham, T., *The Boer War*, London, 1979.

Penning, L., *De Oorlog in Zuid-Afrika: De Strijd tusschen Engeland en de Verbonden Boeren Republieken Transvaal en Oranje-Vrystaat, in Zijn Verloop Geschetst*, 3 Vols., Rotterdam, 1899–1903.

Pienaar, A.J., *Christiaan Rudolph de Wet in die Anglo-Boereoorlog*, Unpublished MA dissertation, PU for CHE, Potchefstroom, 1974.

Preller, G.S., *Kaptein Hindon: Oorlogsavonture van 'n Baasverkenner*, 3rd edition, Cape Town, 1942.

Rompel, F., *Heroes of the Boer War*, London, 1903.

Rompel, F., *Marthinus Theunis Steijn*, Amsterdam, n.d.

Rompel, F., *Uit den Tweeden Vrijheidsoorlog, Schetsen en Portretten*, Amsterdam, 1900.

Rosny, J.H., *La Guerre Anglo-Boer: Histoire et Récits d'Après des Documents Officiels*, Paris, 1902.

Rosenthal, E., *General De Wet*, 2nd edition, Cape Town, 1968.

Scholtz, W.L. von R., *Die Betrekkinge tussen die Zuid-Afrikaansche Republiek en die Oranje-Vrystaat, 1899–1902*, Unpublished MA dissertation, RAU, Johannesburg, 1973.

Scholtz, W.L. von R., *Generaal Christiaan de Wet as Veldheer*, Unpublished DLitt et Philthesis, University of Leiden, Leiden, 1978.

Stamperius, J., *Met Generaal de Wet in 't Veld: 'De Strijd tusschen Boer en Brit'*, Den Boerengeneraal Naverteld, Amsterdam, 1902.

Steevens, F.J., *Complete History of the South African War in 1899–1902*, London, n.d.
Steytler, F.A., *Die Geskiedenis van Harrismith*, Bloemfontein, 1932.
Stirling, J., *The Colonials in South Africa, 1899–1902*, Edinburgh, 1907.
Stirling, J., *Our Regiments in South Africa, 1899–1902*, Edinburgh, 1903.
Tresling, T.P., 'De Generaals Botha, De Wet en De la Rey', in *Mannen en Vrouwen van Beteekenis in Onze Dagen*, Haarlem, 1903.
Valentin, W., *Der Burenkrieg*, 2 Vols., Leipzig, 1903.
Valter, M.P.C., *Generaal Botha tijdens den Engelsch-Afrikaanschen Oorlog in 1900*, Amsterdam, 1915.
Valter, M.P.C., *Louis Botha contra Generaal Christiaan de Wet*, Amsterdam, 1915.
Van der Merwe, N.J., *Marthinus Theunis Steyn: 'n Lewensbeskrywing*, 2 Vols., Cape Town, 1921.
Van Everdingen, W., *De Oorlog in Zuid-Afrika*, 3 Vols., Delft, 1902–1915.
Van Rensburg, A.P.J., 'Die Ekonomiese Herstel van die Afrikaner in die Oranjerivierkolonie, 1902–1907', in *Argiefjaarboek vir Suid-Afrikaanse Geskiedenis*, Vol. II, Pretoria, 1967.
Van Schoor, M.C.E., Malan S.I. and Oberholster, J.J., *Christiaan Rudolph de Wet, 1854–1922*, 2nd edition, Bloemfontein, 1964.
Van Zyl, P.H.S., *Die Helde-Album, Verhaal en Foto's van Aanvoerders en Helde uit Ons Vryheidstryd*, Johannesburg, 1944.
Wilson, H.W., *With the Flag to Pretoria*, 2 Vols., London, 1901.
Wilson, H.W., *After Pretoria: The Guerilla War*, 2 Vols., London, 1902.

Index

Africans
  captured 18
  agterryer flogged 34
  information to British
    to Paget 43
    to Broadwood 46, 48
    to Kitchener 135–136, 163
    to Methuen 145
    to Smith-Dorrien 153
    to Hamilton 181
  inform De Wet of escape route 194
army, Boer (*see* commandos, Boer)
army, British
  1st Argyll and Sutherland Highlanders
    become involved in De Wet hunt 178 (*see also* Hamilton, Gen. Sir Ian)
  Australian Bushmen
    besieged at Eland's River 176 (*see also* Hore, Col. C.O.)
  Australians
    at Karroospruit 53, 54, 61n. 108
    escaped POW re Boers 167
  Bechuanaland Field Force
    guns of, left behind in Olifant's Nek 87 (*see also* Kekewich, Col. R.G.)
  1st Border Regiment
    with Hamilton 178
    left at Commando Nek 180 (*see also* Hamilton, Gen. Sir Ian)
  9th Brigade
    sets off from Frederikstad 168 (*see also* Douglas, Maj.-Gen. C.W.H.)
  12th Brigade
    towards Senekal 24
    Hunter awaits arrival of 36
    short of supplies 36 (*see also* Clements, Gen. R.A.P.)
  19th Brigade
    to OFS railway 18
    to move to Bank to head De Wet 143
    arrives at Welverdiend 148
    leaves Welverdiend 163 (*see also* Smith-Dorrien, Maj.-Gen. H.L.)
  20th Brigade
    to drive OFS forces eastwards 20
    at Bethlehem 24
    sent away from De Wet's escape route 38

21st Brigade
  to march to Bethlehem 26
  Hunter awaits arrival of 36 (*see also* Hamilton, Maj.-Gen. Bruce)
2nd Cavalry Brigade
  at Bethlehem 24
  sent away from De Wet's escape route 38
  at Witklip 44–45
  surprises De Wet at Karroospruit 49–50
  and Boer crossing of Bloemfontein–Pretoria railway 63
  sets off for Vredefort 76
  at Vredefort 79
  in tatters, end July 1900 84
  deployed near Vredefort 86
  covers Colonial Division's move to Winkel's Drift 112
  at Rhebokfontein 114
  at Lindeque's Drift 145
  bivouacks at foot of Gatsrand 147
  reaches Welverdiend 154
  leaves Welverdiend 163
  bivouacks at Uitkyk 167
  departs from Uitkyk 175–176 (*see also* Broadwood, Brig.-Gen. R.G.)
3rd Cavalry Brigade
  to Heilbron 37
  change of commander 46
  to Rundle 46
  at Paardeplaats 48–49, 76
  fails to get in touch with Broadwood at Karroospruit 49
  fails to communicate with Broadwood 50
  contact with Boers crossing Bloemfontein–Pretoria railway 63
  urged by Roberts to overtake De Wet 67
  first communication with Broadwood 76
  trouble with supply convoy 76
  reaches Welgelegen 77
  at Vredefort 79
  deployed near Wonderheuwel 86
  fired at by Boer artillery at Wonderheuwel 87
  covers Knox's right flank near Rhebokfontein 112
  sent back to Paardekraal near Vredefort 112

225

at Lindeque's Drift   145
bivouacks at foot of Gatsrand   147
reaches Welverdiend   154
leaves Welverdiend   163
bivouacks at Uitkyk   167
departs from Uitkyk   175–176 (*see also* Little, Lt.-Col. M.O.)
City of London Imperial Volunteers (CIV)
   arrival of awaited at Bank   87–88
   arrive at Bank   148
   reach Wonderfontein   150
   half left behind at Bank   163
   at Syferfontein   191–192 (*see also* MacKinnon, Col. W.H.)
Colonial Division
   bars De Wet in E. OFS   19
   controls Ficksburg–Biddulphsberg line   26, 36
   reinforces Rundle   37
   at Paardeplaats   48–49
   De Wet sets off to capture   50–51
   to Vaal   89
   at Winkel's Drift   112, 114
   ordered to cross Vaal at Scandinavia Drift   135
   ordered to follow Methuen in attack near Koedoesfontein   136
   starts pursuing De Wet on left flank   145
   leaves supply column behind   146
   bivouacks at Enzelspoort   146–147
   ordered to leave for Frederikstad   147–148
   reaches Frederikstad   161
   departs from Frederikstad   162
   500 remain at Frederikstad   163
   at Modderfontein   165
   at Syferfontein   191–192
   forces Magato's Nek   192 (*see also* Dalgety, Lt.-Col. E.H.)
1st Derbyshires
   to guard baggage   47
   deployed near Wonderheuwel   86
4th Derbyshires
   at Rhenoster River   13
   remain behind when Broadwood sets off for Vredefort   76
1st Division (*see* Methuen, Gen. Lord)
8th Division (*see* Rundle, Lt.-Gen. Sir Leslie)
3rd Durhams
   to join the South Wales Borderers at Roodewal   114
1st Gordon Highlanders
   at Doornkop   11
   left behind at Bank Station   87
2nd Grenadier Guards
   outside Brandwater Basin   37

Highland Brigade
   provisons for, June 1900   13
   joins Hunter   20
   at Bethlehem   24
   to Vaal   89
3rd Imperial Yeomanry
   Methuen leaves Bank with   87
   at Scandinavia Drift   123
   attacks laager at Buffelshoek   137
   arrives at Bank   148
   at Modderfontein   164, 166
5th Imperial Yeomanry
   Methuen leaves Bank with   87
   sets off for Scandinavia Drift   123
   attacks laager at Buffelshoek   137
   arrives at Bank   148
   charges De Wet at Blesbokfontein   164
   at Modderfontein   164, 166
10th Imperial Yeomanry
   Methuen leaves Bank with   87
   sets off for Scandinavia Drift   123
   attacks laager at Buffelshoek   136, 137
   arrives at Bank   148
   at Modderfontein   164–165, 166, 170n. 37
13th Imperial Yeomanry
   Lindley affair   12
71st Imperial Yeomanry
   arrives at Koppie Alleen   89
5th Irish Brigade
   arrives at Koppie Alleen   89
   at Kromellenboogspruit   145
   bivouacks south of Welverdiend   154
Kimberley Mounted Corps   84
1st King's Own Scottish Borderers
   with Hamilton   178
Kitchener's Horse
   at Vredefort   77
9th Lancers
   scout in direction of Rhenoster River   77
   in tatters, end July 1900   84
   illustr.   85
12th Lancers
   casualties near Koedoesfontein   139
17th Lancers
   skirmish with Boers crossing Bloemfontein–Pretoria railway   63, 77
Lovat Scouts
   do not prevent De Wet from escaping   36
1st Loyal North Lancashires
   left behind in Olifant's Nek   87
   with Hamilton to Hekpoort   180
Malta Mounted Infantry
   arrives at Koppie Alleen   89
   action against TVK   97
Marshall's Horse
   arrives at Koppie Alleen   89

INDEX 227

2nd Mounted Infantry
   at Bethlehem 24
   bars De Wet's exit 32
   ordered to assist Paget at Witklip 44–45
   at Karroospruit 54
   sets off for Vredefort 76
   at Vredefort 79
   at Groot Eiland 112
   bivouacks at foot of Gatsrand 147
   leaves Welverdiend 163
   bivouacks at Uitkyk 167
   departs from Uitkyk 175–176 (*see also* Ridley, Brig.-Gen. C.P.)
Naval Brigade
   arrives at Koppie Alleen 89
Northamptonshires
   set off for Scandinavia Drift 123
2nd Northamptonshires
   Methuen leaves Bank with 87
1st Northumberland Fusiliers
   Methuen leaves Bank with 87
   set off for Scandinavia Drift 123
2nd Northumberland Fusiliers
   arrive at Koppie Alleen 89
   occupy line south towards Rhebokfontein 114
   sent to Winkel's Drift 123
1st Oxford Light Infantry
   arrives at Koppie Alleen 89
Rhodesia Field Force
   near Zeerust 143
Rhodesians
   besieged at Eland's River 176 (*see also* Hore, Col. C.O.)
2nd Royal Berkshire Regiment
   with Hamilton 178
Royal Canadian Infantry
   seals De Wet's eastern exit along Vaal 112–114
2nd Royal Dublin Fusiliers
   arrive at Koppie Alleen 89
Royal Engineers
   11th Field Co., leaves Bank with Methuen 87
   repairs railway 88, 162
Royal Irish Regiment
   arrives at Koppie Alleen 89
Royal Irish Rifles
   at Reddersburg 9
3rd Royal Scots
   arrive at Koppie Alleen 89
Scots Fusiliers
   set off for Scandinavia Drift 123
   at Tygerfontein 127–128
2nd Scots Guards
   around Brandwater Basin 37

2nd Shropshire Light Infantry
   left behind at Bank Station 87
   in train derailment 95
   arrives at Bank 148
   leaves for Welverdiend 150
2nd Somerset Light Infantry
   arrives at Koppie Alleen 89
South Wales Borderers
   to be joined by 3rd Durhams at Roodewal 114
Welsh Fusiliers
   captured on Bloemfontein–Pretoria railway 65–66
   set off for Scandinavia Drift 123
   at Tygerfontein 127–128
West Yorkshires
   arrive at Bank 148–149
artillery, Boer
   at Roodewal 13
   exit from Brandwater Basin 34
   at Witklip 44–45
   at Paardeplaats 48–49
   at Karroospruit 53
   and crossing of Bloemfontein–Pretoria railway 64
   at Vredefort 79
   near Wonderheuwel 87
   attack Methuen at Gatsrand 88
   escape with Fourie 107
   sent south from Rhenosterpoort 121
   cross Vaal 123
   at Venterskroon 124, 125–127, 129
   at Gatsrand 146
   at Modderfontein 164
   Borslap's gun abandoned 164, 168
   in rearguard after Modderfontein 173
   in Olifant's Nek 191
   left in Magato's Nek as decoy 192
artillery, British
   at Bethlehem 24
   Hunter short of ammunition 36
   Rundle reinforced with 37
   around Brandwater Basin 37
   at Witklip 44–45
   with Broadwood and Ridley 46, 47, 50
   with Little 46
   at Paardeplaats 48–49
   at Karroospruit 53–54
   at Boer crossing of Bloemfontein–Pretoria railway 63
   at Vredefort 79
   deployed at Vleispruit 86
   at Wonderheuwel 87
   Methuen leaves Bank with 87
   left behind at Bank 87
   arrive at Koppie Alleen 89

force Boers back towards laager south of Vaal 112
Methuen attacks Liebenberg with 115
set off for Scandinavia Drift 123
at Tygerfontein 125–128
Hart's make slow progress south of Vaal 135
naval guns along Vaal with Kitchener 136
attack laager at Buffelshoek 136–138
at Gatsrand 146
naval guns across Vaal 147
with Smith-Dorrien 149
with MacKinnon 150
scouring Gatsrand for sign of Boers 154
depart with Methuen from Frederikstad 162
attack De Wet at Modderfontein 164–165, 168
Royal Canadian Artillery, with Hamilton 178
escort Kekewich 182
Badenhorst, F.C. C.C.J.
to leave Brandwater Basin 28
illustr. 28
at Paardeplaats 48–49
rejoins De Wet at Rhenosterpoort 103
re joining of De Wet and Liebenberg 158n. 63
Baden-Powell, Col. (Maj.-Gen.) R.S.S.
at Mafeking 10
escorted by Hamilton north of Magaliesberg 143
to stay at Commando Nek 143
wants to be besieged in Rustenburg 178
to Rietfontein 178
problems with communication 182–183
Hamilton suggests he moves along northern slopes of Magaliesberg toward Rustenburg 183–184
raises alarm of De Wet's presence near Commando Nek 192
to pin De Wet and Steyn against Pretoria–Pietersburg railway 192
Baltespoort 114, 135
Bank Station
Liebenberg attacks line near 84
Methuen reaches 87
Smith-Dorrien arrives at 148
Roberts under impression De Wet is heading for 149
Barter, Col. 194
Barton, Gen. G.
re strength of Liebenberg 104
re supplies for Methuen 114
and communication 116
supply base for pursuers 143
supplies for Smith-Dorrien 149
on supplies for Kitchener 163
Hamilton awaits supply column 182
Bethlehem 29, 52

Blacks (*see* Africans)
Blesbokfontein 54
Borslap, Bomb. C.
escapes with De Wet 34
at Witklip 44
assists De Wet near Venterskroon 124
gun abandoned at Modderfontein 164, 165
Boshoff, Comdt. K. 185
Botha, Gen. Louis
after the war 3, 4
after Pretoria 12
at Diamond Hill 12
to Machadodorp 12
orders P. Viljoen to assist De Wet 31
encourages De Wet 102
orders P. Viljoen to Machadodorp 104
at Dalmanutha 204
Botha, Gen. Philip
in command of force leaving Brandwater Basin 27
illustr. 27
exit from Brandwater Basin 34
attacks Little at Paardeplaats 48–49
and crossing of Bloemfontein–Pretoria railway 64–65
position near Reitzburg 135
protects laager crossing Gatsrand 146
crosses Krugersdorp–Potchefstroom railway 150
re Steyn 191
returns to OFS with De Wet 193–194
Brakfontein (*see* Eland's River)
Broadwood, Brig.-Gen. R.G.
at Sannah's Post 9
advance from Bloemfontein 11
at Bethlehem 24
sent away from De Wet's escape route 38
at Witklip 44
awaits Ridley's arrival 45–46
sets off after De Wet 46
replenishes from Ewart's convoy 47
little progress 48
surprises De Wet at Karroospruit 49–50, 53
discovers De Wet's identity 49–50
fails to communicate with Little 50
advances along Rhenoster River 56
explanation for success of first week of hunt 56
and Boer crossing of Bloemfontein–Pretoria railway 63
urged by Roberts to overtake De Wet 67
bizarre behaviour of 67–68
arrives at Shepstone 70, 76
realises mistake 75
reaches Roodewal 75
replenishes at Koppies 75

INDEX
229

  to send daily reports to Chermside   75–76
  sets off for Vredefort   76
  first communication with Little   76
  leaves Shepstone   77
  reaches Vredefort   77
  re Boer bravery at Vredefort   78
  rescues Legge at Vredefort   79
  joined by Little   79
  Roberts resumes contact with   83
  illustr.   86
  and horses   86
  requests supplies   86
  deploys forces south of Vaal   86
  reinforcements of arrive south of Vaal   88–89
  at Rhebokfontein   114
  ordered to advance from Rhebokfontein   135
  reaches farm Bloemfontein   135
  treks along Vaal with Kitchener   136
  shells laager across Vaal   138–139
  crosses Vaal at Lindeque's Drift   147
  bivouacks at foot of Gatsrand   147
  Methuen contact with   147
  ordered by Smith-Dorrien to shift right flank closer to Bank   153
  leaves Welverdiend   163
  bivouacks at Uitkyk   167
  departs from Uitkyk   175–176
  halts at Grootfontein   176
  ordered to push on to Olifant's Nek   177
  engages De Wet's rearguard before Olifant's Nek   177
  under impression Hamilton is occupying Olifant's Nek   181, 198
  west of Syferfontein   192
  assessment of   200, 201
Buffelshoek (Gatsrand)   135, 137
Buffelshoek (near Olifant's Nek)   176, 177
Buller, Gen. Sir Redvers
  relieves Ladysmith   8
  ready to enter the Transvaal   11
  enters the Transvaal   19–20
  instructions re Clery   67
  occupies Greylingstad   104
  breaks through at Dalmanutha   204
Bruwer, Corp.   34, 44

Carrington, Lt.-Gen. Sir F.   143, 178
Chermside, Maj.-Gen. Sir H.   75–76
Chesham, Lord   136, 137
Clements, Gen. R.A.P.
  flying column of   19
  ordered to drive OFS forces eastwards   20
  attacks Bethlehem   20
  towards Senekal   24
  Hunter awaits arrival of   36

  short of supplies   36, 199
  delayed before Brandwater Basin   36
  to Vaal   89, 114
  assessment of   200
Clery, Maj.-Gen.   67, 83
Colvile, Maj.-Gen. Sir H.E.   11, 12, 13
Commando Nek
  Roberts under impression De Wet is heading for   148, 178
  Olifant's Nek nearest pass to   175
  Baden-Powell left to hold   175
  1st Border Regiment left to hold   180
  De Wet wants to return to OFS via   192, 194
  guarded by Barter   194
commandos, Boer
  Bethal
    sent to reinforce P. Viljoen   104
  Bethlehem
    to leave Brandwater Basin   28
    at Karroospruit   53
    crosses Bloemfontein–Pretoria railway   65, 66, 70
    at Venterskroon   128
    protects rearguard near Losberg   145
    protects rearguard north of Krugersdorp–Potchefstroom railway   151
    returns to OFS with De Wet   193–194
  Boshof
    to leave Brandwater Basin   28
    at Paardeplaats   48, 49
    rejoins De Wet at Rhenosterpoort   103
  Frankfort
    to leave Brandwater Basin   27–28
    at Witklip   44, 45
    at Karroospruit   53, 54
    returns to OFS with De Wet   193–194
  Griqualand West rebels
    to leave Brandwater Basin   28
    at Venterskroon   124
    left in Magato's Nek as decoy   192
  Harrismith
    ordered to Brandwater Basin   27
    to be joined by Crowther   28
  Heilbron
    to leave Brandwater Basin   27
    at Witklip   44
    at Karroospruit   53
    at Paardekraal   55
    at Venterskroon   128
  Kroonstad
    to leave Brandwater Basin   27
    at Paardeplaats   48, 49
    rejoins De Wet at Rhenosterpoort   103
    protects rearguard near Losberg   145
    to cover laager crossing Gatsrand   146

Potchefstroom burghers
   to leave Brandwater Basin 28
   join Liebenberg 104
Pretoria
   occupies Olifant's Nek 185
Standerton
   sent to reinforce P. Viljoen 104
Vrede
   ordered to Brandwater Basin 27
   to be joined by Crowther 28
   returns to OFS with De Wet 193–194
communication, Boer 11, 70
communication, British
   to be restored after Roodewal 18
   Broadwood 48, 68, 76
   first week of hunt 56
   Roberts' problems 68–69, 75, 87, 200
   around Vaal 89
   disrupted by Liebenberg 94–95, 115–116
   difficult to convey across Vaal 117–118, 135, 139
   Kitchener's restored after seven days 147
   Dalgety does not receive orders from Methuen 147–148
   Smith-Dorrien receives information too late 148, 153
   Methuen does not receive message from Smith-Dorrien 148
   Spens and MacKinnon use signal lamps in contact with Smith-Dorrien 150
   faulty information re De Wet's crossing of Krugersdorp–Potchefstroom railway 153, 154
   Kitchener with Methuen during attack on Modderfontein 167
   Broadwood to Methuen before Olifant's Nek 177
   information to Hamilton false 181
   problems between Roberts, Hamilton and Barton 182–183
   Hamilton's with Roberts re Baden-Powell 183–184
   explanation for De Wet's success 197–198
Craven's Rust 46–47
Crowther, Gen. J. 28

Dalgety, Lt.-Col. E.H.
   to Vaal 89
   at Winkel's Drift 112, 114
   ordered to cross Vaal 135
   ordered to follow Methuen in attack near Koedoesfontein 136
   leaves supply column behind 146
   bivouacks at Enzelspoort 146–147
   ordered to leave for Frederikstad 147–148
   reaches Frederikstad 161

   illustr. 161
   at Syferfontein 191–192
Dalmanutha 204
De Bruyn, artillerist 124, 126, 127
De la Rey, Gen. Koos
   after the war 3
   re guerrilla war 8
   at Doornkop 11
   to Western Transvaal 12
   at Silkaatsnek 31
   Roberts expects De Wet to join him 143
   besieges Hore 176, 182
De Lisle, Col. H. de B. 54, 112, 177
De Villiers, Comdt. C.J. 107
De Villiers, Jacob
   on British scouts 24, 198
   on Boer delegate 109n. 43
   tired, west of Olifant's Nek 174
   on scene before Olifant's Nek 184–185
De Wet, Gen. C.R. (Christiaan)
   early life 1–2
   overview of actions during the war 2–3
   writes memoirs 3
   after the war 3–4
   at Roodewal 7, 8, 12–14
   and guerrilla warfare 8, 9, 12, 193, 202
   at Kroonstad 8
   dissolves forces in March 1900 9
   at Sannah's Post 9
   at Reddersburg 9
   at Wepener 9
   at Swavelkrans 13
   delays Roberts' eastward advance 17, 204
   house of, burnt 19
   retreats into Brandwater Basin 20, 23
   realises danger of remaining in Brandwater Basin 26–27
   reasons for leaving Brandwater Basin 29–30, 63, 99
   and co-operation with P. Viljoen 30–31, 104, 197, 198
   first attempt to pass through Slabbert's Nek 32
   burghers' faith in 32
   exit from Brandwater Basin 34–35
   number of men accompanying him 34, 40n. 41
   orders *agterryer* to be flogged 34
   explanation for escape of from Brandwater Basin 36–38
   diverts British attention from Slabbert's Nek 37
   at Witklip 43–45
   at Craven's Rust 46–47
   agrees to invade Cape Colony 47
   spots Ewart's convoy 47

INDEX   231

attacks Little at Paardeplaats 48–49
identity discovered 49
caught up by Broadwood 50–52
and wagon laager 52–53
parts with P. de Wet 55
at Paardekraal 57
crosses Bloemfontein–Pretoria railway 63–67
illustr. 65, 203, 204, 205
faith of 67, 101–102, 107, 201
promotes Theron to commandant 69–70
reconnoitres towards Vredefort 70
sends wheat to Vredefort 70
and skirmish to save flour 78–79
at Rhenosterpoort 79, 90
and Roberts' new strategy against 84
posts sentries along Vaal 93, 101
receives supplies from Liebenberg 94, 105
complains to Roberts about Stowe 97–98
and Prinsloo's surrender 101, 105–107
Jacob de Villiers on 101
inspired leadership of 101–102
and recommandeering 102–103, 202
learns of P. de Wet's surrender 103
Kestell on 103–104
and Albert Grobler 106
errors in memoirs of 109n. 44
realises necessity to trek through Vaal 114
route through Schoeman's Drift left open by Methuen for 118
crosses Vaal 123
attacked by Methuen at Venterskroon 124–129
at Van Vuuren's Kloof 129
re wagon laager at Venterskroon 134
attacked by Methuen near Koedoesfontein 136–140
Roberts expects he will join De la Rey 143
overtaken in Gatsrand by Methuen 145–146
informed of Smith-Dorrien's presence at Bank 146
crosses Gatsrand 146
slips past Smith-Dorrien over Krugersdorp–Potchefstroom railway 148–150, 154
joins Liebenberg 151–152, 158n. 63, 168–169
intends to join De la Rey 152
description of, on horseback 152
halts east of Ventersdorp 152
Theron parts with 152–153, 158n. 72
attacked by Methuen at Modderfontein 163–169
re abandoned gun 164
sets grass alight 166
as seen by Australian POW 167
British POWs believe he is on his way to L. Botha 167

and pursuers after Modderfontein 173
at Rietfontein 174
expected to be caught before Olifant's Nek 177
learns Olifant's Nek is in Boer hands 184
convoy of leaves Roodewal 184
joined by rearguard on way to Olifant's Nek 184
crosses Olifant's Nek 185
outspans on Kruger's farm 185
news of escape reaches pursuers 185–186
moves north of Magaliesberg 192
wants to return to OFS through Commando Nek 192
Roberts tries to pin him and Steyn against Pretoria–Pietersburg railway 192
returns to OFS 193–194
escapes over Magaliesberg near Wolhuter's Kop 194
realises objectives of trek 197
re British scouts 198
British no match for 200
personal qualities explaining his success 201–202
meets Steyn near Ventersdorp 204
De Wet, Gen. Piet
and Lindley affair 12
pays home a visit 47
in command at Karroospruit 49, 50–52, 55, 56–57, 62n. 127
parts with C. de Wet 55
surrenders 55, 103
illustr. 56
takes up arms against Boers 62n. 121
prediction re railway crossing 63, 67
suggests brother might surrender 106
De Wet's Drift 93, 135
discipline, Boer 24, 34
Doornspruit 63
Douglas, Maj.-Gen. C.W.H. 124, 168, 191
Douthwaite, Comdt. C.M. 31, 88, 91, 104
Du Preez, Corneels 127
Du Toitspruit 151

Elandsfontein 145–146, 158n. 76
Eland's River
Roberts expects De Wet to join De la Rey at 143
De la Rey besieges Hore 176, 182
Roberts orders Hamilton to relieve Hore 183
Roberts orders Methuen and Little to relieve Hore 192
Kitchener relieves Hore 192, 205
Enslin, Lt. Barney 54
Enzelspoort 145
Ewart, Col. J.S. 37, 47

Fleur 65, 203
  illustr. frontispiece
flour incident 70, 73n. 64, 77–79
Fourie, Gen. Piet 107, 202
Fouriesburg 24, 32
Fox, Sgt. 137–138
Frederikstad Station
  train derailed near 94–95
  Methuen reaches and departs from 88, 161, 162
  Dalgety ordered to leave for 147–148
  Smith-Dorrien requires supplies at 148
French, Gen. Sir John 8, 10, 11, 67, 83
Froneman, Gen. C.C. 13, 18, 107

Gaskell, H.M. 125, 145, 165
Gatacre, Maj.-Gen. Sir W.F. 164, 165
Gatsrand
  Liebenberg supplies De Wet from 94
  Liebenberg active in 95, 104
  Methuen overtakes Boer rearguard at 145
  De Wet arrives at 146
  De Wet crosses 146
Gordon, Brig.-Gen. J.P.R. 37, 46, 50, 85
Gordon Lennox, Col. Lord Algernon 97–98
Gough, Maj. A. 76, 88
Grobler, Albert 106, 111
Grootfontein 176
Grootplaats 178

Haasbroek, Comdt. Sarel 107
Hamilton, Maj.-Gen. Bruce 26, 36, 37
Hamilton, Gen. Sir Ian
  advance from Bloemfontein 10–11
  at Doornkop 11
  flying column of 19
  breaks collar bone 20
  involved in De Wet hunt 143, 178
  to Hekpoort to delay De Wet 178, 180
  force of 178
  Roberts does not convey urgency of occupying Olifant's Nek to 180
  bivouacks at Bultfontein 180
  ordered to occupy Olifant's Nek with part of force 180–181
  informed De Wet has crossed Krugersdorp–Potchefstroom railway 181
  fails to appreciate urgency of Roberts' orders 181
  troops of, on three-quarter rations 181–182
  bivouacks near Thorndale 182
  chooses route over Witwatersberg towards Tafelkop 182
  information from Roberts to, is mostly 24 hours old 183
  informed De Wet is heading for Tafelkop 183
  ordered to relieve Hore 183
  illustr. 185
  tries to shift blame re De Wet's escape 186
  at Zandfontein 191
  takes Olifant's Nek 192
  ordered to delay De Wet before Pretoria–Pietersburg railway 192–193
  assessment of 200
Hart, Maj.-Gen. A.F.
  on Boer crossing of railway 67
  arrives at Koppie Alleen 89
  not up to task 90
  occupies line south towards Rhebokfontein 114
  ordered to advance from Rhebokfontein 135
  reaches farm Bloemfontein 135
  treks along Vaal with Kitchener 136
  crosses Vaal 147
  moves fast north of Vaal 147
  bivouacks south of Welverdiend 154
  not involved in hunt any longer 168, 176
  at Groenfontein 192
Hattingh, Gen. F.J.W.J. 28, 107
Hekpoort 143, 178, 180, 181
Hertzog, Gen. J.B.M. 107
Hickman, Col. T.E. 178, 192
Hintrager, Oskar
  diary of 5n. 4
  re railway 63
  on Boer character 69–70
  re Boer storming on horseback 78
  on situation at Vaal 94
  on crossing of wagon laager 121
  at Venterskroon 124, 126
Holfontein Siding 96–99, 166
Honingspruit Station 64, 65
Hore, Col. C.O.
  besieged at Eland's River 176, 182
  Hamilton ordered to relieve 183
  Methuen and Little ordered to relieve 192
  Kitchener relieves 192, 205
horses, Boer
  with exit from Brandwater Basin 35
  at Karroospruit 53
  in deplorable state 56
  and crossing of Bloemfontein–Pretoria railway 64
  distance on horseback 93
  state of, according to British POWs 93, 167
  Malan captures 93
  killed in Gatsrand action 146
  of Liebenberg in poor state 152

INDEX   233

artillery horses killed at Modderfontein   164
   lost at Modderfontein   173
   De Wet sends some into bushveld   191, 193
   little time to rest   192
horses, British
   pursuers badly off for   84–85, 200
   Gordon's report on   85
   rested by Methuen at Tygerfontein   134
   Methuen's at Koedoesfontein   140
   killed in Gatsrand action   146
   Kitchener's spent, Welverdiend   162
   tired after Modderfontein   167
   utterly exhausted after De Wet hunt   192
Howland, F.H.
   at Karroospruit   50, 52
   at Vredefort   77, 79
   re 'thin line of khaki'   86
   sees Boer positions along Vaal   112
   assessment of Boer scouts   198–199
   criticises Methuen   200
   on De Wet hunt   207
Hunter, Gen. Sir Archibald
   advances on Vaal   10
   given command to capture De Wet   20
   arrives at Behlehem   24
   illustr.   26
   ordered to capture De Wet   26
   and De Wet's escape from Brandwater Basin   35–36
   short of supplies   36–37, 199
   warned that Boers might escape   37
   sends Paget away from De Wet's escape route   38
   informed of Boer escape   44
   orders Ewart to cut off Boers   47
   informed that escaped Boers are under De Wet   50
   Prinsloo surrenders to   89
   ordered to send delegate to De Wet   106
   assessment of   200
Hutton, Maj.-Gen. E.T.H.   67

Johannesburg   11, 12

Kaallaagte   64
Karroospruit   47, 50–54
Kekewich, Col. R.G.
   left to hold Olifant's Nek   87, 178
   evacuates Olifant's Nek   178
   with Hamilton to Hekpoort   180
   to escort supply convoy   182
Kelly-Kenny, Lt.-Gen. Sir T.   50
Kestell, Dominee J.D.   52, 103–104
Kitchener, Gen. Lord
   sent to OFS   18
   to take over hunt south of Vaal   84, 89–90

arrives at Koppies   111
organisation south of Vaal on arrival   111–112
orders Methuen to close western cordon   112
cordon of, firmly in place   114
headquarters at Wonderheuwel   114
requested to relay orders to Methuen   116
takes over command north of Vaal too   116
difficult to communicate with Methuen across Vaal   117–118, 135, 139
learns of De Wet's escape across Vaal   134–135
arranges pursuit of De Wet north of Vaal   135
orders of, after De Wet's crossing of Vaal   135
moves headquarters to De Wet's Drift   135
decides to shift most of force east to cross at Lindeque's Drift   135–136
orders Ridley to cross at Lindeque's Drift   136
treks along Vaal   136
unites with Little east of Vredefort   136
at Lindeque's Drift   145
starts pursuing De Wet on right flank   145
crosses Vaal at Lindeque's Drift   147
on wrong track north of Vaal   147
bivouacks at Droogeheuvel   147
Methuen contact with   147
reaches Welverdiend   154
learns of De Wet's escape over Krugersdorp–Potchefstroom railway   154
supply problem at Welverdiend   162–163, 199
resumes hunt from Welverdiend   163
delayed at Mooi River   167
bivouacks at Schoolplaats (Uitkyk)   167
supplies arrive at Uitkyk   167–168
informed that Hamilton would occupy Olifant's Nek   175, 181, 198
departs from Uitkyk   175–176
illustr.   176
does not comply with Methuen's request before Olifant's Nek   176
at Grootfontein   176
learns of De Wet's escape over Olifant's Nek   186
at Syferfontein   191–192
relieves Hore   192, 205
takes Methuen's supplies   192
approaches Wolhuter's Kop   194
assessment of   200
Klein-Bloemfontein   70, 78, 79
Knowles, Lt.   137
Knox, Gen. C.
   informs De Wet of Prinsloo's surrender   105–106
   occupies Rhebokfontein   112
   at Baltespoort   114

ordered to cross Rhenoster 135
to deny De Wet re-entering OFS 136, 145
Koedoesfontein 129, 134
Kruger, Pres. Paul
at Kroonstad 8
leaves for Machadodorp 11
re peace, June 1900 12
re meeting with Steyn 29, 67, 105, 197, 204
requests OFS rearguard attack 30
De Wet outspans on farm of 185, 191
urges Botha to organise guerrilla war 204
granted six months' leave 204
Lagden, Sir Godfrey 36, 37, 38
Leeuwfontein 136, 178
Legge, Col. N. 77–79, 112
Leliefontein 173, 174, 175
Liebenberg, Gen. P.J. (Piet)
ordered in direction of Potchefstroom 31
joint action with De Wet and Theron 63, 197
attacks Krugersdorp–Potchefstroom railway 84, 94–95, 99, 114–115
captures garrison in Klerksdorp 84
opposes Methuen in Gatsrand 88
delays Methuen 88, 114, 115, 129
supplies De Wet 94, 105
joined by Potchefstroom burghers 104
disrupts British communications 115–116
Smith-Dorrien bears brunt of attacks by 148
at Syferbult 149
joins De Wet 151–152, 158n. 63, 168–169
doubles his force 151
illustr. 152
intends with De Wet to join De la Rey 152
rearguard after Modderfontein 173
covers Magato's Nek 191
retires from Magato's Nek 192
follows De Wet north of Magaliesberg 192
returns to Magato's Nek 193
Little, Lt.-Col. M.O.
put in charge of 3rd Cavalry Brigade 46
at Paardeplaats 48–49, 76
fails to get in touch with Broadwood at Karroospruit 49
fails to communicate with Broadwood 50
contact with Boers crossing Bloemfontein–Pretoria railway 63
urged to overtake De Wet 67
first communication with Broadwood 76
trouble with supply convoy 76
determined to pursue enemy 76–77
reaches Welgelegen 77
reaches Broadwood 77, 79
at Vredefort 79
deployed near Wonderheuwel 86
covers Knox's right flank near Rhebokfontein 112

sent back to Paardekraal near Vredefort 112
mans eastern sector near Vredefort 114
ordered to reconnoitre in direction of Reitzburg 135
scouts run into P. Botha near Reitzburg 135
unites with Kitchener east of Vredefort 136
crosses Kromellenboogspruit 138
crosses Vaal 147
bivouacks at foot of Gatsrand 147
leaves Welverdiend 163
bivouacks at Uitkyk 167
departs from Uitkyk 175–176
at Grootfontein 176
west of Syferfontein 192
ordered to relieve Hore 192
Losberg
Boers on road to 134, 137, 138, 139
De Wet spends night at 145
TVK remains at 145
TVK departs from 146

MacDonald, Gen. Sir Hector
under Colvile 11
flying column formed 19
joins Hunter 20
at Bethlehem 24
to Vaal 89, 114
Mackenzie's mill 70, 73n. 64
MacKinnon, Col. W.H.
to Wonderfontein 150
ordered to join forces with Spens 153
drives Boers off north of Welverdiend 153
delayed at Mooi River 167
at Zwartplaats 176
at Syferfontein 191–192
follows Kitchener to relieve Hore 192
Mafeking 10, 178
Magaliesberg
description of 174–175
Methuen blocks road leading west from the foothills of 177
Roberts hopes to block De Wet against 178
Boer sharpshooters in 180, 181
De Wet to be prevented from moving north of 180–181
De Wet moves north of 192
De Wet escapes over, near Wolhuter's Kop 194
Magato's Nek 186, 191
Mahemspruit 66
Mahon, Brig.-Gen. B.T. 180, 182, 192–193
Malan, Wynand 66, 69, 93
Methuen, Gen. Lord
orders in E. OFS 17–18
flying column in OFS 19
in Rustenburg–Krugersdorp area, July 1900 68

INDEX 235

ordered to Potchefstroom   83, 90n. 1, 178
departs from Olifant's Nek   87
gives Roberts too little detail   87
reaches Bank Station   87
leaves Bank   87
at Wonderfontein   88
engages Douthwaite in Gatsrand   88
reaches and departs from Frederikstad   88, 161, 162
awaits supplies at Konieplaats   88
reaches Potchefstroom   88
delayed by Liebenberg   88, 114, 115, 129
threatens Boer co-operation   105
ordered to close western cordon   112
attacks Liebenberg   115
communication of, disrupted by Liebenberg   115–116
illustr.   117
ordered to cross drifts over Vaal   117
difficult to communicate with Kitchener across Vaal   117–118, 135, 139
sets off for Scandinavia Drift   118, 123
leaves route through Scoeman's Drift open   118
joined by Younghusband at Scandinavia Drift   123
reaches Tygerfontein   123
joined by Douglas   124
attacks De Wet between Tygerfontein and Venterskroon   124–129
unable to send detachment to Parys   129
fails to attack De Wet after Tygerfontein   134, 136
attacks De Wet near Koedoesfontein   136–140
starts pursuing De Wet on left flank from Rietfontein   145
overtakes Boer rearguard at Gatsrand   145
at Taaiboschspruit   146
contact with Kitchener and Broadwood   147
orders Dalgety to leave for Frederikstad   147–148
chances of capturing De Wet before Krugersdorp–Potchefstroom railway   161
hears De Wet has joined Liebenberg   162
under impression Hamilton is occupying Olifant's Nek   162, 175, 176, 177, 181, 198
attacks De Wet at Modderfontein   163–169
supplies arrive after Modderfontein   168
from Leliefontein takes route of Boer advance guard   175
sees Boer rearguard from Rietfontein   175
options before Olifant's Nek   176
departs from Rietfontein   177

orders Broadwood to push on to Olifant's Nek   177
reaches Doornlaagte   177
on De Wet's escape   186
remains at Doornlaagte   191
ordered to relieve Hore   192
forces Magato's Nek   192
supplies of, taken by Kitchener   192, 199
praises troops   200–201
assessment of   200–201
Middelfontein   174, 184, 185
Milner, Sir Alfred   23, 97–98
Money, Col. C.G.C.   123
Mooi River   151
Muller, Capt. W.H.
  exit from Brandwater Basin   34
  at Witklip   44
  at Paardeplaats   48–49
  at Karroospruit   53
  at Vredefort   78
  near Wonderheuwel   87
  not present at Venterskroon   124
  joins laager at Venterskroon   129
  position near Reitzburg   135

Naauwpoort's Nek   29

Olifant's Nek
  Kekewich left to hold   87, 178
  Roberts reckons De Wet will head for   143
  pursuers under impression Hamilton is occupying Olifant's Nek   162, 175, 176, 177, 181
  Boers on road to, after Modderfontein   173
  Boers halt west of   174
  Kekewich evacuates   178
  Roberts does not convey urgency to Hamilton of occupying   180
  illustr.   184
  De Wet crosses   185
  taken by Hamilton   192
Olivier, Comdt. J.H.   32, 107, 110n. 53
Osplaat   45, 46

Paardekraal   57, 63, 68
Paardeplaats   48–49, 76
Paget, Maj.-Gen. A.H.
  ordered to drive OFS forces eastwards   20
  attacks Bethlehem   20
  at Bethlehem   24
  escaping Boers pass him   35, 38
  and supplies   37
  at Witklip   43–45
  to pin De Wet and Steyn against Pretoria–Pietersburg railway   192–193
  assessment of   200

Pienaar, Philip 105
Pienaar, Piet 145–146, 155n. 13
Pine-Coffin, Capt. J.E. 97
Potchefstroom
   Methuen ordered to 83
   Methuen departs for 87
   Methuen reaches 88
   De Wet in, *illustr.* 203, 204
Powell, Capt. 164–165
Pretorius, Comdt. H.P.J. 107
Prinsloo, Marthinus
   to guard Brandwater Basin passes 29
   surrenders 38, 89, 105–107
   illustr. 106
Prinsloo, Comdt. Michael
   to leave Brandwater Basin 27
   illustr. 27
   crosses Bloemfontein–Pretoria railway 64
   rearguard north of Krugersdorp–Potchefstroom railway 151
   returns to OFS with De Wet 193–194
prisoners of war, Boer
   near Roodewal 18
   before Olifant's Nek 177
prisoners of war, British
   at Sannah's Post 9
   at Reddersburg 9
   at Lindley 12
   at Swavelkrans 12–13
   at Rhenoster River 13
   at Vredefort Road Station 13
   at Roodewal 13
   near Kroonstad 17
   1 300 in just over a week 17
   north of Rhenoster River bridge 18
   Welsh Fusiliers captured on crossing Bloemfontein–Pretoria railway 66, 67
   officers captured by Theron at Holfontein 96
   Welsh Fusilier escapes from De Wet 135
   POW escapes at Koedoesfontein 138, 139
   escape at Modderfontein 166
   re treatment by Boers 166
   re Boer military situation 166–167, 171n. 49

railway
   Bloemfontein–Pretoria line
      De Wet attacks Roodewal 7, 12, 13–14, 17
      war council of Kroonstad and 7–8
      Kitchener sent to 18
      Kitchener narrowly evades capture on 18
      Roberts' proclamations re 18
      garrisons to protect 19
      De Wet wants to resume raids on, after exodus from Brandwater Basin 29
      Boers cross 63–67

      TVK damages, near America Siding 94
      damages, at Leeuwspruit 95
      damages, at Serfontein 95
      damages, at Wolwehoek 95
      Theron captures train at Holfontein 95–98
      limited time-table 98
      assessment of Boer success on 199
   Delagoa Bay line
      Kruger along, to Machadodorp 11
      Roberts suspects Steyn heading for 67
      Roberts departs along 83–84
      Roberts returns along 84
      British offensive gains momentum 104
      Roberts' advance along, delayed by De Wet 204–205
   Krugersdorp–Potchefstroom line
      Liebenberg attacks 84
      Liebenberg disrupts 94–95, 99, 115–116, 148
      Smith-Dorrien's train wrecked 114
      De Wet slips past Smith-Dorrien over 148–150
      Smith-Dorrien's role against De Wet on 149
      De Wet crosses 150
      TVK wrecks 150
      Barton complains about situation on 163
   Pretoria–Pietersburg line
      Roberts tries to pin De Wet and Steyn against 192
Ramsbottom, Dr A.E.R. 140
rearguard action, Boer
   at Witklip 43–45
   at Karroospruit 52–54, 62n. 127
   at Koedoesfontein 137–140
   at Modderfontein 164–166
   assessment of 199
regiments, British (*see* army, British)
religion, Boer 101–102
Retief's Nek 29, 31
Rhebokfontein 93, 112, 114, 135
Rhenosterkop 94
Rhenosterpoort
   De Wet reaches 79
   belongs to Jan Botha 81n. 45
   base for raids 90, 93, 95, 97
   renegades arrive at 103
   Boers strike camp 114
   Boers return to 121
Ridley, Brig.-Gen. C.P.
   at Bethlehem 24
   bars De Wet's exit 32
   ordered to assist Paget at Witklip 44
   illustr. 45
   joins Broadwood 46

INDEX 237

replenishes from Ewart's convoy   47
at Karroospruit   53, 54
sets off for Vredefort   76
and skirmish at Vredefort   77, 79
deployed at Vleispruit   86
advances closer to Vaal   112, 114
controls drifts around Parys   114
ordered to send patrol over Vaal   135
patrol of, reports De Wet at Buffelshoek   135
ordered to cross at Lindeque's Drift   136
at Lindeque's Drift   145
bivouacks at foot of Gatsrand   147
leaves Welverdiend   163
bivouacks at Uitkyk   167
departs from Uitkyk   175–176
halts at Grootfontein   176
with Kitchener to relieve Hore   192
at Wolhuter's Kop   194
Rietfontein   174, 175, 176
Riversdal   47
Roberts, Gen. Lord
   captures Bloemfontein   7–8
   advance through OFS   8, 10–11
   captures Pretoria   8, 11
   re Wepener   9
   isolated after Roodewal   17
   re Swavelkrans   18
   sends Kitchener to OFS   18
   launches scorched earth policy   18
   proclamataions of   18–19
   orders re De Wet's house   19
   decides to corner De Wet mid-June 1900   19, 20
   re OFS forces cornered in Brandwater Basin   23
   warns Hunter that Boers might escape   37
   orders Little to assist Broadwood   48
   discovers De Wet's identity   49–50
   and Boer crossing of Bloemfontein–Pretoria railway   67
   communication problems with Broadwood   68–69, 75
   orders Broadwood to pursue De Wet 'in what direction he may go'   75
   no communication with Methuen   75
   resumes contact with Broadwood   83
   orders Methuen to Potchefstroom   83
   re capture of De Wet and Steyn   83
   departs and returns along Delagoa Bay railway   83–84
   new strategy against De Wet   84
   communication problems with Methuen   87, 116
   decides to pin De Wet against Vaal   89
   orders Kitchener to take over hunt   89–90
   complains to Botha about capture of trains   99

learns De Wet has crossed Vaal   143, 148
under impression De Wet would move to Olifant's Nek   143
under impression De Wet is heading for Commando Nek   148, 178
orders Smith-Dorrien to Bank   148
under impression De Wet is heading for Bank   149
on supplies for Kitchener   162, 163
orders Carrington to Mafeking   178
costly delay when not sure where De Wet is heading   178–180
orders Hamilton to Hekpoort   180
does not convey urgency to Hamilton of occupying Olifant's Nek   180
illustr.   183
information to Hamilton mostly 24 hours old   183
informs Hamilton De Wet is heading for Tafelkop   183
orders Hamilton to relieve Hore   183
tries to exonerate himself re De Wet's escape   186
tries to pin De Wet and Steyn against Pretoria–Pietersburg railway   192
learns of De Wet's escape near Wolhuter's Kop   194
calls off first De Wet hunt   194
assessment of   200
Roodewal (farm)   174, 177
Roodewal Station   7, 12–14, 30, 63, 202
Ross, Comdt. Alex   28, 44, 193–194
Roux, Gen. Paul H.   28, 29, 32, 107
Rundle, Lt.-Gen. Sir Leslie
   bars De Wet   19
   controls Ficksburg–Biddulphsberg line   26
   able to feed troops from countryside   36
   reinforced   37
   troops at disposal at Ficksburg   37
   engagement of, at Roodekrantz   37–38
Rustenburg   178, 191, 192, 204

Scandinavia Drift   93, 111, 115, 135
Scheepers, Capt. Gideon
   to leave Brandwater Basin   28
   seen in Lindley   49
   and crossing of Bloemfontein–Pretoria railway   63–64
   De Wet relies more on   133
   illustr.   133
   conveys information re Methuen too late   136–137, 140
   returns to OFS with De Wet   193–194
   assessment of   198–199
Schoeman's Drift
   position of   93

Kitchener learns whereabouts of Boer laager at 111
Methuen leaves route open through 118
wagon laager crosses 121
last Boers cross 128
Schoolplaats 167, 175
Schurwe Poort Oost 63
scouting, Boer (*see* TVK *and* Scheepers, Capt. Gideon)
scouting, British
   Jacob de Villiers on 24
   problems for Hunter 36
   no scouts sent out in direction of Slabbert's Nek 38
   set off after De Wet 46
   at Karroospruit 53
   explanation for De Wet's success 198
Sebastopol 35, 38
Selons River 174, 177
Serfontein, Hendrik 63
Serfontein Siding 64–65, 95
Sitwell, Lt.-Col. C. 95
Slabbert's Nek 29, 32, 34–35
Slegtkamp, Henri 126, 150
Smith-Dorrien, Maj.-Gen. H.L.
   to OFS railway 18
   left behind at Bank Station 87
   to escort Methuen's supply column 88
   train accompanying derailed 94, 114
   attacked by Liebenberg 114–115, 148
   ordered to Bank to head De Wet 143, 148
   receives information too late 148, 153
   De Wet slips past 148–150
   sends Spens to Welverdiend 148
   arrives at Bank 148
   role against De Wet spelt out 149
   receives gun 149
   hears artillery duel between Methuen and De Wet 149–150, 161
   hears railway being blown up with De Wet's crossing 150
   illustr. 151
   blows up bridges over Mooi River 151
   measures to prevent De Wet from crossing the railway 153
   learns of De Wet's crossing of Krugersdorp–Potchefstroom railway 153
   leaves Welverdiend 163
   delayed at Mooi River 167
   halts at Zwartplaats 176
   under impression Hamilton is occupying Olifant's Nek 181
   at Syferfontein 191–192
   follows Kitchener to relieve Hore 192
   assessment of 200
Spens, Col. J. 148, 150, 153

Steenekamp, Comdt. Lucas 13, 27, 193
Steyn, Pres. M.T.
   leaves Bloemfontein for Kroonstad 8
   leaves Kroonstad for N.E. OFS 11
   re peace, June 1900 12
   moves to Bethlehem 20
   retreats into Brandwater Basin 23
   wife and children 24, 32
   and war council in Brandwater Basin 27
   intended meeting with Kruger 29, 101, 105, 191
   illustr. 30, 174
   first attempt to pass through Slabbert's Nek 32
   exit from Brandwater Basin 34, 38
   proposes to De Wet that they invade Cape Colony 47
   breakfast at Blesbokfontein 55
   crosses Bloemfontein–Pretoria railway 64, 65
   crosses Vaal 123
   crosses Krugersdorp–Potchefstroom railway 150
   supports Theron 153
   British POW on 166
   Australian POW on 167
   in vanguard after Modderfontein 173
   P. Botha on 191
   Roberts tries to pin him and De Wet against Pretoria–Pietersburg railway 192
   Steyn to proceed to Kruger 193
   visits Kruger 197, 204
   returns to OFS 204
Stormberg 164, 165
Stowe, Col. J.S., consul-general of USA 96–99
Strydom, Lt. P.J.
   exit from Brandwater Basin 34
   at Witklip 44
   at Paardeplaats 48–49
   at Karroospruit 53
   at Vredefort 78
   near Wonderheuwel 87
   at Venterskroon 124–127
supplies, Boer
   required at Roodewal 13–14
   at Rhenosterpoort 94
   Liebenberg sends to De Wet 94
supplies, British
   shortage before Brandwater Basin 36–37
   Ewart's convoy 37, 47
   supply column to follow Broadwood 67–68
   Kitchener's follow north of Vaal 147
   Smith-Dorrien requires, at Frederikstad 148
   arrive for Smith-Dorrien 149
   Colonial Division's eight days behind 162
   Roberts requests, for Kitchener 162, 163
   too late for Kitchener 163

INDEX

arrive at Schoolplaats for Kitchener 167–168
arrive for Methuen after Modderfontein 168
Kitchener leaves behind at Uitkyk 176
Hamilton to feed off Hekpoort valley 180
Hamilton's convoy behind 180
Hamilton's troops on three-quarter rations 181–182
Hamilton awaits Barton's supply column 182
Kitchener takes Methuen's 192
assessment of problems with 199–200
Swavelkrans 13, 18
Syferbult 149

Taaiboschspruit 145, 146, 161
Tafelkop 182, 183
Theron, Capt. (Comdt.) Danie (*see also* TVK)
   addresses men before Karroospruit 52
   rearguard action of, at Karroospruit 52–54
   at Blesbokfontein 56
   at Paardekraal 57
   crossing of Bloemfontein–Pretoria railway 63–67
   captures train near Serfontein 64–66
   illustr. 69
   promoted to commandant 69–70
   De Wet on 69
   uses Rhenosterkop as base 94, 95
   captures train at Holfontein 95–99
   returns to Rhenosterpoort 108
   crosses Vaal 123
   at Venterskroon 126, 129
   appears before war council after Venterskroon 133, 153
   attacked at Koedoesfontein 138
   protects rearguard at Losberg 145
   parts from De Wet 152–153, 158n. 72
   exponent of mobile warfare 193
   collaborates with Liebenberg 197
   assessment of 199
Thorndale 182
TVK (Theron Verkenningskorps)
   task of, in Brandwater Basin 24
   composition of 24, 38n. 5
   discipline of 24
   rearguard actions of 24
   to leave Brandwater Basin 28
   ordered to retreat inside Brandwater Basin 31
   as rearguard in escape from Brandwater Basin 34
   covers Boer retreat from Craven's Rust 47
   reports Little's presence 48
   at Karroospruit 52–54, 62n. 127
   covers Boer retreat from Karroospruit 54
   arrives at Blesbokfontein 56
   arrives at Paardekraal 57

and crossing of Bloemfontein–Pretoria railway 63–67
captures train near Serfontein 64–66
skirmish near Vredefort 78
at Rhenosterkop 94, 95
damages railway near America Siding 94
damages railway at Leeuwspruit 95
damages railway at Serfontein 95
damages railway near Wolwehoek 95
action against Sitwell 95
captures train at Holfontein 95–99
returns to Rhenosterpoort 108
crosses Vaal 123
at Venterskroon 126, 128, 129
accused of not warning laager in time 133
guards attack from Van Vuuren's Kloof 134
attacked at Koedoesfontein 138
protects rearguard at Losberg 145
joins Boers in Gatsrand 146
rearguard during and after crossing of Krugersdorp–Potchefstroom railway 150, 151
rearguard for De Wet and Liebenberg 152
departs from De Wet 152–153, 158n. 72
to Elandsfontein to renew raids 158n. 76
praised by British POWs 167
collaborates with Liebenberg 197
assessment of 199
Tygerfontein 123–129

Uitkyk 167, 175

Van Aard, Comdt. Frans 27, 48, 103
Van Niekerk, Chris 67
Van Vuuren, Comdt. Stefanus ('Rooi Faans') 191, 193
Van Vuuren's Kloof 114, 126, 202
Van Zyl, F.C. J.A. 28, 124, 125, 192
Ventersdorp 152, 164
Venterskroon 123, 124–129
Ver Loren van Themaat, Hendrik
   diary of 5n. 4
   at Karroospruit 61n. 108
   and skirmish at Vredefort 78
   on crossing of Schoeman's Drift by wagon laager 121–123
   on Boer character 128–129
   re endless plains after crossing Krugersdorp–Potchefstroom railway 151
Viljoen, Gen. Piet 30–31, 104, 197
Visser, Comdt. P.J. 107
Vlakkuil 70, 78, 79
Vredefort
   De Wet to proceed to 29
   De Wet heads towards 46, 47

terrain about   70
Broadwood sets off for   76
wagon laager
  decision at Kroonstad re   9, 52
  sent to Fouriesburg   24
  delays first attempt to pass through Slabbert's Nek   32
  exit from Brandwater Basin   34, 38
  flees from Witklip   46
  flees from Karroospruit   52–53
  sent to Honingspruit   54–55
  at Paardekraal   55
  crosses Bloemfontein–Pretoria railway   64–65
  crosses Schoeman's Drift   121
  at Van Vuuren's Kloof   127–128
  number   134
  decision to send back to OFS after Venterskroon   134
  attacked by Methuen near Koedoesfontein   136–140
  crosses Gatsrand   146
  races past Ventersdorp   164
  under pressure at Modderfontein   166
  vanguard after Modderfontein   173
  baggage tossed from wagons before Olifant's Nek   175
  crosses Olifant's Nek   185
  Methuen sees last wagons crossing Olifant's Nek   186
  De Wet sends into bushveld   191, 193
  protected by TVK   199
  success for De Wet despite   201
  in many cases left behind in bushveld   202
  De Wet convinces burghers to get rid of   202
wagons (*see* wagon laager)
War Council, Boer
  at Kroonstad   8, 52
  in Brandwater Basin   27, 39n. 12
  at Riversdal   47
  after crossing Bloemfontein–Pretoria railway   105
  after Venterskroon   133
  Theron appears before, at Venterskroon   153
  at Crocodile River   193
Welverdiend Station
  British telegraph line restored as far as   116
  Boer rearguard and laager join south of   146
  Spens sent to   148
  Smith-Dorrien controls up to 3 km west of   149
  Spens leaves for   150
  De Wet crosses railway 5 km west of   150
  Kitchener arrives at   154
  Kitchener delayed at   162
Wessels, Andries B.   55, 61n. 118
Wessels, Cornelis   55
Winkel's Drift   111, 112
Witklip   35, 43–45
Wonderheuwel   70, 114

Younghusband, Col.   123, 137

Zeekoehoek   180, 182
Zoutpan   194